THEOLOGY OF THE PENTATEUCH

THEOLOGY OF THE PENTATEUCH

Themes of the Priestly Narrative and Deuteronomy

Norbert Lohfink

Translated by
Linda M. Maloney

FORTRESS PRESS MINNEAPOLIS

THEOLOGY OF THE PENTATEUCH

Translated from *Studien zum Pentateuch*, Stuttgarter biblische Aufsatzbände 4, and from *Studien zum Deuteronomium und zur deuteronomistischen Literatur I*, Stuttgarter biblische Aufsatzbände 8, published 1988 and 1990 by Verlag Katholisches Bibelwerk, Stuttgart.

Library of Congress Cataloging-in-Publication Data

Lohfink, Norbert.
[Selections. English. 1994]
Theology of the Pentateuch : themes of the priestly narrative and Deuteronomy / Norbert Lohfink : translated by Linda M. Maloney.
p. cm.
Articles selected and translated from the collections Studien zum Pentateuch and Studien zum Deuteronomium und zur Deuteronomistischen Literatur I.
Includes bibliographical references and index.
ISBN 0-8006-2593-5 (alk. paper)
1. P document (Biblical criticism) 2. Bible. O.T. Deuteronomy–Criticism, interpretation, etc. 3. Human ecology–Religious aspects–Christianity. I. Title.
BS1181.6.L64213 1994
222'.106–dc20 94-25508
CIP

ISBN: 0-8006-2593-5
1-2593

98 97 96 95 94 1 2 3 4 5 6 7 8 9 10

Contents

Preface

It is now more than thirty years since I began learning the tools of exegesis: this was in Rome, in the early 1960s, and my teacher was William L. Moran, who would later be the Assyriologist at Harvard. I still remember the enthusiasm with which he spoke, in his seminar, about Albrecht Alt, the great antipode of his own teacher, William F. Albright. He emphasized above all that Alt was a master of the *small form.* He had written almost no books, practically nothing but articles. But in every article there was more than another author could put in a whole book, and every article was a minor scholarly revelation.

Thar impressed me deeply at the time. Did it have unsuspected consequences? In any case I suddenly realized, many years later, that although I cannot compare myself with Albrecht Alt by claiming that each of my articles has been a minor revolution, still we are alike in the fact that I have not been a typical writer of books. The *small form* seems to suit me better, too.

I have certainly produced a vast number of articles over the years. And naturally, when an article is finished one likes to see it published, and since one must often wait three or four years for an article to appear in the major international journals, one publishes the piece where it will come out sooner: in any journal that offers, even those that are small and known only to experts, in collections, and in festschrifts. It took me a long time to realize that this often results in the article's being effectively buried.

However, that was not the end of the story. Things that were first intended for a wider audience soon attracted the interest of discriminating publishers, first Josef Knecht, and then my friends at Herder. They collected these articles into books. Two of them have been translated into English (*The Christian Meaning of the Old Testament* [Bruce, 1968] and *Great Themes from the Old Testament* [Franciscan Herald Press, 1981 and T & T Clark, 1982]). Other books of that kind, unfortunately the very ones that seem to me to be the most important, have remained unknown to English-speaking audiences. Still, those are my more 'popular' works. No publisher has called me about the strictly scholarly pieces.

And yet, it is these last that in the long run may be the more significant. Consequently, I was very pleased when the Katholisches Bibelwerk in Stuttgart offered me the opportunity, a few years ago, to collect my more important scholarly studies of the Bible for republication in the series 'Stuttgarter Biblische Aufsatzbände.' That process has already begun: at the present time, the fourth volume is in preparation, and it appears that the publication will extend to seven volumes. In these volumes, I have arranged the articles thematically, beginning with studies on the Pentateuch and the Deuteronomic literature. When the first two volumes had appeared, Dr Marshall Johnson of Fortress Press suggested publishing a selection from them in English. I readily agreed, and left the selection to him since he knows better than I what will be most useful in the English-speaking world. Dr Linda Maloney, who already produced an outstanding translation of a small book of mine (*Option for the Poor* [Bibal Press, 1984]), agreed to undertake this translation: and so this volume appeared. It thus contains nothing that is not in the first two of my collected volumes in German, but at the same time it does not contain everything that is in them.

The book begins with a study of Gen. 1:28. It was indirectly occasioned by the first Club of Rome report issued by M.I.T. in 1972. At that time, in Europe at least, the charge began to circulate rather quickly that the exploitation and destruction of the earth's material resources was ultimately based on this text in the Jewish-Christian Bible, because it assures human beings of a complete right to an unlimited domination and exploitation of the sub-human creation. In this study I have attempted to explain clearly what Gen 1:28 says and what it does not say. In subsequent discussion this article, especially the semantic analysis of the roots *kbš* and *rdh*, has for the most part met with agreement, but also with some opposition.

According to classical Pentateuch theory, Gen. 1:28 is part of the priestly historical narrative. For a long time, this stratum of the Pentateuch was scarcely examined. When I was teaching in Rome in the 1960s, and also in the early 1970s when I returned to Frankfurt am Main, I therefore concentrated my work primarily on that stratum. The essays numbered 4 to 7 in this volume stem from that era. At that time what we in retrospect call the 'crisis in Pentateuch criticism' was just beginning, but in the earliest of these essays I was already in contention with the protagonists of the new points of view. I am thinking primarily of Frank Moore Cross and Rolf Rendtorff, both of whom regard the priestly narratives in the Pentateuch only as expansions and additions, and not as an originally independent historical narrative. I believe that my counter-arguments have not been refuted even today.

Otherwise, these studies were shaped especially by the crisis in modern notions of progress that appear to endanger the ecological balance of our planet. I think I can show that the priestly document in the Pentateuch was already faced with analogous questions and offered a theological response to them. Behind the last article, 'The Strata of the Pentateuch and the Question of War' stand both the problems involved in the American discussion of Vietnam and the issues raised by the European peace movement in the last years of the Cold War. In it, I explore the strangely shifting attitude toward war in the various layers of the Pentateuch. I intend to return to this question very soon in a new study of 'State and War in Ancient Israel.'

Before I began to concentrate my scholarly interest on the priestly layer of the Pentateuch, I devoted most of my attention to Deuteronomy and the deuteronomic literature. This interest continues today, as I am working with Georg Braulik on a commentary on Deuteronomy for the 'Hermeneia' series. The articles numbered 8 to 11 in this collection, and even number 7, belong to this area of research. If I were to gather them under a common heading, I would say: I am first of all attempting, in light of the state of Deuteronomy research, which has become completely tangled in hypotheses of different layers, to get a clear synchronic view of the text. The articles printed here were written before the discovery of the 'literary' approaches to the Bible, but their direction is much the same. They are not 'synchronic' in the sense that they only work with the canonical text in its final form, but they do attempt a synchronic view of broader connections and structures in the different diachronic layers of the text. Reference has already been made to these studies of Deuteronomy in some commentaries, such as those of Georg Braulik, Patrick D. Miller, and Duane L. Christensen, and in part in the work of Moshe Weinfeld.

In recent discussions of the Pentateuch, it is primarily the study of Exod. 15:22–27 (number 3 in this collection) that has attracted attention, for example by Erhart Blum. This text has a key function in several different theories of the Pentateuch. To my own surprise, my analysis of the language showed that it is to be assigned to a very late redactional layer of the Pentateuch, possibly the final redaction. But at the same time I must say that my own intention in writing this article was not at all to advance the newer discussions of the Pentateuch. Instead, I was concerned with the connection between just society and human health. The study originated in an exegetical seminar for doctors and nurses.

In closing, I would like to say something about the second article in this collection. It is a minor debate that I conducted with Karl Rahner in 1963, the very first year when I began to teach. I wanted to put a stop to the introduction into systematic theology, by a famous theologian, of a conceptual apparatus that was untenable in the field of biblical scholarship. I succeeded in doing so, but in addition this publication resulted in my entering into a very personal relationship with this great human being that endured until his death. At the end, when we saw one another, we usually spoke about the book of Qoheleth [Ecclesiastes].

This personal note can serve to lead me to the necessary acknowledgments. I am grateful to the many people among whom these studies were developed and for whom they in turn provided an occasion to enter into conversation with me. I thank all those, including some mentioned above, who aided in their publication. In particular I thank Klaus Baltzer of the 'Hermeneia' editorial group, who first suggested this English edition, Marshall Johnson of Fortress Press, who carried out and guided the publication, and Linda Maloney, who, in addition to her own teaching duties in Berkeley, undertook the work of translation.

Norbert Lohfink

Translator's Preface

There is always great satisfaction for me in bringing to American audiences a work of one of the Lohfink brothers, whom I have counted as friends and mentors for nearly ten years. It was in putting into English, first, a small work of Gerhard Lohfink's, *The Work of God Goes On*, and almost immediately afterward Norbert Lohfink's *Option for the Poor*, that I made my first tentative steps in learning the art of translation. The stimulation of their theological insights not only makes the weight of detail and scholarly apparatus lighter, but reveals, as does no other contemporary work I can name, why such attention to detail is necessary.

In my earliest discussions with Norbert Lohfink, we quickly agreed on the necessity for a gender-inclusive translation of the German text. That policy has been pursued in this book. Biblical quotations are based on the New Revised Standard Version, but because of the nature of the argument in many articles it has been necessary to modify the translated text in accordance with the author's own insights. I am particularly grateful to Donna Stevenson for her assistance with Hebrew, her own area of special expertise.

Linda M. Maloney

List of Abbreviations

AnBib	Analecta Biblica
AOAT	Alter Orient und Altes Testament
ArOr	*Archiv orientální*
ASTI	*Annual of the Swedish Theological Institute*
ATD	Das Alte Testament Deutsch
ATh	*Année théologique*
AThANT	Abhandlungen zur Theologie des Alten und Neuen Testaments
BA	*Biblical Archaeologist*
BASOR	*Bulletin of the American Schools of Oriental Research*
BBB	Bonner biblische Beiträge
BC	Biblischer Commentar über das Alte Testament
BEvTh	Beiträge zur evangelischen Theologie
BHS	*Biblia hebraica stuttgartensia*
BhTh	Beiträge zur historischen Theologie
Bibl	*Biblica*
BibOr	Biblica et Orientalia
BIES	*Bulletin of the Israel Exploration Society* (= *Yediot*)
BK	Biblischer Kommentar
BKAT	Biblischer Kommentar: Altes Testament
BTAVO, B	Beihefte zum Tübinger Atlas des Vorderen Orient – Reihe B, Geisteswissenschaften
BWANT	Beiträge zur Wissenschaft vom Alten und Neuen Testament
BWAT	Beiträge zur Wissenschaft vom Alten Testament
BZ	*Biblische Zeitschrift*
BZAW	Beihefte zur *ZAW*
CahRB	Cahiers de la Revue Biblique
CBQ	*Catholic Biblical Quarterly*
EdF	Erträge der Forschung
EH	Exegetisches Handbuch [zum Alten Testament]
EHS.T	Europäische Hochschulschriften. Ser. 23: Theology
EvTh	*Evangelische Theologie*
FRLANT	Forschungen zur Religion und Literatur des Alten und Neuen Testaments
FzB	Forschung zur Bibel
HAT	Handbuch zum Alten Testament

HKAT	Handkommentar zum Alten Testament
HSM	Harvard Semitic Monographs
IDB	*Interpreter's Dictionary of the Bible*
IEJ	*Israel Exploration Journal*
JAOS	*Journal of the American Oriental Society*
JBL	*Journal of Biblical Literature*
JSOT	*Journal for the Study of the Old Testament*
KAT	Kommentar zum Alten Testament
KeH	Kurzgefaßtes exegetisches Handbuch
LThK^2	*Lexicon für Theologie und Kirche*, 2nd ed.
LXX	Septuaginta
MBPF	Münchener Beiträge zur Papyrusforschung und antiken Rechtsgeschichte
MT	Masoretic text
NRSV	New Revised Standard Version
NRT	*La nouvelle revue théologique*
NT Suppl	*Novum Testamentum, Supplements*
OBO	Orbis biblicus et orientalis
Or	Orientalia (Rome)
OTS	Oudtestamentische Studiën
PJ	*Palästiner Jahrbuch*
QD	Quaestiones disputatae
RAC	*Reallexikon für Antike und Christentum*
RB	*Revue biblique*
RHPR	*Revue d'histoire et de philosophie religieuses*
SBLDS	SBL Dissertation Series
SBLMS	SBL Monograph Series
SBS	Stuttgarter Bibelstudien
ScEs	*Science et esprit*
Schol	*Scholastik* (Freiburg)
SFF	Studien zur Friedensforschung
SSN	Studia semitica neerlandica
SupplRivBib	Supplements to Rivista Biblica
SVT	Studia in veteris testamenti
TDNT	G. Kittel and G. Friedrich, eds., *Theological Dictionary of the New Testament*
TDOT	G. J. Botterweck and H. Ringgren, eds., *Theological Dictionary of the Old Testament*
THAT	Theologisches Handwörterbuch zum Alten Testament
ThB	Theologische Bücherei
Theol.St.u.Kr.	*Theologische Studien und Kritiken*
ThLZ	*Theologische Literaturzeitung*
ThPh	*Theologie und Philosophie*
ThRundsch	*Theologische Rundschau*

ThSt	*Theologische Studien*
ThW	Theologische Wissenschaft
ThZ	*Theologische Zeitschrift* (Basel)
TQ	*Theologische Quartalschrift*
UF	*Ugarit-Forschungen*
VT	*Vetus Testamentum*
WMANT	Wissenschaftliche Monographien zum Alten und Neuen Testament
ZAW	*Zeitschrift für die Alttestamentliche Wissenschaft*
ZDPV	*Zeitschrift des deutschen Palästina-Vereins*
ZThK	*Zeitschrift für Theologie und Kirche*
ZWTh	*Zeitschrift für wissenschaftliche Theologie*

I

'Subdue the Earth?' (Genesis 1:28)

In 1972, the journal *Orientierung* published a detailed essay[1] devoted to the topic, 'the limits to growth,' in response to the Club of Rome study[2] commissioned by the Massachusetts Institute of Technology. At the end of his article its author, Paul Erbrich, expressed his conviction that the Christian churches in particular, drawing on their tradition, could offer practical systems of values that might serve to bring about the necessary changes in fundamental human attitudes.[3]

Dennis L. Meadows, an author of *The Limits to Growth,* has a different opinion on this point. For him there are two ultimately conflicting images of the human being. In a lecture given at Frankfurt on 15 October 1973, he formulated his point of view as follows:

> The one image of humanity, maintained by the supporters of unlimited growth, is that of *homo sapiens,* a very special creature whose unique brain gives it not only the capability but also the right to exploit all other creatures and everything the world has to offer, for its own short-term purposes. This is an ancient view of humanity, solidly grounded in Jewish-Christian tradition and recently strengthened by the magnificent technical achievements of the last few centuries . . . According to this belief, the human being is all-powerful . . . The contrary image of the human being is also ancient, but it is closer to Eastern than to Western religions. It assumes that the human, one species among all the rest, is

1. *Orientierung* 1972, nos. 19 and 20, pp. 219–22, 233–36.
2. Donella H. Meadows, et al., *The Limits to Growth: a Report for the Club of Rome's Project on the Predicament of Mankind* (New York, 1972).
3. *Orientierung* 1972 no. 20, 236. For further discussion, cf. also *Orientierung* 1973, nos. 18 and 19, pp. 198–200, 212–16 (article by Heinz Robert Schlette).

> embedded in the fabric of natural processes . . . It acknowledges that humanity, as regards its ability to survive, is one of the more successful species, but that its very success leads it to destroy the supporting fabric of Nature, which it scarcely understands.[4]

How much is Included in Genesis 1:28?

Historically speaking, Meadows may be right. Often enough, Christians themselves have claimed that the great technological and imperial explosion of the West in modern times rests ultimately on an impulse given in the first chapter of the Bible (Gen. 1:28: 'Be fruitful and multiply, and fill the earth and subdue it; and have dominion over the fish of the sea and over the birds of the air and over every living thing that moves upon the earth').[5] But impulses can also issue from misunderstood statements. It may not be unimportant to consider on which side Christians feel they should stand when, in our own time, a decision is to be made about the conditions under which the next generation or two of human beings will experience themselves and the world around them. Therefore, in what follows, we will propose the apparently academic question: what, from the point of view of a contemporary biblical scholar, do the statements about the creation of humanity in Gen. 1:26–28 *cover*, and what do they not include? To anticipate the conclusion: Meadows and all those who think like him had no real need to push Jews and Christians into the wrong camp; and, to the extent that those two groups are already on the wrong side, it may be that a description of the original meaning of their own earliest traditions can lead them to forsake that camp for the other.

'Image of God' in the Context of the Priestly Document

Our analysis of the statements about the creation of human beings in Genesis 1 must begin with vv. 26 and 27:

> 26 Then God said, 'Let us make humankind in our image, according to our likeness; and let them have dominion over

4. Dennis L. Meadows, et al., '*Wachstum bis zur Katastrophe?*' (Stuttgart: dva-informativ, 1974), 28–29. In quite similar fashion, Carl Amery, for example, in *Das Ende der Vorsehung. Die gnadenlosen Folgen des Christentums* (Hamburg, 1972) sees the Bible as the source of the unlimited claims of modern humanity to sovereignty (cf. *Orientierung* 1972, no. 19, p. 213).

5. Translation from the NRSV. It is popular to speak, in this instance, of the 'Creator entrusting the world' to human beings.

the fish of the sea, and over the birds of the air, and over the cattle, and over all the earth,[6] and every moving thing that moves upon the earth.'[7]

27 So God created humankind in God's image,
in the image of God they were created;
male and female God created them.[8]

The *leitmotif* of these sentences is: 'image of God.' Obviously, it is not easy to say what this means, for from ancient times there have been extended discussions of this subject among theologians.[9] We have to deal with this question, since in quite recent times the opinion has spread that this very statement about the human being as 'image of God' asserts human dominion over the universe.[10] Humanity, in a sense, takes God's

6. There is a text-critical problem in this verse. We do not expect to find the earth in the midst of the various groups of animals. The old Syriac translation read: 'cattle, and over *all the wild animals of the earth*, and over every creeping thing . . .' [The NRSV chooses the Syriac version. Tr.] But it is probable that there was no corresponding Hebrew *Vorlage*, and that the translator simply corrected the text. Nevertheless, the Syriac could be a correct reconstruction of the original. In that case, 'dominion' over the earth, as such, would be mentioned only in v. 28. Since it is certainly stated there, the uncertainty of the text at this point is not so decisive for the discussion of our topic. In what follows, we will avoid drawing any particular conclusions based on this passage. Even if 'all the earth' is original, the reference can only be to the living creatures on the earth, since the verb *rdh*, 'to rule,' always refers to living things (even at 1 Kgs. 5:4 and Pss. 72:8).

7. Literally: 'every creeping thing that creeps upon the earth.' But this group of words, taken together, frequently serves to encompass a variety of kinds of animals, once even referring to all of them (Gen. 9:2), so that it seems appropriate to employ a somewhat broader translation.

8. What is at stake here is the fact that there are two genders. The text moves then to the *blessing of fertility* that follows immediately in v. 28. This need not refer to a single human couple, in the sense of Genesis 2; one may just as easily think of a number of original couples – as in Mesopotamian texts – or of humanity as a whole. That is why the phrase is translated 'male and female.'

9. See the bibliographic references in Werner H. Schmidt, *Die Schöpfungsgeschichte der Priesterschrift*, WMANT 17 (Neukirchen–Vluyn, 1964), 132, n. 1. There is a typology of the various explanations in Oswald Loretz, *Die Gottebenbildlichkeit des Menschen* (Munich, 1967), 9–41. Both will be found also in Claus Westermann, *Genesis*, BK 1 (Neukirchen–Vluyn, 1966ff.), 203–14.

10. To give some examples of the various arguments advanced for this thesis: the Jewish exegete Benno Jacob argues from the context (*Das erste Buch der Tora. Genesis* [Berlin, 1934], 59); the Catholic exegete Heinrich Groβ argues from the

place within the world. This assertion is based primarily on Egyptian texts that describe the Pharaoh as the image of the deity. This idea of the king as image of God is said to be somewhat 'democratized' in the biblical creation text, i.e., it is here applied to the role of humanity with respect to the whole sub-human creation.[11]

The biblical statements must be illuminated by the language and culture of the world of their own time, and to that extent there can be no objection to adducing Egyptian texts. But the situation is more complicated at the point where an initial idea like that of human beings as 'image of God' in the ancient Orient is found to appear in different cultural regions and, in part, within different contexts and with different meanings. Then we must pose the additional question: where exactly do we find a context corresponding to the biblical use of this idea?[12] This kind of complication of the inquiry appears in the present case, i.e., the idea of the human being as 'image of God.'

The first chapter of Genesis is part of the so-called 'priestly document,' the latest source document of the Pentateuch. It was probably written during or shortly after the Babylonian exile, and quite likely in Babylon.[13] It is less concerned with Egyptian than with *Mesopotamian*

commentary on Genesis 1 in Pss. 8:5–6 ('Die Gottebenbildlichkeit des Menschen,' in *Lex tua veritas,* Festchrift for H. Junker [Trier, 1961], 89–100); the Lutheran exegete Hans Wildberger comes to a similar conclusion on the basis of extra-biblical, especially Egyptian sayings about the king as image of the deity ('Das Abbild Gottes,' *ThZ* 21 [1965]: 245–59, 481–501).

11. In the mean time, the Egyptian material has been more thoroughly examined: Erik Hornung, 'Der Mensch als "Bild Gottes" in Ägypten,' in Loretz, *Gottebenbildlichkeit* (see n. 9 above), 123–56. There was also a 'democratization' of the idea in Egypt, but it can be documented even before the statements about the king as image of God, and is apparently independent of them (Hornung, p. 150). Where the saying is most intensively interpreted, it does not refer to dominion, but to the similarity between human and divine activity: 'Human beings are images of God in their custom of giving ear to a man's response' (Hornung, p. 153). Thus it may be that the comparable Egyptian material does not support the proposed thesis as readily as we may have thought, quite apart from the question that must now be raised about the appropriateness of using it at all.

12. Westermann makes the same methodological demand: *Genesis* (see n. 9 above), 214; idem, *Genesis 1–11,* EdF (Darmstadt, 1972), 25–26.

13. On the state of the text of the 'priestly document' in the sense of a 'priestly history' (without the narrative additions and legal complexes inserted at a later time), cf. Karl Elliger, *Kleine Schriften zum Alten Testament,* ThB 32 (Munich, 1966), 174–75. Typical texts from the priestly document are, e.g., Genesis 17, Exodus 6 and Exodus 24–31, and Exodus 35 to Leviticus 9.

ideas. This has become increasingly clear, especially since we have finally gained access to one of the most important works of Babylonian literature, the Atrahasis epic.[14] It is from this work that the priestly document adopts its sketch of the beginnings,[15] as well as many of its details.[16] Apparently there was a tradition in Mesopotamia of connecting the notion of the creation of human beings by the gods with the idea of an image of God or a similarity to divinity.[17] It is difficult to locate in the surviving sources, and – as far as I can see – there has been no thorough study done by any Assyriologist. It is possible that it developed in a differentiated fashion, so that the creating divinity first produces an image of itself, as a kind of spiritual model, which then enters into the human beings as a crucial component when they are formed from mud and perhaps other elements (such as a portion of divine blood). There is a well-known text in the Gilgamesh epic, at the creation of Gilgamesh's companion Enkidu. As soon as the goddess Aruru received the order of the sky-god Anu to create Enkidu,

14. W. G. Lambert and A. R. Millard, *Atra-Ḫasis. The Babylonian Story of the Flood* (Oxford, 1969).

15. Even the Yahwist history, which constituted the priestly document's primary *Vorlage* within the literature of Israel, had followed the outlines of the Atrahasis epic's story of the beginning. But the priestly document retained the sequence of events in a purer form: creation of humanity, human expansion, flood, post-flood 'compromise.' Thus it must have had access to the Atrahasis epic independently of the Yahwist work.

16. As examples we may mention two elements in Gen. 1:26–27 itself, neither of which could have entered the priestly document by way of the Yahwist. In the plural form of the divine deliberation ('Let us make the human beings . . .') we can still glimpse the great council of the gods at which, in the epic, a decision is made to create human beings. The deliberate and conscious movement toward the theme of 'fruitfulness and increase' at the end of v. 27 corresponds to the theme of the Atrahasis epic, for there the sole problems are overpopulation and birth control, as William L. Moran, 'Atrahasis: The Babylonian Story of the Flood' (*Bibl* 52 [1971]: 51–61), and Anne D. Kilmer, 'The Mesopotamian Concept of Overpopulation and Its Solution as Reflected in the Mythology' (*Or* 41 [1972]: 160–77) have independently shown.

17. Old Testament scholars were not ignorant of this Mesopotamian tradition, either. See, for example, Gerhard von Rad's article in *TDNT* 2: 381–83; Schmidt, *Schöpfungsgeschichte* (n. 9 above), 137 (with references to other authors); Wildberger, 'Abbild' (n. 10 above), 254–55 (with arguments for rejecting the parallels); Francesco Vattioni, 'La creazione dell'uomo nella Bibbia,' *Augustinianum* 8 (1968): 114–39, at 122–23 and 127. But on the whole little attention has been paid to this tradition, or else a connection with Gen. 1:26–27 has been expressly denied.

she formed an image of Anu in her heart.
Aruru washed her hands, pinched off clay and threw it into the wilderness; . . . she made Enkidu the fighter.[18]

There is a very extensive account of the creation in the Sumerian myth of 'Enki and Ninmaḫ'. Here we read, at a crucial point:

At the word of his mother, Nammu, Enki arose from his bedchamber; the god walked about in the sacred space, and thought, as he struck himself on the thigh;
the wise, the knowing, the prudent, the one who knows all that is necessary and beautiful, the creator (and) the one who shapes all things, emitted the *Sigensigšar;*
Enki brings him the arm(s) and forms his breast;
Enki, the creator, permits his wisdom to enter into the innermost parts of his own (creation);
he speaks to his mother, Nammu:
'My mother, impose on the creatures you have called forth the arduous work of the gods;
when you have mixed the interior of the clay on Apsu, you will form the *Sigensigšar* (and) the clay; let the creature be present, (and) may Ninmaḫ be your helper;
may Ninimma, Egizianna, Ninmada, Ninbara, Ninmug, Sarsadu, Ninniginna, whom you have borne, be at your service;
My mother, decide his (= the creature's) fate; let Ninmaḫ impose (on him) the slave's tasks.'[19]

The text may well be understood to mean that Enki first creates the model of the human being, from which the mother goddess and Ninmaḫ are then to make the human being.[20] It contains Enki's bodily form and Enki's wisdom. Any idea of the human being's having a ruling role is

18. Gilgamesh epic 1.II.33–36, quoted here in the version by John Gardner and John Maier, with the assistance of Richard A. Henshaw, *Gilgamesh* (New York, 1984). See also Giovanni Pettinato, *Das altorientalische Menschenbild und die sumerischen und akkadischen Schöpfungsmythen.* Abhandlungen Akademie Heidelberg 1971, 1 (Heidelberg, 1971), 42.

19. 'Enki and Ninmah', 2–38, quoted from Pettinato (cf. n. 18), 71.

20. Thus Pettinato (see n. 18), 39–40. He understands the Sigensigšar as 'the human form created by Enki'. Cf. also Kilmer, 'Overpopulation' (n. 16 above), 165–66.

completely foreign to the text. Instead, the quoted portion ends with the determination of a totally different purpose for the human being's existence: enslavement to the gods. This text is by no means unique in this regard. Rather, it represents the universal Mesopotamian opinion.[21]

It should not be deduced from its use of the idea of the human being as image of God that the biblical priestly document understands what it says about the human being as image of God in precisely the same sense as the Mesopotamian tradition it is adapting. For it also takes the liberty of altering its statement about the purpose of human existence, which in both cases follows immediately: according to this document the human being exists, not to do the gods' tedious and exhausting work for them, but to rule over the animals. As far as the saying about the image of God is concerned, it offers no further clarification – in contrast to the text from 'Enki and Ninmaḫ,' but in agreement with other Mesopotamian texts, such as those cited from the Gilgamesh epic. It simply makes use here of a fixed component in traditional discourse about the creation of humanity. In doing so, it emphasizes the human being's special closeness to God, in contrast to all other creatures. But it does not explicate the matter further.[22] With regard to our own question we can say that the description of the human being as 'image of God,' in itself, permits no conclusions about a ruling position given to humans or any 'responsibility for the world' on their part.

The Blessing of Creation

The statement in v. 26 about human sovereignty over the animals is repeated in v. 28 in a more elaborate context; therefore it will be discussed first of all in this latter connection. Verse 28, God's blessing of humanity, reads:

> 28 God blessed them, and God said to them, 'Be fruitful and multiply, and fill the earth; take possession of it, and have dominion over the fish of the sea and over the birds of the air and over every living thing that moves upon the earth.'

The blessing of fruitfulness requires no further commentary, except to say that it is a blessing and not a 'commandment.' The increase of

21. On this, see Pettinato's whole book (n. 18 above), though he probably makes too sharp a distinction between the Sumerian and Akkadian conceptions.

22. Cf. the remarks in Westermann, *Genesis* (see n. 9 above), 214–18.

humanity also played a major role in Mesopotamia, especially in the Atrahasis epic.[23] However, we should be cautious in using the blessing of fruitfulness in Gen. 1:28 to legitimate one or another position on our present problem of population explosion. For in the thinking behind the priestly document, the 'blessing of creation' is by no means a blessing that applies to all future human generations. The priestly document supposes that some day the blessing of fruitfulness will have achieved its purpose, that humanity will have reached the necessary numbers and that it will then no longer need to increase any further. It expresses this idea quite simply. In the expository technique of the priestly document, every word of God is followed, at some point, by a statement that it has been carried out or been fulfilled. That applies to this blessing as well. Of course, the story of humanity is told only for a single nation, Israel, to the point at which the necessary number of people has been reached. But undoubtedly Israel serves, in this regard, as an example for all the peoples of the earth. It is said of Israel, at a point when it had been living in Egypt for several generations:

> But the Israelites were fruitful and prolific; they multiplied and grew exceedingly strong, so that the land was filled with them (Exod. 1:7).

Here the individual expressions in the blessing of fruitfulness are reprised. From this point on, the priestly document has nothing more to say about fruitfulness and increase. The topic is exhausted.[24]

The end result of the increase in the number of human beings is to be that humanity fills the earth. From the continuation of the priestly document, especially in Genesis 10, the so-called list of nations, we can see that the growth of humanity is conceived as unfolding itself in various races and peoples. According to the divine plan, these nations may each take possession of their own regions. It seems to me that this is precisely what is meant by the statement that follows immediately in Gen. 1:28,

23. Here let me refer to my article, 'Die Priesterschrift und die Grenzen des Wachstums,' appearing in *Stimmen der Zeit*, July 1974.

24. Previously, the blessing of fruitfulness had been frequently repeated: after the Flood (at which point the verb 'to be prolific' is added to the others in Gen. 9:7; it is then taken up also in Exod. 1:7), and at other places in the history of the patriarchs. In addition, it is only to this point that we find the genealogies that are connected with the blessing of fruitfulness; these are intended to illustrate the growth of humanity. On this, cf. Peter Weimar, 'Die Toledot-Formel in der priesterschriftlichen Geschichtsdarstellung', *BZ* 18 (1974): 64–93, at 89–90.

which is usually translated 'subdue it [i.e., the earth].' In exegetical literature we often read, as regards the verb *kbš* that is used here, that it is a very strong expression for 'conquer' or 'subjugate,' and thus means something like 'trample down.'

We may regard Benno Jacob's exposition as typical: 'With this one word, echoed again in Pss. 115:16, humanity is granted unlimited sovereignty over the planet earth; therefore no work that is done on it, for example drilling or the levelling of mountains, drying up or diverting rivers, and similar things, can be regarded as a violent ravaging that is repugnant to God.'[25]

It is true that, immediately after this, Jacob points out that another important Jewish exegete, S. D. Luzzato, understands the verb *kbš* in a 'much more limited' sense. According to him, human beings are intended to 'occupy' the earth, 'to take control of it, namely from the wild beasts,' in continuity with their filling of the earth. And here Luzzato may, in fact, have come closer to the sense of the text than Jacob and many others. This is true not only because it yields a single, clear and direct series of statements, leading from the growth of humanity to their extension throughout the whole earth, while taking possession of the territories of the earth in which previously only beasts have dwelt, and exercising a function of rulership with respect to the animal world, nor only because this avoids an interpretation that would simply outstrip the imaginative horizon of the author of the priestly document. Rather, Luzzato's point of view seems, in addition, to correspond more closely to the other instances in which the Hebrew word *kbš* is used.

The word must have had an original meaning something like 'place one's foot on something,' 'step on something.'[26] But it occurs in Hebrew only in two derived meanings, both mediated by visual metaphors dependent on the original meaning. With 'sins' as its object, the verb means 'to forgive sins.' Sins are like a fire that God crushes underfoot.[27] With people, nations and lands as its object, the verb means 'to take

25. B. Jacob, *Genesis* (see n. 10 above), 61.

26. The meaning is similar in the other Semitic languages as well, especially Akkadian (*kabasu*) and Arabic (*kabasa*). In what follows I will omit the probably corrupt instance in Zech. 9:15. With that exception, I will treat all the occurrences of the word in the Old Testament.

27. There is only one instance of this: Micah 7:19. However, its meaning is fairly certain, since there is a corresponding development in Akkadian. There we find the neo-Babylonian instance *kabasu ša ḫitišu*, 'extinguish guilt, forgive' (cf. Wolfram von Soden, *Akkadisches Handwörterbuch* [Wiesbaden, 1965ff.] 1:415).

possession of.' It is easy to understand how this meaning arose, if we consider that the word *keḇěs*, 'footstool,' is a related substantive.[28] Conquered foes throw themselves to the ground before the victorious king, and he places his foot on them. In Egyptian pictures of the Pharaoh we can see how lands conquered by Egypt, depicted as persons or war bows, are made the footstool of the enthroned king. This expresses the fact that they have lost their freedom and have become his possession.[29] However, we must consider that in using the Hebrew expression 'to place one's foot on something' people did not give much more scope to it than we do when we speak of 'laying hands on something.' The image can be revivified, but normally it is rather pale. Thus the word is used in a great variety of contexts: when free persons are enslaved and thus become someone else's property,[30] when nations or lands, after losing a war, are in a state of dependence,[31] when, through intercourse, a man makes a woman his 'possession.'[32]

Precisely in a text in which the verb *kbš* appears in a context that has a priestly echo and that has the *land* of Canaan as its object, namely Num. 32:22, 29, the parallel biblical passages in Deut. 3:20, 31:3; Josh. 1:15 show, with the word *yrš* used in the corresponding place, that what is at issue is that the land has become the possession of YHWH or of the Israelites.[33] It is therefore best to translate the text of Gen. 1:28 also as undramatically as possible, somewhat as I have done above: 'Take possession of it [i.e., the earth].' And that is to be understood in such a way that humanity, when it has grown so great that it consists of many peoples, is to expand over the whole earth, and each people is to take

28. This is found in 2 Chr. 9:18, in the description of King Solomon's throne.

29. Cf. Othmar Keel, *Die Welt der altorientalischen Bildsymbolik und das Alte Testament. Am Beispiel der Psalmen* (Zürich, 1972), plates 341, 342, and 342a. Cf. also the other biblical expressions for the same thing, in 1 Kgs. 5:17 and Pss. 110:1. In three places (Num. 32:22, 29; Josh. 18:1, 1 Chr. 22:18), the original image behind *kbš* also emerges through the syntactic construction. Here we must translate literally: '[the land {or some similar word}] found itself trodden underfoot, in the presence of NN.'

30. Jer. 34:11, 16; Neh. 5:5; 2 Chr. 28:10.

31. Num. 32:22, 29; Josh. 18:1; 2 Sam. 8:11; 1 Chr. 22:18.

32. Esther 7:8. It does not seem to me to be necessary here to suppose a third path of development from treading down to oppression to rape.

33. There can be no doubt about the dependence of these texts on one another. It is irrelevant for our purposes to know in which direction the dependence exists. *Yrš* in its basic form, in deuteronomic and deuteronomistic language, simply means 'to take possession of', and is a stereotypical expression.

possession of its own territory. Therefore for the people Israel, too, once it has been established, in Exod. 1:7, that the blessing of fruitfulness has been fulfilled, the next question is how it is to come into and take possession of the land of Canaan, which God has planned for Israel. God immediately offers an answer to this question by giving a promise, in Exod. 6:5–8 (only a few verses later in the priestly document), that Israel will be delivered from Egypt and will be led into the land of Canaan, which will become Israel's possession.

The Human Being and the Animals

If the peoples possess their lands, they should rule there, and that means ruling over the *animals.* Gen. 1:28 closes with this idea. What does it mean? We can begin by excluding every kind of exploitation of the animal world by hunting or slaughter, for according to Gen. 1:29 human beings are permitted only vegetable food. Only after the Flood does God alter this law and also permit animals to be eaten. But at that point the formulation is different: 'the fear and dread of you shall rest on every animal of the earth, . . .' (Gen. 9:2). Thus in the passage we are dealing with the subject must be something much more peaceful and normal. But in the works of most biblical interpreters we read something different. They say that here the verb that is used, *rdh,* has the basic meaning of 'tread down,' still clearly retained in Joel 3:13 [Hebrew 4:13], which talks of the stamping of grapes by those who tread the winepress. Therefore in Gen. 1:28, human beings would also be authorized to exercise a violent, indeed a positively cruel domination. But here again, a more careful examination leads to a less daring conception.

It does not appear to me clearly established that the verb *rdh* is to be found at all in Joel 3:13. It is equally possible that what we have is a form of the verb *yrd,* 'to climb down.'[34] In that case, we would find here a demand to go down into the winepress that has been cut into the floor and filled with grapes – of course, for the purpose of stamping and treading the grapes, but that would have nothing to do with the word *rdh.*

Once we are free of any dependence on Joel 3:13, we can organize the remaining occurrences of the verb with relative ease.[35] The objects of

34. This was the usual interpretation of earlier scholars, and it is still reflected in Salomon Mandelkern's concordance.

35. However, in some instances the text is so uncertain or the content so obscure that we can do little with it: Num. 24:9; Pss. 49:14 [Hebrew v. 15]; Lam. 1:13.

the verb are sheep,[36] slaves,[37] laborers,[38] conquered peoples or their kings.[39] When there is an intention to express a special severity in the action referred to, an extra expression must be added.[40] We may infer from this that the word in itself does not express any special severity or cruelty, but simply means: to rule, to command, to lead, to direct.

There is just one passage that does not clearly fit into this picture: Pss. 68:27 [Hebrew v. 28], 'There is Benjamin, the least of them, leading them, the princes of Judah in a body, the princes of Zebulun, the princes of Naphtali.' This is a description of a festal procession. Undoubtedly, at this point, Benjamin does not rule or command, but simply goes at the head of the line. This recalls the Akkadian word *redû*, which has a related root, and for which the meaning given is 'accompany, lead [with oneself]; go.'[41] It is also used, in particular, for driving and leading animals.

Thus we are led to ask whether the Hebrew meanings of *rdh* may not have developed out of a fundamental notion of accompaniment, particularly of animals. Pasturing a flock is a favorite image for the activity of a king. And Gen. 1:26 and 1:28 can be assumed to contain the normal meaning 'to lead, to rule' from the human sphere, but in such a way that the application of the word to animals serves to reactivate the original meaning. Thus the human beings are designated as those who, on settling in their own land, are to govern the animals, and that apparently is done by leading them to pasture, making use of them as beasts of burden, giving them commands to be obeyed, or, in other words: domesticating them. This seems to be what is intended here, and the implied goal appears to be the domestication of animals in all spheres of reality: in the water, in the air, and on the earth.

When, in the context of the blessing of fruitfulness, the topic is later repeated quite frequently, and finally concluded, and when the direction to take possession of the various realms of the earth shapes the priestly

36. Ezek. 34:4. This is a metaphor for the Israelites. In Pss. 49:14 there appears to be a parallelism with *r'h*, 'to pasture', which also indicates that we are in the context of a pastoral culture.

37. Lev. 25:43, 46, 53.

38. 1 Kgs. 5:15 [Hebrew 5:30]; 9:23; 2 Chr. 8:10.

39. Lev. 26:17; 1 Kgs. 4:24 [Hebrew 5:4]; Isa. 14:2, 6; Ezek. 29:15; Pss. 72:2; 110:1 [Hebrew v. 2]; Neh. 9:28.

40. Lev. 25:43, 46, 53; Isa. 14:6; Ezek. 34:4.

41. Wolfram von Soden, *Akkadisches Handwörterbuch* (Wiesbaden, 1965ff.), 2:965.

document to its end, we should ask whether an extension of the theme of human rule over the animals might also yield insight into the precise meaning of the last part of Gen. 1:28. But, surprisingly, the topic is not reintroduced, unless we can regard the new formulation in Gen. 9:2, already mentioned above, as a continuation: 'The fear and dread of you shall rest on every animal of the earth, and on every bird of the air, on everything that creeps on the ground, and on all the fish of the sea; into your hand [or: power] they are delivered.'

We should probably regard this text, in fact, as a revision of the relationship between human beings and animals as originally defined. The formulations 'fear and dread,' and 'to deliver into [someone's] hand' are part of the language of war.[41a] In the oracle that is reflected here the divinity gave the enemies 'into the power' of those making war on them, and in the battle itself the god took part and thus threw the enemies into 'fear and dread.' The permission to eat meat thus creates a hostile relationship between human beings and animals, in which the human being is the victor. The possibility that whole species of animals might be exterminated, of course, is not considered here, either. With regard to Gen. 1:28 we can only say that there the universal domestication of the animal world is conceived in terms of something like a paradisiacal peace among all species which, however, is no longer possible after the Flood. Whatever measure of animal domestication still existed *after the Flood* must probably be regarded as a remnant of that peace. But it is always mixed with war.

A Pre-Technological Horizon of Experience?

Thus in its original meaning Gen. 1:28 is anything but a justification of the belief that human beings are all-powerful and possess a brain that gives them not only the ability, but also the right to exploit all other creatures and everything the world has to offer, without regard for the consequences. Of course, one might say that the harmless character of Gen. 1:28 in its original meaning was simply conditioned by the author's still innocent horizon of experience. But in principle the authorization to take possession of all parts of the earth and to domesticate the whole animal world could be said to contain the germ of everything that later,

41a. For this entire linguistic field, see Gerhard von Rad, *Der Heilige Krieg im alten Israel*, AThANT (Göttingen, 1952); Manfred Weippert, '"Heiliger Krieg" in Israel und Assyrien', *ZAW* 84 (1972): 460–93.

with a more developed rationality and technical knowledge, reveals itself to be humanity's limitless demand to exploit the cosmos. For in any case, human beings have been promised a unique place in the universe.

This kind of argument cannot be dismissed out of hand, for we must translate from an earlier horizon of experience to our own if we want to understand the real meaning of a text. However, in this concrete instance we must immediately raise the counter-question whether the author of the priestly document really had such a simple, pre-technological horizon of experience. After all, he lived in the highly-organized urban and irrigation culture of Babylon. The world into which exile had thrown him had already been struggling with the problem of overpopulation for several millennia. In the process, it had acquired experience with technology, rational organization of community life, and the limits of human possibility. It had ancient and highly developed traditions of civilization and culture. If the author omits technology from the blessing of creation, it appears that in his opinion it does not belong there. Was he rejecting it?

Again, this appears not to be true. He simply did not find it appropriate to include it within the blessing of creation. But later, at the point when he describes the phase after the expansion of humanity, but before the final stabilization of all nations in their territories as exemplified in the case of the people Israel, he illustrates it in two different contexts, one negative, the other positive.

At the beginning of the book of Exodus, technical civilization is sketched in its negative aspect. Ancient technology was based on slavery and hard manual labor. The people of Israel fell victims to that fate when they had reached their full number, but had not yet entered into their land. The Egyptians 'made slaves of them. They made their lives bitter with hard service in mortar and brick and in every kind of field labor. Thus the Israelites were forced to do the hard labor of slaves' (Exod. 1:13b–14: from the author's translation). This kind of technology, which required slaves in order to reach a higher level of civilization, was of no interest to the God of the priestly document. God hears only that people are groaning under their slavery (Exod. 2:23b–25). Immediately, God effects their liberation from Egyptian slavery, announcing it by saying: 'I will free you from the burdens of the Egyptians and deliver you from slavery to them. I will redeem you with an outstretched arm and with mighty acts of judgment' (Exod. 6:6). Therefore we can say that as soon as the rule of human beings over nature becomes the rule of human beings over other human beings, in the sense of exploitation of some people by others, God says 'no.' Since by no means all human beings receive the same benefit from the increasing exploitation and control of nature that is taking place today, but instead the majority of humanity are more disadvantaged than benefitted by the whole process, so that their physical and spiritual potential are curtailed rather than enhanced, and all for the advantage of the minority, it should be clear what conclusions should be drawn from the priestly document in this respect. And to the extent that, at the present time, human beings are exploiting other human beings when, supposedly, their intention is merely to extend their control over nature, it can assuredly never be said that this situation (if not explicitly, at least in germ) is based on the blessing of creation in Gen. 1:28. The priestly document's description of the exodus proves the contrary.

The Real Meaning of Technology

Technology appears in a positive light in the priestly document's description of the events at Sinai. It is true that Israel has not yet arrived in its land, but the most significant expression of life in the land is already being prepared: the gift of the sanctuary, through which God will dwell in the midst of the people as its own God. The artistic preparation of the sanctuary is evidently meant to express the culmination of human reshaping of the world. In contrast to the remaking of the world that was taking place in Egypt, based on the principle of slavery, in Israel everything rests on the principle of voluntariness. Moses asks that those 'whose hearts move them to do so' should donate the materials for the sanctuary (Exod. 35:5–9). Those who 'are skillful' are requested to come forward and carry out the work (Exod. 35:10).[42] The leading technician is introduced with great enthusiasm:

> 'See, YHWH has called by name Bezalel son of Uri son of Hur, of the tribe of Judah, and has filled him with divine spirit, with skill, intelligence, and knowledge in every kind of craft, to devise artistic designs, to work in gold, silver, and bronze, in cutting stones for setting, and in carving wood, in every kind of craft' (Exod. 35:30–33).

42. The Hebrew expressions are: *kōl nĕdîb libbô* (Exod. 35:5) and *kōl-ḥăkam-lēb* (Exod. 35:10). We could also translate 'generous people' and 'artistic people.' On the first expression, cf. the still broader formulations in Exod. 35:21 and 35:29. Some of the generous Israelites also bring the fruits of their artistic talent: cf. Exod. 35:25–26. On the other hand, it is emphasized in Exod. 36:2 that the technicians and artists undertook the work freely ('everyone whose heart was stirred to come to do the work').

Thus artistic and technical achievement rests on a special giftedness from God that is bestowed on individuals. Perhaps this subject could not be introduced in the beginning, at creation, since there the text spoke of all human beings and not of special individuals. In any case, what is here undertaken as an improvement on nature, differentiated according to the special type of work, but still in a 'classless' society based on spontaneity, is described with the greatest solemnity as something introduced by God's own will into the divine creation. This is accomplished by the priestly document's taking on the enormous task of reciting the whole story of the building and furnishing of the sanctuary, not once, but twice. First Moses is called up to God on the mountain and is given the most detailed instructions on what to do (Exodus 25–31). Then the carrying out of God's instructions is narrated in equal detail (Exodus 36–40). Nowhere else is the priestly document so detailed. This whole procedure looks like a human continuation of the first work of creation on the six days. In fact, at the beginning of the events at Sinai, the glory of YHWH covers the mountain for six days, and on the seventh day YHWH calls Moses, in order to reveal to him the sanctuary that the people are to build (Exod. 24:16).[43] This work is not merely revealed in verbal instructions; rather, Moses is shown a heavenly model of the sanctuary:

> '. . . make me a sanctuary, so that I may dwell among them (= the Israelites). In accordance with all that I show you concerning the pattern of the tabernacle and of all its furniture, so you shall make it' (Exod. 25:8–9).[44]

We cannot help noticing that the human being itself was made in the image of God. The Mesopotamian pre-history of this idea, at least, is acquainted with the notion that this does not simply mean that the human being is an image of God, but that God first produces, from within the Godhead, a heavenly model of the human being who is similar to God, and according to which the individual human beings will then be formed. Of course, the divine model for the sanctuary is not an image of God, but an image of God's heavenly dwelling. Nevertheless, it is thereby made

43. For more detail on the relationship between the week of creation and the theophany at Sinai in the priestly document, which has been sketched in a very simplified form here, see Nicola Negretti, *Il settimo giorno*, An Bib (Rome, 1973), 224–51.

44. The heavenly model is then mentioned once more in connection with the lampstand (Exod. 25:40). Its description hints that it is a symbol for the cosmos.

clear why human beings have been given the ability to alter nature through their own activity. It is so that the earth may be developed to resemble heaven, in order that the earth may become the dwelling place of God. On this basis, we can see what false accents Carl Amery has drawn out of the story in his book, *Das Ende der Vorsehung*:

> Likeness to God is attributed solely to human beings. This privilege is ascribed to no other living thing, to no other creature, not even to the whole harmony of the universe. From the fact that communication with other kinds of living things, as well as with the gigantic, indifferent things of the universe is closed to human beings, it is concluded that a deep cleft has been laid between them and the rest of creation; a cleft that is not regarded as a misfortune, but rather as evidence of the fundamentally higher value of human beings. This is still true today, even for dyed-in-the-wool materialists who consider the origins of our species from a completely physiological point of view. They, no more than believers, have overcome the conviction that the human being, both in theory and in practice, is the culminating point: *telos*, end and goal of world history.[45]

This is the kind of conclusion that is reached when one rips a sentence from the literary context in which it belongs. The priestly document intended Gen. 1:26–28 in a different sense. Its Sinai pericope shows that, while it is true that human beings are meant to change this world, they are to change it into an image of a heavenly model in harmony with the work of the first six days. This alteration is to make it possible for God to dwell among human beings. It is not human beings, but God's dwelling among them, that, according to the priestly document, is '*telos*, end and goal of world history.'

The doctrine of humanity that is often read out of Gen. 1:28 is thus not to be found there. No one may use this text to legitimate what humanity has inaugurated in modern times, the bitterly evil results of which appear to be showing themselves on our horizon. The Jewish-Christian tradition of humanity is different. It regards human beings very highly, but it would never designate them as absolute rulers of the universe.

45. Amery (see n. 4 above), p. 16.

2

Genesis 2–3 as 'Historical Etiology'

Thoughts on a New Hermeneutical Concept

It is customary in Catholic theology to make a deliberate distinction between 'inspiration' and 'revelation.' A biblical text is, for those who read it, the word of God spoken to them, and in that sense it is revelation. But as regards the human authors of the biblical texts it is only true, in the first instance, that they are inspired. The way in which they arrived at their expressions and formulations, that is, what the process of inspired writing looked like from the human side, is another question. Here revelations (of the mystical type) can play a role, but it can also be the case that older traditions were simply incorporated or that the author's own reflections and conclusions led to a particular statement or expression. Thus from the fact of inspiration itself we cannot draw any immediate conclusions about the concrete process by which a biblical text came into existence.

This approach to the theology of inspiration is particularly important in connection with the biblical statements about the beginnings of human history. For the way in which we suppose the biblical author arrived at these statements cannot fail to influence their theological interpretation. If the author of Genesis 2–3 was in a 'vision,' so to speak, moved backward in time some hundreds of thousands of years, and could be said to have 'seen' the events of that period in the true sense of the word, or if the author received a tradition that, by divine providence, had been preserved intact through millennia, and that ultimately rested on eyewitness testimony, the individual formulations and expressions must, of course, be evaluated quite differently than would be the case if the author, reflecting in some ways the notions of the origin of all things that were current in the writer's own time, had independently drawn certain *conclusions* about an 'original sin,' based on experience of the world contemporary to the author as well as on a faith in the one God of Israel and that God's familiar way of dealing with the world, and had then given a concrete, narrative depiction of that idea in his or her own style. Even in this third case, the fact of inspiration, and with it the correctness of what is stated (to the extent that it is really a question of a statement of truth and not of its pictorial concretizing) is not impugned.

Only from the text itself can we determine which of the three cases mentioned above, or what other possible situation, lies before us. The matter therefore falls within the competence of exegesis. Many Catholic exegetes today have made a decision in favor of the third scenario as here described. A.-M. Dubarle, in particular, has done some thorough exegetical investigations of the question.[1] H. Renckens, whose book on the biblical history of origins bears the significant title, 'Israel's visie op het verleden,' ['Israel's view of the past'] has made this point of view accessible to a broad audience.[2] At the same time, the dogmatic theologian Karl Rahner adopted this view as his own, refined its hermeneutical implications in sharper conceptual language, and placed the whole in a larger context of epistemological theory and theology.[3] Rahner's precise standpoint has now become the point of departure for exegetical examination of the question: L. Alonso-Schökel has applied the methods of stylistic analysis anew to the text of Genesis 2–3 from the points of view supplied by Rahner, and found them fully confirmed. In fact, he made a completely new discovery: that Israel's salvation-historical theology of covenant, in particular, greatly influenced the composition of the account of the first human sin.[4] We thus have here an excellent example of the

1. *Les Sages d'Israël*, Lectio Divina 1 (Paris, 1946); *Le péché originel dans l'Écriture*, Lectio Divina 20 (Paris, 1958). In this article, which relates to an internal Catholic problem, I do not wish to enter into a discussion of non-Catholic exegesis.

2. Published in German as *Urgeschichte und Heilsgeschichte. Israels Schau in die Vergangenheit* (Mainz, 1959). Original Dutch edition 1957.

3. 'Ätiologie', *LthK*[2] (1957) 1: 1011–12. He writes in more detail in P. Overhage and K. Rahner, *Das Problem der Hominisation.* 'Über den biologischen Ursprung des Menschen,' *Quaestiones disputatae* 12/13 (Freiburg, 1961), 34–42. This work was translated in part by W. T. O'Hara, under the title, *Hominisation. The evolutionary Origin of Man as a Theological Problem*, QD 13 (London, 1965). Quoted material and page numbers given in parentheses in the text are from O'Hara's translation, but the orthography has been slightly altered to conform to American usage. Cf. also K. Rahner and H. Vorgrimler, *Kleines theologisches Wörterbuch.* Herder-Bücherei 108/109 (Freiburg, 1961), 36.

4. 'Motivos sapienciales y de alianza en Gn 2–3,' *Bibl* 43 (1962): 295–316. Cf. especially the concluding positions on each of Rahner's theses at pp. 312–13. On the traces of covenant theology, see pp. 305–9.

fruitful results that may follow from a cooperation between exegesis and dogmatic theology.

It is certainly desirable that this dialogue be continued. The more concrete the discussion becomes, the fewer problems will exist.[5] Karl Rahner could have been expected to be willing to pursue the dialogue, since he promised a whole book in the series he edited, 'Quaestiones disputatae,' on the subject of the theological interpretation of Genesis 1–3. The remarks below are intended to do nothing more than aid in avoiding the sudden appearance of unexpected difficulties in this dialogue. I do not refer to difficulties concerning the subject itself, but as regards the *terminology* used in this discussion.

Karl Rahner introduced a new terminology to which he gave specific definition.[6] Of course, every author has the right to choose his or her concepts as seems appropriate, and to define them as he or she wishes. But precisely when a dialogue between two different scholarly disciplines is in progress, it would be better for neither of the two partners to introduce terminology already in use in the other field in a new sense that deviates at the outset and by definition from the old meaning. Thus within dogmatic theology there may be no objection when Rahner refers to Genesis 2–3 as a 'historical etiology' and describes this 'historical etiology' as a 'literary genus.' But the conversation with exegesis is unnecessarily burdened by this, since in exegetical studies both words are already in use in other contexts and therefore have other referents. For example, the unease created among exegetes is apparent in the article by Alonso-Schökel mentioned above, at the point where he mentions Rahner's terminology for the first time. He speaks of a 'terminologia personal, que los exegetas no encontrarán muy feliz.'[7] What Alonso-Schökel thus notes briefly should, in what follows, be

5. As one indication, we may cite the pointed plea of the exegete H. Haag (*Hochland* 53 [1960–61] 278) to dogmatic theology that 'the teaching on the 'dona praeternaturalia' be re-examined in light of our present understanding of the biblical narrative.' He makes this request in the context of a review of Rencken's book, where he finds it illogical that the author denies that human beings in Paradise were not subject to suffering, but still maintains that they were immortal. On the question of paradisiacal preservation from death, see the more recent work of the exegete V. Hamp, 'Paradies und Tod', in *Neutestamentliche Aufsätze*, Festschrift for J. Schmid (Regensburg, 1963), 100–109. He is much more cautious than Haag, but it is clear from the article that his reticence is occasioned not by exegetical reasons, but by church documents. This is obviously a point that requires further discussion.

6. The classification used in the bibliography in *LThK*[2] (1957), 1012 gives the impression that the terminology had been taken from Rahner's predecessors.

7. 'Motivos sapienciales' (see n. 4 above), 295.

made somewhat clearer, especially to our partners in this dialogue on Genesis 2–3 from the field of dogmatic theology, and to the audience.[8]

First let us briefly review *Rahner's terminological system.*[9]

(a) Rahner's approach to the concept of 'etiology' begins with the following question: '*Whence* does the author of Genesis know the things he reports?' He answers this question about 'whence' with an 'as': 'He knows it *as* historical etiology' (pp. 35–36).

(b) In his definition, Rahner starts from a rather broad concept of 'etiology' and progressively limits it. 'Etiology in the widest sense is the assigning of the reason or cause of another reality' (p. 36). From there, without an intermediate stage, we are led to etiology 'in a narrower sense.' This is 'indicating an earlier event as the reason for an observed state of affairs or occurrence in human affairs, the observed state of affairs being the means whereby the cause is known' (p. 36). Here the concept has been limited in three ways: (1) The reality to be explained by the etiology is an 'observed state of affairs or occurrence in human affairs;' (2) the proposed originating cause is 'earlier,' and therefore historical; (3) the historical origin cannot be known from one's own recollection or through (reliable or unreliable) historical reports, but must be deduced from the effect that is to be explained. It is this third element that is most important for Rahner. He now seeks in his own field for the principle by which the concept can be further subdivided. He inquires, in a sense, about the success of the deduction from effect to cause. Depending on its failure or success, he distinguishes 'mythological' and 'historical' etiologies. The 'reference back to an earlier event may [a] take the form of a figurative representation of a cause which, however, is only designed vividly to express and impress on the mind the state of things actually observed. That is mythological etiology, and it may be quite conscious and deliberate, or it may be accompanied by belief in the occurrence of the earlier event. Frequently in this matter without consciously realizing it the human mind hovers in an imaginative, meditative way . . .' Otherwise [b] 'The reference back to an earlier event may . . . be genuine, that is to say, the

8. I wish to express my sincere thanks to Karl Rahner for the interest with which he read a first draft of this article, for his objections and suggestions, and especially for the generosity with which he encouraged me to publish my ideas. That was some time ago, and the plan was to publish this article alongside the study by Alonso-Schökel cited in note 4 above. But I held it back so long as it would have been difficult for Karl Rahner to reply in a similarly public forum.

9. The page numbers in the following citations refer to O'Hara's translation (see n. 3 above).

objectively possible, well-founded and successful inference of an historical cause from a present state of affairs. The state of affairs itself is more clearly grasped and the real cause and its consequence are seen in one perspective. The degree to which the true historical cause is grasped in its own concrete reality may vary considerably. Correspondingly, the manner in which the inferred cause of what actually exists is stated is almost inevitably expressed in a more or less figurative manner which . . . derives from the world of experience of the etiologist. This is historical etiology' (pp. 36–37).

(c) Rahner thinks that he has thus defined a literary genre, for at the beginning of a later section he writes: 'What follows if this concept of historical etiology is applied to the account in Genesis as being its literary character?' (p. 39).

The following reflections are undertaken from three points of view: the literary field from and for which the concept of etiology is derived; the role of genuine historical reports in an etiology; the designation and treatment of etiology as a literary genre.

1. The Literary Province of Etiology

In Rahner's work it is clear that he has created this whole system of concepts only with a view to the Genesis stories of Paradise and the Fall.

Thus the attribute 'mythological,' in contradistinction to the word 'historical,' makes almost no sense except in the case of etiological narratives that take place at the beginning of time or before time, and in which heavenly beings appear. Otherwise we do not ordinarily speak of 'myths.' But we would certainly not wish to call, for example, the etiological explanation of the name of 'Edom' in Gen. 25:30 a 'historical etiology' in Rahner's sense; on the other hand, to call it a 'mythological etiology' would surely not be (altogether) appropriate either. It is clear that Rahner arrived at his not wholly adequate pair of opposites (historical vs. mythological) on the basis of a concrete situation within the history of exegesis: in contrast to the 'mythological' explanation of Genesis 2–3 prevailing in Protestant interpretation, he attempts to find a basis for a 'historical' interpretation, not in the usual sense of the term, but with a meaning that is nonetheless genuine. In the process, biblical texts other than Genesis 2–3 are scarcely taken into account.

In fact, Old Testament scholarship has been using the concept of etiology for quite some time,[10] applying it to literary phenomena

10. The usage is similar to, if not precisely identical with that in the general field of religious studies and the study of folklore. As far as I can see, this use of the word (in

distributed throughout much of the Old Testament. Many narratives, especially those of an early period, are pointed toward the fact that, as an effect of the event narrated or in memory of it, a visible sign, a name, or a fixed custom continues '*to this day*' (i.e., until the time when the narrative in question was formulated). Or sometimes it is stated – and we even have an instance of this type of etiological motif in Genesis 2 – '*therefore* a man leaves his father and his mother and clings to his wife, and they become one flesh.' The fixed formula 'to this day,' or a narrative conclusion introduced by 'therefore,' or both together (Gen. 32:32 [Heb. v. 33]) clearly indicate that the past is being described in order to explain something in the present. Here, that is, we find revealed an intention of the narrator, a purpose given by the narrator for telling the story. Whether this is always the only or primary purpose has to be determined by further literary analysis. Not only that, but literary analysis can, of course, sometimes uncover such an intention on the part of the narrator even when these fixed formulae are lacking. In any case: this intention on the part of the narrator is called 'etiological.' 'Etiology' thus refers primarily to the narrator's intent. Two facts are significant: (1) the concept of etiology is, in the field of Old Testament studies, constructed on specific topical formulae that often appear in a narrative context, and (2) the concept is applied to a great many and widely varying types of texts in large parts of the Old Testament.

Hermann Gunkel demonstrated very skillfully how the formative

addition to which there has always been another meaning in natural philosophy, also derived from antiquity) is ultimately traceable to Callimachos of Cyrene (310–240 BCE). His major work was the Αἴτια, 'a "wreath of etiological sayings" (Rohde) . . . in which the origins of cultures and customs, festivals and games, sanctuaries and cities, the names of gods and heroes were traced to events of an earlier time, and in which the limits of mythical history were not always observed . . . His principal aim was to bring to light unknown sayings and to reveal new aspects of those that were known; in this he did not in any way limit himself to those whose origins or nature rendered them etiological in character, but he also knew how to subordinate other types of myths to these purposes' (Herter, in Pauly-Wissowa, *Real-Encyklopädie der classischen Altertumswissenschaft*, Supplement 5 [Stuttgart, 1931), 408. In the scholarly fields mentioned, an etiological reference to the beginning of time is regarded as only one among the possible types of etiology. The article 'Ätiologie,' in Bächtold and Stäubli, *Handwörterbuch des deutschen Aberglaubens* I (Berlin, 1927), 647–66 (Beth), does not, as far as I can see, include any myth concerning the beginning of time among its many examples. Realities that are given etiological explanations are normally cults, names, surprising individual phenomena, and, less often, the basic situation of human beings as such. But in the present article I intend to restrict myself to the use of the term in Old Testament scholarship.

stages of a number of fields of learning can be discerned in the various classes of etiological motifs contained in Genesis.[11] In Genesis 2–3, also, etiological intentions were determinative, in a number of places, for the concrete details of the narrative.[12] But in some of these, at least, it is a matter of subordinated secondary motifs. It is not so easy to demonstrate whether the author's primary and comprehensive intention was etiological, and if so, in what sense.[13]

When starting from such a broad basis, we undoubtedly find it somewhat strange to encounter a concept of etiology that is directed entirely to a single text and its current and urgent hermeneutical problematic. In the long run we have to expect misunderstandings to arise when dogmatic theologians, with their concept of etiology in mind, run across the exegetical concept of etiology – and vice versa, of course. The situation is only made more peculiar by the fact that exegesis at the present time is in the process of developing a kind of concept of 'historical' etiology, but with an entirely different meaning.

2. Historical Reports in Etiological Narratives

To summarize at the outset: For Rahner, the crucial point about 'historical etiology' is that the fact narrated from the past is not derived from

11. *Genesis*, HKAT (Göttingen, 1910). In the creation and Paradise stories are found the beginnings of philosophy and theology, as well as the history of cultures (XV–XVI). In the sagas of the patriarchs we find ethnological sagas forming the origins of philosophy of history, etymological motifs as the origin of linguistics, cultic saga motifs (questions about the beginnings of cultic places and customs) as the origin of the history of religions, and geological saga motifs (such as the explanation of the origins of the Dead Sea) as the first stages of geology (XX–XXV).

12. In Gen. 2:24 and 3:14–19 there are individual etiologies (Eros, human being and serpent; the difficulties of pregnancy and birth; work and its pains; death).

13. According to G. von Rad it might be better to speak of theodicy. Ultimately it is a question of 'acquitting God and his creation of the guilt for all the suffering and tribulation that have entered the world' (*Das erste Buch Mose, Genesis Kapitel 1–12,9*, ATD [Göttingen, 5th ed. 1958], 81–82). Naturally, an intended theodicy also includes, as an internal factor, an intended etiology for all the suffering and tribulations of the world, but it is more comprehensive. In any case, a still broader etiological intention is evident in the structure of Genesis as a whole: the history of origins must 'be understood as one of the most essential elements in a theological etiology of Israel' (G. von Rad, *Theologie des Alten Testaments* I [Munich, 2nd ed. 1958], 178. Translated by D. M. G. Stalker under the title, *Old Testament Theology. I. The Theology of Israel's Historical Origins* [Edinburgh and London, 1962], 164).

historical knowledge, but is *deduced* from the effect that is to be explained. Old Testament scholarship, on the other hand, is struggling at the present time to formulate a concept of etiology that permits us to suppose that the narrated fact from the past can be derived from *genuine historical tradition* and for that very reason can be historical. Of course, this problem is not acute in the case of Genesis 2–3, but arises primarily with regard to texts relating to the period of the patriarchs and the entry into the Land.

Rahner probably took the concept of etiology from a field in which this problem was not yet urgent. For we must admit that Old Testament scholarship (like other scholarly fields as well) for the most part couples the concept of what is etiological almost automatically with what is invented at a later time and therefore is unhistorical. The considerable skepticism about the historical value of the biblical narratives of the patriarchs and the appropriation of the Land is founded on this very connection, and such skepticism is still widespread today. The stories about the entry into the Land, in particular, contain a great many etiological motifs. But it is precisely in this area that, in recent years, a discussion has arisen, within which the relatonship between etiological statements and the historicity of what is narrated has been hotly debated.

The events surrounding the occupation of the land of Canaan by the Israelite tribes are, in fact, accessible, at least in part, to historical-critical methods, as a result of archeological excavations and the possibility of comparison between different biblical traditions. It thus happened that new discoveries aroused debate over the long-held view that the etiological narratives were historically unreliable. Particular objections were raised by W. F. Albright and his students.[14] Then, at the 1959 Oxford International Old Testament Congress, Martin Noth presented, in dialogue with these objectors, what is probably the best definition of the relationship between etiology and history:

> Etiological narratives, of their very nature, have a relationship to history, since they explain a particular circumstance by means of some historical process. In individual cases, certainly, it is doubtful how close or distant the real relationship to history is. It is only on the basis of the observation that historical processes can leave visible or otherwise detectable traces that we can begin to imagine how etiological narrative came into being. In this process, it is

14. The most important of those students was John Bright. See his *Early Israel in Recent Historical Writing* (London, 1956).

> entirely possible that an accurate and concrete historical tradition could take the form of an etiological narrative. W. F. Albright, on the basis of a number of examples from ancient and modern times, has quite rightly indicated that historical memories are especially likely to be retained in a living form in oral tradition if they can be repeatedy connected to consequences of the historical process that are still known . . . But on the basis of this observation of the recognizable continuing effects of historical processes it has also happened that some have moved in the reverse direction, so that, beginning with some remarkable phenomenon, conclusions are drawn about a historical process that appeared capable of explaining this phenomenon. In this case, as well, there is a relationship to history. First of all, the remarkable phenomenon itself, which forms the starting point, is a historical element; and the process by which the phenomenon is explained also rests on historical tradition. The question then is only whether the phenomenon and the process are really connected historically, or whether they have only been combined in hindsight, and whether the historical tradition that serves as an explanation is more or less concrete, or whether it is entirely vague. In general, it is not possible to discern from an etiological narrative the route that the tradition has taken, and how closely it is related to genuine history. We must reckon with a whole spectrum of possibilities.[15]

The fact that the thing to be explained is the sole starting point for the discovery and construction of the explanatory event thus constitutes only a circumscribing limit for etiological narrative. In itself, etiological narrative is indifferent as regards the origin of its contents. We gain access to the essence of etiology as a literary phenomenon, like that in the Old Testament, by asking: Why is the story told? and not: How does the narrator know the things that she or he is telling? The latter question arises only at a later point, and goes beyond what is really meant by the word 'etiology.' Within this question, etiological narrative based on traditional knowledge of the past again appears as the original, and in some sense the 'normal' type. To my knowledge, the phrase 'historical etiology' has not yet been applied to this normal type, and it probably will not be so applied. Instead, in cases where it seems appropriate, we would prefer to speak of a 'historically reliable etiology.' Even so it remains awkward when

15. 'Der Beitrag der Archäologie zur Geschichte Israels,' *NTSuppl* 7 (1960), 279–80.

the very similar-sounding expression 'historical etiology' is applied to the special case of Genesis 2–3, especially when, in the conceptual system being applied in this case, a historically reliable etiology, which deals with genuine traditions, can *ex definitione* not be given the name 'etiology.'

It is interesting to note that, both in the case of Rahner dealing with Genesis 2–3 and in the case of Albright treating the narratives of the entry into the Land, what emerges is an effort to recover the historicity of biblical statements. Thus parallel but independent efforts have, in this instance, led to an opposite application of a particular terminology. In this case, however, the exegetes are probably not only *in possessione*, but they find it more difficult to surrender the field, since they have worked out their concept through a much broader process of induction than that of the dogmatic theologians, who started from a single case and gave no attention to any others. Externally, Rahner's conceptual system in fact looks like an arbitrary, *a priori* arrangement, only subsequently to be verified with reference to the phenomena.

3. Is Etiology a Literary Genre?

Rahner gives his 'historical etiology' its name, but in doing so he places himself in a contradiction to that very classification.

Rahner arrives at 'historical etiology' by distinguishing, within 'etiology in the narrower sense,' between 'mythological' and 'historical' etiologies. This is not the kind of distinction that is customarily used in separating literary genres.

Ordinarily, the procedure is to list differing characteristics of form, different life-situations (*Sitze im Leben*), different typical contents and motifs, and the like. Here, on the contrary, the specific distinction appears to be – at least partly – between true and false. Let me explain.

Although it is very difficult to understand precisely what Rahner means by the word 'mythological,' one thing is clear: the mythological fabricates a fact at the beginning of human history, but does not attain to the reality, not even when it believes that it has arrived at the fact. 'Historical etiology' is 'successful' in its attempt to attain to a historical basis; 'mythological etiology,' on the other hand, is unsuccessful. The two 'etiologies' Rahner distinguishes thus function as successful and unsuccessful attempts, as true and false. Is it possible to distinguish literary genres in this way?

If there are two stories in the morning paper, parallel in structure, one of which (as later appears) is true, the other false, or, to use Rahner's terms, one of which is 'successful,' the other 'unsuccessful,' nevertheless both are examples of the same genre, 'newspaper story.' Truth or falsehood do not effect a division of the genre of the newspaper story into two sub-genres of true and false, historical and unhistorical newspaper story. I can construct these expressions, of course, but in doing so I depart from the field of genre classification. The question of literary genre is certainly useful in determining what *kind of truth* is to be expected (historical report, religious statement, lyric utterance, etc.), but within the realm of truth circumscribed by the genre it remains the task of the individual text, in the sense of 'yes' or 'no,' to be true or false, 'successful' or 'unsuccessful.' The responsibility for this lies with such factors as the veracity or mendacity of the author, available evidence or error. This is at a different level from all the things that determine literary genre.

Thus if Rahner had intended to define a genre, he would not have introduced 'success' into the definition. We could even try out Rahner's distinction between mythological and historical etiology without the characteristic of 'success,' and thus leaving aside the question of truth. We could say, for example, that etiologies of the type found in Genesis 2–3, which attempt to point back to the beginning of history within the framework of history itself, are called 'historical etiologies,' while the name 'mythological etiology' would be applied in cases in which the limits of history are ruptured and, to explain present circumstances, events are narrated that are to be conceived as happening in a kind of timeless time. Of course, if we did that we would get tangled up with the customary notion of myth. But what of it? Even so, this procedure would not be sufficient to give us a definition of the genre. Literary genres are positive facts. Consequently, the next question would be whether these two kinds of etiology can be found in a literary corpus, and in such a way that they can be distinguished from one another by means of definable external characteristics. Presupposing that all this could be accomplished, we could, of course, pose the question of truth to each individual text that could be classified within the genre of 'historical etiology.' In that case it would be – as is proper – not a question for the genre, but for the individual texts. If historians ask a question about truth, they use historical methods; if theologians pose the question of truth concerning a biblical text, they will also, according to the circumstances, need to keep in mind the matter of inspiration. That would be entirely proper in this case. On the other hand, it is quite improper to insert inspiration directly or indirectly into the definition of literary genres, something that seems at least threatened in Rahner's case.

This brings us to a further point: Rahner makes no effort to discover formal or lexical characteristics, motifs, or other traits of the genre he is defining that are tangibly evident in the textual matter itself. While it is true that literary genres cannot be defined on the basis of such external features alone, still they cannot be so defined entirely without them. Literary genres develop historically, they grow over a historical period of time, and they also decline and disappear historically, giving way to other genres. Literary genres belong to the realm of 'institutions,' in the same sense that universities and states are institutions: like these latter, they cannot be defined without reference to some kind of material reality and tangible features. Without a reference to unique features of linguistic form, 'literary composition' would lack what is 'literary.' But such references are entirely lacking in Rahner's definition of 'historical etiology.'[16] (In contrast, cf., for example, the study by J. Fichtner, 'Die etymologische Ätiologie in den Namensgebungen der geschichtlichen Bücher des Alten Testaments.')[17]

In particular, we ought also to observe that Rahner first develops the concept of 'historical etiology' hypothetically, and verifies it only at a second stage. This procedure could be regarded as legitimate in the field of research on literary genres as well. But Rahner does not go on to confront his concept with the biblical text in order to refine its content and make it concrete. Instead, he immediately sets it over against the irreducible demands of the church's teaching. That again is, in itself, fully justified. But it certainly does not belong within the realm of genre research.

Thus we may conclude that Rahner's opinion that he is talking about a 'literary genre' is refuted by his own way of dealing with the subject. But in the concrete case of etiology it is also true that, as regards the Old Testament, we have to ask to what extent 'etiologies' constitute a 'genre.'

This is necessary at least if we understand 'genres' as fixed units with a clearly determinable purpose and *Sitz im Leben*, a clearly determinable type of content and form, appearing in pre-literary cultures and those in an early stage of literary development, and playing a major role in the Old Testament as well.

What is lacking in the etiological elements in the Old Testament is

16. See further on the nature of literary genres: René Wellek and Austin Warren, *Theory of Literature* (New York, 1956), with a bibliography on this question at 341–42. With particular reference to the Old Testament: L. Alonso-Schökel, 'Genera litteraria,' *Verbum Domini* 38 (1960): 3–15; V. Hamp, 'Genera litteraria,' *LTK*² IV (1960), 686–89. Hamp's definition of 'genre' rests primarily on its classifying function, which is also an important point of view.

17. *VT* 6 (1956): 327–96.

often the characteristic of independence or closure. They may have had such characteristics at an early stage of their existence, but now they often constitute only appendages or final elements of stories that would stand as complete and coherent in themselves, even without these 'etiologies.' Thus at the most we can speak of genre-related *motifs*. Sometimes they are also inserted in the middle of a narrative in order to lend an etiological point to something that is merely a subordinate element in the narrative itself. Or, at other times, the etiological element is a coordinated intention of the narrative, but is not solely responsible for the shaping of the narrative units in question.

In his commentary on Genesis, Hermann Gunkel employed the various types of etiological viewpoints only for the purpose of distinguishing some subgroups within 'myth' and the nonhistorical or ethnographical 'sagas of the patriarchs' (as he calls them in his system). He does not appear to include 'etiology' as a special genre.

But even if there are instances of a proper genre of etiologies in the Old Testament, we must again question whether that genre is present in Genesis 2–3. It is true that Genesis 2–3 uses pre-literary genres as elements in its construction, such as the three verdicts of YHWH-Elohim on the serpent, the woman and [all] humanity [Adam].[18] But the whole composition is not at that level. We ought not to be deceived by its 'simplicity.' It is not 'archaic, but rather in sovereign control of its artistry.'[19] The question of genre can then, at most, be posed in a different sense corresponding to this level, and in that case we should, in any case, proceed at a minimum from a survey of the whole 'Yahwist writing.'

However, this question can remain open; my only purpose here is to advise caution. It is by no means established that what Rahner describes, and what he has in mind, belongs in the field of 'genres.' We must at this point demand of the dogmatic theologians, too, a greater degree of precision in the application of concepts drawn from literary theory, or at least a justification of their conceptual language (since, of course, the literary theoreticians are not always in full agreement with one another).

It has become customary among Catholics to speak of the *genus litterarium*. This concept is sometimes expanded to mean something like 'literary phenomenon,' unfortunately even among exegetes. In fact, the 'genre' is, of course, only one – and by no means the most important –

18. Cf. J. Haspecker and N. Lohfink, 'Gn 3,15: "weil du ihm nach der Ferse schnappst,"' *Schol* 36 (1961): 364–70.

19. G. von Rad, *Das erste Buch Mose* (cf. n. 13 above), 80.

aspect of literary reality. The genre is not even the one thing in a literary work that needs to be examined to determine the author's intention, which would certainly be important in a hermeneutics involving a theology of inspiration. This is clear even from the papal documents, which in connection with the question of determining what is intended to be expressed use not only the phrase *genus litterarium* (558, 580, 581)[20] but a whole series of other expressions, such as *dicendi formae* (558, similarly 559, 560, 581), *loquendi modi* or *rationes* (559, similarly 558, 560), *exponendi narrandique artes* (559, similarly 560). These refer in part to individual literary characteristics, and in part to the whole body of such characteristics. This is clear especially in the more technical formulations in Cardinal Suhard's letter: 'les procédés . . . de la pensée et de l'expression' (580), 'les formes littéraires,' 'tous les problèmes littéraires,' 'les procédés littéraires,' 'tout le matériel . . . de la science littéraire,' 'langage' (all in 581). (The encyclical *Divino afflante Spiritu* was apparently not in a position to express itself precisely in the technical language of modern literary criticism, since it was written in Latin.) It is evident that the papal documents are not the reason why *genus litterarium* has become a catch phrase used far more often than is appropriate. Perhaps this was caused by the fact that, at the beginning of this century, that concept for a time was the focus of hermeneutical discussion among Catholics, and that in recent years it was again brought into the foreground by the struggle over form criticism of the gospels. In any case, dogmatic theologians should only use it when it is appropriate to the subject, since otherwise, here again, the long-term result will be another split between dogmatics and exegesis that can only lead to misunderstandings.

These, then, are my misgivings about Karl Rahner's terminology. Let me emphasize once again that it is not a question of the subject matter, but of the words; one could even overlook the unconventional use of language were it not necessary to take a stance in opposition to the steadily growing alienation among the various fields of theology.

It remains, finally, to ask how that which Rahner is suggestng can be better organized and named. I think it is important to note at this point that Rahner begins with the question: *Whence* does the author of Genesis 2–3 know the things that are being described? Rahner's attention is thus directed not at all to the finished biblical text and its ultimate literary shape, but to the process of recognition, of acquisition of knowledge, that

20. These and the following numbers refer to the enumeration in *Enchiridion Biblicum, Documenta ecclesiastica Sacram Scripturam spectantia* (Naples, 3rd. ed. 1956).

precedes the text. And that is the real subject of his remarks. Rahner is thus really speaking of *acquiring knowledge of history*, and, in fact, of a very special case of that acquisition of knowledge: *acquiring knowledge of history by deduction.*

Alonso-Schökel, in his section II, 4, has developed the triangular scheme that serves as the directing principle in this process of acquisition of knowledge.[21] A whole series of facts at a particular historical moment constitutes the basis from which the retroactive question is posed concerning a single cause 'at the beginning.' All lines of causality converge on this one single cause, just as the various lines one could draw from the different points at the base of a triangle can converge at the apex. But modern historical consciousness is guided by a different principle, which is more like the image of a web. Behind the plurality of facts at a given historical moment there stands, at an earlier moment, a plurality of causes that is just as complex and confusing, and behind that another similar plurality, and so forth. It would be a praiseworthy task for a dogmatician interested in the theory of knowledge to provide a solid and convincing proof that the triangular scheme, at least in this one special case of the account of the beginnings of human history, is objectively justified, in contrast to the scheme of multiple interweavings of various parallel causes.

Since we must be careful, in the case of such an intensely literary text as Genesis 2–3, not to draw too great a separation between the process of knowledge and that of composition, and since, in addition, we can only deduce the process of knowledge from the resulting composition, Rahner's statement about the process of historical knowledge behind Genesis 2–3 simultaneously contains some essential implications about the *creative process* through which Genesis 2–3 came to be. Alonso-Schökel, in his section 'Hipótesis sobre el proceso creativo'[22] deliberately drew this conclusion. At the same time it is true that this particular kind of process of knowledge and composition has shaped the *concrete appearance* of the text, even though it may remain an open question whether one should necessarily assign the resulting stylistic characteristics and structures of the text to the level of 'genre.' In any case, these are literary phenomena that aid us in determining the *expressive intention* of the text.

The expressive intention must be determined at the literary level before there is any point in considering the fact of inspiration as part of a

21. 'Motivos sapienciales' (see n. 4 above), 309–12.

22. Ibid. (see n. 4 above), 313–14. I am leaving aside the fact that at this point in his article he has already introduced the fact of inspiration.

theological evaluation of the biblical text.[23] We must, in fact, draw attention to the fact that even with the determination that the author is evidently thinking in terms of the triangular scheme that inquires about a single ultimate cause, the intention of Genesis 2–3, as regards what it means to say about history, is not fully clarified.[24]

In particular, the multiple modes of thinking according to the triangular model collected by Alonso-Schökel raise the question whether this model was always applied solely for the purpose of making genuine historical statements. The model, as model, implies our world of space and time, and therefore always locates the apex of the triangle at a point in space and time. But is it really certain that the whole model, including the space-time scheme, could not also be used simply in order to make statements about the present world of the one making the assertion? If, on the basis of the multiple instances of the use of this model in the Old Testament, we admit the validity of this question, we must pose an additional question to each: namely, whether the author in each case, who, with the aid of the triangular model, presents an event in the past as the cause of present circumstances, genuinely intends to make a historical statement. In the case of Genesis 2–3 this question can scarcely be answered solely by means of a stylistic analysis of these two chapters; what is required is an examination of the larger context of Genesis 2–3, that is, the whole Pentateuch or – if one wants a more restricted field and considers the corresponding theory to be correct – the Yahwistic work. Of course, it is not sufficient to prove that the work as a whole contains a general intention to make historical assertions (a proof that would probably not present too many difficulties), but beyond this, it is necessary to show that the prehistorical prologue is also located within the field wherein the intention is to make genuine historical statements. Only that fundamental affirmation can guarantee the triangular model in Genesis 2–3 its full effectiveness. Only then can one, on that basis, describe the intention of Genesis 2–3 as genuinely historical.

Once the intention of the statements about the sin that stands at the beginning of human history has been literarily clarified in this way, one can introduce the fact of *inspiration* and thus arrive at a genuinely

23. This is stated with emphasis here, since in Rahner's work the line between these two areas, which should be methodically separated, tends to disappear.

24. This is not entirely clear in Alonso-Schökel's work, either. Still, there is at least an indication on p. 300 that a mythical self-understanding on the part of Genesis 2–3 is excluded by the larger context in which those chapters stand.

theological evaluation. In this process, the conclusions we have reached earlier about the methods of attaining knowledge and of composition that led to the biblical text will be of the utmost importance for the purpose of determining and describing the particular statement made by the text in its *individual details.*

3

'I am Yahweh, your Physician' (Exodus 15:26)

God, Society and Human Health in a Postexilic Revision of the Pentateuch (Exod. 15:2b, 26)

At the time when Jesus of Nazareth appeared, Jewish society was groaning under Roman rule. The Jews themselves were divided into warring groups; moreover, the wealthy few confronted masses of poor and hungry people. The Zealot underground movement was preparing for revolt. Their battle slogan was: 'The rule of God alone.' It appeared that only a violent change of rulers offered any promise of justice and humanity.[1] Jesus took no notice of all this and publicly asserted that the reign of God was already appearing. If he was asked how one might recognize this, he pointed to his own miracles, for he was moving through the cities and towns as a kind of healer. Wherever he had been, people could point to those who had been restored to health. At least, that is what the gospels tell us. The amount of space they devote to miraculous healings is quite embarrassing for us today – very much so, since we, as post-Enlightenment people, have a hard time imagining miracles of any kind. But we can overcome this to a degree when we consider that the gospels, of course, contain popular and legendary types of discourse. Thus we need not accept everything that is narrated there as historical fact. Certainly there remains a kernel of fact that cannot be simply eliminated. Here psychosomatic theories, applied to the appearance of a strong personality, are an additional aid. Oddly

1. Cf. Martin Hengel, *The Zealots*, translated by David Smith (Edinburgh, 1989). On the programmatic slogan of the sole rule of God, see pp. 90–110.

enough, after we have performed these mental operations there still remains a remnant of embarrassment. It is evident that what really bothers us most is that Jesus was in any way concerned about physical health. With all the emphasis we place on human bodiliness, it still seems to us more important to concentrate on other things: better social structures, room for human self-development, new and more immediate approaches to the divine realm. 'Jesus, the Savior' – that is still acceptable. We can understand it in a spiritual sense. But 'Jesus, the Healer' – who would dare to go so far as to restore an intelligible meaning to the archaic word 'savior' [German: Heiland], which for many remains nothing more than an empty religious formula?[2]

The task of this contribution to the anniversary volume of the Stuttgarter Bibelstudien is to inquire into language about God in the Pentateuch. In the space allowed, it is impossible to treat the question in a comprehensive way, but at most by way of examples. In view of the difficulty posed for us by Jesus' appearance, as just described, it seemed to me an interesting idea to look into a short statement about the God of Israel that is known to few people, and is for the most part not assigned to any of the major source levels of the Pentateuch. To readers attuned to the major events of salvation it appears only as a kind of dab of mortar inserted between the great blocks of the literary edifice, but in a surprising way it anticipates the image that the gospels offer us of the reign of God that is breaking forth around Jesus. I am speaking of the concluding phrase in Exod. 15:26, which Luther translated as 'I am the LORD your physician.'

This statement interested me all the more, inasmuch as Wilhelm Pesch, in partnership with whom I developed the idea for the Stuttgarter Bibelstudien in the year 1964, and to whom I dedicate these pages in grateful friendship, has just ended his academic teaching career prematurely in order to undertake the duties of pastoral care in a large hospital.[3]

2. On the background of this difficulty with Jesus of Nazareth, cf. E. Biser, 'Das Heil als Heilung. Aspekte einer therapeutischen Theologie,' in J. Sudbrack et al., *Heilkraft des Heiligen* (Vienna, 1975), 102–39.

3. When I asked Wilhelm Pesch for his permission to make this dedication, he indicated that I should not neglect the opportunity also to mention Herr Hermann Farnung, who directed the publishing house Katholisches Bibelwerk at that time. That is quite correct. Other publishers thought that the idea had no merchandising future and, with polite smiles, showed us the door. Herr Farnung, on the contrary, recognized the importance of the subject, set aside his marketing considerations, and

The two verses, Exod. 15:25–26, which close with this phrase, play scarcely any part in surveys of Old Testament theology. On the other hand, they have attained a certain importance in Pentateuch theory during the last century, and for that reason they are not uncontroversial from several points of view. Beyond this, we may ask whether, even among these viewpoints, there may not be some still unnoticed elements that may be brought to light. We will thus have to approach these verses carefully, slowly, sometimes almost by roundabout routes, before we have them in focus in such a way that they really reveal themselves and begin to speak to us of God, society, and human health.[4]

1. Israel at the Waters of Marah

When the Israelites, as early as Exod. 12:37, move from Rameses to Succoth, in 13:20 from Succoth to Etham on the edge of the wilderness, and in 14:2–4 to the place of the sea miracle, all this is still closely connected for the readers with the events in Egypt, and it is only after the destruction of Pharaoh in the Sea of Reeds, when Miriam and the Israelite women have danced their victory song in Exod. 15:20–21, that the readers' attention turns to the new theme of 'wandering in the wilderness,' which apparently begins at 15:22 with another statement about departure and travelling:[5]

thereby proved himself the better merchant after all. For at that time none of us would have dared to hope that this series would survive so long and, after fifteen years, would already have reached its hundredth volume.

4. As far as I can see, there has not yet been any study dealing thematically with Exod. 15:25–26. J. Hempel, '"Ich bin der Herr, dein Arzt" (Ex. 15,26),' *ThLZ* 82 (1957): 809–26, has a kind of motto-title and really deals with the whole field of ancient Israelite medicine and the ideas connected with it. On Exod. 15:26, see p. 823 of that article.

5. The preceding seems to me the only permissible description of the total impression given readers of the definitive text of Exodus. It is true that G. W. Coats, in particular, has offered a number of good arguments for thinking that the Sea of Reeds story should be attached to the desert complex rather than to the departure, not only in terms of tradition history but also in the thinking of the later redactors of the Pentateuch: cf. his 'The Traditio-Historical Character of the Reed Sea Motif,' *VT* 17 (1967): 253–65; idem, *Rebellion in the Wilderness* (Nashville, 1968), 133–36; idem, 'The Wilderness Itinerary,' *CBQ* 34 (1972): 135–52; idem, 'An Exposition for the Wilderness Traditions,' *VT* 22 (1972): 288–95. But the stratum that most strongly shapes the definitive image, the priestly historical narrative, made the miracle at the sea the climax of the exodus event: cf. (against Coats) B. S. Childs, *The Book of*

> Then Moses ordered Israel to set out from the Sea of Reeds, and they went into the wilderness of Shur.

It may not be accidental that the root *yṣ'*, 'set out,' the word associated with the exodus from Egypt, is quite unusual in ordinary statements about travel, but occurs once again at this point.[6] With the departure from the place where the Egyptians perished, the last phase of the exodus is accomplished. But there is not, as is usually the case in travel notices, an immediate announcement of their arrival at a new place, only a statement about the direction they are taking. This is, of course, toward a *wilderness* (that of Shur). The narrative that follows develops out of this crucial word as a matter of course, and in order to prepare for what will happen after the arrival at a stopping-place on the journey it has to begin while the people are still on the march:

> They went three days in the wilderness
> and found no water.

Thus the people immediately have an experience typical of the desert: thirst. But the great miracle story that responds to this need does not by any means follow right away: God's gift of water is not the subject until Exodus 17. Still, at least a tiny foretaste of it must be told immediately, in order that the true character of the wilderness will assume its narrative shape. In the next part of the story, there is an apparent solution to the problem: they come to a place where there is water. But this only brings

Exodus. A Critical, Theological Commentary. OT Library (Philadelphia, 1974), 222–24; also the newest and most thoroughgoing analysis of the exodus story in the priestly historical narrative: J. L. Ska, 'Les plaies d'Égypte dans le récit sacerdotal (P^g),' *Bibl* 60 (1979): 23–35. The filling out of the narrative text with historicized ritual directions in Exodus 12–13, and the hymn in Exod. 15:1–18, which serves as a poetic conclusion to a large composition, act still further to connect Exodus 14 to the Egyptian events. Besides, it is an open question whether what follows in the books from Exodus to Numbers can be combined in the sense of the priestly document and later redactions under the title 'wandering in the desert.' I am using it here in a very preliminary sense.

6. The subject shifts (Moses causes them to set out; the people departs). The exodus from Egypt can easily be described in the *qal*: cf. Exod. 12:41; 14:8. The Samaritanus and LXX versions have the *hifil*, and Moses remains the subject. It is also possible for Moses to be the subject of the exodus event: cf. Exod. 14:11 (although this is polemic). But the Masoretic text is probably original. The *hifil* reading is an accommodation to the subject, and may also represent the establishing of a textual reference for Exod. 16:3.

disappointment and intensifies the problem, since the water is unpotable:

> When they came to Marah, (= bitter)
> they could not drink the water of Marah (= bitter)
> because it was bitter (= *mārîm*).
> That is why they[7] called this place[8] (also) Marah (= bitter).

The *leitmotif* in this sequence is 'bitter,' a word that designates not only a quality of taste. It is ordinarily found in rhetorical contexts where the subject is sickness, death or despair.[9] In connection with bitter water, the 'water of bitterness that brings the curse' (*mê hammārîm ham'ārĕrîm*)[10] in the jealousy ritual in Num. 5:11–31 is important, and perhaps other rituals of divine judgment that have not been preserved. These associations may have arisen immediately for the original readers, at the borders of their consciousness. Thus the water of this oasis was not simply bitter. It was water that could bring sickness, and even death. And the effect – curse or blessing – may even have depended on how the one who drank of it stood before God, on the basis of his or her previous actions and attitude. That, at least, is a horizon opened for the subsequent narrative by the sharply emphasized word 'bitter.' The play on the word permits the action to be arrested momentarily by the etiology of a name.[11] Now it continues immediately:

7. Another possible translation is 'he' (Moses).

8. I am reading according to the LXX (and probably the rather free translation of the Vulgate at this place): *qārā' šēm hammāqôm hazzeh mārāh.* The Masoretic text and Samaritanus have: *qārā' šĕmāh mārāh,* 'they called her [Mara is feminine] name Marah.' It is true that normally, in the Pentateuch, a shorter reading in the Masoretic text, especially when it also coincides with Samaritanus, deserves preference over a longer text in the LXX. Besides, at this point the LXX presumes the usual formulation, while the Masoretic text is unusual. Still, greater weight should probably be given to the fact that the longer text permitted the eye to jump from *hm* in *hammāqôm* to the second *h* in *hazzeh,* with the following *m* in *mārāh.*

9. Examples can be found in the concordance. The common expression *mar nepĕs* may also be connected with this. It is not metaphorical; *nepeš* means the throat, and it refers to all those physical conditions and psychic moods in which the throat constricts and becomes dry, hard and bitter. Cf. T. Collins, 'The Physiology of Tears in the Old Testament,' *CBQ* 33 (1971): 19–38, 185–97 (at 35–37).

10. We should note that, based on the logic of sounds, the two words for 'bitter' and 'curse-bringing' were practically identified.

11. This etiology of name is not the point of the narrative, but has a subordinated function – something that is sometimes overlooked. Correctly: B. O. Long, *The Problem of the Etiological Narrative in the Old Testament,* BZAW 108 (Berlin, 1968), 12.

And the people complained[12] against Moses, saying:
'What shall we drink?'
He[13] cried out to the Lord;
and the Lord told him about[14] a piece of wood;
he threw it into the water,
and the water became sweet.

The 'complaining' here does not connote an improper or even rebellious attitude. It is the normal reaction of the followers to their leader when something is not as it should be; and after the leader's appeal, God immediately produces a remedy for the problem.[15] When the water has been changed from its unpotable condition to potability, the narrative tension previously established is resolved. It could still be said that the Israelites drank the water and quenched their thirst, or that they believed in YHWH (cf. Exod. 14:31, the end of another complaint story). But that is not absolutely necessary, and it better fits the diction of this story (which although genuinely narrative is very spare) that it concludes at the point at which the water becomes sweet.[16] It is not a broadly detailed narrative, but

12. The Masoretic text has the verb in the plural, although 'the people' is singular. Samaritanus has changed the verb to singular. The Masoretic text is grammatically possible (breaking down a collective expression), and besides, it is to be preferred as the more difficult reading. Samaritanus must then make the subject (Moses) explicit at the beginning of Exod. 15:25.

13. The shorter reading of the Masoretic text is to be preferred. See n. 12. The LXX text corresponded to Samaritanus, probably also in view of the problem treated in n. 12.

14. Following the Masoretic text, *wayyôrēhû* Samaritanus, LXX and the other ancient versions have *wayyar'ēhû*, 'and he showed him (a piece of wood).' The decision between the two readings is not easy. Against the Masoretic text is the isolated witness. In addition, the widely-attested reading is quite adequate to the story and sounds more natural. But the reading of the Masoretic text is undoubtedly the *lectio difficilior*. Verses 25b–26 also follow more naturally on it, as well as 16:4, *bĕtôrātî*. However, the latter could also witness to a subsequent accommodation in the Masoretic text.

15. It seems to me important to distinguish between two different types of 'complaint stories': Type 1, in which God eliminates the cause of the 'complaining,' and Type 2, in which the 'complaining' is condemned and punished as rebellion: cf. Childs, *Exodus* (see n. 5 above), 258–60. The root *lwn* appears to designate revolt against an authority; the word itself leaves open the question whether, in the concrete situation and according to the rules of a given society, this revolt is legitimate or illegitimate. Even in groups under authoritarian leadership there may well be 'democratic' models of procedure, although their actualization often seems rather risky.

16. U. Cassuto, *A Commentary on the Book of Exodus* (Jerusalem, 1967), 185, points out that there are a total of seven occurrences of the letter-sequence *mym* in Exod. 15:22–

rather something like a brief thematic introduction that a storyteller who produces new variations at every session of tale-telling must always keep in mind.[17] In its relationship to the other wilderness stories, it is similar to the Isaac stories in Genesis 26 in relationship to the much broader Abraham and Jacob narratives before and after. Probably it originated as a story by means of which the people in Israel explained why it was that in a place called Marah ('bitter') there could be potable water.[18] Here, in the narrative context of the Pentateuch, it emphasizes that Israel in the wilderness is beset by dangers and difficulties, but that YHWH is in control of those problems. The sequence of narrative beginnings with 'and' can now roll quietly along, for example with a renewed mention of a departure and a journey. But that does not happen. Suddenly, the language breaks sharply upward. In a manner that simply cannot be documented in narrative texts of the ancient type,[19] a new, quite different piece of information is

27 (once *miyyam*, 'from the sea,' the rest *mayim*, 'water'). The theme of water thus shapes the story throughout, but up to v. 25a there are five instances of *mym*, and the other two occurrences only appear when the text again speaks of the journey, at v. 27. Thus the water narrative really ends at Exod. 15:25a.

17. On the narrative techniques presumed here, see the fundamental study by Albert B. Lord, *The Singer of Tales* (New York, 1965, c. 1960).

18. This idea, proposed by E. Meyer, *Die Israeliten und ihre Nachbarstämme* (Halle, 1906), 102, seems to me more plausible than the widely accepted notion that this was a place called Marah, whose water really was unpotable, but could be made drinkable for travellers by the use of a particular kind of wood. This astonishing technique is supposed to have been traced by the storytellers to Israel's period in the wilderness. In that case it is possible to discuss where Marah might be located and what kind of tree this might be. The position I am adopting permits neither speculation. The spring at Jericho, where Elisha worked a miracle comparable to that of Moses at Marah, remained, according to 2 Kgs. 2:22, 'wholesome to this day.' M. Noth, 'Der Wallfahrtsweg zum Sinai (4. Mose 33)', in *Aufsätze zur biblischen Landes- und Altertumskunde* (Neukirchen–Vluyn, 1971) 1:73, n. 61, also supposes there was potable water in Marah (Marah = *ʿēn marra*, east of the gulf of *el-ʿaqaba*).

19. In poetry, *šām* ('there') without a preceding *wĕ* at the beginning of the sentence is found quite often. But in narrative prose, additional or coordinate information related to a place begins, almost without exception, with *wĕšām*, 'and there.' I have found only the following exceptions, distantly comparable with Exod. 15:25b: Deut. 10:6 (in a fragment from a description of a route for travellers, comparable in type to Num. 21:12–13, rather than to the usual style of travel notices, and really for the purpose of introducing additional information); Ezek. 23:3 (where, however, the parallelisms favor poetry instead; note also the inversion in the immediately preceding sentence); Gen. 49:31 (but it is questionable whether these are independent sentences at all: the threefold *šāmmāh* ['there'] could be simply there

introduced asyndetically. The most we can say is that the preparation for this statement was only in the very deep background:

> There he made for them a statute and an ordinance,
> and there he put it[20] to the test.

This statement is thus made with the greatest emphasis, but at the same time mysteriously, since the subject is not stated. It is only from the more general use of the language that the readers can infer that it is Moses who gave Israel a statute and an ordinance – for us, since we can only refer to the books of the Old Testament, the parallel in Josh. 24:25 is the key – and also from the two other possibilities that occur in wilderness stories, namely that either the people puts YHWH to the test (cf. Exod. 17:2, 7; Num. 14:22; Deut. 6:16), or else YHWH puts the people to the test (cf. Exod. 16:4; 20:20; Deut. 8:2, 16; 13:3 [4]). On the basis of the preceding story, only the second possibility can apply in this case.[21] Even the

for the purpose of picking up the preceding place references; cf. the situation in Gen. 25:10, where apparently the preceding reference to a place in v. 10a is summarily reintroduced with *šāmmāh* ['there'] at the beginning of v. 10b). All these instances are late, and their context is not formulated in typical narrative style.

20. The reference is to Israel [cf. NRSV: 'them']. Theoretically, 'he,' referring to Moses, would be possible, but in the context it is unlikely. Even Liedke (cf. n. 22 below), who has 'they' [German 'man'] as subject and refers the testing to the statute and ordinance, claims only that this interpretation applies to a prior stage of the text.

21. Neither in the wilderness texts nor anywhere else is there any instance of Moses as the subject of a 'testing' by Israel or YHWH. Among those who opt for YHWH as the subject of both clauses are Baentsch, Strach, Eissfeldt, and Noth. A further observation speaks in favor of the interpretation suggested here. If we take Moses as a subject in Exod. 15:26 as well (cf. n. 24 below), the result is a palindromic ordering of the subjects of the statements in 15:24–27:

people
    (Moses)
        YHWH
            (Moses)
                water
            (Moses)
        (YHWH)
    (Moses)
(people)

Parentheses are used where the subject is not expressly mentioned. But in v. 27 the plural makes clear (cf. v. 24a) that the people is again the subject, and in the first half of the palindrome it is evident from the verbal content and interweaving of suffixes that Moses is the subject of the second and fourth members. Cf. n. 12 above.

expression *śym ḥōq ûmišpāṭ*, here tentatively translated as 'impose a statute and an ordinance,' was probably perceived as unusual, even by readers who already knew all the statutes and ordinances that were about to follow in the Pentateuch.[22] But the continuation of the text, with its more usual

22. The double expression is usually in the plural, and in the deuteronomic/deuteronomistic field as *ḥuqqîm ûmišpāṭîm*, 'statutes and ordinances;' in the priestly writings as *ḥuqqōt*, 'laws,' and *mišpāṭîm*, 'ordinances.' Cf. the tables in G. Liedke, *Gestalt und Bezeichnung alttestamentlicher Rechtssätze. Eine formgeschichtlich-terminologische Studie.* WMANT 39 (Neukirchen–Vluyn, 1971), 13–17. In the same book, on pp. 180–84, may be found the most thorough study of all the examples of *śym* + *ḥōq* / *mišpāṭ* / *ḥōq ûmišpāṭ*. Liedke deletes *lô* ('him,' dative) to arrive at the original text, and thus interprets: There (= in Kadesh) they established obligation and entitlement, and there they tested them/it (= obligation or entitlement). But 'the deuteronomic redactor of v. 26, at the latest' interpreted it differently and inserted *lô* ('him,' dative). However, even the interpretation of the supposed prior stage cannot be proved. It is derived by way of Josh. 24:25 from an interpretation of the double expression in 1 Sam. 30:25 that is possible there, but by no means necessary. Cf. the skeptical remarks of H. Ringgren in *TDOT* 5: 142–43. M. Weinfeld, *Deuteronomy and the Deuteronomistic School* (Oxford, 1972), 152, applies to Exod. 15:25 and Josh. 24:25 a direct parallel in Akkadian, *mīšaram šakānum*, 'to issue a reforming edict,' something that can scarcely be founded in the context in either of these instances. Cf. N. P. Lemche, 'The Manumission of Slaves – The Fallow Year – The Sabbatical Year – The Jobel Year,' *VT* 26 (1976): 38–59, at 39–40. Other interpretations as well, such as that of R. Hentschke, *Setzung und Setzender. Ein Beitrag zur israelitischen Rechtsterminologie*, BWANT 83 (Stuttgart, 1963), 29, 'Kultordnung und Recht,' narrow the content of the two terms more than can be proven, at least on the basis of the occurrences of the double expression, which is evidently a fixed one. H. M. Orlinsky, *Notes on the New Translation of the Torah* (New York, 1969), 171, thinks this is a hendiadys, 'a fixed rule.' But since *śym*, 'to impose,' can also occur with only one of the two terms contained in the double expression, and by no means certainly with precisely the same meaning, this may be going too far. In the double expression, the second term could also qualify the first more precisely ('in fact'). But we can scarcely clarify that any more, and perhaps we need not, since, at least as regards the horizon of understanding of readers of the finished Pentateuch, there is another avenue of access. The plural double expression for the ordinances of Israel contained in the Pentateuch is presumed to be something familiar. In order not to contradict the obvious fact that Israel's ordinances were first given at Sinai, the double expression is still placed in the singular here. It means the same thing, but it cannot appear to be exactly the same. The possibility of this linguistic refinement is furnished by the fact that the same singular expression already exists for Joshua (Josh. 24:25) and David (1 Sam. 30:25), each of whom – after the time at which Israel received its rule of life from YHWH – established new laws in an analogous situation. The fact that the following verse 26 uses the same expressions that will later be applied to the laws of Sinai and the deuteronomic laws is not an objection to this position, for at that point the text is not speaking of what happened at Marah, but is establishing a general principle that, as matter of course, will apply to all the laws of

expressions for 'law' (v. 26), makes it clear what meaning is to be read here. In this kind of context, the word *nsh*, 'put to the test,' also acquires a meaning related to God's demand: God tests, in a desperate situation, whether Israel will hold to God's law; if it does so, God relieves the need through a blessing. In this connection, we can think especially of Exod. 16:4; Deut. 8:2; 13:4; Judg. 2:22; 3:4.[23] The following verse 26 can thus be regarded as a kind of explication of what is meant by 'put to the test,' and therefore follows quite logically:

He said,
'If you will listen: listen to the voice of the Lord your God, A
and do what is right in his sight, B
and give heed to his commandments C
and keep all his statutes – D
of the diseases that I inflicted in Egypt, E
none will I lay upon you. F
For I am the Lord, the one who heals you. G

It appears that the speaker here is Moses, not YHWH.[24] Although

YHWH that may be mentioned. This may be the best explanation for the special nuance of the double expression in the singular in the definitive text of the Pentateuch. The question whether we should, beyond this, look for the meaning of the expression in Exod. 15:25 in an earlier stage of the text may remain open at this point.

23. If we add the examples of Deut. 8:16 and Judg. 3:1, which in their contexts are to be understood in the same sense, and if we observe that Exod. 20:20 is preceded by the proclamation of the Decalogue, that the immediate context of Deut. 33:8 speaks of observing YHWH's words and covenant (33:9), and that the testing of Abraham referred to in Gen. 22:1 consists of carrying out a divine command, we will encompass the whole group of instances of *nsh*, 'to test,' with God as subject in the Pentateuch and former prophets, all of which point to a single conception of the testing of Israel by its God. It is closely related to the will of God, as normally given in the 'law,' and with its observation. O. Eissfeldt, 'Zwei verkannte militärtechnische Termini,' *VT* 5 (1955): 232–38, at 235–38, suggests for Exod. 15:25, Deut. 33:8 and Judg. 3:1 the translation 'practice, train.' But at no point does the context really suggest that. Cf. L. Ruppert, 'Das Motiv der Versuchung durch Gott in vordeuteronomischer Tradition,' *VT* 22 (1972): 55–63, at 58.

24. The stylization of the speech itself permits no absolute certainty. At the beginning it speaks of YHWH in the third person, while at the end YHWH speaks in the first person. In Deuteronomy it is possible for the 'I' of YHWH to interrupt speeches that are styled as words of Moses: cf. Deut. 7:4; 11:13–15; 17:3; 28:20; 29:4–5. But on the other hand it is possible in a deuteronomic narrative, when a word of YHWH is

the language of this speech sounds different from that in v. 25b, it also stands out in contrast to the old, terse narrative style. In spite of the evident parallelisms, this can scarcely be poetry. What we have here, rather, is high-historic prose.[25] A conditional promise of blessing[26] is founded on a divine self-presentation.[27] The conditional part of the promise of blessing is particularly well developed. On the basis of the verbs, we twice find the sequence 'to hear – to do' (AB and CD), once in the prefix conjugation (AB), and once in the suffix conjugation (CD). Whereas verbal sequences beginning with *šm'*, 'to hear,' are frequently found in conditioned texts of blessing and cursing,[28] nowhere else is there

quoted, for YHWH to make a self-reference in the third person: cf. Deut. 1:8. Thus there are stylistic freedoms here that are not allowed in our own language. It may be that the following considerations favor Moses over YHWH as the speaker in Exod. 15:26: (1) At the beginning of the speech it sounds more as if Moses is speaking, and since the speaker is not expressly introduced, the first impression should probably be determinative. (2) If it is true that, before this, a palindromic structure of expectations is presented (see n. 21 above), Moses is now the subject of the action, and thus of the speech. Finally, the difference between the two possibilities is not very great, since Moses in any case is the mediator of a word from God.

25. On this type of prose, see the most thorough study to date: G. Braulik, *Die Mittel deuteronomischer Rhetorik erhoben aus Deuteronomium 4,1–40*, AnBib 68 (Rome, 1978). Of course, what we find here is not precisely the same technique, and there is a certain affinity to the rhetoric of the priestly laws as well. There is, as yet, no monograph on that subject. On the narrative style of the priestly writing, cf. S. E. McEvenue, *The Narrative Style of the Priestly Writer*, AnBib 50 (Rome, 1971).

26. Other instances of conditional promises of blessing are Exod. 19:5; 23:22, 25; Lev. 26:3; Deut. 4:29; 7:12; 11:13, 27; 13:19 [18]; 15:5; 21:9; 28:1, 2, 13; 30:1, 2, 10, 16 (LXX); 1 Kgs. 3:14; 9:4; 11:38; 2 Kgs. 21:8; Job 36:11; Prov. 2:1, 4; Jer. 17:24; Zech. 6:15. (In each case, the verse where the condition begins is cited.) Similar texts are: Gen. 22:28; 26:5; Lev. 26:14, 18, 21, 23, 27, 44; Deut. 4:25; 8:20; 11:28; 28:15, 45, 58, 62; 30:17; Josh. 23:12, 16; 24:20; 1 Sam. 12:15; 2 Sam. 7:14; 1 Kgs. 9:6; Ps. 81:14; Job 36:12; Jer. 13:17.

27. On this, see the classic studies: W. Zimmerli, 'Ich bin Jahwe,' *Geschichte und Altes Testament. Albrecht Alt zum 70. Geburtstag*, BhTh 16 (Tübingen, 1953), 179–209; K. Elliger, 'Ich bin der Herr – euer Gott,' *Theologie als Glaubenswagnis. Festschrift zum 80. Geburtstag von Karl Heim* (Hamburg, 1954), 9–34. In Exod. 15:26 we find the long formula (Zimmerli), or the formula of favor (Elliger). The qualification of YHWH as *rōpĕ'ekā* 'your healer,' is unique among the self-presentations in the OT. Corresponding I-statements of YHWH, but not in the framework of self-presentation formulae, can be found in Deut. 32:39; 2 Kgs. 20:5; Jer. 20:17; 33:6; Hos. 11:3; 14:5. All these, except for 2 Kgs. 20:5 and perhaps Jer. 33:6, are metaphorical.

28. Of the 52 instances in n. 26 above, 33 begins with *šm'*, 'to hear!'

such a rhetorical doubling of the schematic sequence.[29] In addition, the reinforcement of the verb *šmʿ*, 'to hear,' with the preceding infinitive, *šāmôaʿ*, is at least rare.[30] The two verbs for hearing, *šmʿ* and *ʾzn hifil.* (AC), like the two verbs for doing, *ʿśh*, 'to do,' and *šmr*, 'to take heed' (BD) are both sets of words that belong together in parallel.[31] The object of each of the four verbs is an expression referring to the will of YHWH, but in this case it is more difficult to identify fixed pairs of words.[32] At most we can say that it is only in the second step (CD) that words for 'law' begin to appear. The meaning of the successive units is narrowed and pointed toward the end.[33] Nevertheless, the initial clause gives the impression of being a carefully constructed chiastic-parallel unit. It is balanced by a quite differently constructed final clause, originating in the divine speech. This begins asyndetically. The word *kol*, 'all,' 'each,' before the last word of the first clause and the first word of the final clause signals a precise correspondence between condition and promise,[34] as well as the

29. At most, Prov. 2:1–2 could offer a remote comparison.

30. Otherwise only in Exod. 19:5; 23:22; Deut. 11:13; 15:5; 28:1; Jer. 17:24; Zech. 6:15.

31. *ʾzn* exists almost exclusively as a parallel word for *šmʿ* or other expressions of hearing. The only exceptions are Isa. 8:9; 51:4; Pss. 77:2; 80:2; 135:17; 140:7; 141:1; Job 32:11; 37:14; 2 Chr. 24:19 among 41 total examples. Also, the word is found almost exclusively in poetry. *šmr*, 'to take heed,' and *ʿśh*, 'to do,' are closely related, both in deuteronomic and priestly diction, as expressions for observation of the law. Cf. N. Lohfink, *Das Hauptgebot. Eine Untersuchung literarischer Einleitungsfragen zu Dtn 5–11*, AnBib 20 (Rome, 1963), 68–70.

32. The word pair *miṣwôt* + *ḥuqqîm* (in that order) is otherwise attested only in Deut. 27:10 (with preceding *šmʿ* + *qôl YHWH*; but *ḥuqqîm* is only found in the Masoretic text, while the Samaritan – although it is probably assimilating to the usual reading – has *ḥuqqôt*) and in Ezra 7:11 (in a kind of title for Ezra!). Is it possible that the more likely *ḥuqqôtāyw* was avoided for reasons of assonance? It would have formed a very close rhyme with *miṣwôṭāyw*, while the three-word chain of *bĕʿênāyw* / *lĕmiṣwôtāyw* / *kol-ḥuqqāyw* thus appears somewhat looser, and the middle part, BCD, holds together in contrast to the more powerful framing rhyme on *-êkā* in AFG. Another aim in choosing *ḥuqqîm* instead of *ḥuqqôt* could have been a desire to take up the *ḥōq* from v. 25b.

33. A: 6 words; B: 3 words; C: 2 words. But D has three words again, because of the added *kol*, 'each,' 'all.' It blocks the movement we have indicated here, establishes a kind of end-point, and, since it is immediately taken up again in E, it in a sense triggers the final clause. Moreover, we may observe a corresponding length in the lines of the final clause: E: 5 words; F: 3 words; G: 4 (= 2 x 2) words.

34. One can speak here of 'talion style.' Cf. N. Lohfink, 'Zu Text und Form von Os 4,4–6,' *Bibl* 42 (1961): 303–32, at 311–25. Here there is a forced movement from

universality and fundamental character of the whole statement. Moreover, the statement in the final clause is artfully drawn out. It begins with an object displaced to the front of the line, which is then explained in a relative clause: '[all] of the diseases that I inflicted in Egypt' (E). That requires the expenditure of a whole breath, and the speech has to begin again with the principal clause. Then the verb from the relative clause is repeated, this time negated,[35] so that what emerges is a sharp contrast between YHWH's actions in Egypt and in Israel, evident also in the sound of the words. But this verb was already found in Exod. 15:25, where it was sharply emphasized by the harshly-constructed rhyme, echoed again afterward: *šām śām – wĕšām*, 'there he inflicted . . . and there . . .' In this way, the repetition of words also serves to underscore the fundamental statement: YHWH, who inflicted sickness on the Egyptians, imposes on Israel a rule of life, and if they live by it, YHWH will inflict no sickness on Israel. The principal clause, F, ends with *-êkā,* the rhyme for *YHWH ʾĕlōhêkā*, 'YHWH, your God,' at the end of A, and this in turn triggers the triumphal conclusion, G, connected by a consequent *kî*, 'for,' which reveals YHWH in person, in essence: 'I am YHWH, the one who heals you.' It ends again with the rhyme, *-êkā*.

The concrete content of the blessing (the preservation of Israel from sickness) and its foundation (YHWH, the physician of Israel) establishes the connection between the bitter water of Marah that has been made potable and the suddenly introduced theme of 'the imposition of law and ordinance and the testing of Israel.' This is true, at least, if one has already heard the undertones in the key word *mar*, 'bitter,' as pointed out above. Similarly, the motif of 'teaching,' with its echo of the word 'Torah,' is seen to be anticipatory. Through YHWH's Torah the water is made wholesome; Israel is not brought by bitter water into the realm of

the otherwise repeated verb to the tiny word *kol*, 'all,' 'each,' while the repetition of the verb, which has its place within the final clause and the promise of blessing, reaching back into Exod. 15:25, assumes a different function. (On this, see below.)

35. *śym*, 'to inflict,' 'to lay upon,' is constructed in v. 25 with *lĕ*, in v. 26 (E) with *bĕ*, and in v. 26 (F) with *ʿal*. I have attempted to indicate this by a slight variation in the translation of each. But it could be that there is only an attempt at stylistic variation here, and that no particular nuances of meaning are present. It would be most likely that, with the object *ḥōq ûmišpāṭ* ('law and ordinance'), the language could exert pressure for *lĕ* of the person: cf. Josh. 24:15; 1 Sam. 30:25; Ps. 81:5; also Prov. 8:29. But there are possible counter-instances in Isa. 42:4; Pss. 78:5; 81:6 (for *bĕ* with words for law) and Gen. 47:26 (for *ʿal*). With regard to illnesses, both *bĕ* and *ʿal* are possible. Perhaps in Exod. 15:26 *bĕ* refers more to the territorial, and *ʿal* to the personal aspect. But cf. Deut. 7:15 as a counter-instance.

death; and thus it will always remain free of sickness if it holds to YHWH's order. A single event has clarified something much more comprehensive and universally valid, and vv. 25b and 26 make this explicit. In so doing, they also significantly broaden the horizon beyond that of the preceding narrative. While in Exod. 15:22 what is about to be narrated is located by the words *wayyēṣĕʾû*, 'they set out,' and *midbār*, 'wilderness,' between the departure from Egypt and the wilderness that now stretches out before Israel, now the relative clause in Exod. 15:26 E reaches farther back, into the time when Israel was in Egypt. It speaks of the plagues that YHWH caused to fall upon Egypt, for Israel's sake. In Deut. 28:27, in a context similar to that in Exod. 15:26, it is said that YHWH will strike Israel, if it fails to observe YHWH's laws, with the 'boils of Egypt;' in Deut. 28:60, YHWH will 'bring back upon you all the diseases of Egypt, of which you were in dread.' In the blessing text in Deut. 7:15 it is said that YHWH will not inflict on Israel 'all the dread diseases of Egypt that you experienced.' The fear and knowledge of Egyptian diseases can also be understood in these texts as fear and knowledge stemming from hearsay.[36] Here in Exod. 15:26, on the other hand, it is not a question of commonly known, typical diseases from Egypt; instead, there is a narrative recollection. And in the context of the book, this is a reference to the so-called plague narratives. There YHWH imposed sicknesses on Egypt.[37] It is true that the key word 'sick,' which one refers spontaneously, in the first place, to human beings, plays

36. However, this is not entirely certain for Deut. 28:60. Cf. n. 79 below.

37. The reference of the relative clause to the plague narratives has not been generally recognized by commentators. For example, cf. B. Baentsch in HKAT (Göttingen, 1903), ad loc., 'With *mḥlh*, cf. 23:25E, one should here think especially of diseases that are characteristic of Egypt (elephantiasis, eye diseases, dysentery, etc.). Or is the author making making a reference to the plagues? But frogs, hail, darkness, etc. are not really *mḥlh*; at most one could think of the death of the firstborn. Still, *kl* shows that the author is thinking of a number of different diseases, cf. Deut. 7:15.' However, from the fact that the boils in Exod. 9:8–12 are not mentioned at all we may recognize that it is not the plague narratives in the definitive book of Exodus, but those in the older sources of the Pentateuch that are being used as a standard of measurement. If we pose the question under these presuppositions, it is not every commentator who has the courage that we find, for example, in W. Fuß, *Die deuteronomistische Pentateuchredaktion in Exodus 3–17*, BZAW 126 (Berlin, 1972), 331–32. According to Fuß, the relative clause certainly refers 'to the Egyptian plagues. But the corresponding reports had nothing to do with diseases! Therefore our reference does not correspond to the requirements of harmony (= JE), but instead to a deuteronomistic statement of faith according to which defection from YHWH brings disease in its wake.'

virtually no part in the 'plague narratives' in Exodus 7–12.[38] But the climax of the whole narrative complex, the killing of the Egyptian firstborn, must surely be imagined concretely as a sudden illness leading to death.[39] The darkness that precedes it is the inbreaking of the realm of death.[40] The sixth plague (soot that causes boils) is an illness that affects everyone.[41] The fifth plague is pestilence, but it only attacks the cattle, while people are spared.[42] This, consequently, raises the question whether the reference to the diseases that 'I inflicted in Egypt'[43] can be restricted to human sickness. As soon as that question is posed, it becomes clear that this reference may encompass the whole complex of plague stories, which are summarized and interpreted under the general concept, foreign to the stories themselves, of 'disease' laid on the land by YHWH. If we take this as our starting point, we perceive still another relationship. The plagues in Egypt began, in fact, with the water of the Nile becoming undrinkable. It is emphasized three times (Exod. 7:18, 21, 24) that the Egyptians cannot drink the Nile water. Thus at the beginning of the series of plagues, the Egyptians find themselves in a very similar situation to that of the Israelites in Marah, where again the water is unpotable. But for them it is changed

38. In the definitive book of Exodus one should probably extend the plague complex to the twelfth chapter.

39. Let me refer here to S. E. Loewenstamm, 'An Observation on Source-Criticism of the Plague Pericope (Ex. vii–xi),' *VT* 24 (1974): 347–78, at 376–77. He presents arguments for the idea that there must once have been a schema of plagues in which pestilence for human beings followed the pestilence of the cattle, and was then succeeded by the final plague. The basic texts for his analysis are Exod. 9:13–15 and Ps. 78:48–51. But it may be questioned whether Ps. 78:51 must really be describing another, new plague in contrast to 78:50. Could the psalmist's meaning not be that the killing of the firstborn occurred precisely as a result of *deber*, 'pestilence'? Equipped with such an idea, the final redactors of Exodus 9 might also have regarded vv. 13–15 as by no means a blunted motif, but as a hint at the forthcoming death of the firstborn. Even if they did not understand it in that way, it could be so interpreted at a later time.

40. Cf. the later interpretation of this plague in Wisdom 17, whose basic notion undoubtedly corresponds to the intention of the text.

41. Exod. 9:8–12. This text belongs exclusively to the plague cycle in the priestly historical narrative. For that reason, there is usually no reference to it in interpretations of Exod. 15:26. Incidentally, it is here that the only verbal correspondence with the 'Egyptian' diseases in the book of Deuteronomy occurs: *šeḥîn*, 'boil,' found in Exod. 9:9, 10, 11 (2x), and Deut. 28:27(35).

42. *deber*, 'pestilence,' in Exod. 9:1–7, 13–15. Cf. n. 39 above.

43. On the problem of translation, see n. 35 above.

into potable water, and thus the whole series of plagues that drove toward disease and death is interrupted at its very beginning, because they receive a Torah, thereby allowing themselves to be put to the test and withstanding that testing. This is the initial beginning of the new reality of their lives. However, in Exod. 15:26 this truth is stated in a very fundamental fashion and without connection to a particular incident. Thus from Marah forward, the horizon is broadened toward the future. It extends far beyond the time in the wilderness, to every point at which the law that will be preached from Sinai to Moab is to have its effect. It will always be true that YHWH is the one who cares for Israel's health. What has been shown at Marah, at the beginning of the wilderness journey, is universally valid. From this comprehensive perspective, the subsequent verse, Exod. 15:27, turns its gaze backward again, returning to the simple and succinct style of the journey narrative. There is also an insertion in v. 27 to explain immediate circumstances, but in contrast to Exod. 15:25b it is introduced by the *wĕšām*, 'and there,' that is normal for the old narrative style. This is then taken up in the next clause by *šām*, 'there,' after the verb:

> Then they came to Elim,
> and there there were twelve springs of water and seventy palm trees;
> and they camped there by the water.

What is unusual, in comparison to Exod. 15:22 and other similar passages, is that there is no mention of a departure from Marah,[44] and the text speaks immediately of an arrival at another place, which, moreover, represents a positive contrast to Marah in terms of the central theme of water. It seems as if there had been no real pause in Marah. Only at Elim, for the first time since the departure from the Sea of Reeds, do the people make camp. Thus the narrative unit is rounded off at this point. U. Cassuto has pointed out that the consonant groups *mym* and *š/śm* each occur seven times in Exod. 15:22–27, which is surely no accident. But in both cases, the number seven is only reached in v. 27.[45] YHWH has led

44. Cf. especially, in addition, Num. 33:9.

45. Cf. n. 16 above. The two elements, each of which is present seven times, are brought together only in Exod. 15:27. Moreover, *mym* is found only in Exod. 15:22–25a, the Marah story told in the old narrative style, and *š/śm* is only in vv. 25b, 26, the universalizing of the story in terms of law and health, whose style stands out from the rest. From this point of view, the two text fields in v. 27 are connected to one another. The picture is not changed if, with Cassuto, we assign the occurrences of *šmʿ*, 'to hear,' and *šmr*, 'to give heed,' to the instances of the letter-combination *š/śm*, thus arriving at a total of ten.

Israel from the water of the Sea of Reeds through the desert to a new source of water.[46] During this journey through the wilderness, at a mysterious and dangerous place, there occurred a kind of confrontation with the life-threatening situation that earlier, in Egypt, had characterized the plague narratives. Israel was brought by God into a situation of testing. A connection emerged, wide-ranging in its significance, between Israel's health and its free acceptance of the order of life promised it by YHWH. YHWH stands self-revealed as the one who gives bodily health to Israel. History is illuminated in its full sweep, both past and future, through a very particular event. The single incident was more than just a single incident.[47]

2. Layering of the Text

As we now read the text of Exod. 15:22–27 in the Bible, it presents a carefully composed unit, as we have already seen. Its statement is as clear as it is deep and full. It is more than a historical report. This 'more' is clearly expressed by the text itself.

The same statement could probably be made differently, in its language as well: in particular, the language could be more unified. This brings us to the literary-critical question. While many things in the text produce meaning, they do so in a way that indicates to someone analyzing it that this text was created in stages. It had a pre-history.

The most obvious tension exists between the simple Marah narrative, up to v. 25a, and its continuation beginning in v. 25b. Here a new kind of language begins, and new content elements, which could scarcely have been anticipated, are introduced. The narrative is subsumed in statements of general validity. The historical horizon expands.

Beyond this, one may ask whether there are seams within Exod.

46. Could it have anything to do with that kind of latent level of background meaning that after Elim the Israelites, in Num. 33:10, come again to the Sea of Reeds? Cf. M. Noth, ATD, on Num. 33:10, though he sees here an 'improper conclusion from the misunderstood remark in 2 Moses 15:27 that, after their arrival in Elim, they camped by the water.' Only at the historical level could this be called 'improper.'

47. Let me also indicate that, through Exod. 16:4bβ, the manna narrative is also brought within the context of YHWH's testing of Israel. YHWH wishes to see whether Israel 'will follow [YHWH's Torah] or not.' Again in this story, which begins as a narrative of murmuring, Israel as a whole stands fast and is gifted by God with food, not only for this occasion, but for the whole period of the wilderness journey, in fact, as an abiding memorial.

15:25b–26. Did vv. 25b and 26 originally belong together? Has an older self-presentation by YHWH perhaps been secondarily expanded, in v. 26, to form the present, conditional blessing with its attached explanation?[48]

Besides this central literary-critical problem complex, there is a peripheral one as well. Did the journey framework originally belong to the Marah narrative, or was it secondarily introduced?[49] The latter could be favored by the absence of a notice of making camp at and departing from Marah. In this case, more wide-ranging hypotheses about the layers of the Pentateuch and their redactional composition affect the argumentation.[50]

48. If we decided in favor of further differentiations here, the question may arise whether either v. 25b or the self-presentation in v. 26 can still be isolated from the old Marah narrative only in terms of tradition history, but not from a literary-critical point of view. For Wellhausen it was important that v. 25b, although an old 'poetic fragment,' was part of one of the ancient sources. This was an essential building block for him in postulating a tradition of lawgiving at the oasis of Kadesh: cf. J. Wellhausen, *Prolegomena zur Geschichte Israels* (Berlin, 6th ed. 1905), 342. For E. Meyer, on the other hand, (see n. 18 above) it was important that the presentation of YHWH as a god of healing belonged to the old tradition. That made it easier to identify Marah with the principal fountain of Elim, which is supposed, in fact, to be the Phoinikon of Agatharchides of Cnidos (ca. 130 BCE): pp. 100–103.

49. Thus, for example, M. Noth, *Überlieferungsgeschichte des Pentateuch* (Stuttgart, 2nd ed. 1948), 18, and ATD, Commentary, ad loc. He assigns Exod. 15:22aα, 27 to the basic priestly document. The degree to which those knowledgeable in the linguistic style of the Pentateuch are sensitive to the absence of a notice of making camp and departing is indicated by the desperate positing of two lacunae in the text by R. Smend, *Die Erzählung des Hexateuch auf ihre Quellen untersucht* (Berlin, 1912), 146. O. Eissfeldt, *Hexateuch-Synopse* (Leipzig, 1922), first accepted this in the synopsis, but abandoned it again before the work was printed (see the Introduction, pp. 44–45) in favor of another, no less daring hypothesis.

50. See, for example, J. Wellhausen, *Die Composition des Hexateuchs und der historischen Bücher des Alten Testaments* (Berlin, 3rd ed. 1899), 77–78: 'To begin with, 15:22, 23, 27 are assigned to Q. It is true that Q contained these stations; it is just as true that JE also contained them, for if Elim, here present, can no longer be demonstrated elsewhere, the situation is no different for Yam Suf in Q. What right has anyone to make JE incomplete at this point, in order to make Q complete? Rather, from the contexts, JE has the more probable right to these verses, as v. 22b and v. 23 stand in a clear relationship to v. 24ff. Very significant formal grounds would have to favor Q in order to justify this excision. But precisely the contrary is true. In v. 22, *wysʿ mšh* is foreign to this source, just as is *yśrʾl* (instead of *bny y* . . . or *byt y* . . .); in v. 23 the characteristic *wysʿw mn* at the head is lacking. Similarly in v. 27: in the latter verse also, the episodic content better fits JE than Q. Nothing can be proven from Numbers 33, unless one can produce proof in advance that it would be impossible or unlikely that the author of this catalogue was more recent than JE.'

The identification of the posited layers with fixed items in one or another Pentateuch theory further complicates the picture of authorial intentions.[51]

The peripheral literary-critical problem cannot be discussed here. I personally believe that Exod. 15:25aα, 27; 16:1 belong within the system of journey notices by means of which the priestly historical narrative divides the 'toledot of Jacob' (the title of Gen. 37:2), which, quantitatively, make up the second half of the work.[52] This implies that the Marah narrative, in its earlier shape, cannot certainly be assigned to a broader and older narrative context, although that is not excluded either. Thus it could have been part of an old Pentateuch source, but it could also have been a story handed down in isolation, inserted during the redaction of the Pentateuch, or even later, into the journey description in the

51. Nöldeke, Steuernagel, Gressmann, Noth, Elliger, and Fritz suppose a more or less extensive share of P on the borders of the unit. Otherwise, scholars tend to follow Wellhausen's argumentation. Without exception, text from older Pentateuch sources is considered to account for vv. 23–25a, and sometimes for more. Wellhausen did not venture to decide which sources these were. Later scholars, with the exception of Steuernagel, were more cautious in their divisions. Kuenen and Baentsch assign to E; Jülicher, Gressmann, Noth, Fritz, Cazelles, and Childs (for example) to J_1; Smend, Eissfeldt, Beer, and Fohrer opt for L or N. Steuernagel, Gressmann, and Cazelles suppose a change of source (between the old Pentateuch sources) in v. 25b from J or JE to E. Almost universally, v. 26 is assigned to R^{JE} R^{D}, or D. Here scarcely any doubt has been indicated since Wellhausen. According to him, 'it appears that the Jehovist [Deuteronomist?] freely added v. 16' (*Composition*, 79). Jülicher, Baentsch, Beer, Noth, Fritz, and H. H. Schmid, however, have the deuteronomic addition begin as early as v. 25b. According to Smend, Eissfeldt, E. Meyer, Gressmann, Cazelles and Childs, there is source material retained in the saying about a healing God at the end of v. 26. A recent proposition is that vv. 25b, 26 should be more precisely designated as early or proto-deuteronomic: cf. H. Gese, 'Bemerkungen zur Sinaitradition,' *Vom Sinai zum Zion. Alttestamentliche Beiträge zur biblischen Theologie*, BEvTh 64 (Munich, 1974), 32n. 10; A. Reichert, *Der Jehowist und die sogenannten deuteronomistischen Erweiterungen im Buch Exodus*, Diss. Tübingen, 1972, 90–91 (not accessible to me during the preparation of this essay).

52. Cf. N. Lohfink, 'Die Priesterschrift und die Geschichte,' *Congress Volume Göttingen* 1977, SVT 29 (Leiden, 1978), 189–225, at 203–207. Wellhausen's arguments, cited in n. 50 above, lose much of their force when we abandon the absolute necessity of proving the continuous character of 'JE' at this point. In order to do so, Wellhausen postulates for 'Q' a measure of stereotypical style that is possibly too great. Cf., against this, McEvenue, *Narrative Style* (n. 25 above), 185: 'Rather the priestly writer seems to be at pains, not only to vary when he repeats, but also to confuse and interlock symmetries, and to disturb balance.'

priestly historical narrative.[53] The assignment of the outside frame, the journey notices, to the priestly historical narrative is quite in accord with the remaining literary-critical data, which remain to be examined. But these are not dependent on that assignment, nor would they become questionable, if the frame were assigned to an old Pentateuch source – the same one to which the text also, at least as far as Exod. 15:25a, would belong.

It should have become clear from the analysis of the present text presented above that there is a break between Exod. 15:25a and 15:25b. What appears at this point is not only a new content; the classical narrative language stops at the same moment.

Wellhausen, and many others after him, would admit that right away. But they still thought it possible to assign Exod. 15:25b to one of the old sources of the Pentateuch. Wellhausen spoke of a 'poetic fragment' inserted here (apparently by one of the authors of the sources).[54] Then, despite the linguistic interruption, there would be, at least, a very early connection between the Marah narrative and Exod. 15:25b.[55] In fact, *šām*, 'there,' at the beginning of a sentence corresponds to this kind of poetic usage. On the other hand, as already stated, there are a number of marginal occurrences in prose that can be adduced, even though they are never in texts that are indebted to the old narrative style.[56] Beyond this, the poetic fragments that can be found inserted in texts in the classical narrative style, from Genesis to 2 Kings, are always explicitly designated as quotations.

53. With some such beginning as 'When the Israelites marched out of Egypt, they journeyed towards the wilderness of Shur . . .' such a Marah narrative could certainly have been told by itself, even at a later time. It would of course be possible, independently of any connection with a larger narrative context by means of journey notices, to begin with the language and motifs within the field of the story itself and here to discover connections with definitive texts, either from 'J' or from 'E,' for example. This is done by, e.g., H. Cazelles in his review of V. Fritz, *Israel in der Wüste* (Marburg, 1970), *VT* 21 (1971): 506–14, at 510. But should we really believe that the place name 'Marah,' which besides is given a popular etymological explanation, designates Moses' sister Miriam in other J texts, while YHWH as healing god indicates the E texts Gen. 20:17 and Exod. 23:25, so that at this point *two* old Pentateuch sources are evident?

54. Cf. in 48 above. It is also apparent from Wellhausen, *Composition* (cf. n. 50), 79 that he assigned all of v. 25 to the old sources.

55. Today it could be that another conception would appear more likely: that a tradition-historical tension is visible behind the literary unity. But this could not explain the break at the purely linguistic level.

56. Cf. n. 19.

Never does the text move from prose to poetic diction without noting the fact.[57] Add to this that in Exod. 15:25b there is no poetic parallelism at all, at least none that is certain. Thus Wellhausen's often-repeated thesis remains unprovable, and even improbable. It is more probable that v. 25b was secondarily introduced into the Marah story, and that this happened in a later period when it was no longer considered necessary to formulate in the old narrative style; when, in fact, the author may deliberately have formulated against the old style in order to attract attention.[58]

Was only v. 25b introduced at that time, so that v. 26 represents a still later layer? The question about a break between v. 25b and v. 26 arises primarily because it is thought that deuteronomistic language characterizes v. 26 almost entirely, while at least some scholars deny this for v. 25b. In fact, *ḥōq ûmišpāṭ*, 'law and ordinance,' is not deuteronomic: Deuteronomy always has this double expression in the plural.[59] The question, however, is whether we are at all justified in applying labels like 'early deuteronomic,' 'proto-deuteronomic,' 'deuteronomic,' or 'deuteronomistic' to v. 26.

The reasons why this labeling has been or could be applied will now be summarized and given an immediate critical evaluation:[60]

57. Cf. Num. 21:27, 'Therefore the *mōšĕlîm* say;' Josh. 10:13, 'Is this not written in the *sēper hayyāšār*?' Here the quoted poetic fragments themselves have narrative character (within Josh. 10:12–13, this is true at least of Josh. 10:13). In both cases, moreover, the matter that is cited poetically at first (Num. 21:26) or afterward (Josh. 10:13–14) is repeated in prose. The frequent poetic pieces that are put in the mouths of persons in the narrative as word-for-word discourse, and thereby do not in themselves express actions within the narrative, are not introduced in this comparison. I know of no clearly recognizable poetry into which the old narrative prose would, in a certain sense, shift without further reflection, as for example when Qoheleth's prose is suddenly transformed into a fixed linguistic form, and even into broad poetry.

58. H. H. Schmid, *Der sogenannte Jahwist. Beobachtungen und Fragen zur Pentateuchforschung* (Zürich, 1976), 66 n. 20, has emphasized that the singular expression *ḥōq ûmišpāṭ*, 'law and ordinance' is not sufficient even to demonstrate an early deuteronomic basis. According to Cazelles (see n. 53 above) *nsh*, 'put to the test,' shows that here the Elohist is speaking. But Ruppert, 'Versuchung' (see n. 23 above), who has devoted a monograph to the investigation of *nsh*, 'put to the test,' in the Elohist, does not refer to Exod. 15:25. He regards v. 25b as 'typically deuteronomistic' (p. 55). In light of the occurrences of *nsh*, 'put to the test,' in Deut. 8:2, 16; 13:4; Judg. 2:22; 3:1, 4, Cazelles' argument is unpersuasive.

59. Cf. n. 22 above.

60. A quite thorough study is that of Baentsch, HKAT, (Göttingen, 1903), 140. The matter is often treated quite simplistically; in fact, for many authors the situation

1. On the basis of the form, what we have here is a conditional promise of blessing, ending with a self-presentation by YHWH that gives foundation to the blessing. The conditional promise of blessing is, from early deuteronomic texts onward, part of the deuteronomic field of language,[61] and for all the non-deuteronomic instances one may suspect more or less obvious deuteronomic influence.[62] However: YHWH's self-presentation is *not* typical of deuteronomic language, while within the Pentateuch it appears primarily in the priestly language.[63] The combination of conditional promise of blessing and formula of self-presentation is found only in the blessings in the holiness code, Lev. 26:3–13 (without a conjunctive *kî*, 'for'). The holiness code presumes Deuteronomy,[64] but is itself part of the priestly literature. We may also compare Lev. 26:44 (45), the conclusion of the unconditional promise of blessing that is attached to the announcement of the curse in the holiness code (with *kî*, 'for'). In addition, there are distant comparisons with Deut. 4:24, 31 (though the predications of YHWH are in the third person!) and Ps. 81:11 (because of its similarity to vv. 14–17). Deuteronomy 4 is part of a very late layer in Deuteronomy that must be closely associated with the priestly document.[65]

seems perfectly clear. The simplest formulation is that of A. Jülicher, 'Die Quellen von Exodus VII, 8–XXIV, 11,' *Jahrbücher für protestantische Theologie* 8 (1882): 79–127, 272–315, at 275–76: 'pure deuteronomic phrases all in a heap.' If, in what follows, I do not list parallel verses for individual words, I presume it is evident that there are enough in deuteronomic and deuteronomistic texts that could be cited. Anyone who wants to be sure may refer to the concordance. On the other hand, I will give verse citations where the parallels that may be discovered are not immediately persuasive, or when the further discussion demands it.

61. Cf. Exod. 23:22, 25. For a classification of the text as proto-deuteronomic, see J. Halbe, *Das Privilegrecht Jahwes. Ex 34, 10-26. Gestalt und Wesen, Herkunft und Wirken in vordeuteronomischer Zeit*, FRLANT 114 (Göttingen, 1975), 483–502. For a general list of occurrences of conditional promises of blessing, see n. 26 above.

62. This is even true of Job 36:11, 12; Prov. 2:1, 4.

63. Cf. the investigations by Zimmerli and Elliger (n. 27 above).

64. More precisely, with specification of layers: A. Cholewinski, *Heiligkeitsgesetz und Deuteronomium. Eine vergleichende Studie*, AnBib 66 (Rome, 1976); for particulars on Lev. 26 see pp. 310–19 of this work. Cf. also N. Lohfink, 'Die Abänderung der Theologie des priesterlichen Geschichtswerks im Segen des Heiligkeitsgesetzes. Zu Lev. 26, 9.11–13,' in H. Gese and H. P. Rüger, *Wort und Geschichte, Festschrift für K. Elliger zum 70. Geburtstag*, AOAT 18 (Neukirchen–Vluyn, 1973) 129–36.

65 Cf. N. Lohfink, 'Kerygmata des Deuteronomistischen Geschichtswerks,' *Die Botschaft und die Boten. Festschrift für H. W. Wolff zum 70. Geburtstag* (Neukirchen–Vluyn, 1981), 87–100, at 100.

Psalm 81 stands in a loose relationship to the deuteronomic field of language; in fact, the parallels point rather to a late stage.[66] Thus the form of Exod. 15:26 does presume the deuteronomic field of language, but the verse itself belongs to a post-, or at the most a late deuteronomistic stage of development.

2. *šmʿ*, 'to hear,' + *qôl*, 'voice,' cannot be designated as a typically deuteronomic combination of words. It is more probably a common idiom in ordinary speech.[67] It is true that the appearance of this word combination in the introduction to a conditional blessing or curse is typically deuteronomic. But then we always find the combination *šmʿ bĕqôl*, never *šmʿ lĕqôl*, as in Exod. 15:26;[68] *šmʿ lĕqôl* for obedience to God appears in the deuteronomistic language field only in Judg. 2:20; 1 Sam. 15:1; Ps. 81:12. (The total appearances are about 60.) In non-deuteronomic language, *šmʿ lĕqôl* is never found for obedience to God, but it does occur twelve times for obedience to other beings. The instances of the intensification of *šmʿ*, 'to hear,' through an initial infinitive in conditional promises of blessing, which are not very numerous,[69] extend from proto-deuteronomic texts to the post-exilic period. Altogether, what we have here, despite a clear imitation of deuteronomic language, is an unconventional variant.

3. The fact that *YHWH ʾĕlōhêkā*, 'YHWH, your God,' is typically, but not exclusively deuteronomic requires no further discussion.[70] In Deuteronomy itself the suffix is in the singular or the plural, depending on

66. The most important parallels are collected in J. Jeremias, *Kultprophetie und Gerichtsverkündigung in der späten Königszeit Israels*, WMANT 35 (Neukirchen–Vluyn, 1970), 126. Its conclusion, pointing to levitical circles in the royal period, and associated with the Deuteronomy theory of A. Bentzen and G. von Rad, does not appear to me to be verifiable on the basis of the parallels.

67. Cf. A. K. Fenz, *Auf Jahwes Stimme hören. Eine biblische Begriffsuntersuchung*, Wiener Beiträge zur Theologie 6 (Vienna, 1964), 26–27 (Übersicht I) and 33 (Übersicht III).

68. Cf. ibid., 38–39 (Übersicht IV). In the Cairo Geniza there was a fragment similar to the usual linguistic usage: cf. *BHS*, apparatus, ad loc. Otherwise the Masoretes succeeded in protecting the unusual formulations through a special list: cf. G. E. Weil, *Masorah Gedolah iuxta codicem Leningrandensem B 19a* I (Rome, 1971), no. 23.

69. Cf. n. 30 above.

70. Cf. N. Lohfink, 'Die These vom 'deuteronomischen' Dekaloganfang – ein fragwürdiges Ergebnis atomistischer Sprachstatistik,' in G. Braulik, ed., *Studien zum Pentateuch. Festschrift W. Kornfeld* (Vienna, 1977), 99–109, at 106.

whether Israel is addressed in singular or plural form. In the holiness code (and in the priestly writing as a whole), where plural address is always presumed, the double expression with plural suffix is also quite frequent.

4. *ʿśh*, 'to do,' + *hayyāšār bĕʿênê NN*, 'what is right in the eyes of NN,' seems to have been part of the language of public discourse and dealing.[71] With reference to the eyes of God, it is a stereotypical formula in the deuteronomistic characterization of kings.[72] In Deuteronomy, however, the expression seldom occurs. It appears only once in an injunction to observe the commandments, at Deut. 6:18.[73] Then there are four more instances, in legal layers that are probably late: Deut. 12:25, 28; 13:1; 21:9. In all four cases we find it in clauses that announce conditions for YHWH's blessing or the causes of that blessing. They could certainly have been influenced by the stereotypical royal judgments in the deuteronomistic history. In any case, we may suppose that they, in turn, contributed to the appearance of the expression in Exod. 15:26, since they reveal the same theme and the same internal logic. Here, then, we seem to have a deuteronomistic expression which is not attested anywhere in the priestly language. However, it must be located as late as possible.

5. The word *ʿśh*, 'to do,' together with *šmr*, 'give heed to,' constitutes another typical deuteronomic word pair for observing the law. Hence the deuteronomic character of the two words, related to one another in parallel here, should be investigated. But this character seems doubtful. For in Deuteronomy, by contrast, the fixed sequence is *šmr* – *ʿśh*. In addition, the two verbs are most often closely connected (*šmr laʿăśôt*, 'give heed by doing'), only then followed by a series of words for 'law.' But later, probably on the basis of Deuteronomy, the word pair achieved a certain significance, within the paraenesis of the holiness code as well. And here there is rather a tendency to parallel division, in which a different expression for the law as object can be associated with each of the two verbs. Twice, moreover, in Lev. 18:4 and 25:18, the canonical sequence of the verbs is reversed.[74] That corresponds precisely to the situation in

71. Cf. Deut. 12:8; Josh. 9:25; Jer. 26:14; also Judg. 17:6; 21:5. Without *ʿśh*, 'to do,' also at 2 Sam. 19:7; Jer. 40:4–5. In Josh. 9:25 and Jer. 26:14 we find *ṭôb*, 'good,' + *yāšār*, 'right.'

72. Fourteen times (with nine parallels in Chronicles).

73. Augmented by *ṭôb*, 'good,' placed second, in unusual fashion. I would assign Deut. 6:18 to DtrN, a probable late-exilic reviser of the deuteronomistic history detected by R. Smend in Joshua and Judges. Cf. Lohfink, 'Kerygmata,' (see n. 65 above), 98.

74. In Lev. 25:18 the first verb is repeated again, in the typical 'short-circuit style' of the priestly document (McEvenue).

Exod. 15:26: a reversed sequence, a stronger division by means of a complicated parallelism, and each verb with its own expression for 'law' as object. Thus at this point we find the linguistic flavor of the priestly document, and not the deuteronomic style.[75]

6. *'zn hifil*, 'to hear,' is called a deuteronomic word, with reference to Deut. 1:45; 32:1. But those are completely different contexts. It is certainly not a deuteronomic word for obedience or observation of the law. In the greater majority of instances it is a poetic parallel word for *šmʿ*, 'to hear,' and other words for hearing.[76] It is introduced in Exod. 15:26 because at that point something occurred that is otherwise not attested in Deuteronomy and its field of influence: namely, the doubling of the element of 'hearing' in a conditional clause of blessing to form a parallelism. This compositional move is within the trajectory of the stylistic tendencies of the priestly document.

7. *miṣwôt*, 'commandments,' as a designation for YHWH's laws stands alone both in Deuteronomy and in the priestly laws. The same is true of the isolated plural *ḥuqqîm*, 'laws,' even though the examples are few.[77] *miṣwôt*, 'commandments,' + *ḥuqqîm*, 'laws,' as a word pair is only comprehensible in the deuteronomistic realm, but rarely even there: in the sequence found in Exod. 15:26, the only other instances are in Deut. 27:10 and Ezra 7:11; it is found in the reverse order in Deut. 4:40 and 1 Kgs. 3:14; in the order in Exod. 15:26, but with the insertion of *'ēdôt*, 'decrees,' it is in Deut. 6:17 and 2 Chr. 34:31. No sort of special dependence can be demonstrated; this is simply a selection from among the many possibilities for combining expressions for 'law.'[78]

8. For the whole first clause of the conditional expression we could adduce Deut. 13:19 [18] as the nearest parallel:

> – if you obey the voice of YHWH your God
> by giving heed to all his commandments that I am commanding you today,
> doing what is right in the sight of YHWH your God.

75. For the detailed citations for this description of the situation, see Lohfink, *Hauptgebot* (n. 31 above), 69–70. The ordering of the witnesses from the holiness code given there as instances of an older 'preaching tradition' in Israel preceding all the layers of the Pentateuch represents a position I no longer hold.

76. Cf. n. 31 above.

77. Lev. 10:11; Deut. 4:6; 6:24; 16:12; 17:19. The first three are with *kol*, 'every.'

78. Cf. also n. 32 above.

This may be the model for Exod. 15:26a. But then it is clearly evident what is being done. The double infinitive has been converted into a juxtaposition of equal clauses. The system of three clauses has been altered, through the introduction of a clause parallel to 'hearing,' into a chiastic parallelism of four clauses. In the process, some elements had to be exchanged and others introduced. The formula of promulgation was dropped. From the perspective of Deuteronomy, all this represents an accommodation to the linguistic style of the priestly document.

9. As already mentioned above, the promise of blessing, with its reference to the diseases imposed by YHWH in Egypt, recalls the promise of blessing in Deut. 7:15 and the threatened curses in Deut. 28:27, 60, although in these there is no express reference to the plague narratives. The three passages in Deuteronomy are all in the same type of formal context: a conditional blessing or curse. It is true that, in the cases of Deut. 7:15 and 28:60, it is not entirely certain that these texts are older than Exod. 15:26.[79] But even if only Deut. 28:27 were left, it would have to be

79 From a comparison of the texts of Exod. 15:26 (= A in the following discussion), Exod. 23:25 (= B) and Deut. 7:15 (= C), which certainly belong together, the following facts can be derived: A has as its verb *śym*, 'to lay upon,' and the term for disease is *maḥălāh*, 'disease.' B has as its verb *swr*, 'to take away,' and the term for disease is *maḥălāh*, 'disease.' C has as verbs *swr*, *śym*, and *ntn*, 'to give,' and its terms for disease are *ḥŏlî*, 'disease,' and *madweh*, 'epidemic.' The terms for disease in C could stem from Deut. 28:59–61, and *ntn* from the whole chapter Deuteronomy 28, but *swr* and *śym* could not. The fact that A has taken over the rare *maḥălāh* from B (see n. 81 below), but not *swr*, is explainable: the total of seven instances of *š/śm* had to be reached, and a link backward to 15:25b had to be established. The combination of verbs from B (*swr*) and A (*śym*) in C is most easily explained if C is the most recent of the three texts. But the situation can also be explained otherwise, though not more simply, if other reasons should compel us to locate C before A. We must take account of the fact that Deuteronomy 7 is a text that was revised at a very late date. It contains priestly theologoumena: cf. Lohfink, 'Kerygmata' (n. 65 above), n. 44. Deut. 28:60 is apparently presumed by 7:15, but, on the other hand, it also belongs to a late layer of Deuteronomy. C. Steuernagel (HKAT[1] 1900), 99, is correct in viewing Deut. 28:56–61 as a text fragment that at one time constituted the conclusion of the whole cursing section. But when, because of the lack of any mention of the exile, he dated this part shortly before the conquest of Jerusalem (p. 104), he demanded of the concluding sentences something that can scarcely be postulated. On the contrary, the reference to the threats of disease and plagues described as 'not recorded in the book of *this* Torah' (*hazzō't* with the Masoretic text against Samaritanus and other witnesses!) could perhaps indicate knowledge of other existing written laws with threatened curses, such as the holiness code, even though this again is not necessarily the case. If we make that supposition, it is still more likely, on the basis of the formulation, that we should think of a period of time in which, for example, the holiness code and Deuteronomy had not yet been collected

supplemented by the conditional promise of blessing in Exod. 23:25, which does not directly mention Egypt. The latter is proto-deuteronomic.[80] And in this web of passages we probably have located the tradition to which Exod. 15:26 belongs. It undoubtedly lives within the deuteronomic realm. That may be presumed. But it still remains open whether Exod. 15:26 itself must be described as deuteronomic or deuteronomistic, or whether the principal statement within this text refers back to a deuteronomic tradition and carries it farther. A linguistic dependence in detail can at most be suspected in the case of the word *maḥălāh*, 'disease,' which is also in Exod. 23:25.[81]

10. A self-description of YHWH as 'physician of Israel' is unique in the Old Testament. In order nevertheless to explain this as deuteronomic, reference is sometimes made to Deut. 32:39. But apart from the metaphoric use of *rp'*, 'to heal,' in this passage, it otherwise represents the 'song of Moses,' which one may adduce only with the greatest caution, and never without parallel passages from deuteronomic prose, to establish the deuteronomistic character of a motif. And those are lacking here. The appeal to YHWH as a 'physician' dwelt in a different field of tradition within Israel: more on that later.

We may now summarize. In its form, its use of words, and in its meaning, Exod. 15:26 is related in multiple ways to the deuteronomic and deuteronomistic texts. That is the kernel of truth in the usual labeling of this verse as 'deuteronomistic,' or something like it. But at the same time there are such profound differences between this and everything deuteronomic, differences that constantly point toward documents in the later style and language of the priestly writing, that in the end we must reject this labeling. The author must, rather, belong to a period and a situation that had access to both the deuteronomic and priestly writings. More precisely: this verse was probably formulated, in dependence on and with reference to the deuteronomic texts, by someone who personally was more at home in the linguistic world of the priestly writing. While not

into a single Pentateuch. If Deut. 28:58–61 added to the powerful text of curses, which must already be presupposed at that point, a conclusion that was deliberately aimed at diseases, it indicates an attitude similar to that which interpreted the Egyptian plagues as 'diseases' in Exod. 15:26. In fact, the expression 'the diseases of Egypt' raises the question whether the well-known narratives of the Egyptian plagues should not be interpreted as a latent part of the text. Cf. n. 36 above.

80. Cf. n. 61 above.

81. Otherwise in the OT only at 1 Kgs. 8:37 (deuteronomistic history) = 2 Chr. 6:28, in a context that alludes to texts of cursing.

with absolute necessity, still with great probability, we must therefore think of the Pentateuch redactors themselves, or else a still later revision of the text.

If that is the case, the reasons for seeking a seam between Exod. 15:25b and 15:26 evaporate. The unusual 'narrative style' in v. 25b also can best be understood in terms of the priestly linguistic world.[82] On the other hand, there are good deuteronomic parallels for the motif of the 'testing' of Israel by YHWH,[83] and these are an excellent aid to understanding Exod. 15:26 as a natural explication of the final statement in 15:25b. Thus the intention of Exod. 15:25b, 26 is to be a single expansion of the old Marah narrative, and one that is to be located relatively late in the history of the Pentateuch.[84]

At most one may ask whether this could not be an insertion before an already existing conclusion to the Marah narrative, namely *wayyōʾmer ʾănî YHWH rōpĕʾekā*, 'And he (= YHWH) said: I am YHWH, who heals you.'[85] That is not impossible. As 2 Kgs. 2:21–22 shows, the cleansing of a water source by God, so that it no longer causes deaths and miscarriages, can be described as its healing. But neither can this be positively proved. We will have to leave the question open and suppose that even if that were true the hand of the reviser has fully identified with the textual basis on which it has expanded.

It is also possible to give a partial description of the expander's literary technique. He appears to have had two purposes: to embed his statement in the context, and at the same time to set it off clearly from that context. In the text as given, Exod. 15:22–25a, 27, he discovered that

82. Cf. the texts from the priestly historical narrative and Ezekiel introduced for comparison in n. 19 above.

83. Cf. Deut. 8:2, 16; 13:4; (33:8); Judg. 2:22; 3:1, 4.

84. Since Wellhausen there has been an opinion, constantly repeated but never supported by any newer types of proof, according to which *nsh*, 'to put to the test,' in Exod. 15:25 originally stood in connection with an etymology of the place name *massāh*, 'Massah' (Exod. 17:7; Deut. 6:16; 9:22; 33:8; Ps. 95:8). This serves to support the so-called Kadesh hypothesis, according to which Kadesh (with which Massah is to be connected) was the original location of judicial pronouncements, and even of the giving of law in the wilderness. However it may otherwise be with this hypothesis – cf. the report by H. F. Fuhs, 'Quades – Materialien zu den Wüstentraditionen Israels,' *Biblische Notizen* 9 (1979): 54–70, which indicates a certain skepticism – Exod. 15:25b should no longer be cited in support of it.

85. Cazelles (cf. n. 53 above) locates the YHWH discourse in the older text after *bĕmiṣrayim*, 'in Egypt.' But what is the meaning of the clause *lō ʾāśîm ʿālêkā* supposed to be?

the text was held together as if by a key word, through seven occurrences of the consonant group *mym*. Thus he produced something similar for his new text. He began with the second consonant group that appears twice in the concluding verse, Exod. 15:27, *šm*. He constructed his insertion in such a way that this consonant group immediately appears three times in Exod. 15:25b and occurs a total of seven times (ten times by another reckoning). In this way his own text was connected with the closing verse in exactly the same way as was the old Marah text. But since the key words were different, the two texts simultaneously stood out in contrast to one another. For the total composition of the insertion in Exod. 15:25b, the expanding author took additional inspiration from the two clauses with *šām*, 'there,' which continue the text with the notice of arrival in Elim in v. 27. But he did not use the ordinary older narrative style, since he wished to create a high degree of attention to his statement in v. 25b. He linked his text to the preceding, older Marah narrative in a different way: by creating a palindromic puzzle out of the subjects of his individual clauses.[86]

The backward reference to the plague narratives in Exod. 15:26b is probably more plausible if we presume as its background not only the old Pentateuch sources, but the priestly writing as well. The plague narratives could much more easily be interpreted as 'diseases' if they already contained the plague of boils in Exod. 9:8–12, and that plague is part of the priestly writing. Thus on the whole it is more probable that the expanding author was either the redactor of the Pentateuch itself, or else a still later editor.[87] Therefore the text that interests us here probably dates from the Persian period.

3. Was there an Old Tradition about YHWH the Physician?

In Exod. 15:26, YHWH is not only called 'physician,' but also 'the physician of Israel.' In spite of this, it is possible that we can frame the question of tradition history, which must now be asked, in a somewhat broader framework. In fact, we really must do so, if only because our sentence, in this strict form of a divine self-presentation, is unique in the

86. Cf. nn. 21 and 24 above.

87. If he was the Pentateuch redactor himself, and if the framing journey notice stems from the priestly historical narrative, the seven occurrences of the consonant group *mym* would be accidental, or else he would have achieved that number by a minor manipulation of the materials before him.

whole Old Testament. What, however, precedes it in the way of statements about YHWH the physician as such, and about YHWH the physician of Israel?

First let us set aside a discussion that has flared up again in recent years. There is a word, *rĕpā'îm*, which is used at several places in the Old Testament to describe a legendary, pre-Israelite original race in Palestine. At other points, it refers to the spirits of the dead or to dead ancestors. There are reasons to think that the legendary people of the Rephaim constitute a misunderstanding of the *rĕpā'îm* (= spirits of the dead); but there are other grounds for thinking that there was an original pronunciation of this word that identifies it with the biblical word that is now vocalized, in the plural, as *rōpĕ'îm*, and means 'healer, physician.'[88] The spirits of the ancestors, beings that exist in the divine realm, were probably called upon, in the pre-Israelite region of Canaan, as healing powers. The Ugaritic equivalent, *rā'pī'u*, has aroused lively discussions. In all this, theories have been developed according to which there was an individual god called *rāpī'u*, or that superior gods – some say it was Ilu, others that it was Baal – were called *rāpī'u*, and that YHWH is thus to be identified with such a *rāpī'u*-divinity. Such theories are quite hypothetical in themselves, and the fact that they are so hotly disputed among scholars is scarcely compatible with the circumstance that the designation of YHWH as 'healer' was apparently not so immediate or so direct as this. Consequently, having made brief mention of this whole discussion, we will not pursue it further.

Neither have we any reason to believe that YHWH had ever been specifically identified as properly, or so to speak 'professionally' a healer god, comparable to Asclepius, or ever had become such. E. Meyer attempted to deduce from Exod. 15:22–27 that the Israelites had regarded YHWH as the healer god of the spring of Marah, the primary water source of the oasis of Phonikon.[89] Still, even he supposes that YHWH was not originally thought of in that way, but only here, in order to displace the 'demons of the place' and to make it possible for the Israelites to make

88. See, as the best documented, most succinct and most balanced treatment of the problem in all its dimensions, including what follows: M. Dietrich, O. Loretz, and J. Sanmartin, 'Die ugaritischen Totengeister *RPU(M)* and the biblical Rephaim,' *UF* 8 (1976): 45–52. A particularly strong interpretation of YHWH on the basis of a supposed healing god, Baal, is found in J. C. de Moor, 'Rāpi'ūma – Rephaim,' *ZAW* 88 (1976): 323–45. His argument rests primarily on Deut. 32:39 and Hos. 11:2–3 (p. 337).

89. Cf. n. 18 above.

pilgrimage there and to seek healing at the spring. In addition, the hypothesis presupposes that the final clause of Exod. 15:26 is very old. But not even the bronze image of the serpent Nehushtan, which is traced to Moses (Num. 21:4–9), which stood in the Temple at Jerusalem and was banished from it by Hezekiah when he reformed the cult (2 Kgs. 18:4) can bear the burden of proving that YHWH was properly a god of healing.[90] When, after suffering an accident, Ahaziah of Israel sends servants to inquire of Baal-zebub of Ekron,[91] and the prophet Elijah accuses him for having sent messengers to a strange god, '[as if] there is no God in Israel to inquire of his word?' (2 Kgs. 1:16) it appears that the Baal of Ekron was quite clearly a god of healing who was frequently consulted, while on the contrary, at least in the minds of the upper classes, no special responsibility in that field was attributed to YHWH. When in the later period YHWH was called the 'sun of righteousness . . . with healing in its wings' by those who revere the divine name (Mal. 4:2; Heb. 3:20) we have a clear example

90. The connection of the serpent image with sickness and healing is clear only from Numbers 21, and not in 2 Kgs. 18:4. Among those who have rejected this method of interpretation are K. R. Joines, 'The Bronze Serpent in the Israelite Cult,' *JBL* 87 (1968): 245–56. In Numbers 21 the problem, to be precise, is only snakebite. YHWH saves the lives of those who look up to the bronze serpent after having been bitten by a snake. This is complicated: originally it was probably the bronze serpent itself that symbolized the healing divinity. Thus, obviously, YHWH has here been secondarily introduced into an originally transparent symbolism for a god of healing. That YHWH never clearly belonged in this context can probably be deduced from the elimination of this cultic image during Hezekiah's reform. It was evidently not entirely orthodox in the sense of strict YHWH-monolatry. There may also be connections between the removal of Nehushtan and the throne vision of Isaiah, whose image-statement, as O. Keel has shown, consists in the fact that the numinosity of the much-revered serpent being, which now nevertheless cowers before YHWH, is only signalized by the much greater holiness of YHWH: O. Keel, *Jahwe-Vision und Siegelkunst. Eine neue Deutung der Majestätsschilderungen in Jes 6, Ez 1 und 10 und Sach 4.* SBS 84/85 (Stuttgart, 1977), 113. This may be true, although the seraph-serpents of Isaiah do not directly reflect the serpent type of Nehushtan, but rather that of the winged serpent (ibid., 81ff.).

91. It is not quite clear what was the real name of the divinity to be consulted at Ekron. We can stick with *ba'al zĕbûb*, and thus understand it to mean either 'lord of the flies' or 'lord of the flame.' The first fits a healing god very well, while the latter corresponds to a primary motif in the narrative itself and in the broader context of the Elijah stories. We can also suppose here a parody on the name Beelzebul, known to us from the NT, and thus understand the name as 'lord ruler,' 'lord of the house/temple,' or (again parodied), 'lord of the dung.' The best overview, with documentation, is that of C. Fensham, 'A possible explanation of the name Baal-Zebub of Ekron,' *ZAW* 79 (1967): 361–63.

of the way in which ideas originally connected with the sun god, who was revered as a healer in Babylon and elsewhere, have been secondarily applied to YHWH; but this does not mean that YHWH was therefore necessarily regarded as properly a god of healing.[92]

There is simply no need to suppose that YHWH was a professional healing god. Gods of that type, in fact, are often located in the lower ranks within a divine pantheon, or else they have a very localized importance. W. W. Graf Baudissin concluded, as early as 1911: 'I am not able to prove with certainty that there was any special god of the healing arts in the Semitic regions; but it is expressly stated of different divinities, and with special emphasis, that they heal the sick.'[93] He then presents the material on this topic that was available at the time. As soon as he reaches the point of evaluating personal names, one gets the impression that even this thesis was too restrictive. It seems almost as if healings could be predicated of every god who was genuinely revered.

In the mean time it has become clear why we should have this impression. Phenomena like health, sickness and healing are, religiously speaking, by no means to be attached to particular divinities. Prior to that, they have their place within a certain type of religion.[94] We must distinguish between official religion, ordered to the city, the state, and the major temple as center of official life, and that type of religion that was carried out by individuals, or, more precisely, within families. Sickness, efforts at healing, and recovery of health all took place primarily in the family sphere. Of course, oracles were consulted in order to determine

92. Cf. F. Vattioni, 'Mal. 3,20 e un mese del calendario fenicio,' *Bibl* 40 (1959): 1012–15, at 1015.

93. W. W. Graf Baudissin, *Adonis und Esmun. Eine Untersuchung zur Geschichte des Glaubens an Auferstehungsgötter und an Heilgötter* (Leipzig, 1911), 311. The expanded material is found on pp. 310–24. Compare the broad statement of P. Humbert, 'Maladie et médecine dans l'Ancient Testament,' *RHPR* 44 (1964): 1–29, at p. 21, that the theme of the 'healing god' played a major role in Israel.

94. The following remarks rely primarily on two studies: E. S. Gerstenberger, *Der bittende Mensch. Bittritual und Klagelied des einzelnen im Alten Testament*, WMANT 51 (Neukirchen–Vluyn, 1980), a somewhat older version of which was available from the author after 1971; and R. Albertz, *Persönliche Frömmigkeit und offizielle Religion. Religionsinterner Pluralismus in Israel und Babylon*, Calwer Theologische Monographien, A 9 (Stuttgart, 1978). Because of its strict criteria of selection, a work especially important for the identification and interpretation of Israel's psalms of illness is: K. Seybold, *Das Gebet des Kranken im Alten Testament. Untersuchungen zur Bestimmung und Zuordnung des Krankheits- und Heilungspsalmes*, BWANT 99 (Stuttgart, 1973). Further bibliography may be found in these works.

whether the sickness would lead to death or whether one could have hope. For the necessary penitential and prayer rituals at the sickbed or (in the absence of the sick person) at the sanctuary, the indispensable professional aids were called upon: physicians, priests, prophets. Often, the lines of distinction among these professional designations cannot be clearly drawn. Sacrifices were also brought, and when health has been restored it could happen that a thanksgiving celebration was held at the sanctuary, a ceremony that at the same time restored the sick person to society. Nevertheless, the family is the center of the whole process. This does not enter into the official cult as such, and despite all the connections that are necessarily present, even the theoretical ideas that emerge in the prayers and songs reveal some clear differences.

One route of access to this family religion is by way of personal names, since among Semitic peoples they are almost all religious confessional statements. They are formulated and given in the context of the birth of a child, which again is an occurrence that is totally centered in the family. The god to whom the name is referred is thus the numen revered in that particular family as their personal god. In polytheism, this is usually one of the gods worshipped in the public cult. In monolatrous Israel we can expect that normally it is YHWH, the only god of the official religion, who is also the god of individual families. It is true that YHWH is also addressed as El, and in some periods perhaps even as Baal.

The distinction among the various divinities worshipped in families is not very important for understanding family religion. The structure of activities and the religious experiences undergone in the process did not differ to the degree that might be inferred from the names of the divinities that were worshipped. With all the caution that is demanded, we may even suppose that there was a considerable affinity between family religion in Mesopotamia and in Israel – in sharp contrast to the striking differences in the religious acts, theorems and experiences that characterized official religion in the two areas.

Family-related activities in the religious realm within Israel are harder for us to grasp than official religion, since it is the latter that is primarily reflected in the Old Testament writings. Still, on the basis of Israelite personal names we can suppose that family religion also was El-YHWH-oriented from a very early date. This orientation could be repeatedly threatened: think of the worship of the 'Queen of Heaven,'[95] whoever she

95. Jer. 7:18; 44:17, 19, 25. It is obscured in the Masoretic text by the vocalization *mĕleket haššāmayim*, which in some manuscripts even became *mĕle'ket* (work of the

may have been, which is attested in the book of Jeremiah and apparently is rooted in families.[96] But for our question concerning the worship of YHWH as healer and physician in Israel it is sufficient if we can suppose that there was some sort of general YHWH-oriented family piety.

There are enough indications that, in Israel as well as elsewhere, this family religion encompassed the experiential realms of health, sickness and healing, and thus as a matter of course turned to YHWH as personal god in the life of the individual.

First of all, it was customary to obtain a prognosis, preferably from prophets, to ascertain whether the illness would lead to death or not.[97] One did penance and spoke prayers of petition oneself.[98] But one also secured the intercession of powerful prayers, especially from prophets.[99]

heaven = heavenly host). But the translation 'queen of heaven' in Jer. 7:18 [several versions] and in 51:17 LXX points to an original *malkat haššāmayim*, 'queen of heaven.' For the internal family character of this cult, cf. especially Jer. 7:18 and 44:19.

96. See the recent study by M. Weinfeld, 'The Worship of Molech and of the Queen of Heaven,' *UF* 4 (1972): 133–54.

97. 1 Kgs. 14:1–18 (the wife of Jeroboam of Israel inquires of the prophet Ahijah because of the illness of her son); 2 Kgs. 1:2–17 (the prophet Elijah reproaches Ahab of Israel for having consulted the god of Ekron in his illness, '[as if] there is no God in Israel to inquire of his word'); 8:7–14 (Ben-hadad of Damascus is ill and inquires of the 'man of God,' Elisha – probably told in imitation of what was usual in Israel); 20:1–6 (Hezekiah of Judah, mortally ill, receives first a negative and then a positive message from Isaiah); Ps. 107:20 (YHWH 'sent out his word' to the mortally ill 'and healed them' – the form of the oracle is not visible here).

98. 2 Sam. 12:15–23 (David's prayer and fasting for his dying child should probably not be interpreted as petition of behalf of another, but rather as the prayer of the father who is himself touched, through and in the child, since according to v. 14 David himself is punished by the child's death); 2 Kgs. 20:2–3 (the sick Hezekiah prays and weeps, while turning to the wall); Ps. 6:2–8 (prayer of a sick person); Ps. 41:5–11 (quoting a prayer within a song of testimony from a celebration of thanksgiving); Ps. 107:19 (the sick 'cried to YHWH'); Job 33:26 (the sick person 'prays to Eloah, and is accepted by him'). Cf., in imitation of such prayers, with the root *rp'*: Jer. 15:18; 17:14.

99. Gen. 20:17 (where Abraham is portrayed as a prophet: 20:7); Num. 12:13 (where the issue is that Moses is more than a prophet: 12:6–8); 1 Kgs. 13:6 (the man of God in Bethel); 1 Kgs. 17:19–21 (Elijah; prayer surrounded by ritual); 2 Kgs. 4:33–35 (Elisha; prayer surrounded by ritual); Ps. 35:13–14 (penitential ritual and prayer of the one who prays the psalm for others who are ill); Job 33:23–25 (*mal'āk*, 'angel,' *mēlîṣ*, 'mediator': probably a priest – cf. Seybold, *Gebet des Kranken* [n. 94 above], 60–62); 2 Chr. 30:18–20 (King Hezekiah, in face of a threat of disease as punishment). The figure of the 'servant of God' in Isaiah 53 has as its background both the sick person and prayerful intercession for him or her (*rp'*, 'heal,' in 53:5).

After healing, one thanked YHWH at the sanctuary and was restored by YHWH to community.[100] In all these contexts it was a matter of course that YHWH is the one who effects healing[101] and restores life.[102]

This is the basis for all discourse about YHWH as the physician in Israel, extending throughout all time periods and continually endowed with a new and living power by constant experience of sickness and healing.[103] Undoubtedly, there are close analogies to family religion outside of Israel. But what is typical of the Old Testament, in contrast, is the extent to which, especially among the various writing prophets, we encounter a 'transferral' of the statement about YHWH the healer.[104]

'Transferral' is here to be understood in a twofold sense. First, it is not a matter of the sickness of an individual human being. The subject who is sick, and who needs YHWH for healing, is Israel, Judah, or Jerusalem – in any case, a collective entity greater than the bounds of the family. Second, the concept of sickness itself is extended. To the bodily illness of individual persons, other elements are added, i.e., social and economic disturbances, distress and diminishment of life in all forms. All

100. Seybold, *Gebet des Kranken* (n. 94 above) has shown that this is the central purpose of the psalms of sickness and healing.

101. This is especially clear in the legends of the prophets, since the prophets of YHWH themselves also served as 'doctors' in our sense of the word. They breathed life into the sick (1 Kgs. 17:21; 2 Kgs. 4:34–35) and applied medicines (2 Kgs. 20:7), although, in the context of the story, there cannot be the least doubt that YHWH is the true physician. A clear theoretical formulation is found in Job 5:18; Pss. 103:3; 147:3.

102. Baudissin, *Adonis und Esmun* (see n. 93 above) has, in his depiction of YHWH as the 'rescuer from sickness and death' (pp. 385–402), which still repays reading, a section, 'YHWH heals,' in which he focuses on the root *rp'*, 'to heal' (pp. 385–90), and follows this with another section, 'YHWH "gives life" in sickness and distress,' in which he centers his remarks primarily on the root *ḥyh*, 'to live' (pp. 390–97). Since sickness was regarded as being seized by death, healing means being brought back to life. It is only on the basis of this concept that we can achieve a full understanding of the OT statements about YHWH, who liberates from illness. Further important texts are introduced in this perspective, such as 2 Kgs. 5:7 and 1 Sam. 2:6. Restricting myself to the vocabulary in Exod. 15:26, I will not enter into a specific discussion of this broader field of expression.

103. Even when, later, angels appear as numina who mediate healing, and demons are their direct opponents, the final and absolute responsibility of the God of Israel for sickness and healing is not diminished. A good example is the book of Tobit, in which the very name of the angel says everything: Raphael = El has healed.

104. Of the total of 80 instances of the root *rp'*, 'heal,' in the OT (excluding names), 42 belong to this category, according to my count.

this together is Israel's sickness. This is sometimes referred to as a metaphorical use of the words for sickness and healing. That is correct in a sense, and in a sense it is not. For sickness in the strict sense constitutes a part of the more comprehensive phenomenon that is here called 'sickness.' The kernel of this all-encompassing sickness of Israel (or, secondarily, of Egypt or Babylon) is a disrupted relationship with God. But that in itself is nothing new or contrasting with the concept of sickness in family religion.

The examples of this way of speaking about the sickness and healing of Israel are to be found primarily in the books of Hosea, Isaiah and Jeremiah.[105] It appears to have been urgently important for the first writing prophets in the eighth century, at least for two of them, Hosea and Isaiah. It entered the books of Jeremiah and Ezekiel in the oracles on the alien peoples.[106] This kind of speech is directly continued when the healing of every illness, full health and long life then become a theme of eschatological promise.[107]

In this many-layered complex of statements, the idea of YHWH the physician has moved outside the realm of family religion and entered the context of Israel's national religion. The connecting links, undoubtedly, are the prophets. They belonged to the fixed personnel of family piety, and in particular they seem to have preserved and carried on the practical and theoretical knowledge belonging to that sphere. They then acquired, little by little, a new task on behalf of all Israel, and in the process they probably made use of their old sphere of knowledge as well, in order to make themselves understood within the new dimension.[108]

105. Hos. 5:13; 6:1; 7:1; 11:3; 14:5; Isa. 6:10; 57:18–19; Jer. 3:22; 6:14; 8:11, 15, 22; 14:19; 19:11; 30:13, 17; 33:6; also Ezek. 34:4; Zech. 11:16; Deut. 32:39; Ps. 60:4; Lam. 2:13. The Chroniclers' history has also adopted this kind of speech in its prose: cf. 2 Chr. 7:14; 36:16, and probably also 21:18. (In this context, king and people constitute a unit.) Here and in the next two footnotes I will only mention the examples of *rp'*, 'heal,' in these contexts. The instances of the whole complex of such statements are much more extensive, especially for eschatological sayings. For the historical Isaiah, who is not adequately represented by the instances of *rp'*, 'heal,' let me however mention Isa. 1:5–6.

106. Jer. 46:11; 51:8–9; Ezek. 30:21.

107. Isa. 19:22; 30:26; Ezek. 47:8, 9, 11; Mal. 3:20. Jesus of Nazareth would refer his healings, interpreted as eschatological, to the promise of the healing of concrete illnesses in the book of Isaiah: cf. Matt. 11:5, *par.* Luke 7:22 with Isa. 29:18; 35:5–6; 42:7, 18–20; 43:8. These instances belong in the present context.

108. The situation could have been still more complicated. In Hos. 6:1–3 and Jer. 14:19–22, penitential songs of the people are quoted (although without any kind of formal

Thus there was an old idea of YHWH the physician, always vivid because bound up with immediate, personal religious experience. Beyond this there was, at the time when Exod. 15:26 was written and inserted in the Pentateuch, a way of speaking about YHWH the physician of Israel that had already existed for a long time within prophetic speech. It was bound up with the interpretation of the collapse, first of the northern and then of the southern kingdom, the Babylonian deportation and return from exile, and finally with the expectation of God's great, eschatological action on behalf of Israel and the whole world. Is all that taken up in Exod. 15:26 and introduced into the ancient Pentateuch?

We need to know all this as background to Exod. 15:26. But at this point we must indicate one difference.

Exod. 15:26 portrays YHWH, not as the healer of individual persons, but as the physician of Israel. Yet, on the other hand, this does not seem to represent the sort of 'metaphorical' expansion of the concept of sickness and healing that is also typical of prophetic usage. What is at stake here is apparently sickness, healing and health in the stricter sense, even if the reference to the plague stories seems to insinuate an extension of the concept in this instance as well.

Exod. 15:26 is a special formulation in contrast to the prophetic sayings about YHWH, the healer of Israel. The special character of the saying also has a background of its own, namely the deuteronomic tradition.

4. Israel's Health in the Deuteronomic Tradition

Deuteronomy seems to mark the high point in a tradition whose oldest witness is retained for us in the 'code of YHWH's privilege' in Exod.

designation as quotations), and these songs are clearly imbued with motifs of sickness and possible healing of the people. They may have been formulated in summary fashion by the prophets themselves, who could have brought their own imagery into the songs. Or else, at least in Hos. 6:1–3, they are penitential songs composed as an echo of prophetic proclamation (cf. Hos. 5:13). But there remains a third possibility: that these are existing formulae from the repertoire of popular penitential songs. Then it would be the case that, in the sphere of penance and popular lament, the theorem of YHWH as physician had already moved from the realm of family piety into public religion, even before the prophets. It might also be possible to bring Ps. 60:4 into the argumentation as well, although there are major problems of dating with regard to this psalm. But even if all this were true, a genuinely productive extension of this idea beyond the family sphere appears to have been first effected by the prophets of the eighth century, especially Hosea and Isaiah, and later mainly by Jeremiah.

34:10–26. Even here it is connected with the key word *bĕrît*, 'covenant, contract.' Several years ago an unusually thorough and judicious study of this text was provided by J. Halbe.[109] The earliest layer of the text may stem from the pre-monarchical period. The community of the adherents of YHWH that stands behind this text extends beyond the boundaries of family or tribe. It distinguishes itself sharply from the other population groups in Canaan and from their gods, and conceives its relationship to its god, YHWH, in analogy to the laws governing human relationships such as the rights of chieftains or fathers, i.e., as a law of privilege. The groups that are accepted into the sphere of YHWH's privilege live under YHWH's blessing. Even in the period before the establishment of the state, there appears to have developed, in connection with the sanctuary at which this tradition of the law of privilege was cultivated, a basis for uniformity of laws among the groups involved, and a formulated acknowledgment of laws protecting the poor and the weak. The sanctuary could have been Gilgal; the concept claimed the power of determination for the whole entity of 'Israel.'

With the foundation of the state, this self-understanding was forced into an underground status, or one of opposition.[110] The 'book of the covenant,' Exod. 20:23–23:33, may have been written as an attempt to rescue this pre-state social impetus from oblivion and to preserve it for a more clear-headed future. Here the old covenant text of Exodus 34, expanded and rearranged, forms the frame within which a kind of collection of laws indicates the stateless, now even anti-state social idea of ancient Israel. At the end of the frame, in Exod. 23:20–27, 31b–33,[111] YHWH's crucial demands of the community that is bound to YHWH are formulated, reiterating Exod. 34:10–15a: no worship of other gods (23:20–24) and no mingling with other population groups (23:27, 31b–33). It was precisely these two things that were abandoned in the transition to the Davidic state: now non-Israelites live with Israelites in the same nation, and now other gods are worshipped within the same society. But the most distressing thing for those who did not want to participate in this change was that the state had apparently brought prosperity and

109. *Das Privilegrecht Jahwes. Ex 34, 10–26* (see n. 61 above). Earlier literature is listed in this book.

110. On these processes, cf. now, especially, F. Crüsemann, *Der Widerstand gegen das Königtum. Die antiköniglichen Texte des Alten Testaments und der Kampf um den frühen israelitischen Staat*, WMANT 49 (Neukirchen–Vluyn, 1978).

111. Exod. 23:28–31a is a later expansion: cf. Halbe (n. 61 above), 483–86.

comfort in its wake. In order to deal with this fact, vv. 25–26 are inserted into the middle of the text. They confirm that Israel, if it holds to YHWH's 'angels' or 'messengers'[112] and remains true to the old community of privilege directly bound to YHWH, will by no means be bereft of these blessings. If first place is given to serving YHWH, everything else will be given as well. The verses are not even formulated, from a strictly syntactical point of view, as a conditional promise of blessing. Summarizing what went before, the text simply presumes as obvious that Israel again turns entirely to YHWH, and the fourfold blessing follows as a matter of course:[113]

> You shall worship YHWH your God (alone),
> and he will bless your bread and your water;
> and I will take sickness away from among you,
> and there shall be no woman who shall miscarry or be childless in your land;
> I will fulfill the number of your days.[114]

Freedom from disease is the second of the four blessings, and the third and fourth are also closely connected with it. A number of things in this passage are important for our inquiry: health is one among many blessings; the subject clearly is bodily health, and any metaphorical expansion of the concept is excluded; this blessing is not yet conditioned on the observation of individual commandments, and yet the book of the covenant begins with the sketch of a stateless order of society, and the demands of YHWH that immediately surround this passage are the fundamental pillars of the YHWH-community based on the code of YHWH's privilege. Thus at this point the real, physical health of the community of Israel is immediately associated with a 'yes' to a form of society oriented to YHWH, which makes Israel a contrast-society in relation to the normal societies in the world around it. With regard to Exod. 15:26, we may again point out that the first blessing includes clean water. Recall that Exod. 15:25b, 26 is attached to an old narrative about the healing of unhealthful water.

The proto-deuteronomic conception of Israel attested here is not part

112. On 'messengers,' especially in connection with the Gilgal traditions, as 'charismatic authority that made cultic proclamation of YHWH's will,' cf. Halbe (n. 61 above), 360–63, 369–76.

113. On the preceding cf. Halbe (n. 61 above), 484–99.

of family religion. It has to do with a more comprehensive community, a society. On the other hand, it is difficult to include it in the concept of official religion. In the pre-royal period the official religion of those who dwelt in the land was precisely that from which one was expected to distance oneself, in the name of YHWH. After the founding of the state, official religion was centered in the Jerusalem temple and other royal sanctuaries – and it is precisely that which the book of the covenant sets itself against, at the very beginning, with its law of the altar.[115] There is no point, in this instance, in adding another concept to the theory of plural religions in Israel, but one must be aware of the situation.[116] For it was at the point when the state was approaching its end, and when an attempt was made in Jerusalem to revitalize it with the power of the old, pre-national YHWH covenant, that 'Deuteronomy' was created. It was written in order that this tradition might now become the official religion.

In this process of linguistic reformulation, the thought models, motifs and formal elements of the Assyrian culture then dominant in Jerusalem exercised a powerful influence. The privileged relationship between Israel and YHWH was viewed analogously to feudal or vassal

114. The change in number and person does not indicate literary layering, but rather is a rhetorical means of division and a method of attracting attention. Cf. Halbe (n. 61 above), 497.

115. For more detail, see Halbe (n. 61 above), 378–82.

116. The preceding sentences are deliberately formulated in opposition to the position presented by Albertz, *Persönliche Frömmigkeit* (n. 94 above): cf. esp. 165–69, 'Übersicht über die Entwicklung,' and the sections that follow. The two-part division into 'official religion and personal piety,' which is probably too simplified even for Babylon, certainly misses the factual situation in the religious history of Israel. The religious worlds that emerge variously in the writing prophets and in the deuteronomic movement have ancient roots in the pre-national social and religious project of Israel, and the latter distinguishes itself from an 'official' religion, without, however, having been a religion of small groups. With the foundation of the state a new 'official' religion was created, first in Jerusalem, and then again in the North; these combined, in different ways, elements of the old official religions and the religion of YHWH. In the deuteronomic reform it was not the case that official religion sought to gain influence over family religion; instead, the underground YHWH religion, which was always strongly tied to family religion, was superimposed upon and drawn into the official religion in order to revitalize it. At least up to this point in Israel's religious history, therefore, we ought to introduce a special term for the popular YHWH religion that was neither tied to individual, smaller groups nor resident in the official state sanctuaries. The term should also offer opportunity for further differentiation. Incidentally, Albertz himself indicated, in a postscript written at a later date, that he was open to a differentiation of his view of things (p. 297).

relationships laid down in a 'covenant' or 'contract.'[117] The 'blessing' that had been spoken of from of old could be regarded, within the style of such contracts, as a conditional blessing and more clearly defined through an opposition with conditional curses. In accord with the Assyrian models, it appears that more space was allowed for the curse than for the blessing.[118]

Accordingly, in Deuteronomy, in the version on which Josiah's reform was based, the promise of the deflection of sickness from Israel, connected with service of YHWH, is formulated in one instance as a promise of blessing, and in another, and primarily, as a threatened curse in the case of disobedience.

We can only speculate about the promise of blessing. The texts concerning the centralization of the cult, which represent an early version of the deuteronomic lawbook, are developed on the basis of the calendars of feasts in Exodus 34 and Exodus 23; consequently we may suppose that the central formulations of the old covenant text in these chapters were also in Deuteronomy at an early period. They are now to be found, in a late-deuteronomic revised form, in Deuteronomy 7.[119] The promise of blessing from Exod. 23:25–26 is given here in a more developed form:

> 7:12 If you heed these ordinances, by diligently observing them, YHWH your God will maintain with you the covenant

117. On this concept of the origins of Deuteronomy, cf. N. Lohfink, 'Deuteronomy,' *IDB Supplementary Volume* (Nashville, 1976), 229–32. On the special aspects relating to the sociology of knowledge, see N. Lohfink, *Unsere großen Wörter. Das Alte Testament zu Themen dieser Jahre* (Freiburg, 2nd ed. 1978), 24–43: 'Theologie als Antwort auf Plausibilitätskrisen in aufkommenden pluralistischen Situationen, erörtert am Beispiel des deuteronomischen Gesetzes.' [English translation by Ronald Walls: *Great Themes from the Old Testament* (Edinburgh, 1982), 17–37, 'Theology as the Answer to Plausibility Crises in Emergent Pluralistic Situations Taking the Deuteronomic Law as the Basis for Discussion.'] That 'contract' and 'oath of fidelity' were typical features of Assyrian culture is shown, for example, by A. Moortgat's remark: 'At scarcely any time were so many contracts made, so many oaths of fidelity sworn and broken' (A. Scharff and A. Moortgat, *Ägypten und Vorderasien im Altertum* [Munich, 1950], 401).

118. Martin Noth in particular, in '"Die mit des Gesetzes Werken umgehen, die sind unter dem Fluch,"' included in his *Gesammelte Studien zum Alten Testament*, ThB 6 (Munich, 1957), 155–71, has emphatically pointed out the excess weight of the curse even in the earliest form of Deuteronomy 28 (distancing his position from that of C. Steuernagel, who supposed that the two were originally balanced).

119. Cf. my analysis of Deuteronomy 7 in *Hauptgebot* (n. 31 above), 167–88. Further information on the history of research will be found in Halbe, *Privilegrecht* (n. 61 above), 16–19.

loyalty that he swore to your ancestors;
13 he will love you, bless you, and multiply you;
he will bless the fruit of your womb and the fruit of your ground, your grain and your wine and your oil, the increase of your cattle and the issue of your flock, in the land that, as you know, he swore to your ancestors to give you.
14 You shall be the most blessed of peoples.
Neither man nor woman nor beast – nothing will be barren among you.
15 And YHWH will turn away from you every illness;
all the dread diseases of Egypt that you experienced, he will not inflict on you, but he will lay them on all who hate you.

There is a good deal in favor of the idea that the present form of Deut. 7:15 is the result of a revision, the author of which may even have known and presupposed the addition in Exod. 15:26 to which we have referred.[120] Still, it remains probable that even the older text of Deuteronomy 7 contained the blessing of health, and in a formulation that lay somewhere between Exod. 23:25 and the present text. In the text as it stands, the first three of the four items in the blessing in Exod. 23:25–26 are already clearly evident. Abundance of food is expressed in formulae that are probably taken from Deut. 28:4, 51. Then the motif of fruitfulness is brought to the fore. For the theme of 'health,' it seems that formulations from Exod. 23:25, Exod. 15:26, and Deut. 28:27, 35, 60 are combined. The summary of Deut. 7:12–13 under the label, 'promises to the ancestors,' and of 7:14–15 under the title, 'difference from other peoples' is certainly due to the revision, which here creates links to what has preceded and what will follow. Thus it is difficult to see what originally stood at this point on the subject of disease and health, but we must suppose that some passage of this type was present.

In contrast, the formulation of the deuteronomic law in the text of blessing and curse in Deuteronomy 28, written in the Assyrian period, is immediately obvious. It is true that the blessing in Deut. 28:1–13 lacks the theme of 'health.' But in the much more broadly conceived cursing text in Deut. 28:15–45, there are long passages threatening disease in an Israel that does not listen to YHWH's voice. We must suppose that at this point a given series of curses has been included

120. Cf. n. 79 above.

(with a repeated 'YHWH will afflict you with . . .'), as well as that the text relies on Assyrian texts of cursing and their stereotypical principle of succession; the technique of the redaction does not appear to me to have been given a persuasive explanation as yet.[121] The curses related to sickness read:

> 28:21 YHWH will make the pestilence cling to you until it has consumed you off the land that you are entering to possess.
>
> 22 YHWH will afflict you with consumption, fever, inflammation, with fiery heat and drought, and with blight and mildew; they shall pursue you until you perish . . .
>
> 27 YHWH will afflict you with the boils of Egypt, with ulcers, scurvy, and itch, of which you cannot be healed.
>
> 28 YHWH will afflict you with madness, blindness, and confusion of mind;
>
> 29 you shall grope about at noon as blind people grope in

121. The series of curses has certainly been correctly reconstructed from a form-critical point of view. See especially (with somewhat different reconstructions) J. G. Plöger, *Literarkritische, formgeschichtliche und stilkritische Untersuchungen zum Deuteronomium*, BBB 26 (Bonn, 1967), 151–54 (Deut. 28:22, 27, 28–29, 35 as 'affliction series'); G. Seitz, *Redaktionsgeschichtliche Studien zum Deuteronomium*, BWANT 93 (Stuttgart, 1971), 278–82 (original contents of Deut. 28:20, 21, 22, 27, 28, 35). For the Assyrian parallels, cf. especially M. Weinfeld, 'Traces of Assyrian Treaty Formulae in Deuteronomy,' *Bibl* 46 (1965): 417–27, later republished in idem, *Deuteronomy* (cf. n. 22 above), 116–26, integrated in the text in a revised form; for the curses at Sin, the survey by D. R. Hillers, *Treaty-Curses and the Old Testament Prophets*, BibOr 16 (Rome, 1964), 15–16, is helpful. The argument that the sequence of particular curses in Deuteronomy 28 cannot be explained from within Deuteronomy itself, but probably on the basis of Assyrian models in which particular curses are connected with particular divinities, and that these divinities must appear in a particular order within sequences of curses, is persuasive. The decisive parallel text, 'Asarhaddon-Nachfolgeverträge,' *VTE* 6: 419–30, however, does not yield as much information as Weinfeld thinks. For 425–27, the series has not been maintained; 428–30 relate to a single divinity, and the sequence in Deut. 28:30–33 (interrupted in the middle by something different) is supposed to correspond to it, but a close comparison arouses skepticism. But we may consider as proved that the sequence of plagues in 28:27–30 depends on the connection, demonstrable elsewhere in the Assyrian field as well, of typical moon god and sun god curses. Cf. Seitz, 279. Probably we must posit an author of the cursing text who, on the one hand, essentially worked with traditional Israelite curse material, but on the other hand knew Assyrian texts and had internalized their laws of sequence.

darkness, but you shall be unable to find your way; and you shall be continually abused and robbed, without anyone to help . . .

34 [you shall be] driven mad by the sight that your eyes shall see.

35 YHWH will strike you on the knees and on the legs with grievous boils of which you cannot be healed, from the sole of your foot to the crown of your head.

In the whole of the cursing text there are broad-ranging counter-statements to all four blessings in Exod. 23:25–26. But it all culminates in the threat of oppression by enemies, rule, exploitation and even deportation by foreigners. And the real interest of the text may well lie here. Sickness is part of the plagues that announce, introduce and accompany the still greater misery caused by Israel's enemies. To that extent it is also quite natural that 'blindness' stands in the middle of a series of three, between 'madness' and 'confusion of mind,' and, in dependence on the multi-layered symbolism of the sun god, is immediately interpreted in terms of the fading of light in the social context, the inbreaking of lawlessness and social chaos. Thus at this point a metaphorical application of the predictions of disease is developed. But on the whole, the diseases are regularly intended as physical illnesses. YHWH sends them upon Israel if 'you do not listen to the voice of YHWH, your God, by diligently observing all his commandments and decrees, which I am commanding you today' (Deut. 28:15, cf. 45). Thus here, going beyond the very basic formula in Exod. 23:25 (serve YHWH), the social order and life in accordance with it, the essential features of which are sketched in the deuteronomic law, are made the conditions of blessing. The carrying out of the principles of the old contrast-society of YHWH as the order for the state of Judah is the precondition to be observed, if in this 'Israel' of the Assyrian period the diseases and other plagues are not to erupt and finally culminate in the people's destruction at the hands of more powerful enemies.

The theme of cursing that is adopted here, part of which is the threat of disease, certainly has a broad basis in the ancient Orient.[122] But the ordering of the whole imaginable arsenal of curses toward a very particular new society, designed in contradistinction to other societies and living entirely in relationship to a single god, such that the imposition of the curses is made dependent on a nation's 'yes' or 'no' to that society, does

122. Cf. especially Hillers, *Treaty Curses* (n. 121 above).

seem to be something new.[123] Here God, program for society, and human health are brought together in the clearest way imaginable.

At a later period, probably during or after the Exile, a historical shift occurred within the framework of this deuteronomic idea. In an expansion of the cursing text, which we may not attribute to the mood of the writer or to some accident, but which must certainly be ascribed to an authoritative decision, it received a conclusion in which disease in a certain sense represents the summary of all curses:[124]

> 28:58 If you do not diligently observe all the words of this teaching (*tôrāh*) that are written in this book, fearing this glorious and awesome name, YHWH your God,
>
> 59 then YHWH will increase the afflictions laid both on you and on your offspring beyond all measure, and will afflict you with severe and lasting afflictions and grievous and lasting maladies.
>
> 60 He will bring back upon you all the diseases of Egypt, of which you were in dread, and they shall cling to you.
>
> 61 Every other malady and affliction, even though not recorded in the book of this law, YHWH will inflict on you until you are destroyed.

Here 'afflictions' are identical with 'diseases.' This can be true because an Israel is being addressed that has returned home from exile, is living peacefully within the Persian empire, and is more likely to be destroyed by diseases and plagues than by anything else. Or it can also be that the Diaspora is presumed as a matter of course. In that case, disease would also be the severest affliction to be feared.

One may well reckon with similar presuppositions in Exod. 15:26, if the text, for other reasons, is thought to stem from the Persian period. For here also the whole complex of possible evils and the multiplicity of the Egyptian plagues are viewed entirely in terms of the phenomenon of illness. The condition of the blessing is that one listen to the voice of YHWH. This is well known, just as in Deuteronomy. It is made explicit in the laws that sketch Israel's social order. In Exod. 15:26 it is no longer

123. There is something analogous in the prophets of Israel, who also have recourse to threats of plagues: e.g., Amos in Amos 4:6–12 (with W. Rudolph, HKAT 1971, 173–75, and against Wolff, BK, who sees here a text from the period of Josiah).

124. Cf. also n. 79 above.

merely the laws in Deuteronomy that are intended, but all the laws in the Pentateuch. This is the order that the Jewish community living around the rebuilt temple in Jerusalem has received both from its God and from the Persian king as its rule of life. If this community holds to the voice of YHWH, which is so concrete and so audible, its God will heal it; it will be a locus of health, and the diseases that, in the form of plagues, visit the rest of the world's societies, symbolized by Pharaoh and Egypt, will not touch them.

However, this is stated in terms that are much too static. For the fundamental statement of Exod. 15:26 is embedded in a narrative, and thus belongs to an event in process; and in the connective clause in Exod. 15:25b that process is interpreted as Israel's testing by YHWH.

5. The Theodicy of Testing

There is really no point in attempting to discover anything like a 'tradition' about YHWH putting the people of Israel to the test. We should avoid trying to trace it through other words besides *nsh*, 'put to the test,' such as *bḥn*, 'test,'[125] since the nuances of meaning are probably too broad.[126] Ps. 26:2 must be excluded, since there *nsh* is parallel to *bḥn* and takes on the meaning of the latter. What may be the oldest example of YHWH putting someone to the test is in the tribal blessing of Levi. Levi is to be YHWH's true follower, 'whom you tested at Massah, with whom you contended at the waters of Meribah' (Deut. 33:8).[127] The events from the early period of the tribe of Levi that are hinted at here and in the following verse can only be aligned with partially parallel reports in Exodus 17 and 32 with the aid of a good deal of speculation. The normal etymology of the name 'Massah,' a place visited during the wilderness wandering, indicated that it was there

125. Even Ps 81:8[7], 'I tested you at the waters of Meribah (*'ebḥānĕkā*),' which evidently could equally well have *nsh*, 'put to the test,' and where there are references to Exod. 15:25–26 throughout the psalm (cf. section 2 above), does not justify us in adducing additional instances. We cannot give plausible reasons for seeing Psalm 81 itself as older; it could equally well presuppose Exod. 15:25–26.

126. Cf. M. Tsevat, *bāḥan*, in *TDOT* 2: 69–72.

127. For the widest variety of ideas about the age, internal layering, statement and historical background of the blessing of Levi, see, e.g., F. M. Cross and D. N. Freedman, 'The Blessing of Moses,' *JBL* 67 (1948): 191–210; H.-J. Zobel, *Stammesspruch und Geschichte. Die Angaben der Stammessprüche von Gen 49, Dtn 33 und Jdc 5 über die politischen und kultischen Zustände im damaligen 'Israel,'* BZAW 95 (Berlin, 1965), 29–34, 67–70; A. Cody, *A History of Old Testament Priesthood*, AnBib 35 (Rome, 1969), 114–20; Ruppert, 'Versuchung,' (n. 23 above), 56–59.

that Israel put its God, YHWH, to the test.[128] What exactly was meant by YHWH's testing of Levi can no longer be clearly discerned. Above all, it is a question of the tribe of Levi, and not of Israel. Therefore this example must also be dropped from any survey of occurrences. There remain Gen. 22:1 (beginning of the narrative of the sacrifice of Isaac: 'After these things God tested Abraham') and Exod. 20:20 (Moses says to the people, during the theophany at Sinai: 'God has come only to test you and to put the fear of him upon you so that you do not sin'). These are two of the key theological passages from the Elohist fragments in the Pentateuch. Otherwise, the remaining instances are Exod. 15:25; 16:4; Deut. 8:2, 16; 13:4; Judg. 2:22; 3:1, 4; 2 Chr. 32:31.[129]

In both of the Elohist passages[130] the model Israelite, Abraham, and the people of Israel itself are put to the test by God. The sense of the testing is to discover whether the one(s) tested are God-fearers. Fear of God is the central theologoumenon of the Elohist texts. The interpretation of two critical situations, in one case involving the ancestor of all Israel, in another Israel itself in its critical hour, is pointed toward this theologoumenon, through the use of the motif of 'testing.'[131]

128. The explanation of the name, 'Massah,' as a place where Israel put YHWH to the test is found in Exod. 17:7; Deut. 6:16; and Ps. 95:8–9. Otherwise this place name is found (apart from Deut. 33:8) only once, in Deut. 9:22. It is true that from Ps. 81:8 [7] (where, however, the parallel name, Meribah, is also mentioned, and which contains the verb *bḥn*, 'test') one might conclude to a tradition according to which, at Massah, YHWH had tested Israel (and thus not Levi!). But Ps. 81:8 [7] can also be otherwise explained (even without conjectural alterations in the text!). Thus Massah, as a place, is not very well attested, even if we need not go so far as S. Lehming, 'Massa und Meriba,' *ZAW* 73 (1961): 71–77, who explains the whole matter as a misunderstanding of Deut. 33:8. The normal explanation of the place name is based on the idea that Israel put YHWH to the test.

129. One could also consider whether the designation *massôt*, 'testings' (?), referring to the Egyptian plagues in Deut. 4:34; 7:19; 29:2, should be adduced. But this word is highly problematic, and I do not see how it can offer us further help with our question. J. L'Hour differs in his 'Une législation criminelle dans le Deutéronome,' *Bibl* 44 (1963): 1–28 (at p. 5, n. 2).

130. There is, for the field of Pentateuch criticism, a surprisingly high degree of unanimity in assigning these two passages to the Elohist stratum. This is also the case for Exod. 20:20a. Cf. E. Zenger, *Die Sinaitheophanie. Untersuchungen zum jahwistischen und elohistischen Geschichtswerk*, FzB 3 (Würzburg, 1971), 212 (table).

131. Cf. H. W. Wolff, 'Die Thematik der elohistischen Fragmente im Pentateuch,' *EvTh* 29 (1969): 59–72, at 62–67; Ruppert, 'Versuchung' (see n. 23 above), 59–63. Ruppert indicates an extension of this line as well: failing the test leads to 'sin,' that is, to falling away from YHWH.

The remaining examples are all deuteronomistic or presuppose the deuteronomistic literature. While the motif of 'fear of YHWH' is important from early stages of Deuteronomy onward, there appears to be no immediate desire, within that sphere, to combine it with the idea of the testing of Israel by YHWH. When it does appear, it is, at least in its immediate context, rather ordered to the theme of observation of the law.

In Deuteronomy 5, of course, Exodus 19–20 is retold. But here Moses gives no answer to the speech of the people, who have been thrown into panic by YHWH's thunder. God in person answers (Deut. 5:28–31). And God says nothing about having wanted to use the thunder to put the people to the test. However, it seems that the motif of fear is further developed. In equal balance with the love of God, it becomes one of the principal themes of Deuteronomy 5–6.[132]

In the late deuteronomistic texts in which the motif of Israel's testing by God recurs, it is directly connected with love for YHWH and the keeping of the commandments, and at most indirectly with fear of God. Dependencies among these texts cannot be demonstrated with any kind of certainty. Some things can be inferred, but these remain inferences. Almost all the texts seem to belong to approximately the same time and to respond to the same set of problems. In most cases they represent additions and expansions. Those that are most firmly anchored in their context are the passages in Deuteronomy, especially Deut. 8:2, 16. However, Deut. 8:16 is only a shortening and slightly variant reprise of 8:2 within a chapter that is artfully constructed throughout.[133] I consider

132. Cf. Lohfink, *Hauptgebot* (n. 31 above), 158–59; idem, *Höre, Israel! Auslegung von Texten aus dem Buch Deuteronomium*, Die Welt der Bibel 18 (Düsseldorf, 1964), 70–71.

133. Cf. Lohfink, *Hauptgebot* (n. 31 above), 189–99. See also the most recent treatment of this chapter in F. Garcia López, 'Yahvé, fuente última de vida: análisis de Dt. 8,' *Bibl* 62 (1981): 21–54, with bibliography from the intervening years. He believes that the chapter originated in four steps, and in such a way that in each stage the previous text was augmented and expanded. He also believes that 8:2 and 16 (except for the first three words) are from the same hand, and that v. 16 is a shortening of and reference back to v. 2. These verses are in his third layer. I doubt that the distinction of the two oldest layers can be maintained, despite differences in syntax and vocabulary. These can be explained in other ways. The rest of the history of composition, as he sees it, is possible. But again I do not believe that one can prove the identity of the author of Deut. 8:2–6, as he sees it, with the author of Deut. 6:20–24 (in a preliminary stage that he reconstructs). His reasoning on this point in idem, 'Analyse littéraire de Deutéronome, V–XI*,' *RB* 84 (1977): 481–522 and 85 (1978): 5–49 (at 507–9) does not convince me. Moreover: precisely in his oldest layer he indicates a relationship to

it a relatively late text in the paraenetic chapters of Deuteronomy, for there are signs that here the swing from the deuteronomic Horeb-covenant theology to the patriarchal-covenant theology of the priestly document is already in progress.[134] The context of Deut. 8:2–6 presents an overall theological interpretation of Israel's time in the wilderness:[135]

> 2 Remember the long way that YHWH, your God, has led you these forty years in the wilderness, in order to humble you,[136] testing you to know what was in your heart, whether or not you would keep his commandments.
> 3 He humbled you by letting you hunger, then by feeding you with manna, with which neither you nor your ancestors were acquainted, in order to make you understand that one does not live by bread alone, but by every word that YHWH's mouth speaks (= YHWH's commandments).
> 4 The clothes on your back did not wear out and your feet did not swell these forty years.

Deuteronomy 32–33 that is not to be found in the rest of Deuteronomy at all. Is it really more probable that we should think of a dependency of a single 'proto-deuteronomic' text (in contrast to all the other proto-deuteronomic and deuteronomic texts) on these poems, at some indeterminate earlier time, rather than seeing the influence of these poems on a relatively late text of Deuteronomy, at the point when the poems were incorporated into the literary context of the present book of Deuteronomy? Undoubtedly, this happened only at a late period in the history of the book's evolution. Does this not favor the opinion that not only Deut. 8:1, 11b, 19–20 (according to García López's idea) but more or less the whole of chapter 8 is late, even if one may still wish to distinguish different phases of formation internally? But if it is not necessary to split Deut. 8:2–6 and 8:7–18* widely apart, and if both are late, one could even suppose that Deut. 33:8 had at least furnished the impulse for developing the idea of Israel's testing by YHWH in Deut. 8:2, 16.

134. Cf. Deut. 8:18, *lĕma'an hāqîm 'et-bĕrîtô 'ăšer-nišba' lā'ăbōtêkā*, 'so that he may confirm his covenant that he swore to your ancestors.' Similar passages are found only in Deut. 4:31; 7:8, 12; 9:5. Otherwise the text speaks simply of YHWH's oath to the ancestors, without the verbal expression being made dependent on a nominal term meaning 'covenant' or its equivalent. Incidentally, García López attributes Deut. 8:18b to the author of 8:2–6.

135. For a stylistic analysis of the text, cf. Lohfink, *Hauptgebot* (n. 31 above), 190–91.

136. *'nh* II *piel* is difficult to translate, especially in Deuteronomy, since it is also used for the man with respect to the woman in sexual intercourse. Depending on the context, it has nuances such as to bend someone down, to degrade, to humiliate, to weaken, to subjugate, to rape, etc. The emotional flavor, whether negative, positive, or indifferent, is apparently determined by the context.

5 Know then in your heart that as a parent disciplines a child so YHWH your God disciplines you.
6 Therefore keep the commandments of YHWH your God, by walking in his ways and by fearing him.

In this context we can perceive, to some degree, what is meant by the testing of Israel. God brings Israel into a desperate situation. Israel's proving itself, as demanded in this situation, consists in its placing its only hope for life (since the desperate situation brings Israel to a critical moment between life and death) in keeping to YHWH's word, i.e., YHWH's commandments. God responds to this self-proving with the miracle of a life without care, even in the face of the absence of the natural conditions for it. The purpose of this testing initiated by God is a recognition on both sides: God sees how Israel decides about the order of life that God has given to the people; Israel recognizes that it exists through the miracle. This whole complex is then interpreted further through the category of educational discipline.

If we ask why such an interpretation of the wilderness period was developed, Deut. 8:2–6 in itself provides no information, but what follows is more helpful. For here a situation of natural wealth and fullness is addressed, in complete contrast to the wilderness situation. This could be the state of the audience. Well-being is neither a matter of course, nor is it one's own achievement. It remains YHWH's miracle, guaranteed to those who have shown themselves through testing to be those who wish to live according to YHWH's will. Fundamentally, the well-being they enjoy in the land remains for Israel the miraculous existence they experienced in the wilderness.

However, I am not entirely certain whether this understanding of Deuteronomy 8 is accurate.[137] It could also be the case that the addressees are in a situation that is more comparable with the wilderness. This state would be presented to them as a situation of being tested by YHWH, and in which they are to prove themselves by making their entire life

137. To the present, I have presented it in this way: cf. Lohfink, *Höre, Israel* (n. 132 above), 72–86. One problem is that the well-being and wealth is painted in colors that really do not fit the land of Israel (Canaan). Should we, perhaps, think that this chapter was written for a diaspora that had grown rich (thus Lohfink, 'Dekaloganfang' [n. 70 above], 104 n. 17)? But there are things that can be said against that, also. Thus we are led to ask whether this is not a sketch of a Utopia in which the rich land only comes into existence through YHWH's miraculous act. In that case, it would in no way be present to the addressees of the text.

dependent on obedience to YHWH's social order and giving no thought to anything else. Then the miracle will happen for them, and they must know that what they may then experience – projected as a utopia by the text of Deut. 8:7 – will always be nothing else but the miracle in the wilderness, accomplished by YHWH and not by themselves, and which they must therefore never forget.

In a certain sense, the saying about testing would then be a kind of theodicy given to an Israel living in misery, so that it may not despair of its God and may be assured of that to which it must hold fast: You Israelites, you are now in a situation of testing, and what YHWH desires from it is to be able to work a miracle for you!

If this second proposal about the trajectory of Deut. 8:2–6 is correct, it fits more obviously among the passages now to be discussed than in the first proposal, for in these other passages the intended theodicy is more clearly evident.

In any event, Deut. 13:4 is late.[138] It is preceded by a really shocking idea: namely, that a prophet or diviner of dreams might call on the people

138. An overview of the layering in Deuteronomy 13, which will reveal something like the *communis opinio* of present research, can be found in M. Rose, *Der Ausschließlichkeitsanspruch Jahwes. Deuteronomische Schultheologie und die Volksfrömmigkeit in der späten Königszeit*, BWANT 106 (Stuttgart, 1975), 45–46. The most thorough analysis and best foundation for the lateness of many elements is in R. Merendino, *Das deuteronomische Gesetz. Eine literarkritische, gattungs- und überlieferungsgeschichtliche Untersuchung zu Dt 12–26*, BBB 31 (Bonn, 1969), 62–76. It appears to me certain that there was a pre-deuteronomic basic text, but it does not seem so clear whether one must distinguish between a deuteronomic and a deuteronomistic layer. Since Meredino's observations point rather to a late period, it is possible that everything that is not pre-deuteronomic is deuteronomistic. The principal reason for further isolating Deut. 13:4b, 5 from the surrounding revision of the old law is, e.g., the plural address that begins in v. 4b. However, v. 6 also begins with a plural address. It is usual to follow Samaritanus and LXX here. But these versions, which change the number at the beginning and end of the sentence, represent the *textus facilior*; consequently the Masoretic text is to be preferred. But if Deut. 13:6 could jump from plural to singular in the middle of a verse, so that both numbers can represent an address to Israel, the plural address in vv. 4b, 5 is no longer a reason for seeing here a later hand. It may be, therefore, that the laws in Deuteronomy 13 are rather late in the deuteronomic corpus. If we attribute a specific significance for the layer of occurrence to the fact that Israel's being led out of Egypt is expressed in participial form in Deuteronomy only in 8:14 and 13:6, 11 (the citations in García López, 'Analyse littéraire,' [cf. n. 133], 41, are incomplete), we must associate the principal layer of Deuteronomy 13 with Deuteronomy 8. In that case, the reference in Deut. 13:4b to Deuteronomy 8 would be still more in favor of assigning Deut. 13:4b, 5, and 6 to the same, and not to two different layers.

to turn away from YHWH and serve other gods, and that such a person would prove the justice of this call by promising a miraculous sign that, in fact, is fulfilled. How can one deal with such an idea, even intellectually, without renouncing one's allegiance to YHWH? The answer is:

> YHWH your God is testing you, to know whether you indeed love YHWH your God with all your heart and soul.

Such problems are not proposed unless corresponding experiences lie behind them. We are aware of situations, especially in the book of Jeremiah, in which prophets opposed other prophets, or in which serving other gods was justified in public discussions by the fact that 'we used to have plenty of food, and prospered, and saw no misfortune. But from the time we stopped making offerings to the queen of heaven and pouring out libations to her, [and instead have served only YHWH] we have lacked everything and have perished by the sword and by famine' (Jer. 44:17–18). The interpretation of such situations as YHWH's testing is a theodicy in YHWH's favor.

The introductory anticipation of the period of the judges in Judg. 2:11–16, 18–19, which is deuteronomistic, was expanded and augmented, probably late in the exilic period, by a reviser and reinterpreter of the deuteronomistic historical work, whom his discoverer, R. Smend, calls 'DtrN' (the nomistic deuteronomist).[139] This person added Judg. 2:17, 20–21, 23; 3:5–6. In the deuteronomistic historical work, Israel's occupation of the land was originally viewed as having been completed under Joshua. These new elements of interpretation shift that perspective. According to this point of view, YHWH decides, as, in the period of the Judges, the Israelites again defect from YHWH, 'Because this people have transgressed my covenant that I commanded their ancestors [= first commandment of the decalogue], and have not obeyed my voice, I will no longer drive out before them any of the nations that Joshua left when he died' (Judg. 2:20–21). This could have been written with Israel in its Babylonian exile directly in view. In principle, Israel had never really entered completely into its land. If it was now living in a state of deportation, that was really just the ongoing, incomplete state of

139. 'R. Smend, *Das Gesetz und die Völker.* Ein Beitrag zur deuteronomistischen Redaktionsgeschichte,' in H. W. Wolff, ed., *Probleme biblischer Theologie. Gerhard von Rad zum 70. Geburtstag* (Munich, 1971), 494–509, at 504–6. For a thorough analysis of the layers in this part of Judges 2–3, see W. Richter, *Die Bearbeitungen des 'Retterbuches' in der deuteronomischen Epoche*, BBB 21 (Bonn, 1964), 28–40.

occupying the land, even though the situation was newly intensified. YHWH is still allowing other nations to live in Israel's land, because Israel has not been faithful to YHWH.[140] Such a statement can only mean that the deported people should finally begin to adhere to YHWH's laws; then YHWH will finally give them the land that has so long been promised to them. This is expressly stated in other passages that are to be assigned to the nomistic deuteronomist, although naturally it is always projected back into the historical situation of the beginning.[141]

Such a radically negative view of Israel's many centuries of history with its God must have left people at a loss in their understanding of this God. Thus it is understandable that at this key point also, at the beginning of the description of the time of the judges, another commenting hand (if not several) expanded the text and sought for an intellectual explanation. This was again achieved by applying the concept of Israel's testing by YHWH: YHWH will not proceed to destroy the remaining nations,

> In order through them to test Israel, [to learn] whether or not they would give heed to the way of YHWH, to walk in it[142] as their ancestors did, or not (Judg. 2:22).

140. This kind of sweeping reinterpretation of the whole history of early Israel and the Israelite state was not original with DtrN. In the basic Ezekiel writing, as found in Ezekiel 20 (according to Zimmerli, *BK*, in Ezek. 20:2–26, 30–31), exactly the same thing occurs, in fact even more drastically. Even to the generation that occupied the land, when they were still in the wilderness, YHWH had sworn, because of their disobedience to YHWH's laws, to 'scatter them among the nations and disperse them through the countries' (Ezek. 20:23). The seven intervening centuries are simply erased. Perhaps they are described in the shocking statement: 'I gave them statutes that were not good and ordinances by which they could not live. I defiled them through their very gifts, when they brought all their firstborn through fire, in order that I might horrify them' (Ezek. 20:25–26).

141. Cf. Smend, *Gesetz* (n. 139 above; cf. n. 65 above), on Deut. 6:17–19; 11:8, 22–25.

142. The translation is imprecise. While the antecedent (way) is singular, the consequent is plural (in them). The manuscript tradition and the old translations harmonized in various ways, and the Masoretes made a list of these harmonizations in order not to allow the difficulty to be lost (see Weil [n. 68 above], No. 1404). It is certainly necessary to hold to the Masoretic text. Could it be that an intervening phrase that explained YHWH's 'way' in a plural form (for example, through a word for laws) disappeared at a very early time? One would rather think of something like truncated notation without a literary interest, for in Judg. 3:1 there are still more difficult phenomena of the same period. At this point we are almost in the realm of clumsy late glosses.

Verse 23, which follows, stems from the nomistic deuteronomist. After it, the theme is taken up again, and a list of the nations not destroyed is announced:

> Now these are the nations that YHWH left, in order through them to test Israel (Judg. 3:1a).[143]

After the information thus announced about the peoples not destroyed, the whole added section concludes with the repetition of the principal theme: the remaining nations

> were for the testing of Israel, that he [= YHWH] might know whether they [= Israel] would obey the commandments of YHWH, which he commanded their ancestors by Moses (Judg. 3:4).

Then the older text of the nomistic deuteronomist continues. Once again, the whole addition expresses a theodicy of testing.

The deuteronomistic examples of the idea of the testing of Israel by YHWH that have thus far been discussed are in other literary works than Exod. 15:25.[144] The last example still to be examined, Exod. 16:4b, is

143. What follows in v. 1b is a series of explications of v. 1a, possibly from still another hand, but in any case couched in language that is very difficult to decipher. On the syntactic situation, one may best consult C. F. Keil (BC), ad loc. Cf. also the preceding footnote. As regards content, there is a tendency at work here to dissolve the previously established connection between the idea of testing and obedience to the law. That, in particular, favors a still later additional glossing.

144. I see no possibility of assigning all the texts of the series under discussion to some kind of general redaction extending throughout the Pentateuch and the historical books. The Exodus examples, those in Deuteronomy, and those in Judges are separate entities within different works. That does not exclude references among them, but these are more subtle than mutual belonging to the same 'layer,' or mutual dependence. In order not to leave unmentioned any positive references, let me, in passing, draw attention to several matters: Deuteronomy 8 is very strongly related to the Exodus examples by the identity of the theme of distress in the wilderness. In Deuteronomy 13, at the end (13:19) we find the passage which we said was most worthy of consideration as a possible model for Exod. 15:26a. The examples in Judges are not far removed from Josh. 24:25, from which Exod. 15:25b may have drawn the inspiration for its formulation, 'to impose statutes and ordinances.' Schmid, *Jahwist* (n. 58 above), 64–69, sees the following common features between the Marah narrative in Exodus 15, the story of the gifts in Exodus 17, and Judges 2–3: (1) they all reveal the 'judge schema;' (2) in all of them, 'testing' is added as an

only a few verses away in the following chapter. This is primarily from the priestly document.[145] However, most authors, though with sharp divergences in detail, analyze this text as containing an old manna story, if only fragmentarily. For the most part, it is assigned to the Yahwist historical work.[146] Exodus 16:4b is located in the middle of the Yahwist text, but is an addition,[147] and should rather be regarded as stemming from the principal redaction of the Pentateuch than from the older Pentateuch before the priestly writing.[148] Together with another addition

interpretive element (though Schmid overlooks the fact that in Exod. 17:7 it is not YHWH who 'tests' the Israelites, but the Israelites who put YHWH to the test). His purpose is to have the old narrative remnants in Exodus 15 and 17, whenever possible, appear as almost 'deuteronomic-deuteronomistic,' but the argument contains over-hasty conclusions at a number of points. Still, we can affirm that there are some kind of loose analogies (if not exactly the 'judge schema') between the older texts to which are added the expansions containing the motif of Israel's testing by YHWH.

145. Within the priestly writing there are, besides the text of the priestly historical narrative, a number of later expansions that are, however, of the priestly type. This story was not originally located after the Sinai events in the priestly historical narrative, as is often supposed. It is a narrative of a first theophany, parallel to that at Sinai. Here, YHWH reveals the Sabbath. Cf. Lohfink, 'Priesterschrift' (n. 52 above), 206 n. 40. The sequence of speeches, in turn, has not been subsequently altered. What we find here is a sequential schema that is proper to the priestly document: cf. Childs, *Exodus* (n. 5 above), 279–80.

146. On the different types of literary-critical theories and their principal representatives, cf. Childs, *Exodus* (n. 5 above), 274–80. I would assign to the non-priestly text Exod. 16:4–5, 27–31, and perhaps parts of verses 13–15 and 21.

147. Apart from some expansions within the priestly writing, within Exodus 16 it is usual to regard vv. 4b and 28 as additions. Both are found in a non-priestly context, and both are ordinarily attributed to a 'deuteronomistic' redactor. Childs's attempt (p. 286) to show that v. 4b is part of the original text does not convince me. Baentsch (HKAT) ad loc., posits for Exod. 16:28 the same 'spiritual orientation' as for Exod. 15:26b.

148. The terminology in v. 4b (*hlk bĕtôrat YHWH*, 'to walk according to YHWH's instruction), is more widespread at a late, post-deuteronomistic period (examples are 2 Kgs. 10:31; Jer. 26:4; 32:23; 44:10, 23; Pss. 78:10; 119:1; Neh. 10:30; 2 Chr. 6:16; of these, the oldest is probably Ps. 78:10, but Neh. 10:30 shows when the expression became official terminology). We must regard the additions in vv. 4b and 28 as related to one another. As distributed through the chapter, they appear to be a reference to Ps. 78:10b. There, in a glance forward, Ps. 78:12–41, a theological interpretation of Israel's time in the wilderness, is related to this concept. In this interpretation, the combined manna and quail stories in vv. 17–31 are given the central place, with the events in Numbers 11 developed most fully. Verse 10b,

in Exod. 16:28, Exod. 16:4b interprets the gifts of manna and quail as a testing of Israel by YHWH, in which Israel earns YHWH's reproach. YHWH promises to rain bread from heaven, and orders that the people is to gather its daily portion each day.

> In that way I will test them, whether they will follow my instruction or not (Exod. 16:4b).

Although on the sixth day a double daily portion of manna is found, some of the people still go out on the seventh day to gather manna. They find nothing, and are subjected to the divine reproach:

> How long will you refuse to keep my commandments and instructions? (Exod. 16:28)

ûbĕtôrātô mēʾănû lāleket, 'and they refused to walk according to his instruction,' is split between the additions in Exodus 16: *hlk bĕtôrat YHWH* in 16:4b, *mʾn* in 16:28. *mʾn piel*, 'to refuse,' is an un-deuteronomistic word. With reference to obedience to YHWH it is found concentrated in two areas: in the Yahwist plague narratives (where Pharaoh 'refuses'), and in (largely authentic) texts in Jeremiah. The addition of *lišmōr miṣwôtay wĕtôrōtāy*, 'to pay heed to my commandments and my teachings,' has, if I see the matter correctly, no exact parallel. Closest, though broader, is Gen. 26:5b, a text from a 'very late' addition with echoes of the chronistic historical work. Cf. R. Kilian, *Die vorpriesterlichen Abrahamsüberlieferungen literarkritisch und traditionsgeschichtlich untersucht*, BBB 24 (Bonn, 1966), 201–06 and 317–20. Overall the system of additions in Exod. 16:4b, 28 is used, by way of Psalm 78 (apparently presupposed as known) to establish a cross-reference to Numbers 11. The reader is challenged to recognize Exodus 16 as a preview of Numbers 11. This would certainly be more readily possible if, at the time when this system of cross-references was brought into the text, the motif of disobedience to Moses's orders was already present. But that motif belongs to those parts of the text that are from the priestly writing. And since the two additions were made in the Yahwist context, it cannot be definitively excluded that they had belonged to the text of the old source, even before the redaction of the Pentateuch. If they are late, we could ask whether they are from the same hand as Exod. 15:25b, 26. But there are differences in the language. Exod. 16:4b introduces the motif in typically deuteronomistic style, with an infinitive construction, while Exod. 15:25b uses juxtaposition, which tends rather to belong to the priestly style. If we take Exod. 16:4b and 28 as a unit, it is still not easy to bring them under a common heading with Deut. 8:2–6, since in the latter the testing of Israel leads to the miracle, while in the former the miracle occurs, but Israel does not prove itself, and the effect of the reference linking it to Numbers 11 is that it ends with punishment. Thus it will also be difficult to establish dependency between the statements about testing in Exodus 16 and Deuteronomy 8, or even between their intentions.

The critical point on which the theologoumenon about the testing of Israel here turns is the limitation of the possibility of setting aside necessities to the precise amount that is needed for a single day, and in connection with this, the laying aside of the work of providing for one's needs on the seventh day. If we consider what might have been the social situation of need into which such an interpretation might have been injected, we could, for example, suppose that it was a state of general poverty in Judah at the time of the exiles' return, the opposite of the magnificent lifestyle that would have been expected after the return on the basis of prophetic promises like those of Deutero-Isaiah. Secure provision for the basic necessities of life never reached much beyond the present day in which one was living, and to this situation was added the demand that no work be done on the Sabbath. What kind of God was it who allowed this God's own people to live in such conditions? The theodicy of testing turns the question back on the questioners. Are they not, after all, experiencing the miracle of having a sufficiency for life every day? Do they not recognize it as a testing that is intended to evoke from them their fidelity to YHWH's planned order of things, in particular the central Sabbath commandment? Must God not accuse them now of refusing to accept the gift of God's law?

All these texts,[149] together with Exod. 15:25-26, constitute a loose fabric. We cannot propose any clear structure of dependencies, and yet they all appear to emerge from approximately the same period and to address a comparable set of problems experienced by readers, for whose use texts were augmented or expanded. It always appears that YHWH does not act as one believes one ought to expect. Always, YHWH and YHWH's actions have to be made comprehensible to those who are groaning over them. The category of 'testing,' familiar to everyone from the way in which fathers were accustomed to train their sons in Israel, served this purpose: fathers gave their sons the opportunity to prove themselves in difficult circumstances by holding fast to the advice of their fathers as previously given. The proving then culminated in a still greater paternal affection (cf. Deut. 8:2–6, 16).

The addition in Exod. 15:25b, 26 serves to make the narrative of the cleansing of the bitter water in Marah also transparent for some such

149. 2 Chr. 32:31 could also belong to roughly the same period. The problematic that is evoked here by means of the motif of testing seems to be more intellectual in scope: the story of Hezekiah in the books of Kings presented difficulties for the Chronicler, whose intention was at all points to demonstrate YHWH's just direction of history. For more detail, see Rudolph, HKAT.

meaning. Here the special aspect is sickness and health. In Ezekiel's vision of the fountain rising in the temple, the bitter water of the Dead Sea became fresh (Ezek. 47:8–9), it was filled with fish, and the whole desert of Judah was transformed into a garden of fruits. Now, after the return from Babylon, the people lived again in their land, around the rebuilt temple, but the water of the sea to the south, in the valley, remained salty, and epidemics passed over the land, children died as they always had, and only a few people lived to a great age.[150] The question was addressed to YHWH, and our text complex answers with a theodicy of testing. It solemnly renewed the teaching about the connection between fidelity to the special order of society given Israel by its God and the emergence of the miracle of universal health. And if the miracle had not yet made itself manifest, Israel was on the threshold of experiencing it, for its God was in the very process of putting Israel to the test.

If this tentative interpretation of the intention behind Exod. 15:25b, 26 is accurate, it is also relevant that this expansion of the text was inserted at the outset, in the very first narrative of the wilderness period, at the beginning of the four chapters in which Israel is travelling through the desert.

6. Final Considerations

The place where this expansion of the text occurs has always attracted notice. The usual explanation presupposes that the law was first proclaimed at Sinai, and thus assumes something like a holy impatience on the part of a glosser who in some sense could not wait for that point and therefore made a slight correction in the course of the story. A. Jülicher wrote in 1882: 'Law and justice are so indispensable that their proclamation could not be postponed until Sinai. From the very beginning of its existence Israel, as the free people of God, had need of them.'[151]

Now, it should have become clear that what is at issue here is by no means merely the 'law.' To put it in a better way with a more positive ring: it is not just a matter of Israel as God's contrast society over against the nations of the world, although that in itself would be a great deal. In

150. Cf., from approximately the same period, Zech. 8:4–6, where a prophet for once speaks of the period of salvation, as he imagines it, not in imagery but in direct description.

151. A. Jülicher, 'Quellen' (see n. 60 above), 275.

addition, it is a question of the blessing that can arise for humanity within the scope of that society, summarized as freedom from all diseases – also in contrast to what is possible for the peoples of the world. And it is a matter of the overcoming of a situation in which all this is absent, so that the question arises: what kind of God is it who gives something so marvellous, and then does not give it after all?

Moreover, this is not a historical question, i.e., about when Israel received its 'law.' In this late phase of the history of the Pentateuch, its texts were intended as a lectionary for the congregation. Every individual pericope always represents and expresses the whole. But the whole is the project of Israel's order of life; it is Pentateuch as 'Torah.' Thus every pericope, including those about the events at Sinai, can, if necessary, be made transparent toward the whole. It is not at all as if, in this late work of commenting the text, the 'law' was anticipated only as far forward as Marah. Comparable glosses are to be found as early as the story of Abraham, and the priestly document advances its first laws immediately after the Flood, then for Abraham, and at the exodus from Egypt. As soon as the history of humanity begins to concentrate itself in some way in Israel, which is God's special and proper work, there begins the initial idea of a contrasting behavior, and the possibility of speaking about a new society, about the 'law' of YHWH.

Thus what seems notable is not that there is talk of law and the giving of law already at the beginning of the wilderness journey. But what is worth pondering is that this theme is presented just here, at the beginning, and in this constellation of statements.

We have already seen that here a kind of opposition is being constructed. Now the narrative of the events in Egypt is finished. It was a story of a sick society in which human beings were enslaved and exploited, where those in positions of authority did not listen to YHWH's voice, and where, as a result, plague after plague erupted – a society that must ultimately sink down into sickness and death. Now there begins (and this is the reason for positioning the statement at the beginning) the story that can be told about the proper society, the one in which people do listen to YHWH's voice and in which, as a result, no diseases break out; where, instead, is realized what the prophets have promised as the salvation that YHWH will create in Israel: Israel as a healthy, living people. I believe that the statement that YHWH is the 'physician' of Israel, unusual in the real pre-Pentateuch traditions, but indicative of the experiential world of family piety and of the prophetic speeches of warning and promise, really intends to connect the law and the prophets. In the briefest possible hint, we find named here, as the fruit of surrender to YHWH's social will, the promise of salvation announced by the prophets. At this key station, at Marah, the sojourn in Egypt is connected and contrasted not only to the wandering in the wilderness, but even to eschatological expectation.

Thus this late gloss aids still another purpose: that nothing in the prophets' eschatology need be rescinded. The journey through the blooming and changing wilderness promised by a Deutero-Isaiah had really happened, when people moved out of Babylon toward Jerusalem, in painfully assembled caravans, to resume their life there. But at the same time, it had not happened, for there was nothing of those miracles of transformation to be seen. The desert had remained desert, and the bitter waters bitter. But had the essential miracle really happened anyway, and was the rest to be attributed to exaggerated poetic fantasy? Our gloss seems to contradict this.

If the original end of the Pentateuch, with the report of Moses' death, that is, the narrative of taking possession of the land, was simply determined by the fact that afterward no more laws were added, and perhaps also by the fact that the Persian ministerial bureaucracy never granted a written set of particular laws for this rather peculiar province, certainly not a set that, in its sixth part, contained a glorification of the province's own military power – nevertheless, our glosser made use of the fact that the sketch of the YHWH society in which he himself lived was embedded in a narrative about a wilderness journey, and not in a situation within the promised land itself, in order to shape this in a certain sense into an image of the presently existing YHWH society in Jerusalem and Judah. It is true that the people have arrived in Jerusalem, are dwelling around the Temple and attempting to live according to YHWH's law. But really the miraculous desert journey promised by the prophets has only begun. They have not even reached the first station. And everything looks as it did in Egypt: unpotable, disease-ridden water. But it is precisely at this point that everything depends on listening to YHWH's voice and living according to YHWH's order for society. This is the hour of testing, and it must be acknowledged as such. If Israel proves itself now, it will be rescued from the world situation of plagues and diseases; YHWH will be self-revealed as Israel's wonderful healer, as foretold by the prophets. The expansion of the text that we have been considering would thus have been something like an explosion of the static Pentateuch toward the unsatisfied dynamic of the prophetic promises.

Of course, this is a daring interpretation of these few sentences. It may be wrong. Ultimately, we cannot arrive at any unshakable security in dealing with these late, brief glosses. But I think it is more proper to let one's fantasy play a little, as I have attempted to do, than simply to overlook the glosses. Laconic and compact as they are, they intend to offer an interpretative key that often applies to huge bodies of text. They may give us more information about the consciousness according to which people understood the whole tradition in the centuries of the second temple than do the many units of the commented text itself. In this concrete case, such a gloss, however nomistic it sounds at first, may even call into question the thesis of a 'late Judaism' that became frozen in 'legalism,' or that other thesis of clearly distinguishable currents in second-temple Judaism, one theocratic-legalist and one prophetic-eschatological. If the 'theocratic' basic texts of the Torah were read in the congregation, they may have been heard with quite different ears from those we would like to imagine.

When Jesus appeared, it was apparently a matter of course for him and his contemporaries that God's new, eschatological society, now called the 'reign of God,' would be recognizable primarily by the fact that diseases vanished and health miraculously appeared in Israel. The situation of 'testing' was now past, as everyone could see. The Lord was revealed as Israel's physician.

In our society, in spite of the constant progress of medicine, the power of disease is increasing, and the places that are supposed to heal the sick are creating their own new diseases. Anyone who has given thought to the notion of psychosomatic connections knows that it is the society that produces its own sickness or health. In its inability to vanquish sickness, despite many individual victories, the society is revealed as that which is referred to in the book of Exodus as 'Egypt.' God's contrast society, stemming from Jesus and now existing in our world, must shine forth, over against this world, as a place of healing and of health. Is this the case? If not, it must ask itself whether God has let it fall back into a situation of 'testing.' But can such a thing happen? Jesus brought the eschaton with him, and after him there is no further condition placed on salvation; therefore did he not teach his disciples to pray: 'Do not put us to the test' (Matt. 6:13; Luke 11:4)?[152]

152. This appears to be the only place in the New Testament where God appears as one who tests, and perhaps that is not true even here. Otherwise, it is the devil who 'tests.' On this, cf. K. G. Kuhn, 'Πειρασμός – ἁμαρτία – σάρξ im Neuen Testament und die damit zusammenhängenden Vorstellungen,' *ZthK* 49 (1952): 200–22.

4

Original Sins in the Priestly Historical Narrative

The Yahwist, Israel's first major theologian of history, began his historical work with a narrative about original sin (Gen. 2:4–3:24). It contains a complete hamartiology (a theology of sin), and all later sins are somehow anticipated within it.[1] The Deuteronomist, the theologian of history who wrote at the beginning of the exilic period, also began with an original sin: Israel's unbelief in the oasis of Kadesh (Deut. 1:6-8, 19–46). Here, too, Israel's later sins are already sketched in advance.[2]

But neither of these historians stops with a depiction of original sins. After all, they are in large part not writing independently, but are expanding older sources. And these sources often tell of sins and consequences that are brought forth by sins. Beyond that, through composition and commentary they build trajectories into the course of the entire story, shaping their whole history in such a way that it takes on

1. On Gen. 2:4–3:24 as the Yahwist's portrayal of original sin, cf. recently: J. Scharbert, 'Prolegomena eines Alttestamentlers zur Erbsündenlehre,' *QD* 37 (Freiburg, 1968), 60–77. Notes on older literature can be found there.

2. On the first chapter of the deuteronomistic historical work, cf. N. Lohfink, 'Darstellungskunst und Theologie in Dtn 1, 6–3, 29,' *Bibl* 41 (1960): 105–34; idem, 'Wie stellt sich das Problem Individuum-Gemeinschaft in Deuteronomium 1 6–3, 29?' *Schol* 35 (1960): 403–07. Older literature is listed in these essays. Since their publication the following have appeared: W. L. Moran, 'The End of the Unholy War and the Antiexodus (Dt 2, 14–16),' *Bibl* 44 (1963): 333–42; J. G. Plöger, 'Literarkritische, formgeschichtliche und stillkritische Untersuchungen zum Deuteronomium,' *BBB* 26 (Bonn, 1967), 1–59; H. Cazelles, 'Passages in the Singular Within Discourse in the Plural of Dt 1–4,' *CBQ* 29 (1967): 207–19; J. L. McKenzie, 'The Historical Prologue of Deuteronomy,' *Fourth World Congress of Jewish Studies, Papers* (Jerusalem, 1967), 1: 95–101; N. Airoldi, 'Le 'sezioni-noi' nel Deuteronomio,' *Rivista Biblica* 16 (1968): 143–57.

something of the character of a 'history of sin.' For the Yahwist, it is the beginning of history in particular that is shadowed by sin; then, starting with Abraham, it is the blessing now entering history that tends to become the center of attention. But even then the theme of sin is not forgotten. Thus in Gen. 18:22–32 Abraham discusses with YHWH the possibility of rescuing Sodom and Gomorrah in spite of their sins. The very fact that one blessed by YHWH now enters the darkened creation compels renewed reflection on the fact of sin.[3] In the deuteronomistic historical work the theme of sin moves still farther into the foreground. Since Deuteronomy is placed at the beginning of the work, a standard is established by which everything else is to be measured. In particular as regards the kings of Israel and Judah a strict accounting is taken, according to that standard, over the constantly increasing power of sin. At the end, even the pious Josiah can no longer extinguish YHWH's burning rage: Jerusalem falls.[4]

Thus in Israel's major versions of history preceding the priestly historical document, the narrative contained a story of sin heaped upon

3. On the redactional theology of the Yahwist, cf. especially R. Rendtorff, 'Genesis 8,21 und die Urgeschichte des Jahwisten,' *Kerygma und Dogma* 7 (1961): 69–78; H. W. Wolff, 'Das Kerygma des Jahwisten,' *EvTh* 24 (1964): 73–98, repr. in his *Gesammelte Studien zum Alten Testament*, ThB 22 (Munich, 1964), 345–73; L. Ruppert, 'Der Jahwist – Künder der Heilsgeschichte,' in J. Schreiner, ed., *Wort und Botschaft* (Würzburg, 1967), 88–107.

4. Fundamental to the theory of the deuteronomistic historical work is M. Noth, *Überlieferungsgeschichtliche Studien* (Darmstadt, 2nd ed. 1957). For the discussion up to ca. 1960, see E. Jenni, 'Zwei Jahrzehnte Forschung an den Büchern Josua bis Könige,' *ThRundsch* 27 (1961); 1–32; 97–146 (at 97–118). The most important works on the redactional theology of the deuteronomistic historical work after Noth are: G. von Rad, 'Deuteronomium-Studien,' *Forschungen zur Religion und Literatur des Alten und Neuen Testaments* 40 (Göttingen, 2nd ed. 1948), 52–64, repr. in his *Gesammelte Studien zum Alten Testament*, ThB 8 (Munich, 1948), 189–204; H. W. Wolff, 'Das Kerygma des deuteronomistischen Geschichtswerks,' *ZAW* 73 (1961): 171–86, repr. in his *Gesammelte Studien zum Alten Testament*, ThB 22 (Munich, 1964), 308–24; H. Timm, 'Die Ladeerzählung (1 Sam 4–6; 2 Sam 6) und das Kerygma des deuteronomistischen Geschichtswerks,' *EvTh* 26 (1966): 509–26; E. Zenger, 'Die deuteronomistische Interpretation der Rehabilitierung Jojachins,' *BZ* 12 (1968): 16–30. The theory of a deuteronomistic historical work was given new dynamic by F. M. Cross, 'The Structure of the Deuteronomic History,' *Perspectives in Jewish Learning* 3, Annual of the College of Jewish Studies (Chicago, 1968), 9–24. Cross distinguishes between a triumphalistic and missionary 'deuteronomic historical work,' culminating in the establishment of a new Davidic kingdom under Josiah, and stemming from the time of Josiah himself, and its exilic expansion and reinterpretation into a full 'deuteronomistic historical work.' Against this background, what is said in this essay applies to the redactional intention of the exilic version.

sin. Moreover, it was fixed practice to prefigure at the beginning of the work everything that was to follow, in the guise of a kind of original sin. Finally, there was redactional interest in the theme of sin, and to that extent one can even speak of a doctrine of sin expressed by the authors in their historical works. But then, still another version of the history of the world and the beginnings of Israel was produced – probably during the Babylonian exile – by an author unknown to us by name, the so-called priestly writer.[5] What role does sin play in this work? What has this author

5. For opinions on the priestly layer of the Pentateuch, cf. the newer introductory works on the Old Testament. Since there is no consensus at present, it makes sense at this point for me to give a brief sketch of my own position. I believe there was a priestly historical narrative (P^g), to which was added, but only at a later date, the complete legislative priestly material (P^s). It cannot be traced in the biblical text beyond the death of Moses (though this does not exclude the possibility that there may be later priestly texts contained in the book of Joshua), and in all probability it originally ended with Moses' death. At least for the purposes of this essay, as restrictive a limitation as possible is appropriate, in order that none of the contours be blurred by questionable material. When not otherwise noted, I am following the limits set by K. Elliger, 'Sinn und Ursprung der priesterlichen Geschichtserzählung,' *ZthK* 49 (1952): 121–43, at 121–22, repr. in his *Kleine Schriften zum Alten Testament*, ThB 32 (Munich, 1966), 174–98, at 174–75. These are generally coextensive with those proposed by M. Noth in various publications. The results of my investigation appear to me to offer a further confirmation of this position. G. von Rad, *Theologie des Alten Testaments* 1 (Munich, 2nd ed. 1958), 262–72 (= *Old Testament Theology. I. The Theology of Israel's Historical Origins*, 262–72) has impressively described the priestly document's notion of sin under the title, 'Sin and Atonement.' But it is entirely different from the presentation in this essay. The contradiction is resolved as soon as one recognizes that the ideas described by G. von Rad are typical of the P^s material (some of which is, of course, quite old). In P^g, some traces of these ideas are evident in the cultic material used in Exodus 28–29 and Leviticus 8–9, but they exercised no influence at all on the theology of sin that has been redactionally introduced into the historical work. The composition of the priestly historical narrative could well be located in the Babylonian diaspora, and in the 6th, or perhaps as late as the 5th century. Cf., in more recent literature, K. Elliger, 'Sinn und Ursprung;' R. Kilian, 'Die Hoffnung auf Heimkehr in der Priesterschrift,' *Bibel und Leben* 7 (1966): 39–51. Here also, the results obtained in the present essay will offer further support. J. G. Vink, 'The Date and Origin of the Priestly Code in the Old Testament,' *The Priestly Code and Seven Other Studies*, OTS 15 (Leiden, 1969), 1–144, makes another attempt to eliminate the distinction among literary layers within the priestly material, and offers the turn of the 5th to the 4th century as the time of the composition of the 'priest's codex.' Despite all respect for individual interesting observations and arguments, one cannot avoid noting, as regards the conclusion of the whole, that a great many of the arguments present possibilities, at most, and that there is no genuine dialogue with literary criticism, which has been at work on the priestly material since the time of Wellhausen.

made of the individual sins that are narrated, of original sins and the doctrine of sin redactionally applied by his predecessors? How much did he accept, to what extent did he make choices and changes, and how far did he introduce his own new teaching on sin into his work?

As far as I can see, there has not yet been a thorough investigation of the theme sketched out by these questions.[6] What I will present in the following pages can only be an initial attempt and a suggestion.[7] It is dedicated to Heinrich Schlier, as a symbol of gratitude for his writings, but especially for a series of unforgettable discussions and a great deal of good advice.

1. The Priestly Narrative and its Models[8]

(a) If we compare the priestly historical narrative with its models as regards the theme of sin, what is most apparent is the absence of an amazing amount of material and of some astonishingly important matters. Thus, for example, the Yahwist story of original sin is omitted.[9] Also, the narrative of the breaking of the covenant through worship of the golden calf immediately after the revelation on Sinai (which, though there is some dispute over the distribution of the story among its sources, was certainly available at the time the priestly narrative was composed) has been left out.[10] A good many things have been similarly omitted,

6. Scharbert, 'Prolegomena' (see n. 1 above), 97–102, still offers the most extensive discussion of these questions.

7. The following has emerged for me, over time, as a bonus from a number of seminars on problems in the priestly document, and I am indebted to a whole series of students and doctoral candidates at the Pontifical Biblical Institute for their contributions to the discussion and their individual studies, which stimulated me to reflect on the problems of the doctrine of sin in the priestly writing.

8. The presupposition of this section is that P^g knew both JE and the deuteronomistic history. This presupposition is ordinarily, and quite rightly, made wherever an author P^g is accepted, and it is repeatedly confirmed for anyone who makes a close study of the texts of P^g.

9. Gen. 2:4b–3:24. Recently Herbert Haag, in particular, has pointed to the fact of a conscious omission: *Biblische Schöpfungslehre und kirchliche Erbsündenlehre*, SBS 10 (Stuttgart, 3rd ed. 1967), 49.

10. Exodus 32 and Deut. 9:9–10:11. The basic material of Exodus 32 is usually assigned to E. According to M. Noth, *Das zweite Buch Mose, Exodus*, ATD 5 (Göttingen, 2nd ed. 1961), 202–03, it is probably a 'secondary literary addition to the J narrative.' Recent literature on this chapter of Exodus is listed in O. Eissfeldt, *Einleitung in das Alte Testament* (Tübingen, 3rd ed. 1964), 269 n. 1.

such as Cain's murder of his brother or the shamelessness of Canaan.

Many of these omissions may be credited to the tighter narrative style of the priestly history. But the dropping of the Yahwist original sin and the worship of the calf at Sinai, at least, can scarcely be explained by that stylistic trait alone. Here we have someone who deliberately avoids telling about the sin of humanity and that of Israel in the traditional manner.

(b) In other cases, narratives or the content of certain stories are taken from the model documents, but the mention of sin is eliminated from them.

For the Yahwist, the scattering of human beings over the earth was motivated by the story of the building of the tower at Babel.[11] The priestly narrative contains, in Gen. 10:32, at the end of the table of nations, a note that is entirely objective, and can even be understood as referring to a divine blessing: 'These are the families of Noah's sons, according to their genealogies, in their nations; and from these the nations spread abroad on the earth after the flood.'[12]

With the story of the destruction of the cities of Sodom and Gomorrah, the Yahwist also wove into the Abraham narratives a great story of guilt and punishment, and used the dialogue between Abraham and YHWH in Gen. 18:17–33 to expand it into a piece of theological teaching.[13] In the priestly narrative, all this is reduced to the most compact possible note, with no mention of sin. Even YHWH's destructive action is mentioned only in a subordinate clause: 'So it was that, when God destroyed the cities of the Plain, God remembered Abraham, and sent Lot out of the midst of the overthrow, when God overthrew the cities in which Lot had settled.'[14]

In the old Pentateuch sources, the story of Jacob was also saturated with motifs of guilt and nemesis, even though in a much more restrained and expansive manner than the compact guilt-and-punishment stories in the history of origins. Jacob incurs guilt through the betrayal that wins

11. Gen. 11:1–9. According to G. von Rad, *Das erste Buch Mose, Genesis,* ATD 2–4 (Göttingen, 6th ed. 1961), 124, this is the story of a 'secret titanism.'

12. The table of nations in P^g: Gen. 10:1–4a, 5aβ–7, 20, 22–23, 31–32. Within the context of the priestly narrative we must understand Gen 10:32 as the realization of the blessing of fruitfulness given to Noah in Gen. 9:1, 7, even if the typical vocabulary of blessing (as found, for example, in Exod. 1:7) is not employed here.

13. Cf. Gen. 13:13; 18:16–33; 19:1–28.

14. Gen. 19:2. In P^g, this verse probably followed immediately after Gen. 13:6, 11b, 12abαβ (topic: separation of Lot from Abraham).

him the blessing. That costs him twenty years of his life, as his father-in-law makes a fool of him in a way that repeats his own act of betrayal, and the family collapses as a result of all this.[15] The priestly author rewrote this story altogether. Jacob has to travel to Paddan-aram because he must not take a Hittite for his wife, as his brother Esau did (Gen. 28:1–2). He receives Isaac's blessing, in a sense, as a blessing for the journey (Gen. 28:3–4). But Esau too, even though he took the wrong woman to wife, is not a bad son: according to Gen. 28:6–9, he makes up for his fault by quickly taking another wife from among his own relatives.[16] He also remains in the land until he has joined his brother Jacob, after the latter's return, in burying their dead father (Gen. 35:28–29). Then he moves away to Seir, because the wealth of the two brothers is so great that the land cannot support them both together (Gen. 36:6–8). There is not the slightest trace of any disagreement.[17]

In the stories from Israel's time in the wilderness, the Yahwist included the miracle of the quail (Numbers 11), a narrative about the people's sinful murmuring and divine punishment.[18] In the priestly narrative, the quail miracle in Exodus 16 is built into the manna story, whereby the new narrative complex has acquired a different point: the disclosure of the Sabbath.[19]

(c) The narrative of the leading of the people out of Egypt requires a special investigation. It is true that in the old sources, Exodus 1–15 was a story of rescue, not of guilt and punishment. But still, the motif of guilt, in the sense of the culpability of Pharaoh, was echoed once in Exod. 10:16–17 (J), and, in the exilic world in which the oracles of Jeremiah and Ezekiel on the foreign nations were in circulation, the idea could easily

15. For this point of view, let me refer especially to the commentary by G. von Rad (cf. n. 11 above).

16. The whole text in P^g is: Gen. 26:34–35; 27:46; 28:1–9 . . .

17. For more detail on the reshaping of the old Jacob story by P^g, see W. Gross, 'Jakob, der Mann des Segens, Zur Traditionsgeschichte und Theologie der priesterschriftlichen Jakobsüberlieferungen,' *Bibl* 49 (1968): 321–34, at 339–43.

18. According to M. Noth, *Überlieferungsgeschichte des Pentateuch* (Stuttgart, 2nd ed. 1948), 129–30 and 135, there was indeed an original quail story without the motif of murmuring and punishment, but in J these motifs are already fully integrated into the material.

19. The P^g text combined with J texts (manna), is found in Exod. 16:1–3, 6–7, 9–13a . . . 14bα . . . 16abγ–20, 22–26, 31a, 35b. It is possible that Moses' anger about an incorrect procedure in gathering the manna in Exod. 16:20 is a reminiscence of older motifs that are otherwise suppressed in this story.

arise that the destruction of the firstborn of the Egyptians and the drowning of the Egyptian army in the sea were YHWH's judgment on them because of their treatment of the Israelites. It is therefore important to recognize that the priestly narrative not only gives no impetus to this reasonable interpretation, but appears even to attempt to steer away from it.[20]

What the Egyptians did to the Israelites is described in Exod. 1:14 thus: '[they] made their lives bitter.'[21] This corresponds almost literally to what Esau's Hittite wives meant to Isaac and Rebecca.[22]

In the programmatic text Exod. 6:5–8,[23] the exodus from Egypt becomes a liberating deed of YHWH and the acceptance of the Israelites as 'YHWH's people.'[24] Moreover, the individual phases of liberation are not portrayed as narratives of sin. The continual refusal of YHWH's demand for the people's release has been separated from the plague stories drawn from the old sources. Thus the plague narratives become a description of a struggle between the Egyptian magicians and the representatives of YHWH, in which it soon becomes clear that YHWH can accomplish greater miracles.[25] The fact that Pharaoh does not allow himself to be influenced is traced to YHWH's action. The terminology

20. The exodus story in P^g: Exod. 1:7, 13–14; 1:23aγb, 24–25; 6:2–12; 7:1–13, 19, 20aα, 21b, 22; 8:1–3 . . . 11aδb, 12–15; 9:8–12; 13:3–14, 28, 40–41; 14:1–4, 8a, 10abγ, 15–18, 21aαb, 22–23, 26, 27aα, 28–29.

21. *waymārĕrû 'et ḥayyēhêm.*

22. Gen. 26:35: *wattihĕyênā mōrat rûaḥ lĕyiṣḥāq ûlĕribqâ.*

23. Just as in the second programmatic text, Exod. 7:1–5, which contains a more detailed preparation for the exodus story.

24. On this, see my essay, 'Beobachtungen zur Geschichte des Ausdrucks *'am jhwh,*' in H. W. Wolff, ed., *Probleme biblischer Theologie, Gerhard von Rad zum 70. Geburtstag* (Munich, 1971), 275–305.

25. We learn only in Exod. 6:11 and 7:2 why the miracles are performed: in fact, Pharaoh should be moved by these demonstrations of power to release the Israelites. The fact that Pharaoh does not permit himself to be impressed by any miracle is designated as disobedience to Moses and Aaron, not to YHWH as such (Exod. 7:13, 22; 8:11, 15; 9:12). This corresponds to what is said about the Israelites themselves in Exod. 6:9: 'they would not listen to Moses.' If, at that point, this disobedience is excused because their spirits have been broken by hard labor, it could be that the explanation of Pharaoh's attitude – that it results from YHWH's having hardened his heart – might almost be intended as a personal excusing of Pharaoh. Here, YHWH is accomplishing something in history. Questions of guilt or innocence are outside the horizon of the story.

used here could hardly mean (as is sometimes supposed) anything like 'unrepentant hardening in sin,' but instead that YHWH sharpened Pharaoh's lust for combat.[26] The destruction of the Egyptian firstborn is called YHWH's 'judgment' (Exod. 12:12). But the judgment is not on the sinful Egyptians; rather it falls on Egypt's gods.[27] The destruction of the Egyptians in the Sea of Reeds means that YHWH is gaining glory,[28] because in this event the Egyptians must acknowledge that YHWH is YHWH.[29]

26. *qšh hifil*: Exod. 7:3 (programmatic text); (*ḥzq qal*: Exod. 7:13, 22; 8:15); *ḥzq piel*: Exod. 9:12; 14:4, 8, 17. The typical expression in J (*kbd qal*: Exod. 7:14; 9:7; *kbd hifil*: Exod. 8:11, 28; 9:34; 10:1) is avoided. It is true that P^g can find support for *ḥzq* even in passages in the old sources (Exod. 4:21; 9:35; 10:20, 27; 12:33 – even if one joins Noth in attributing some of these examples to P, there remain Exod. 4:21 and 12:33, and it does not appear relevant for our context that they lie outside the plague narratives as such). But the introduction of *qšh hifil* at a crucial point, the elimination of *kbd* in favor of *ḥzq*, and the extension of the use of this idea and terminology in the narrative of the sea miracle favor the notion that P^g intends to apply a new accent. We should suppose it most likely that P^g is taking up the terminology of the deuteronomic history regarding boldness for battle: for *qšh hifil*, cf. Deut. 2:30; for *ḥzq qal*, cf. Deut. 31:6, 7, 23; Josh. 1:6–7, 9, 18; 10:25; 2 Sam. 13:28; for *ḥzq piel*, cf. Deut. 1:38; 3:28; Josh. 11:20; Judg. 16:28; 1 Sam. 23:16. Some of these examples belong within a schema of installation in office: cf. N. Lohfink, 'Die deuteronomistische Darstellung des Übergangs der Führung Israels von Moses auf Josue,' *Schol* 37 (1962): 32–44. But most of these, too, in the context in which they appear in the deuteronomistic history, are challenges to courage in battle.

27. One may conclude from Exod. 12:12 that the *šĕpāṭîm gĕdōlîm* in Exod. 6:6 and 7:4 refer also to the killing of the Egyptian firstborn. Consequently, the expression should also be understood there as a judgment on the gods. The word *šepeṭ* is otherwise found almost exclusively in Ezekiel.

28. Exod. 14:4, 18 (*kbd nifal*). In Ezekiel, *šepeṭ* and *kbd hifil* are found together in the saying against the people of Sidon (Ezek. 28:22), which, before the insertion of the oracle against Egypt, probably constituted the conclusion of Ezekiel's collection of national oracles (cf. W. Zimmerli, *Ezechiel*, BKAT 13 [Neukirchen, 1962], 693). Here again there is no concrete indication of national guilt. In contrast to the individual national oracles preceding it, here the accent lies entirely on YHWH's self-revelation in history.

29. The 'formula of recognition' (cf. W. Zimmerli, 'Erkenntnis Gottes nach dem Buche Ezechiel, Eine theologische Studie,' AthANT 27 [Zürich, 1954], repr. in *Gottes Offenbarung, Gesammelte Aufsätze*, ThB 19 [Munich, 1963], 41–119; idem, 'Das wort des göttlichen Selbsterweises [Erweiswort], eine prophetische Gattung,' in *Mélanges Bibliques rédigés en l'honneur de André Robert*, Travaux de l'institut catholique de Paris 4 [Paris, 1957], 154–64, repr. in *Gottes Offenbarung*, 120–32) is found in the following passages in P^g: Exod. 7:5 (announcement); 14:4, 18. With

Thus in the Exodus narratives everything has been done that could possibly be done in order that they should not be misunderstood as stories of guilt and punishment.

(d) The priestly narrator certainly did not undertake all the operations thus far described, which undoubtedly took extensive liberties with the traditional narrative corpus, in order to avoid telling stories about sin. This writer clearly treats the theme of sin and punishment in three traditional narrative contexts.

In two cases, the author only continues what was already in the old sources: the story of the Flood[30] and the story of the scouts.[31] In the third instance, the motif of sin is even introduced into a narrative in which it was not present before: the water miracle in the desert.[32]

The removal of all the other traditional stories of sin causes these

this formula, P^g takes up an interpretation of the event that already had its basis in the old sources: cf. Exod. 7:17; 8:6, 18; 9:14, 29; 11:7. But P^g eliminates this formula within the plague narratives and transfers it to the revelatory miracle at the Sea of Reeds. The acknowledgment of YHWH becomes the high point of the whole series of events. In addition, as far as the point of view under consideration is concerned, we find that within the plague narratives, a recognition of YHWH by Pharaoh would have pointed to Pharaoh's guilt, and in that event the subsequent events would have automatically appeared as punishment.

30. In the Flood narrative, P^g includes: Gen. 6:9–22; 7:6, 11, 13–16a, 17a, 18–21, 24; 8:1, 2a, 3b–5, 13a, 14–19; 9:1–3, 7–17, 28–29. Elliger also assigns Gen. 9:4–6 to P^g, as do most authors, but I follow the opinion of R. Smend Sr. and H. Holzinger concerning these verses. In the near future, S. McEvenue will present new arguments for this position. [See below, ch. 5, n. 31.]

31. In the scout, or spy, narrative, P^g includes Num. 10:11–12; 13:1–3a, 17aβ, 21, 25, 26a, 32; 14:1a, 2, 5–7, 10, 26–29aα, 35–38.

32. The narrative of the water miracle contains the following material from P^g: Num. 20:1aα, 2, 3b, 4, 6–7, 8aβγbβ, 10, 11b, 12. But the texts concerning the deaths of Aaron and Moses are also to be assigned to the same narrative context: Num. 20:22, 23aα, 25–29; Deut. 32:48–50, 51b–52; 34:1a . . . 7–9. In assigning Deut. 32:48–50, 51b–52 to P^g (instead of the usual mention of Num. 27:12–14a, 15–23), I am following a still unpublished [1970] study by E. Cortese. Contrary to a widely held opinion, most recently and clearly upheld by G. W. Coats, *Rebellion in the Wilderness* (Nashville, 1968), it seems to me that the root *lwn* does not, in and of itself, imply the notion of sinful rebellion. There appears also to be a justified 'complaining' and 'crying out,' to which YHWH reacts by bringing aid (cf., for example, Exod. 15:24–25; 16:1–35 in all layers!). It is only the context that at each point can show whether in a concrete case this amounts to a sinful complaint. This is all the more true of the root *rib*. Consequently, the water narrative from the old sources in Exod. 17:1b–7 only became a story of sin through the introduction (probably later) of the Massah passages in vv. 2 and 7. However, P^g did not develop the tradition of the water

three narratives in the priestly document to stand out all the more sharply, an effect that is undoubtedly intended.

It is also immediately clear that they are related to one another and are intended to constitute a system. The story of the Flood is found in the history of origins, which talks about humanity as a whole. It is evidently an example of the sin of all human beings. The two stories from the desert period are located near the end of the second part of the work, where the subject is only the people of YHWH. At this point, the things YHWH has established for Israel's good are, with one exception, already given: the covenant with Abraham, the constitution of the people by means of the Exodus, the discovery of the sabbath as a result of the manna miracle, YHWH's presence in the sanctuary from Sinai forward.[33] All that remains is for the people to enter the promised land of Canaan. At this moment, the priestly narrative introduces examples of Israel's sins: in the story of the scouts, it speaks of the sins of the political leaders and of the whole people; in the story of the water, it tells of the sin of Moses and Aaron, the mediators between the people and YHWH.

In view of this obvious system, we must even ask whether these are only 'examples,' as we first cautiously suggested. It would seem that the three stories of sin are not intended only as examples, but also in a typological sense. They could be something like three 'original sins.'

Of course, such an interpretation of the three stories has broad implications. It demands a very special understanding of the 'genre' of the priestly narrative, a conception that needs to be worked out on a broader basis. But it appears to me probable, nevertheless, as regards the treatment of the topic of sin, that the priestly historical narrative has no intention of reporting history in our sense (nor even in the sense understood by the Yahwist and the Elohist). It seems likely that the work as a whole is, as regards its genre, one great 'history of origins.' Everything narrated in it is told as 'beginning' and 'prototype.' While the Yahwist only recited 'history of origins' at the beginning, and then continued with 'history,' here in the priestly document *everything* is 'history of origins.' Therefore the original sin related by the Yahwist, which is then elaborated by many historical

miracle in any way as a sin of the people expressed in 'complaining,' but instead caused the 'complaint' to be followed by YHWH's response, which has nothing in the way of punishment about it. The sin, rather, follows through the agency of Moses and Aaron in carrying the miracle through to completion.

33. On the basic structure and meaning of the priestly Sinai pericope, see M. Oliva, 'Interpretación teológica del culto en la perícopa del Sinaí de la Historica Sacerdotal,' *Bibl* 49 (1968): 345–54.

sins, must be eliminated; in its place, three original sins are inserted, and these are distributed through the whole work and systematically related to one another. There are, then, no historically necessary individual sins that follow on these three.

In the remaining parts of this study, the three stories of sin in the priestly historical narrative will be discussed individually. We must inquire of each one: what did the author take from existing sources, and what has been changed? What is the author's inspiration for the new elements that are inserted? What was the intention in each case? What concrete situations of the readers did the author have in mind?

2. The Sin of all Human Beings before God: Violence

(a) When the Yahwist came to write the story of the Flood, there had already been a good deal said about many sins. Therefore in this case the story of the Flood could begin simply with the statement that YHWH looked down from heaven to earth (Gen. 6:5), and in doing so, saw sin and therefore determined on destruction.

It is different in the priestly document.[34] Here, in Gen. 1:31, after the days of creation, God looks at the work that has been done and says: 'See, it is very good.' What follows is a purely objective genealogy from Adam to Noah.[35] After this, the story of the Flood must be told. But before God can look down to earth and discover sin, it is necessary to establish the fact that there really is sin on earth.

The author does this by setting up the contrast between the virtuous Noah and the rest of creation. It is said of Noah in Gen. 6:9: 'Noah was a righteous man, blameless in his generation: Noah walked with God.' The contrasting statement in Gen. 6:11 is: 'Now the earth was corrupt in God's sight, and the earth was filled with violence.'

The formulae are carefully chosen. Sin is called 'violence' (*ḥāmās*), which is a key word in prophetic rhetoric of accusation. It refers to the deliberate oppression and ruthless violation of fellow human beings.[36] The earth is full of it: *wattimmālē'*. The latter is also a prophetic

34. The best study of theology of sin in the priestly flood story is that of L. Van den Wijngaert, 'Die Sünde in der priesterlichen Urgeschichte,' *ThPh* 43 (1968): 35–50.

35. Gen. 5:1–28, 30–32.

36. Examples are given by Van der Wijngaert (see n. 34 above). On *ḥāmās*, see also S. Marrow, 'Hāmās in Jer. 20:8,' *Verbum Domini* 43 (1965): 241–55.

expression, especially in Ezekiel.[37] Just as, during the plague of flies in Egypt, the land is corrupted by the flies that fill it, so here the whole earth, which was 'very good' when it was made, is spoiled by the violence that fills it: *wattiššāḥēt.*[38] In fact, human deeds of violence against other humn beings cause the creation to lose its goodness not only for itself, but also 'before God:' *lipnê hāʾĕlōhîm.* That one sentence contains an entire doctrine of sin.

The narrator prolongs the echo of this brief statement by means of repetitions and word-plays, and in the process makes some minor additions to this doctrine of sin. As in the work of the Yahwist, God looks at the earth and discovers sin there: 'And God saw that the earth was corrupt; for all flesh had corrupted its ways upon the earth' (Gen. 6:12). What is added here is that violence is being exercised by *kol bāśār*, i.e., by all living things, represented by their highest race, all human beings.[39] In God's resulting decision to punish, which in the priestly document is dramatically integrated into the command to Noah to build the ark,[40] the whole is echoed once again: 'And God said to Noah, 'I have determined to make an end of all flesh, for the earth is filled with violence because of them;[41] now I am going to destroy them[42] along with the earth' (Gen.

37. Ezek. 7:23; 8:17; 12:19; 28:16; Mic. 6:12; Zeph. 1:9. For examples of this expression with other words for 'sin,' see Van den Wijngaert (n. 34 above), 40, n. 16.

38. Apart from Gen. 6:11–12 and Exod. 8:20 (plague of flies), *šḥt nifal* is found only at Jer. 13:7 (symbolic action: the ruined loincloth); 18:4 (comparison: vessel spoiled in the potter's hand); Ezek. 20:44 (corrupt deeds). We cannot call this a specifically prophetic use of language. P^g is already beginning, at this point, a play with the root *šḥt* that will be carried on later with *hifil* and *piel* forms as well. The use of *nifal* to characterize the consequences of human sin for all creation is an innovation by P^g. But we should point out that the root *šḥt* also appears in the prophetic text Ezek. 28:1–19, which is decisive for Gen. 6:9–13 (see below): it is in Ezek. 28:17.

39. On the meaning of *kol bāśār*, see A. R. Hulst, '*Kol baśar* in der priesterlichen Fluterzählung,' *OTS* 12 (1958): 28–68, and the corrections added by J. Scharbert, *Fleisch, Geist und Seele im Pentateuch*, SBS 19 (Stuttgart, 2nd ed. 1967), 51–54.

40. In J it was an independent element and constituted the beginning of the whole flood story: Gen. 6:7.

41. *mippĕnêhem*, literally, 'beginning with them.' The plural explicates *kol bāśār.*

42. *mašḥîtām* contains a suffix with a dative function. Once that is recognized, there is no need for emendations, and the nemesis character of the proceeding becomes clear: people have spoiled God's good earth, and now God will spoil that same earth for them in a quite different fashion.

6:13). The expression *qēṣ bā'* also takes up an element of prophetic language.[43]

On the whole, it can be said that here the language of Israel's prophets is employed to define what sin means for all human beings. Sin is the wrong that people do to one another. But precisely as injustice among human beings it is a challenge to God, because it corrupts God's good creation.[44]

(b) The observation that the priestly writing has, at this point, introduced prophetic formulations into the ancient narrative of the flood

43. Cf. Amos 8:1–2; Ezek. 7:2, 3, 6.

44. If the theory proposed by G. Pettinato in 'Die Bestrafung des Menschengeschlechts durch die Sintflut, Die erste Tafel des Atramhašis-Epos eröffnet eine neue Einsicht in die Motivation dieser Strafe,' *Or* 37 (1968): 165–200, should prove to be correct (though W. G. Lambert and A. R. Millard, *Atra-hašis, The Babylonian Story of the Flood* [Oxford, 1969], vi, consider the key point of the theory 'not well founded philologically'), the Babylonians considered the Flood a punishment for human beings' rebellion against the gods. The people rebelled against the proper purpose of their existence, namely, to work as slaves for the gods, and that was a serious trespass. Pettinato concludes his essay with some rather strange remarks about the inferiority of the biblical reasons given for the Flood in comparison to those of Babylon as he interprets them. If for the moment we set aside the Yahwist narrative, which requires a separate discussion, and if we then presuppose Pettinato's theory and compare the priestly conception with the 'Babylonian,' a calm comparison yields something like this: In both cases the sin that is punished by the Flood is an injury done to the order of creation. The difference is in the order of creation itself. Babylonian is 'slave labor as the real purpose of the creation of humanity' (Pettinato, 198); proper to the priestly writing is the exercise of governance over other creatures within a created world that is 'very good' (Gen. 1:28, 31). Babylonian is the human being 'made to do the work that had become too arduous for the gods themselves' (Pettinato, 181); the human being has a 'tragic existence' (Pettinato, 190). In the priestly document the human being is supposed to be 'blameless' and 'walk before God' (Gen. 6:9; 17:1). Since in the Babylonian version the gods exploit humanity by virtue of creation itself, the injury done to the order of creation is necessarily a social revolt against the gods. In the priestly writing, on the contrary, the injury to the order of creation is first of all an evil within the world itself, namely antisocial behaviour, and it is only on behalf of the creation that is thereby being damaged and destroyed that God takes a hand. The Babylonian gods have to defend themselves, and in actuality they remain in the role of the accused. The God of the priestly writing defends the good world, and it is human beings who stand under indictment. However, this comparison requires one further correction, since the Atraḫašis epic is evidently more strongly subject to mythical forms of speech than is the priestly writing: a translation of all the mythical symbols in terms of a rational language more similar to that of the priestly writing might change the picture. Beyond this, of course, there remains the question of how further research will react to Pettinato's theory.

can be given an additional dimension, for it is almost certain that, here especially, the author of the priestly narrative is drawing on one of the oracles to the alien peoples in Ezekiel: the oracle against Tyre in Ezek. 28:1–19.[45]

Certainly, this text, in turn, makes use of an old, pre-Israelite myth of the fall from paradise of a once-perfect being – probably the same myth that, in the same or some other form, furnishes a tradition-historical background to the Yahwist story of the Fall.[46] The priestly writing had access to the myth in the allegorizing form found in Ezekiel, already shot through with prophetic motifs.

Thus by a roundabout way through a prophetic text, the priestly document retained the connection to ancient, mythological-exemplary thought. This may confirm the thesis that, although it had previously omitted the Yahwist's narrative of original sin, its intention at this later point is to speak, not of particular sins at a particular period, but of the sin of humanity as such.

(c) Still another approach lends support to the idea that what is said here is meant to apply to all human beings. The counter-image to the sin before the Flood is that of the blameless Noah. Gen. 6:9 says of him: 'Noah was a righteous man, blameless in his generation; Noah walked with God.'[47] What is here predicated as reality of Noah, however, is at a later period demanded of Abraham in the form of a command, before El Shaddai will make a covenant with him: 'I am El Shaddai; walk before me, and be blameless' (Gen. 17:1).[48] Given the systematic character of the priestly historical writing, we may presume that the sins that Abraham is

45. In what follows I am in agreement with Van den Wijngaert (see n. 34 above), 40–48. His opinion appears to me to be more accurate than the contrary position, that makes Ezekiel 28 dependent on P^g. This seems to be the opinion of W. Zimmerli, *Ezechiel* (see n. 28 above), 686.

46. The question whether this myth can be more clearly identified and reconstructed from other ancient witnesses is not very important in the context of the present essay. R. de Vaux, 'Les prophètes de Baal sur le mont Carmel,' *Bulletin du Musée de Beyrouth* 5 (Paris, 1941): 7–20 (at 13–16 and 20), repr. in *Bible et Orient* (Paris, 1967): 485–97 (at 490–92 and 496–97) refers to a myth concerning Baal Melquart of Tyre.

47. See, before this, Gen. 5:22, 24 concerning Enoch. For this terminology, cf. Ezek. 28:14–15.

48. On form and function in P^g, see N. Lohfink, 'Die priesterschriftliche Abwertung der Tradition von der Offenbarung des Jahwenamens an Mose,' *Bibl* 49 (1968): 1–8 (at 6–7).

to avoid in fulfilling this demand are the same as the sins in Gen. 6:11–13. They are thus the sins that threaten human beings of every era.

(d) Of course, the readers of the priestly history, in the Babylonian exile or in the Babylonian diaspora, looked back on the prophets' preaching of doom as something in the past. In reading the priestly narrative of the Flood, they could see that they had been justly accused by their prophets and punished by their God. But at the same time they were to know that they had not merely transgressed some special regulations that applied only to the children of Abraham. When they practiced violence and injustice and were accused of these deeds by their prophets, they had committed sins that were forbidden to all human beings because they corrupted God's good creation.

But beyond these sins, in respect to which the Israelites were on the same level with all other human beings, the priestly historical writing recognizes others that can only occur when YHWH has bestowed special affection on a group of people. These the priestly writing defines in the stories of sin in the wilderness era.

3. The Sin of Israel's Political Leaders and of the Whole People: Slandering the Land

(a) The story told in Numbers 13–14 about the scouting of Palestine from the south remained a war story, in spite of repeated expansions and reworkings in the old sources of the Pentateuch. In the deuteronomistic history, where, in Deuteronomy 1, it furnishes the beginning of the whole narrative, it is the real original sin of Israel. Its character as a war story is, in fact, heightened. It is the story of a perverted holy war.

In the priestly historical narrative, by contrast, any connection with war and conquest has been eliminated. There is no military necessity that requires the sending of scouts. YHWH personally orders that a delegation be sent through the land of Canaan. Its members are not 'scouts.' Rather, they are supposed to traverse the land in a procession lasting exactly forty days,[49] from its southernmost to its northernmost point, to view it and survey it.[50] They are, as representatives of all Israel, to take a position regarding YHWH's last and greatest beneficence, the 'land of Canaan, which I am giving to the Israelites.' For this reason a representative from

49. *wayyāšūbû* in Num. 13:25 does not refer to the return home, but to the change in the direction of the march at the northernmost point of the route.

50. In this interpretation of the root *twr* I am following an unpublished study by S. McEvenue.

each of the tribes of Israel must be present: each must be a *nāsî'* (Num. 13:2).[51]

It is in the process of surveying and valuing YHWH's beneficent gift that sin occurs.[52] Employing the technique we have already noted in the story of the flood, the author gives the sin a precise name. It is *dibbat hā'āreṣ*, 'giving a bad report about the land,' i.e., slandering or calumniating it.[53] The land is YHWH's beneficent gift. The sin therefore consists in slandering the concrete, good gift that YHWH offers.

The slanderous words are quoted in Num. 13:32: 'The land . . . is a land that devours its inhabitants; and all the people that we saw in it are of great size.' The second half of this sentence is an expanded motif from the old sources that is not precisely covered by the naming of the sin as 'slander of the land,' but the first part is new, and it leads us again to Ezekiel.

(b) Ezek. 36:1–15 is a prophecy of salvation from YHWH to the land of Israel, which is taken into YHWH's protection against the slanders and reproaches of the nations.[54] The nations' insults are summarized in Ezek. 36:13 as follows: 'You devour people, and you bereave your nation of children.' In Ezekiel, of course, it is the other nations who speak in this way, and they do so at a time when Israel has, in fact, been devoured. But that makes Israel's sin all the worse, when that nation itself uses such words, and precisely at the moment when the land is to be given to Israel.

(c) We may readily suspect that at the time of the exile and at the beginning of the post-exilic diaspora, it was not only Israel's enemies who slandered YHWH's good gift, the land of Canaan. Probably the priestly writing is speaking here of a sin that threatens its own Israelite readers, if they had not already succumbed to it: that when they were called to return to their land, they did not listen and had no desire to have and to dwell in

51. It is also part of the demilitarizing of the story that P^g completely omits the defeat at Hormah (JE: Num. 14:39–45; deuteronomistic history: Deut. 1:41–45) by which sin is punished, or at most hints at it, for those familiar with the old tradition, in the general condemnation in Num. 14:29, 35 and the note about the death of the 'spies' in Num. 14:36–37.

52. According to the old sources and Deuteronomy, the sin consists of fear, revolt, and unbelief. In what follows I am adopting some observations from an unpublished work by E. Cortese on the theme of 'land' in the priestly writing.

53. Num. 13:32; 14:36–37. for *dibbāh* as 'slander,' cf. Gen. 37:2 P^g; Prov. 10:18; 25:10. Otherwise the word is found only in Ezek. 36:3; on this, see the following note.

54. The words used are *dibbāh* (Ezek. 36:3); *kĕlimmāh*, 'insult' (Ezek. 36:6, 7, 15); and *ḥerpāh*, 'disgrace,' (Ezek. 36:15).

that land any more, since they no longer valued it. Perhaps this was precisely the temptation of the leaders of these exiles and of the groups in the diaspora, and they persuaded the masses to think the same way.

(d) At any rate, at this point in the priestly narrative, those who have inspected the land draw the whole people into their sin. This seems to be the meaning of Num. 14:36.[55] In its despair, the people wishes that they had died in Egypt, or here in the wilderness (Num. 14:2). This desire is fulfilled to the letter.[56] In Num. 14:28–29, 35, YHWH condemns them to die in the wilderness.

Only Joshua and Caleb do not participate in this sin. They had declared: 'The land is exceedingly good' (Num. 14:7). In Joshua and Caleb, therefore, the reader of the priestly writing recognizes the proper attitude, as with Noah in the flood story. Consequently, later in the story, Joshua and Caleb will also join another generation in receiving YHWH's beneficent gift. Besides them, Moses and Aaron also were not participants in the sin. But their not sinning has a different function, founded on the economy of the whole narrative. In these spiritual leaders of Israel a different sin is depicted. This takes place in Numbers 20, in the third and last story of sin.

4. The Sin of the Religious Leaders of Israel: Lack of Trust

(a) In the priestly text of Numbers 20 we find a cleanly executed story of a miraculous gift of water in the desert.[57] Water is in short supply. The

55. This interpretation of Num. 14:36 is not entirely certain. *lĕhôṣîʾ dibbāh ʿal hāʾāreṣ* could as easily be referred to what the 'scouts' did as to the action to which they enticed the whole community. But, according to P^g, in any event the community had identified itself with the 'scouts'' opinion of the land of Canaan by their desire for death in Num. 14:2.

56. On the attitude behind the description at this point, see S. McEvenue, 'A Source-Critical Problem in Nm 14, 26–38,' *Bibl* 50 (1969): 453–65, at 464–65. A similar attitude was indicated earlier, in Gen. 6:13: cf. n. 42 above.

57. I consider G. W. Coats's interpretation (*Rebellion in the Wilderness*, 71–82, cf. n. 32 above) – in terms of a story of rebellion, in which Moses and Aaron are punished as representatives of the whole rebellious people – unsuccessful. It is true, however, that interpreters' paths diverge very early, with the determination of the content of the P text and with the methodological question whether it is appropriate to apply to the interpretation of a particular biblical layer the viewpoints of other layers, e.g., the deuteronomistic historical writing, in a harmonizing fashion. It is certain that in Deuteronomy 1–3 Moses, as representative of the people, is prevented from entering the promised land: cf. N. Lohfink, 'Individuum-Gemeinschaft in Deuteronomium 1, 6–3, 29' (n. 2 above). But the question is: what does that mean for P^g?

community assembles and complains. Moses and Aaron go to the tent and pray. YHWH's glory appears, and YHWH tells them to gather the community in front of the rock and to speak to the rock; then it will yield water. They do so, and streams of water flow from the rock. People and animals can drink from it.

But at two points a completely new element intrudes in the narrative, which otherwise proceeds according to a familiar schema. When Moses speaks to the rock (Num. 20:10), he does not utter a command that it should yield water, but instead proposes a question that betrays his uncertainty: 'Listen, you rebels, shall we bring water for you out of this rock?'[58] In spite of this, water flows out. But then the story concludes in Num. 20:12 with YHWH's judgment on Moses and Aaron: 'Because you did not trust in me, to show my holiness before the eyes of the Israelites, therefore you shall not bring this assembly into the land that I have given them.'[59] As a result of these additions, which must be ascribed in their entirety to the priestly author, the original narrative becomes a story of a sin and a divine judgment.

(b) As in the first two narratives, here also the sin has a special name: *lō' hẹ'ĕmantem bî*, that is, unbelief, lack of trust in YHWH's miraculous power and will to help, and in this case in regard to *lĕhaqdîšēnî lĕ'ênê bĕnê yiśrā'ēl*, failure in carrying out the duty to treat YHWH as the Holy One before YHWH's people.[60]

This introduction of the motif of YHWH's holiness brings into the context a feature that is undoubtedly important for the priestly historical writing. This motif becomes still more prominent in the 'holiness code,'

58. There is a longstanding argument in exegetical literature about what really constituted the sin of Moses and Aaron. But it should be abundantly clear from the narrative logic of P^g that it is the *words* of Moses in Num. 20:10 that must be regarded as the sin of both men. In Deut. 32:51, as in Num. 20:12, the sin described in Num. 20:10 is ascribed to both Moses *and* Aaron (as also in Num. 27:14, in case one prefers to assign the parallel passage in Numbers 27 to P^g). But in Numbers 20, P^g, there are no common actions of Moses and Aaron that can be considered in this category, except for the assembling of the people in front of the rock and the words of Moses. It is true that the words are spoken by Moses alone, but he says 'we,' speaking in the names of both of them, Aaron included. Since we must posit an internal narrative logic in P^g, the sin must consist in these words.

59. J. L. McKenzie, 'Historical Prologue' (see n. 2 above), 97, seems to assign both Num. 20:12 and Num. 1:2 to JE; on this basis, he develops a special interpretation of Moses' sin in Deuteronomy 1 (DtrG). But that Num. 20: 12 belongs to P^g should not be subject to any doubt, in light of Deut. 32:51 (and Num. 27:14).

60. There is a similar formulation, in the *piel*, in Deut. 32:51.

which stems from the same tradition. Nevertheless, there may be some suspicion that the root *qdš* is employed *at this point* in particular because in the old tradition the story was geographically connected with the oasis of Kadesh. The priestly narrative does not mention this localizing, probably because according to its theory Kadesh was part of the land of Canaan,[61] into which, at this stage of their history, the Israelites cannot yet have entered. But the incidental use of the root *qdš* could be an external nod, typical of the priestly writing, to an element in the content of the old sources that has been bypassed. Thus the decisive description of the sin remains: it consists in a lack of faith and trust. That is the sin of the mediators between Israel and God.

(c) Why is this sin not only narrated, but in fact created? The usual answer is that this historical writer, who is such a systematic thinker, has offered an adequate explanation for the fact, known from tradition, that Moses and Aaron did not enter the promised land. The explanation found in the work of the Deuteronomist, that Moses was barred from the land because he served as a kind of hostage for his sinful people,[62] did not fit in with this author's much more individualistic theology.[63]

But perhaps, even if we accept this reasoning, we may see still another analogy to the other two stories of sin. Here, as there, the priestly writing would have been directed to its own readers in exile or in the diaspora. It called their attention to the special danger that threatened, in particular, their prophets and spiritual leaders. If the people and their political leaders were in danger of failing to recognize the value of a return to the land of Canaan, the religious heads of the exiles and the people in the diaspora may gradually have begun to forget to proclaim the miraculous power of YHWH, for whom even the impossible is possible.

Conclusion

The priestly historical work thus speaks of sin in a very considered manner. It does not introduce any universal concept of sin; rather, each of the sins described has its own special name. There is the sin of all people,

61. Cf. Num. 34:4. Num. 34:1–12 should (against Noth, but according to an unpublished essay by E. Cortese) be assigned to P^g.

62. Cf. Deut. 1:37; 3:23–26; also 4:21–22. Moreover, this has to do with Moses, and P^g also needed a rationale for the exclusion of Aaron, who is so important to this writer.

63. On this feature of the theology of P^g, which again demonstrates its connection with Ezekiel, see Scharbert, 'Prolegomena' (n. 1 above), 99–100.

which contravenes the order of the good creation: violence among human beings. Then there is a special sin of the chosen people of God; it, too, can be materially described. This is contempt, on the part of the political leaders and the whole people, for the good gift that is offered them; it is the slandering of the land of Canaan. And for the spiritual leaders, it is a failure to fulfill their mission to believe in YHWH's miraculous power and to show YHWH to the people as the Holy One who is present and active in their midst. The three sins seem to have been formulated to speak to a particular situation in the life of Israel, and at the same time they are so well marked out and systematically related to one another within the historical narrative that we must believe that they are meant to indicate 'original sins,' from which the essential elements of a doctrine of sin can be derived.

5

God the Creator and the Stability of Heaven and Earth

The Old Testament on the Connection between Creation and Salvation

First let me indicate how I conceive the purpose of this gathering. Some years ago, Gerhard Nebel published a volume of essays entitled *Sprung von des Tigers Rücken.*[1] He was referring to a Chinese proverb according to which it is impossible to dismount from a tiger while in motion. The fate of anyone riding a tiger is unavoidable. Nebel says that for him the tiger is the image of technological civilization. It races forward so swiftly that it even jeopardizes the habitability of the earth and raises doubts whether Adam will reach the third millennium. We are reminded of the tiger because the process that has begun is one of enormous active and 'biting' power. We have to agree with the Chinese proverb, at least so far as it applies to humanity in general: 'I see no possibility of a return to the archaic; I can neither believe in the return of the gods nor in a coming liturgy and revelation; neither in a destruction of industry nor in a cleansing of the water and the air; nor can I believe in an overcoming of boredom and the anarchy that is born of it – that is, in some future ethic. I consider the overall situation hopeless, and I also believe it is comparatively unimportant whether our downfall occurs through capitalism or planning, democracy or fascism.'[2] But every human being is an individual, and as such does not need to submit to the general decline. '[He or she] can leap from the back of the ferocious beast, but

1. Stuttgart, 1970.

2. Ibid., 5–6.

only for him- or herself or for a small circle of friends.'[3] He prefers to speak of such opportunities to dismount, things such as reverence for God, or fantasy, drunkenness, sports, the enjoyment of ruins, or walking in the forest.

This deeply reflective denial by a sorrowful humanist of any ethic for this world is not only similar, in its despair, to the leap out of the world characteristic of all the gnostic movements at the end of the ancient period, but is at the same time *one* form of expression of a mood of detachment that is much more widespread at the present time, a distancing from responsibility for the world in favor of salvation of the individual and perhaps of a small group of friends. It may be combined with Zen or yoga or with a retreat into the private home and garden, or equally – and that is what is important here – with a traditional Christian system of values in which words like salvation and redemption are writ large, but where other words like earthly reality, humanity, and creation appear seldom or only in the margins. This is true in spite of the many contrary, and very popular, theologies of recent years.

Our gathering, as I understand it, is intended to pose the counter-question whether our faith, founded on the Bible, does not challenge us, despite all proverbial wisdom to the contrary, to attempt to curb the racing tiger on which we are riding. This responsibility our faith places upon us, if it is true that the message of salvation has something to do (not only superficially, but at its heart) with a word about God the creator and about the world as God's creation. That is why we pose, in this context, the question of a *theology of creation.*

Our view of this question is at the present time *socially obscured.* Religion is a minor segment in postmodern society. The other spheres of life have their own independent basis in knowledge. As a consequence, talk about salvation no longer refers to the whole. No matter what theologians and pastors may say, it is necessarily connected to the individual or the small community in which people come together. Talk about creation has no foothold at all in our lives today, no place in which it could be usefully located. For the multiplicity of separate segments of life are, as we know, only held together by some vague general notions.[4] If we properly intend to connect salvation and creation and to establish the responsibility of faith for this world and its future, then not only is the

3. Ibid., 6.

4. Here let me refer especially to Thomas Luckmann's theses in the field of sociology of religions.

privatistic notion of salvation shared by many of our contemporaries wrong, but the whole structure of our society appears questionable, and even dangerous. I wanted to have that said so that no one will regard the theological project that we have undertaken as something harmless.

In addition, I am here as an Old Testament scholar. Consequently, you should not expect any synthesis that will immediately address the concrete problems of the present. Instead, what I will present are some suggestions that are utterly strange to us, drawn from a literature from the distant past that, however, because of its strangeness together with the biblical authority that persists for us Christians despite all this, offers ideas that are able to derail our usual trains of thought and to move us to new ways of thinking. Further steps must remain for other speakers after me to take.

I have no interest in offering information about everything that the Old Testament has to say on this subject, and I intend to set aside the discussions of the topic that have preoccupied our scholarly field in recent decades, despite their interest and importance. Here I am referring, for example, to the regularly reappearing question of the *theological position* of belief in creation within the whole of Old Testament faith concerning salvation. Since its origin in the year 1935, when Gerhard von Rad proposed this theme for the first time at a meeting in Göttingen,[5] it has been far too closely connected with the narrowing of the question necessitated by the conflict of the Confessing Church with the tendencies of the churches to accommodate themselves to the ideology of the Third Reich, an accommodation that sought legitimation in a theology of creation, even though this is scarcely evident in the subsequent literature. Another question is that of the *antiquity* of Israel's belief in creation. In recent years this has focused primarily on the question of the time at which one may reckon with an identity between YHWH, the liberating god of Israel, and El, the Canaanite creator god. The date is being pushed steadily backward as more is known about Canaanite religion. Quite recently, the excavations at Ebla have revealed a religious-historical turning point in local personal names at around the year 2400 (more than a millennium before Moses), in the period of King Ebrum, at which time the god El is called by the new name of Ya(w). This finding is utterly dizzying: in Ebla at that early period, the name Mi-kà-Il was being replaced by the name Mi-kà-Jà, and for the name Iš-ra-Il was being

5. 'Das theologische Problem des alttestamentlichen Schöpfungsglaubens,' in *Werden und Wesen des Alten Testaments*, BZAW (1936), 138–47.

substituted the name Iš-ra-Jà.[6] But those are problems in the history of religions. We are more interested in the definitive Old Testament, which encounters us as message. That should also be said with reference to the important dissertation by Rainer Albertz, written at Heidelberg in 1972, in which he shows that in Israel people originally spoke of creation in two very different contexts: not only the creation of the world, in the context of the cultic praise of God, but also the creation of the individual human person by that person's own God, in the context of lament and rescue.[7] Here, then, we have a context in which rescue (that is, redemption and salvation), was immediately and originally connected with knowledge of creation and the creator, and where it is not at all evident how the two motif-complexes can be kept separate from one another. But in the first instance all this is primarily interesting from a religious-historical point of view.

For the following considerations I would like to isolate a single literary and theological complex and develop the contours of its proclamation: I refer to the 'priestly historical narrative' in the Pentateuch. Despite recent counter-arguments, including those of Frank Moore Cross[8] and Rolf Rendtorff,[9] it can be clearly distinguished both from the old sources of the Pentateuch and also from priestly legal material that was added later: it is an originally independent document.[10] There can be little doubt that it originated near the end of the Babylonian exile or shortly afterward. It begins with Genesis 1, the best defined creation

6. See the article by G. Pettinato in *Biblical Archeologist* 39 (1976): 48.

7. *Weltschöpfung und Menschenschöpfung,* Calwer Theologische Monographien 3 (Stuttgart, 1974).

8. *Canaanite Myth and Hebrew Epic* (Cambridge, Mass., 1973).

9. 'Das überlieferungsgeschichtliche Problem des Pentateuch,' BZAW 147 (1976).

10. For the external limits, one may most practically consult K. Elliger, 'Sinn und Ursprung der priesterlichen Geschichtserzählung,' *ZthK* 49 (1952): 121, reprinted in his *Kleine Schriften zum Alten Testament* (Munich, 1966), 174–75. It is true that Elliger follows Martin Noth's theory, according to which the priestly historical narrative ends in Deuteronomy 34. In contrast, I believe that the concluding passages of this document are found in the book of Joshua, although P had no theory of a violent seizure of the land. It is important for the following exposition that Josh. 18:1 was part of the original priestly historical narrative. Within Genesis–Numbers also, my assignment of passages differs from Elliger's in some places, but these differences are unimportant for what follows. A selected printing of the priestly historical narrative as a single document can be found in R. Smend, *Alttestamentliches Lesebuch,* Siebenstern-Taschenbuch 182 (Hamburg, 1974), 88–124.

text in the whole Old Testament, as well as the best known. In fact, it is an all too common mistake to interpret this text in isolation. In contrast, in what follows I wish to regard it (to put the matter in a nutshell) as only a single building block in the entire systematic expression that is the priestly writing. The priestly writing's doctrine of creation is only completed with its last words within the book of Joshua.

If what I am about to say sounds different in some respects from what is to be found in exegetical literature, it is only because I wish to attempt to interpret the priestly writing as a *single* systematic expression. What is the relationship of the realities known as 'creation' and 'salvation' to one another within this work from the end of the sixth century BCE, which presents itself, in literary terms, as a historical narrative, but in its content is thoroughly theological and systematic in its intention? What are the consequences for our world of this relationship between God's attitude and human responsibility?

The first step to be taken is introductory in nature.

1. *The priestly writing envisions the world not as something thrusting dynamically forward, but as a system that moves from dynamism to stability*

We should probably regard the priestly writing as a kind of counter-project to the eschatological view of history that arose during the Babylonian exile among the prophets and branches of the deuteronomistic movement, culminating in the intense expectation of the rapidly approaching end that is evident in Deutero-Isaiah. This represented a dynamic projection of history toward the future. The old had passed away, and something new and greater was approaching, something that God was in the very act of creating in the midst of the nations. The covenant with the ancestors was past and a new covenant unlike the old was about to appear.

Here the priestly narrative offers resistance. From its point of view, no new covenant is necessary. The *covenant* that God had promised to *Abraham*[11] was an eternal bond, entirely the initiative and promise of God that could not be abrogated by any human sin. A sinful generation might fall away from it. In that case, death would pursue them; they would be destroyed in the desert.[12] But the old promises are simply renewed for the next generation.

11. Genesis 17.

12. Cf. Numbers 14.

And the Abrahamic covenant, in turn, is encompassed by the *Noachic covenant.*[13] It, too, is an eternal covenant. All human beings and all beasts, in fact the whole universe, has received God's promise never again to bring forth a flood – that is, never again to cause a collapse of the whole world order. The Egyptians, who had built their cities out of the sweat and groanings of an enslaved Israel, are swallowed by the waters of the sea.[14] But the edifice of the world endures, and rescued Israel can begin its trek to the land God has assigned to it. The covenant with Abraham and, before it, the covenant with Noah, are the theological guarantees of the world's stability.

One might object that the priestly writing also depicts a constant dynamic and development. Here, too, shortly after creation we find the enormous threat to the continuity of the world represented by the Flood, which is only halted at the last minute.[15] And besides, the history of the people of Israel from Abraham to Joshua, as depicted here, is all a single movement and dramatic development. Thus the world and the history of the priestly writing are also dynamic rather than stable.

In fact, what the priestly narrative relates is a forward-thrusting dynamic. But the question is: what is the significance for its entire world view of that period in world history that the priestly writing describes? I would like to approach an answer to this question by a roundabout route: by way of our present dynamizing of the world and the ancient Mesopotamian struggle with a similar set of problems.

The increasingly powerful processes that threaten to destroy the fabric of our world depend, to a considerable extent, on the growth of population that is on the verge of becoming a veritable explosion. It presses us to continually broader urbanization, to a production of foodstuffs that does increasing violence to the land, to a steadily accelerating exploitation of our planet's stores of energy and raw materials. As a result, the question of dynamism versus stability is at the present time not solely, but very urgently a question of a continued increase of the human population or of setting goals toward a stabilization of our numbers.

However, this problem of overpopulation appeared, in analogous fashion, in the ancient world: analogously, because given the available forms of transportation in that period such a problem could occur within a

13. Genesis 9.

14. Exodus 14.

15. Genesis 6–9.

limited geographical area, and also because at that time there were still fewer technical means at hand to avert famine from a population that was increasing too rapidly. In any case, the early development of the Mesopotamian culture based on cities and irrigation could be traceable to population pressure. Even after this culture was in place, it appears that the threat of overpopulation arose periodically anew.

One witness to this, which is interesting for us precisely in connection with the priestly writing, is the Atrahasis Epic, the most important work of that genre that we possess from the dawn of Mesopotamia. In the version we know best, it contains 1,245 verses and was composed by the scribe Ku-Aja in the seventeenth century BCE, but in the middle of the first millennium BCE, when the priestly document was written in Babylon, it was still one of the best known and most widely read works of ancient literature.[16] If my teacher, Professor William L. Moran of Harvard University,[17] and Professor Anne D. Kilmer of the University of California at Berkeley[18] have not gone completely off the track in their exciting interpretations of this epic, the problem of overpopulation is one of the major themes of the poem, and is treated in connection with the question of the endurance and stability of the world.

The epic begins with the gods in the already existing but still humanless world. There is work that needs to be done in the world, and the superior gods force the inferior ones to do all the work alone. After a while, the inferior gods revolt, and it is for that reason that human beings are created. From this point on, they are to do the work, and in order that there will be enough humans for the purpose, they are equipped to reproduce themselves. But this mechanism is so effective that soon the number of human beings is so great and the noise they make is so loud that some of the gods can no longer sleep in their palaces; they decide to decimate or even destroy humanity. Since other gods take the side of the humans, the first attempts at destruction (famine and plagues) fail. Then a radical final solution is attempted: the Flood is brought forth. But Atrahasis, the favorite of the god of Wisdom, is also rescued from the Flood, and for his sake and that of his progeny the rival divine parties come to an agreement. They produce what I would call the great post-

16. There is a scholarly edition with an English translaton: W. G. Lambert and A. R. Millard, *Atra-Ḫasis. The Babylonian Story of the Flood* (Oxford, 1969).

17. 'Atrahasis: The Babylonian Story of the Flood,' *Bibl* 52 (1971): 51–61.

18. 'The Mesopotamian Concept of Overpopulation and Its Solution as Reflected in the Mythology,' *Or* 41 (1972): 160–77.

Flood divine compromise: on the one hand, in the future human beings will have the right to exist, since, after all, the gods need them to do the work of the world. But on the other hand, their number is fixed at a third of the previous total. So that they will not again increase beyond it, means are introduced for limiting the population: the barrenness of many women, infant mortality, and the institution of unmarried and therefore childless priestesses. Thus the contrary forces in the world itself have swung to a midpoint – for these Mesopotamian gods are the fundamental forces of the universe itself.

Here the Atrahasis epic ends. It need tell nothing further, since now the world is the way it should be and will remain. The dynamic of the world's coming to be, as regards the existence, function and number of human beings and the fundamental danger they have posed to the world-edifice is ended. The stable condition of the world in which humanity now lives, and in which it is to remain, has begun. The message of the Atrahasis epic is thus that of a stable world, even though the subject of the narrative is that world's dynamic prehistory.

The same is true of the priestly writing. Even the older strata of the Pentateuch (the 'Yahwist,' as is usually supposed) took inspiration from the Atrahasis epic for the account of the world's origins, for example in treating the topic of 'work' and in the narrative of the Flood. But here the dependency was more superficial. In contrast, the priestly writing appears to adopt the basic form and fundamental statement of the epic, in addition to some of its content, in its attack on its contemporaries' dynamic vision of the future.

It is true that in the priestly writing, the dynamizing element is not the excessive increase of population, but human and animal *deviation from the God-given order of things*. But apart from this, it also has the narrative scheme according to which, by way of a series of critical and dynamic situations, a kind of final compromise is achieved that leads to stable relationships. This structure is even repeated two successive times in the priestly writing, once for the fabric of the world itself, and again for the world's population.

The world is made in such a way that both human beings and beasts are meant to use only the plants for food.[19] But the creatures do not abide by this order. Violence escalates, and as a result the world, which was created as good, in fact very good, is in a decaying condition.[20] God, by

19. Gen. 1:29.

20. Gen. 6:9–13.

bringing the Flood (a genuine reduction of the world to the original chaos) only carries the decay of the world, which is already in progress, to its conclusion. But God saves Noah, who had not adopted violent ways, from the catastrophe and, at the last moment, halts the destruction of the world. After the Flood comes the compromise that, under the monotheistic presuppositions of the priestly writing, obviously cannot be made between rival groups of gods, but instead is proclaimed by the one, transcendent creator God in a sovereign decree. It is the introduction of something like a second-best world order. The peace between human and animal that was characteristic of Paradise is replaced by a new order of war: note, a war between human and animal, not between human beings. Concretely, this means that meat can be eaten and the consumption of flesh is no longer regarded as a deed of violence.[21] This in turn decreases the measure of possible violence so much that God is in a position to give an eternal promise, in the Noachic covenant, never again to bring forth a Flood.[22] Thus is the fabric of the world made stable.

But a further dynamic emerges among the inhabitants of this structure. According to God's plan of creation ('Be fruitful and multiply, and fill the earth')[23] humanity, now at a tiny, new beginning, must multiply, expand, and enter, nation by nation, into the places planned for them by God. This is not described in the priestly document as it applies to all peoples, but only in the people Israel as an example. Abraham receives the land of Canaan as his portion.[24] In the next generation, his tribe multiplies. But then, when the full number of the people is reached and the blessing of fruitfulness therefore comes to an end,[25] this people is living in a foreign land, in Egypt, where it is enslaved.[26] Thus a new dynamic and a new instability arises. YHWH delivers the people from Egypt and leads them through the wilderness into their designated land. There are still complications along the way, because of the sins of the people themselves. But finally, at the border of Canaan, the dynamic

21. Gen. 9:1–6.

22. Gen. 9:7–17.

23. Gen. 1:28. On the meaning and function of this important verse, see N. Lohfink, ''Macht euch die Erde untertan?'' *Orientierung* 38 (1974): 137–42 (Chapter 1 of this book).

24. Gen. 17:8.

25. Exod. 1:7.

26. Exod. 1:13–14.

period is at an end. The nation's leadership structures are revised by God: now, in the Land, the priests can assume leadership, since dynamic leaders like Moses are no longer necessary.[27] This is something like a second compromise in the priestly document, concluding a second dynamic situation and bringing a transition to stability.

The analogy of this narrative structure to that of the Atrahasis epic is obvious. Hence the same basic statement is also present: however dynamic the beginnings may have been, once the world and humanity have arrived at their full dimensions and proper order, the world can and should *remain as it is.* And when the addressees of the priestly writing, although they are Israelites, are no longer *de facto* living in the land of Canaan, this is a temporary disruption that should be alleviated by God as soon as possible, if human resistance does not intervene to hinder the process. As a whole, our world is conceived as a stable entity, and God's eternal covenant promises are an expression of that stability.

If, as Carl Amery and others suppose,[28] there is a biblical influence on our thoroughly dynamized world of today, it ultimately derives from the dynamic view of history proposed by the exilic prophets. If we at the present time cry out for stability, the priestly writing is already ahead of us. Within this message about a world that is willed to achieve stability in the wake of its original dynamism, we must now inquire about the relationship between creation and salvation [Heil].

2. *According to the priestly writing, salvation is primarily a successful creation: the good life of the nations in their lands*

We can pose the question about salvation in the priestly writing at two different points: either with Abraham, when a land is given to the people God desires as a particular possession, or with the leading of the people out of Egypt, where salvation appears as rescue, deliverance and redemption. At both points the priestly document offers highly reflective basic theological texts, for Abraham in Genesis 17 and for the deliverance from Egypt in Exodus 6. The two texts contain clear signals referring them to one another. In Genesis 17, God gives a covenant to Abraham, and in Exodus 6 Moses learns from God of God's intention to deliver Israel from Egyptian oppression because God remembers that covenant. In fact, there is identity in the content of what is promised to Abraham and that for

27. Num. 27:12–23.

28. See especially C. Amery, *Das Ende der Vorsehung. Die gnadenlosen Folgen des Christentums* (Hamburg, 1972).

which Israel is to be delivered from Egypt. In Gen. 17:7–8, we read God's words to Abraham:

> I will establish my covenant between me and you, and your offspring after you throughout their generations, for an everlasting covenant, to be God to you and to your offspring after you. And I will give to you, and to your offspring after you, the land where you are now an alien, all the land of Canaan, for a perpetual holding; and I will be their God.

Here the statement that the God who is appearing will be Israel's God frames the other promise to give Israel the land of Canaan. We find the same double promise in Exod. 6:6-8:

> I am YHWH, and I will free you from the burdens of the Egyptians and deliver you from slavery to them. I will redeem you with an outstretched arm and with mighty acts of judgment. I will take you as my people, and I will be your God. You shall know that I am YHWH your God, who has freed you from the burdens of the Egyptians. I will bring you into the land that I swore to give to Abraham, Isaac, and Jacob; I will give it to you for a possession. I am YHWH.

Thus we can describe the twofold content of salvation in the sense of the priestly writing as *the land of Canaan* and *the special relationship between God and Israel.* Let us first consider the entity 'land of Canaan.' The fact that this refers not merely to the possession of the land, but to the people's peaceful and happy life in this land, is a matter of course for the priestly writing, which summarizes everything in the simplest possible concept. It requires no lengthy proof.[29]

The great significance for the priestly writing of the *land as YHWH's good gift* is spotlighted by one of that document's rare, but therefore all the more important narratives concerning sin: the story of the sending out of the scouts in Numbers 13 and 14.[30] In the pacifistic priestly writing it is

29. On 'land' in P, see E. Cortese, *La terra di Canaan nella storia sacerdotale del Pentateuco* (Brescia, 1972).

30. On this and other narratives of sin, see N. Lohfink, 'Die Ursünden in der priesterlichen Geschichtserzählung,' in G. Bornkamm and K. Rahner, eds., *Die Zeit Jesu,* Festschrift for H. Schlier (Freiburg, 1970), 38–57 (Chapter 4 of this book).

not a hostile troop of spies, but a sort of sacred group of land inspectors who, in the name of their people, are to look over the gift of God that lies before them.[31] This they do in a procession, lasting forty days, from the extreme South to the extreme North of the land, and then, on their return, they proclaim their verdict over the land before the assembly of the people. It is negative. Canaan is said to be a land that devours its inhabitants. The congregation joins in this judgment with a loud cry. The result is that this whole generation is condemned to die in the wilderness. Only the following generation will be able to enter the land, because for them YHWH's old promise to Abraham will be revived. The priestly writing also has a precise definition for this sin: it is 'calumny of the land' in the sense of a slander of YHWH's specific, good and saving gift.[32]

The next generation does not commit this sin, and at the end of the priestly writing they enter into the promised land. In one of the last sentences of the whole work, after the people have taken possession of the land (a process that is to be conceived as entirely peaceful), we find an expression that brings us to the question we have posed concerning the relationship of salvation and creation. For in Josh. 18:1 we read:

> Then the whole congregation of the Israelites assembled at Shiloh, and set up the tent of meeting there. The land lay subdued before them.

The fact that they had taken possession of the land is expressed here, at the end of the priestly document, with the aid of a word that had not been used in the whole narrative before this, except at the very beginning, at the climax of the description of creation. This is the word *kābaš*, literally meaning something like 'to set one's foot on something,' not, however, to be understood in the sense of subjugating, exploiting, or trampling; instead, especially when applied to a territory, it should be understood to mean 'to take possession of.'[33] As Odil Hannes Steck has shown,[34] God's words in

31. Cf. S. E. McEvenue, *The Narrative Style of the Priestly Writer* (Rome, 1971), 117–23. He demonstrates how an original narrative of a military spying expedition has been demilitarized by P. Something similar could be shown for the narrative of the Reed Sea (Exodus 14). Besides this, there is no military capture of the land: its absence in P has often served as a ground for calling into question the presence of any P texts at all in the book of Joshua. Taken altogether, P narrates not a single war or battle.

32. Num. 13:32.

33. For more detail, see the article cited in n. 23 above.

34. *Der Schöpfungsbericht der Priesterschrift* (Göttingen, 1975).

the creation account in Genesis 1 are by no means immediately and fully accomplished in the act of creation. Instead, God here sets forth the final condition of the world at which God is aiming; the creative work that follows immediately after these words of creation only establishes the beginnings from which, then, rapidly or slowly, the fully accomplished creation will come to be. This is also true of the blessing that God speaks over the first human beings immediately after their creation. In Gen. 1:28 God says:

> Be fruitful and multiply, and fill the earth and take possession of it.

This can only mean that humanity, so small at the beginning, is to increase, to become many peoples that spread out over the earth and then each, nation by nation, take possession of their own territory.

In Joshua 18 we reach the culmination of this development, as the goal established at creation achieves its fulfillment in the final stage of the world's development. The fully narrated example is that of the people of Israel. A nation has reached its completed development and has entered into its own land and taken possession of it. That the creation has here reached its successful outcome and that Israel has achieved its salvation are one and the same thing.

This salvation is, at least as far as its first element, 'land,' is concerned, not something added to creation, but rather is the fulfillment of creation itself. When the world's reality is as creation's God wished it to be, salvation is present. Rescue and redemption leading to salvation fall within this frame. Israel only has to be delivered from Egypt because Egypt is not the land destined for it, and because slavery represents the exact opposite of free life in the people's own land.[35]

Any concern for a salvation that is not identical with responsible concern for the success of God's creation is therefore, as far as we have seen to this point, unthinkable within the framework of the theology of the priestly writing.

Of course, we still must ask whether the second part of the content of the covenant with Abraham and the promise of the exodus changes the picture: namely, the statement that YHWH desires to be Israel's God.

3. *According to the priestly writing, salvation is also the immanence of the transcendent God in a creation extended by human labor: the encounter with God in cultic worship*

Since the priestly writing relates its key texts clearly to one another by the

35. See the programmatic text Exod. 6:2–8.

use of fixed cue words, there can be no doubt what it means by the apparently obscure formula, 'I will be their God.' After being liberated from Egypt, Israel proceeds to Sinai. There the glory of YHWH rests on the mountain; Moses is summoned to the mountain top, into the burning fire, and there he receives instructions for the building of the sanctuary. In the original priestly document, these instructions conclude with Exod. 29:43–46:

> I will meet with the Israelites there [in the tent of meeting], and it shall be sanctified by my glory; I will consecrate the tent of meeting and the altar; Aaron also and his sons I will consecrate, to serve me as priests. I will dwell among the Israelites, and I will be their God. And they shall know that I am YHWH their God, who brought them out of the land of Egypt that I might dwell among them. I am YHWH their God.

Therefore the fact that YHWH is Israel's God means concretely that YHWH *can be encountered within Israel, in cultic worship.* Now it is also understandable why in Josh. 18:1, toward the end of the priestly document, where it is said that Israel has taken possession of its land, it is reported at the same time that the tent of meeting has been set up within this land, in Shiloh. That is the second element of salvation as the priestly document sees it. Both these things are fulfilled at the end of the priestly narrative: taking possession of the land and the cultic presence of God. Of course it appears that the second element is something that was not, like the first, already prepared for in Genesis 1; it seems that it cannot be traced so simply to creation and its realization.

In fact, at this point we have touched on one of the most difficult problems in interpretation of the priestly narrative, although Old Testament scholars have scarcely noticed that a problem exists. This is the question whether, for the priestly writing, Israel is really a special, chosen people of God, or whether it is only a nation whose history is narrated as an example, even though, strictly speaking, a similar history would have to be traced for every nation on earth. I must admit that I do not see a clear answer to this question. I suspect that the priestly writing itself leaves the matter open. Our preconceptions are so strongly shaped by the deuteronomic theology of election that we often overlook the fact that there are also other initiatives in Old Testament thought, for example in the Wisdom literature, in older historical narratives, or in the words of prophets like Amos. Hence it is not absolutely clear that the priestly writing held the opinion that there could be no cultic presence of God in the world beyond Israel. It would at least not be excluded that the cultic presence of God as salvation has something to do with all nations and, consequently, with the creation that encompasses the whole world.[36]

But we can make a good deal more progress if we pay closer attention to the priestly Sinai pericope, which contains the priestly theology of cultic worship. Here we make the astonishing discovery that its narrative structure is related to Genesis 1, the description of creation.[37]

Genesis 1 is constructed as a depiction of the work of God in six working days, to which is added the day of divine rest as a seventh day and completion of the whole. The same theme of six days plus a seventh begins the whole Sinai pericope. In Exod. 24:15–18 we read:

> Then Moses went up on the mountain, and the cloud covered the mountain. The glory of YHWH settled on Mount Sinai, and the cloud covered it for six days; on the seventh day YHWH called to Moses out of the cloud. Now the appearance of the glory of YHWH was like a devouring fire on the top of the mountain in the sight of the people of Israel. Moses entered the cloud . . .

Thus the seventh day is not only the day of rest from labor, but at the same time it is the day when God and creatures meet within the fire.

At first, this encounter is reserved for Moses. But the central significance of the Sinai narrative is to demonstrate how this encounter is made transferable, so that it can happen for the whole congregation. Therefore Moses, within the fire, receives the model for the sanctuary, which undoubtedly is heaven itself, the place where God's own glory shines forth.[38] Therefore the tent of meeting is built, and the cloud of God's presence moves from Sinai, the world mountain, into the sanctuary, where it is possible for all to encounter God in cultic praise.[39]

When the work of construction is complete, and when the tent has

36. In this connection, however, let me expressly point out that no theology of other religions can be derived from the Noachic covenant in the priestly narrative (as a covenant with all humanity) – something that is occasionally proposed nowadays. The Noachic covenant has nothing to do with cult or other religious institutions.

37. On what follows, see especially M. Oliva, 'Interpretación teológica del culto en la perícopa del Sinaí de la Historia Sacerdotal,' *Bibl* 49 (1968): 348–51; N. Negretti, *Il settimo giorno* (Rome, 1973), 224–51.

38. Exod. 25:30.

39. Lev. 9:24.

been set up and the builders present it to Moses, another series of verbal echoes of Genesis 1 appears.[40] Moses finishes the work as God finished the work of creation. And just as God had looked at each individual work and seen that it was good, so Moses now surveys the work on the sanctuary, and see, everything has been made exactly as YHWH commanded. And when the work is done and the tent stands ready, on the festival day, the encounter of the community with the present God begins.

Therefore there should be no doubt that in the priestly document the building of the sanctuary is paralleled with the divine building of the world, and the encounter with God in cultic worship within the sanctuary is paralleled with the divine rest on the seventh day after the completion of creation. We might even say, from a variety of narrative considerations, that they are identified.

To see this still more clearly, however, we need to take up a further theme that in the priestly writing is inextricably bound up with those of creation and cult: *labor* and *rest.*[41]

In Mesopotamian anthropology, human beings were made by the gods in order that there might be an entity in the world that would bear the yoke and the carrying basket, that would shoulder the burdens and do the work. Originally it was gods who did this. Hence the human beings were made as *images* of *god,* so that they could carry out this onerous, but originally divine task. In this way, the gods were freed from work and became leisured beings.

In the priestly writing the creator god is a god who works and rests, who expresses the divine self outwards and also remains within that self. The human beings are made in the image of this god. Are they made merely to work, as in Mesopotamia? The priestly narrative raises the first doubts about such an understanding when it shows the creator blessing the rest of the seventh day.[42] For in the priestly writing, blessing means the power of increase. But where can the divine sabbath increase and multiply, if not within creation itself?

40. Exod. 39:32, 42–43; 40:17, 33–35.

41. See more on this topic in my book, *Unsere großen Wörter. Das Alte Testament zu Themen dieser Jahre* (Freiburg im Breisgau, 1977), ch. 12: 'Freizeit: Arbeitswoche und Sabbat im Alten Testament, insbesondere in der priesterlichen Geschichtserzählung,' 190–208. [English translation by Ronald Walls: *Great Themes from the Old Testament* (Edinburgh, 1982), chap. 12, 'Leisure. The Work Week and the Sabbath in the Old Testament, and Especially in the Priestly Chronicle,' 203–21].

42. Gen. 2:3.

The theme is taken up again much later, when Israel is in Egypt. There the people are enslaved to work in the fields, that is, to care for the basis of life, and to labor in building cities, which indicates care for the transformation of the existing world through culture.[43] It is hard work. Nothing is said about rest. This is the image the priestly narrative paints of false work contrary to God's intention, work that degrades creation and alienates human beings. It is from this work that God delivers and redeems the people of Israel.

During its wandering in the wilderness, Israel then learns about true labor that does not alienate and that corresponds to the work of creation. First there is labor for food: the manna narrative in Exodus 16 serves this purpose. Here the Israelites learn to adapt themselves to nature. The key word is 'gather.' People gather what the earth offers them. They gather only what they need, and surprisingly enough, they find just as much as they need. In particular, on the sixth day they find a double portion, and on the seventh day nothing at all. That means that when Israel, in its labor, approaches creation with the calm composure of liberated human beings, creation in turn will reveal to the people its previously hidden secret of the rhythm of work and celebration.

But human labor is not only for the purpose of extracting food from nature. It is also and essentially a creative transformation of the world. The truth of this is underscored by the Sinai pericope as a story of the building of the sanctuary. This, too, is a counter-narrative to the work world of Egyptian slaves. In the texts covering the building of the sanctuary there is a piling up of words describing generosity, hearts that are stirred, willing offerings, and individual skills that are brought into play.[44] Here labor is done in a way that develops humans themselves as creative beings. This is true even though, or precisely because they adhere scrupulously to what God commanded Moses on the mountain, so that the sanctuary is built according to its heavenly model in every detail. It is only this work, which fulfills creation in a creativity that is human, but at the same time is entirely oriented beyond itself and toward God, that makes it possible for God's transcendence to become immanence, so that in the festival God becomes present and thereby also becomes Israel's God.

Our initial question was how that element of salvation which the priestly writing depicts as the cultic nearness of God to Israel relates to the

43. Exod. 1:13–14; 2:23–25.

44. Exod. 35:5, 21, 29; 36:2.

order of creation. It has appeared that matters are more complicated and subtle in this second instance than in the first element of salvation, the happy life in the land. What is at stake here is the immanence of the transcendent. But in the priestly narrative it is brought into close connection with the human as a creative being that labors, with the human as image of God, and with the transformation of creation by human labor. The cultic nearness of God comes about when human beings, as image of God, achieve a rhythm in their work of transforming the world, a rhythm between labor and leisure, and when their labor achieves a transformation of the world within which festival makes encounter possible.

We might say that the priestly narrative leaves open the question whether God remains free, even after the sanctuary has been built, to enter into it in divine glory or not; that is, whether the promise to Abraham to be Israel's God is not something that cannot be necessarily deduced from the creation as described in Genesis 1. But on the other hand, without that word of God to Abraham and without what then happens on Sinai as a result, the most important lines of this creation narrative, namely the saying about the human being as image of God and the designation of creation as a week composed of labor and festival, would remain unconnected. They would be left hanging in the air. We can at least say that when God gives salvation as nearness to God, then this only happens in combination with the completion of the creator's *creatio* by the cultural creativity of human beings that makes the world a temple. But that is as close a connection between salvation and creation as we could possibly imagine.

Conclusion

This brings me to some concluding thoughts. The author of the priestly narrative was not faced with the questions that the world now presses upon us. He was not terrified either by a population explosion or by a threat that the planet might become uninhabitable through irresponsible exploitation. Consequently, he does not provide us with a direct answer to our question regarding human responsibility toward the earth.

But indirectly he projects an image of human beings in the world, especially in his teaching about human labor, its attachment to the heavenly model and its direction toward the cult of praise, that condemns every kind of dynamic that is destructive of the world, every kind of disruption of the stable goods of this world brought about by the assertion of human autonomy, as blasphemous and anti-human. Beyond this, in the priestly narrative salvation and creation are so closely related to one another that those who spoil creation forfeit their own salvation.

Hence there is no salvation for human beings apart from creation. There is no way to jump down from the tiger, such that the individual or a small group of friends can withdraw from responsibility for this world.

Of course, we must take account of the relativity of the theology of the priestly narrative. Even though it may be the most impressive theological proposal in the whole Old Testament, it is still only one among many. It is in flat contradiction to all eschatological projects, which at least at first glance seem to have gained the upper hand in the New Testament. I say 'at first glance,' because when it is proclaimed that in Jesus everything is fulfilled, and that with him time has reached its end, that is also the assertion, once again, of a halting of the historical dynamic that is supposed to have happened at least at the time of Jesus.

At a minimum, this theology needs to be lifted to a higher level of abstraction. In place of the nearness of God in cultic worship, there appears the nearness of God in the human being, Jesus, and his community.[45] The proposition that the beginning of the transformation of the world from a dynamic to a stable condition was accomplished when the Israelites crossed the Jordan was somewhat too clever. For a number of reasons, it may have become necessary only at the beginning of the third millennium.

And even if we transpose the priestly narrative in this way, we cannot deny that certain 'last things' are still concealed in it. It is true that it acknowledges no further war, but it is simply silent on the subject rather than condemning it, and its God is still a God who kills. Hence this God legitimates the shedding of blood at least in one dimension, the relationship between human and animal, apparently because it was not yet possible to contemplate a completely nonviolent world. Correspondingly, the cult accepts bloody sacrifices. All this needs to be rethought from the perspective of Jesus of Nazareth, the witness to God's nonviolence, even if we try otherwise to think within the perspective of the priestly narrative. Thus its formula for the world remains preliminary.

But even if we figure in all these relativizing caveats, we must say: what a great mistake was made by those who have wanted to use the priestly narrative's 'be fruitful and multiply, and fill the earth and subdue it,' to legitimate what is being done to God's earth in our day. How much

45. This transposition has been accomplished in the New Testament especially, in its own fashion, by the letter to the Hebrews.

we need, in these days, the images and narrative sequences in the priestly narrative, so that gradually we may construct within ourselves counter-myths against the myth of progress that the modern era has planted so deep in our souls. How clearly it shows us that we will find our salvation only in creation!

6

The Priestly Narrative and History

In Memory of Peter Charlier

Jewish tradition calls the first five books of the Bible 'the Law.' The New Testament does the same.[1] Christian tradition inclines rather to associate these books with the 'historical books' that follow them,[2] but the same treatment is evident in the work of Flavius Josephus: see *Contra Apionem* 1. 8. Behind this distinction are some fundamental differences in understanding. 'Law' points to an order that is given, that endures, and that is to be preserved. 'History,' in contrast, refers to a development that, while highly important, is nevertheless past. It does not exclude the possibility that subsequently there might be new and very different developments, and that it is quite right that it should be so.

It is the task of our profession to ask how the Pentateuch understood itself. This question must be posed primarily to the so-called priestly narrative, for it is quantitatively the longest stratum in the Pentateuch, according to common opinion the latest in time, and certainly the most influential.[3] In fact, during the truly productive phase of Pentateuch

1. Matt. 5:12, 18, 7:12; 11:13; 12:5; 22:36, 40; 23:23, etc.
2. Jewish tradition was not tempted to do anything like that, since the books from Joshua to 2 Kings, together with the prophetic books proper, constituted the group designated 'prophets.' A division of this group into 'earlier' and 'later' prophets appears only since the eighth century CE: cf. O. Eissfeldt, *Einleitung in das Alte Testament* (Tübingen, 3rd ed. 1964), 766. 'Historical books' as a group begin to be distinguishable beginning with the Septuagint, which, however, seems to have viewed the Pentateuch as a special unit and the only one that, in the strict sense, was canonical. Cf. E. Sellin and G. Fohrer, *Einleitung in das Alte Testament* (Heidelberg, 10th ed. 1965), 537.
3. The distinction of strata that has been generally accepted derives from T. Nöldeke, *Untersuchungen zur Kritik des Alten Testaments* (Kiel, 1869), 1–144: 'Die sogenannte Grundschrift des Pentateuch.' There is a summary there on pp. 143–44.

research, in the nineteenth century, interpretation of the priestly narrative was largely shaped by the contrast between 'law' and 'history,' even when the terms themselves were not always the same.

The first person to pursue the question in depth was de Wette in his 'Kritik der Mosaischen Gesetze' of 1807.[4] He discovered both law and history and made no distinction between them. On the one hand, he spoke of an 'epoch of hebraic theocracy' (p. 31), in which a 'poet' sang the 'origins and development of the people of God and their holy constitution,' just as later did 'Virgil the origins of holy Rome' (p. 32). On the other hand, this poet had one primary objective: he wanted 'to deduce the theocratic laws' from history (p. 51).

The delicate balance of the two aspects shattered in subsequent years, yielding two opposed positions. Let me introduce a pair of examples especially appropriate in Göttingen: Ewald and Wellhausen, a teacher and his pupil.

H. Ewald dedicated 32 sequential pages in the first volume of his seven-volume *Geschichte des Volkes Israel*[5] to what he called the 'Book of Origins,' and in subsequent parts he also referred to it repeatedly. He did observe that 'the author only tells the story at length, and with the warmest and most unmistakable devotion of his own heart, when he is able to pursue a lawgiving purpose and explain legal or customary regulations . . . within the framework of the narrative' (p. 123). But the 'principal purpose' (p. 117) of this 'most glorious of all Hebrew historical works' (p. 116) was 'to review the whole historical material to the fullest extent and to trace it back to the earliest beginnings of all that would be,' just as 'the Greeks [did] after the Persian victories' (p. 117). This historical work intends to subsume everything 'under the concept[s] of origin and development' (p. 121). It also points to a meaningful shape of history, for the author used as a principle in the construction of his description the theory of the four ages of the world, which was current among many ancient peoples. He organized history according to Adam, Noah, Abraham and Moses. The 'book of origins' intended to represent the same thing that was symbolized in the work of Hesiod by gold, silver, bronze and iron. It tells the tale of a 'humanity that, in the same stages,

4. The following citations are from W. L. M. de Wette, *Kritik der Israelitischen Geschichte* 1: 'Kritik der Mosaischen Geschichte,' which is identical with his *Beiträge zur Einleitung in das Alte Testament* 2 (Halle, 1807).

5. In what follows, this work is cited according to the third edition (Göttingen, 1864); the first edition appeared in 1843.

was continually spreading outward and advancing in the arts, but that at the same time was internally tearing itself apart at an ever-increasing pace' (p. 118).[6]

The teacher's interpretation still echoes in the symbol Q (quattuor), which his student, Julius Wellhausen, sought to introduce.[7] He believed that God had made four covenants: with Adam, Noah, Abraham, and Moses, and that the work is divided according to those four.[8] But Wellhausen would by no means speak of declining ages of the world. Instead, the 'priestly codex,' as he now calls it, only 'entered its own mainstream with the Mosaic law, and from that point the narrative is suppressed by the weight of legislative material' (p. 362). In addition, everything narrated previously was 'subordinated to legislative purposes' (p. 361). The 'law' is 'the key to understanding the narrative in the priestly codex as well' (p. 383). In a word: 'Only the form is historical; it serves as a framework for the legal material, providing its arrangement, or as a mask to disguise it' (p. 7).

Later authors sought to mediate between the extremes, often by use of Kuenen's formula calling this the 'historical-legislative document.'[9] Most of us have probably adopted a formula like that of Gerhard von Rad, who called the object of the priestly historical narrative 'the emergence of particular cultic institutions in the course of history.'[10] From this point of view, the history that is narrated is certainly more than merely a

6. There is more detail on pp. 368–73.

7. 'Die Composition des Hexateuchs,' *Jahrbücher für Deutsche Theologie* 21 (1876): 392: 'Abbreviation for the book of four covenants (quattuor), the name I suggest as appropriate for it.'

8. *Geschichte Israels* 1 (Berlin, 1878), 356–60; identical with his *Prolegomena zur Geschichte Israels (Zweite Ausgabe der Geschichte Israels, Band I)* (Berlin, 1883), 358–61; subsequent citations follow this edition. The symbol Q was not adopted. Cf. A. Kuenen, *Historisch-kritische Einleitung in die Bücher des alten Testaments hinsichtlich ihrer Entstehung und Sammlung* I, 1 (Leipzig, 1887), 62: 'G I, 28–30 is not really a covenant, but rather a blessing.'

9. Kuenen, *Einleitung* (see n. 8 above), 78 and frequently elsewhere. This mediating compromise is perhaps most evident within the Wellhausen school in the work of H. Holzinger, *Einleitung in den Hexateuch* (Freiburg im Breisgau, 1893). He calls P a 'legal writing in historical form and with a historical substructure' (p. 335).

10. *Theologie des Alten Testaments* 1 (Munich, 7th ed. 1978), 245 (= *Old Testament Theology. I. The Theology of Israel's Historical Origins*, 232). Cf. idem, 247 [Engl. 233–34]: 'P is utterly serious in wanting to show that the cult which entered history in the people Israel is the goal of the origin and evolution of the world.'

'framework,' and much more than a 'mask.' But ultimately it is still told with an 'etiological purpose,' as a 'historical legitimation' of a later Israel.[11] Consequently, even if we have no hesitation about talking of a priestly depiction of 'salvation history'[12] as well, it appears that since Wellhausen, on the whole, the 'law' has carried the day. But, to leap into the categories that are current today, that means that we are sustaining the opinion that, while the priestly narrative made use of history, it was only for the purpose of stabilizing the established social relationships of its own time by means of a narrative legitimation.[13] It would thus be anti-progressive and opposed to any social change.

In what follows I do not intend simply to adopt one of the established possible positions with regard to the classic question as sketched above and to offer new foundation for that position. It is now possible to take a different stance. In the intervening time new facts have emerged, and new observations have been made, questions raised, and points of view been enunciated regarding the topic of 'the priestly narrative and history.' We need to describe and reorder them. In any case, at the end I will necessarily return to the classic question, although from a new point of view.

First let me point to a few things that, in the course of recent decades, have distinguished or even exploded the classical ways of approaching the question. I will list only the most important.

1. It is true that the distinction between a priestly historical narrative proper and the remaining, primarily legislative material, has existed since Wellhausen.[14] But really Martin Noth offered the first genuine

11. G. von Rad, *Die Priesterschrift im Hexateuch* (Stuttgart and Berlin, 1934), 187–88.

12. An example chosen at random: J. Scharbert, 'Der Sinn der Toledot-Formel in der Priesterschrift,' in H. J. Stoebe et al., eds., *Wort – Gebot – Glaube*, Festschrift for W. Eichrodt (Zürich, 1970), 76, speaks, in regard to P, of 'salvation history in which blessing and promise are from time to time condensed, until the divine sovereignty of YHWH manifests itself in the hierarchically organized people of God.'

13. This is also the case when at the present time, following Y. Kaufmann, the priestly narrative is regarded as pre-exilic. Cf. M. Weinfeld, 'Pentateuch,' *Encyclopaedia Judaica* 13 (Jerusalem, 1971), 235: 'The priestly material in Genesis serves only the priestly and sacred purpose of emphasizing the basis for the sanctity of Israel and its institutions.'

14. Wellhausen distinguished, both in the *Composition* (see n. 7 above) and in the *Prolegomena* (see n. 8 above), between Q and RQ. But since he did not find it easy to establish a dating of Q independently of the laws, in the *Prolegomena* he again brought the two bodies of material into very close relationship. In the *Composition,*

investigation of the theology of P^g apart from P^s, in his *Überlieferungsgeschichte des Pentateuch* (Stuttgart, 1948).[15] In response to the subject matter itself, however, it is absolutely necessary to restrict the question, at least initially, to P^g. Fixation on the tension between 'law' and 'history' could, in fact, be occasioned by the very combination of P^g and P^s.[16]

2. In the same work, Noth expressed the opinion that Israel's cultic order (the depiction of which in the Sinai pericope he continued to regard

455–56, he summarized his analysis of the 'priestly codex' as follows: 'Its core is Q, but this core has expanded in many ways, in a sense in an organic and hypertropic manner, to the extent that the expansions are everywhere tied into the core and derive from it their tendencies, ideas, formulae and manners. Q and its secondary and tertiary offspring arise from the same basis, the same circles and the same era.'

15. See pp. 7–9 (where he even denies to a large portion of the legislative material any attribution to the designation P^s) and pp. 259–67. Of course authors like Holzinger (*Einleitung*, see n. 9 above) have taken care to investigate the 'general giving of the law' and the 'secondary contents' of P. But one does not receive the impression that they have been very influential. G. von Rad, *Priesterschrift* (see n. 11 above), 188, even thought that the legitimating connection between history and law emerged more clearly in P than in P^s.

16. This is pointed out by K. Elliger, 'Geschichtserzählung (see n. 19 below), 129. Of course, some aspects depend on the amount of 'law' that is left to P^g when distinguishing P^g and P^s. In this regard, Noth is certainly more radical than his predecessors as respects the middle books of the Pentateuch. But perhaps we should be even more radical than Noth, especially for the portion between Genesis 1 and Exodus 14. For Gen. 9:4–6, see S. McEvenue, *The Narrative Style of the Priestly Writer* (Rome, 1971), 68–71; for Gen. 17:14, P. Grelot, 'La dernière étape de la rédaction sacerdotale,' *VT* 7 (1957): 176–77, 188; for Exod. 12:1–14, J. L. Ska, 'Les plaies d'Égypte dans le récit sacerdotal (P^g), et la tradition prophétique' (to be published in the near future [1977]), Excursus: 'Ex 12, 1–14. 28 fait-il partie de P^g?' (with a negative response). Then, for the revelations in the wilderness the 'legal material' that remains is really confined to the sabbath theme that had begun in the creation text but reaches its climax only in the Sinai pericope, and circumcision, which, however, is incorporated in the theme of the covenant sign and to that extent is not an independent theme. On the Sabbath, cf. N. Negretti, *Il settimo giorno, Indagine critico-teologica delle tradizioni presacerdotali e sacerdotali circa il sabato biblico* (Rome, 1973), 147–251; N. Lohfink, 'Die Sabbatruhe und die Freizeit,' *Stimmen der Zeit* 194 (1976): 395–407; for the Sabbath structure of the Sinai pericope, see also M. Oliva, 'Interpretación theológica del culto en la perícopa del Sinaí de la Historia Sacerdotal,' *Bibl* 49 (1968): 345–54. The Sabbath as law appears first in P^g: cf. Negretti, 252–306. On circumcision in Genesis 17, recent articles include: E. Kutsch, 'Ich will euer Gott sein,' *ZThK* 71 (1974): 361–88; M. V. Fox, 'The Sign of the Covenant,' *RB* 81 (1974): 557–96; C. Westermann, 'Gen 17 und die Bedeutung von berit,' *ThLZ* 101 (1976): 161–70; W. Groβ, 'Berit in der Priesterschrift,' (soon to appear in the *Trier theologische Zeitschrift* [1977]).

as the true center of P^g) is described rather as an 'ideal' plan for the cult, a 'program for the future.'[17] In this way, he demonstrated the possibility of seeing the union of history and law as the expression of a tendency to change, and not to stabilize, the system.[18]

3. While Noth adhered to the traditional opinion that the priestly narrative arrived at 'its real goal' with the description of 'the order established on Sinai' (*Überlieferungsgeschichte*, 8), Karl Elliger, in his essay, 'Sinn and Ursprung der priesterlichen Geschichtserzählung,' has entered a plea that cannot easily be rejected in favor of the proposition that the real theme of P^g, despite the breadth achieved in the Sinai pericope, was not at all the cult or the cultic community, but rather the land of Canaan. The 'epitome of the divine ordering of history' is said to be 'the possession of the land of Canaan as the material and ideal basis on which the life of the people and, as a matter of course, the cult as its most important function can really and properly develop.'[19] This thesis is all the more persuasive

17. Noth, *Überlieferungsgeschichte* (see n. 15 above), 260 and 263. For a summary of authors who, following Noth, no longer posit the post-exilic community as a given for P^g, see W. Wood, *The Congregation of Yahweh: A Study of the Theology and Purpose of the Priestly Document*, Dissertation, Union Theological Seminary, Richmond, Virginia (1974), 30–39. But the uncoupling of the 'priestly codex' from the post-exilic Temple had already been accomplished, long before Noth, by Y. Kaufmann: cf., as a first publication, J. [= Y.] Kaufmann, 'Probleme der israelitisch-jüdischen Religionsgeschichte,' *ZAW* 48 (1930): 23–43, at 42: 'But the work of P has nothing at all to do with the realities of the post-exilic period.'

18. In the end, Noth himself arrived at the theory that P^g lacked any specific interest in history. P^g wanted to 'expand and correct' the 'cultic priestly tradition' of the 'dwelling and presence of God in the Temple' by means of the 'numinous element of the God of Sinai,' who 'merely appears.' It was only because the Sinai tradition does not appear except within the 'great narrative whole' of the old Pentateuch sources that the author was forced to 'offer a summary recapitulation of the whole of the old Pentateuch material' (*Überlieferungsgeschichte*, 266–67). This seems to be nothing other than Wellhausen's 'frame' and 'mask,' but this time no longer on behalf of the law; now it favors a particular theory of the divine presence that is to be propagated. It scarcely does justice to the great care P^g devoted to the 'summary recapitulation' of the Pentateuch narrative, nor to the previous statement about a 'program for the future.'

19. *ZThK* 49 (1952): 129. See the similar remarks of R. Kilian, 'Die Hoffnung auf Heimkehr in der Priesterschrift,' *Bibel und Leben* 7 (1966): 39–51; E. Cortese, *La terra di Canaan nella storia sacerdotale del Pentateuco* (Brescia, 1972). Following the summary by P. Diepold, *Israels Land* (Stuttgart, 1972), 7–8, G. D. Macholz, *Israel und das Land*, Diss. habil., Heidelberg (1969), seems to posit a tendency in P to separate Israel's existence from its attachment to the land of Canaan.

since Elliger still accepts Noth's literary-critical proposition that P^g ended with the death of Moses and did not describe the entry into the land, a presupposition that, in my opinion, is not necessary.[20] In contrast to the cult, which P^g acknowledges only for Israel, dwelling in their own land is something proper to every nation. Hence the history of origins, which deals with all peoples, again comes more strongly to the fore when he addresses the question of the theme of P^g: it could be something more than a mere prelude.[21]

4. Elliger's thesis makes it possible at the same time to concretize something else that, in fact, was clear since de Wette's time: in P^g the choice of material and the technique of the presentation continually make what is narrated 'transparent' to the intended readers and their situation. The aim is to 'steer' the readers' thinking 'to the backgrounds.'[22] Elliger was thinking of readers in the time of the Babylonian exile. It is possible that the transparency of the priestly narration can be better demonstrated if we also take into account the relationships between this text and the exilic and early post-exilic prophetic literature, especially the book of Ezekiel.[23] In any event, what emerges here is the possibility of a historical vision that may not have been interested any longer in the causal or final ordering of various events on a time line, but instead looked to something

20. For more detail, see n. 30 below.

21. W. Brueggemann, 'The Kerygma of the Priestly Writers,' *ZAW* 84 (1972): 397–413, is similar to Elliger in seeing the message of P as being 'that the promise of the land of blessing still endures and will be realized soon' (p. 41). But he looks for the key to this at the beginning of P, especially in Gen. 1:28. Starting at a different point, J. Blenkinsopp, 'The Structure of P,' *CBQ* 38 (1976): 276–92, also arrives at a much closer unity between the history of origins and the history of Israel in P than is usually posited. On this, see also L. Dequeker, 'Noah and Israel,' in C. Brekelmans, ed., *Questions disputées d'Ancien Testament* (Gembloux, 1974): 115–29.

22 'Geschichtserzählung' (see n. 19 above), 189. De Wette indicated this situation by speaking constantly of 'myth,' 'poetry,' and 'epic.' For Wellhausen it was a matter of course 'that the situation of the Babylonian exile influenced the priestly shaping of the sagas of the ancestors;' despite 'all the archaic appearances, . . . the present of the narrator was also positively expressed in the depiction of the time of the patriarchs' (*Prolegomena,* 362). But the earlier authors were preoccupied with the idea of an influence from the time of composition that impeded genuine reporting. They were less interested in the idea of a kerygmatic intention on the part of the author.

23. A. Eitz, *Studien zum Verhältnis von Priesterschrift und Deuterojesaja,* Dissertation, Heidelberg (1969), does not exhaust the topic. It would be especially important to have a thorough investigation of the relationship between P^g and the book of Ezekiel. This is still lacking.

like fundamental, paradigmatic constellations that had appeared in the past and that might have importance for the present.

5. In this connection we should not fail to mention that McEvenue's study, *The Narrative Style of the Priestly Writer*, has finally filled a scandalous gap and has for the first time put us in a position to trace the literary technique of P^g and thus to give individual observations their proper place in the larger picture.[24] This remains true in spite of the skepticism one might maintain in face of the opinion that this is something like an Israelite children's literature.[25]

6. A highly important parallel, at least to the priestly history of origins, is the Atrahasis myth. Although a small portion of it has long been known, it was only a few years ago that a major portion of the work became generally available.[26] Its importance for the interpretation of P^g does not seem to me to have been adequately recognized as yet.[27]

7. Quite recently there have been increasing attempts to see in the narrative texts of the priestly writing not an originally independent document, but only commentary and reinterpretative additions to the older Pentateuch materials, or perhaps the work of the redactor(s) of the

24. See n. 16 above; also his 'Word and Fulfilment: A Stylistic Feature of the Priestly Writer,' *Semitics* 1 (1970): 104–10; idem, 'The Style of a Building Instruction' (unpublished). There was a dissertation written earlier at Heidelberg, and still unpublished: R. Borchert, *Stil und Aufbau der Priesterschriftlichen Erzählung* (1956).

25. Most clearly expressed in 'Building Instruction:' 'a document for the children of the exiles who were not to be allowed to become assimilated in Babylon.' In spite of the striking similarity in style between P^g and modern children's literature for preschoolers, and despite the great potential value of this observation in sensitizing us to the point of view behind the language of P^g, the question of origin, prehistory and function of this style in the priestly literature remains open. Children's literature as such is thus far known only as a modern phenomenon.

26. W. G. Lambert and A. R. Millard, *Atra-Ḫasīs, The Babylonian Story of the Flood* (Oxford, 1969). For a review article, see W. L. Moran, 'Atrahasis: The Babylonian Story of the Flood,' *Bibl* 52 (1971): 51–61. For further literature see the annual 'Keilschriftbibliographie' [bibliography of cuneiform] in the periodical *Orientalia.*

27. Comparisons with the biblical text either ignore the existence of literary layers in the Pentateuch, as for example A. R. Millard, 'A New Babylonian "Genesis" Story,' *Tyndale Bulletin* 18 (1967): 3–18; I. M. Kikawada, 'Literary Convention of the Primaeval History,' *Annual of the Japanese Biblical Institute* 1 (1975): 3–21 (with bibliography), or they concentrate on non-priestly passages, as for example I. M. Kikawada, 'Two Notes on Eve,' *JBL* 91 (1972): 33–37. For comparisons with P^g I can only mention N. Lohfink, 'Die Priesterschrift und die Grenzen des Wachstums,' *Stimmen der Zeit* 192 (1974): 435–50; idem, 'Sabbratruhe' (see n. 16 above); Blenkinsopp, 'Structure' (see n. 21 above), 282.

Pentateuch.[28] Thus far they have not succeeded in convincing me. But they do appear to me to make one thing more clearly evident: even a priestly historical narrative that was originally self-contained should perhaps not be regarded simply as an independent tradition parallel to the other, older Pentateuch traditions; instead, it may be seen as a new conception that consciously relates itself to and distinguishes itself from the others. Such a deliberate reference to the 'old sources,' of course, does not necessarily demand that we adopt a theory of expansion, but is also conceivable in the case of an independent writing if the 'old sources' were familiar to the author and the readers.

Even though I may adopt suggestions from these and many other recent initiatives that are not specifically mentioned, in what follows I do not wish to attach myself to a particular position and use it as a basis for continuing thought; instead, I see it as important that the central questions themselves be posed anew. Before I begin this process, however,

28. The first to express this view regarding the narrative parts of the priestly writing as well was K. H. Graf, in the last twist he gave to his theory on the sequence of the layers in the Pentateuch: according to him, what we find here is a series of 'additions made to the "Yahwist" work at a later time.' He speaks thus in 'Die s.g. Grundschrift des Pentateuchs,' in A. Merx, ed., *Archiv für die wissenschaftliche Erforschung des Alten Testaments* 1 (Halle, 1869), 474. But then Wellhausen's theory of an originally independent priestly historical narrative was accepted. In Graf's line, although most of them wrote without knowledge of their predecessor, we may mention: S. Maybaum, *Die Entwicklung des altisraelitischen Priesterthums* (1880), 107ff. (not available to me); B. D. Eerdmans, *Alttestamentliche Studien* I–IV (Gießen, 1908–1912); idem, 'Ezra and the Priestly Code,' *Expositor*, 7th ser., 10 (1910): 306–26; R. H. Pfeiffer, 'A Non-Israelite Source of the Book of Genesis,' *ZAW* 48 (1930): 66–73; idem, *Introduction to the Old Testament* (New York, 1942); P. Voltz, 'P ist kein Erzähler, in P. Volz and W. Rudolph, *Der Elohist als Erzähler, ein Irrweg der Pentateuchkritik?*, BZAW 38 (Gießen, 1933): 135–42. Sometimes M. Löhr, *Untersuchungen zum Hexateuchproblem I, Der Priesterkodex in der Genesis*, BZAW 38 (Gieβen, 1924) is also mentioned in this context. But Löhr sees P rather as a redactor of many individual traditions (= Ezra); that is, he holds a kind of fragment hypothesis. P is also seen as the final redactor of the Pentateuch by I. Engnell. The newer authors who should be mentioned here are: F. M. Cross, 'The Tabernacle: A Study from an Archaeological Approach,' *BA* 10 (1947): 57–58; idem, *Canaanite Myth and Hebrew Epic* (Cambridge, Mass., 1973): 293–325; R. Rendtorff, 'Der "Jahwist" als Theologe? Zum Dilemma der Pentateuchkritik,' *Congress Volume Edinburgh 1974*, SVT 28 (Leiden, 1975): 158–66; idem, *Das überlieferungsgeschichtliche Problem des Pentateuch*, BZAW 147 (Berlin, 1977): 130–42 and 160–63; J. Van Seters, *Abraham in History and Tradition* (New Haven, Conn., 1975), 279; Blenkinsopp, 'Structure' (see n. 21 above), 280. On the whole of the new discussion of the sources of the Pentateuch, see *JSOT* issue 3 (July, 1977), with various contributions.

I am obliged to give at least a brief account of the literary-critical presuppositions that I perforce must simply take for granted here.

Thus I take it as given that in the Hexateuch one can extract, from within the priestly material (P), an almost complete priestly historical narrative (P^g).[29] Its last sentences extend (here I differ from Wellhausen and Noth) into the book of Joshua.[30] It was originally composed as an

29. Gen. 1:1–2:4a; 5:1–27, 28*, 30–32; 6:9–22; 7:6, 11, 13–16a, 17a , 18–21, 24; 8:1, 2a, 3b–5, 13a, 14–19; 9:1–3, 7–17, 28–29; 10:1–7, 20, 22–23, 31–32; 11:10–27, 31–32; 12:4b, 5; 13:6, 11b, 12*; 16:1, 3, 15–16; 17:1–13, 14*, 15–27; 19:29; 21:1b–5; 23:1–20; 25:7–11a, 12–17 . . . 26b; 26:34–35; 27:46–28:9; . . . 31:18*; 33:18a; 35:6a, 9–15, 22b–29; 36:1, 2a . . . 6–8, 40–43; 37:1–2; 41:46a; 46:6–7; 47:27b, 28; 48:3–6; 49:1a, 28b–33, 112–113. Exod. 1:1–5, 7, 13–14; 2:23*, 24–25; 6:2–12; 7:1–13, 19, 20*, 21b, 22; 8:1–3 . . . 11*, 12–15; 9:8–12; 11:9–10; 12:37a, 40–42; 13:20; 14:1–4, 8–9, 10*, 15–18, 21*, 22–23, 26, 27*, 28–29; 15:22*, 27; 16:1–3, 6–7, 9–12, 13* . . . 14* . . . 16*, 17, 18*, 19–21a, 22*, 23–26, 31a, 35b, 17:1*; 19:1, 2a; 24:15b–18a; 25:1–2, 8, 9*; 26:1–30; 29:43–46; . . . 31:18; 34:29–32; 35:4, 5a, 10, 20–22a, 29; 36:2–3a, 8*; 39:32–33a, 42–43; 40:17, 33b–35. Lev. 9:1*, 2–3, 4b–7, 8*, 12a, 15a, 21b–24. Num. 1:1, 2*, 3*, 19b, 21*, 23*, 25*, 27*, 29*, 31*, 33*, 35*, 37*, 39*, 41*, 43*, 46; 2:1*, 2, 3, 5*, 7a, 10a, 12*, 14a, 18a, 20a, 22a, 25a, 27*, 29a, 34; 4:1* . . . 2*, 3, 34*, 35–36, 37*, 38–40, 41*, 42–44, 45*, 46*, 47–48; 10:11–13; 12:16b; 13:1–3a, 17*, 21, 25, 26*, 32; 19:1a, 2, 5–7, 10, 26–28, 29*, 35–38; . . . 20:1* . . . 2, 3b–7, 8*, 10, 11b, 12* . . . 22b . . ., 23*, 25–29; 21:4*; 10–11; 22:1; 27:12–14a, 15–23; 34:1–18. Deut. 1:3; 32:48–52; 34:1* . . . 7–9; . . . Josh. 4:19*; 5:10–12; 14:1, 2*; 18:1 . . . 19:51. This division is developed from Elliger's, with which I had originally worked. Cf. Elliger, 'Geschichtserzählung' (n. 19 above), 121–22. The changes from Elliger's version rest partly on my own observations and older commentaries, and partly on the following recent literature: Blenkinsopp, 'Structure' (n. 21 above), 249 n. 16 and 290–91; Cortese, *Canaan* (n. 19 above), 41–51; W. Groß, 'Jakob, der Mann des Segens', *Bibl* 49 (1968): 335–37; D. Kellermann, *Die Priesterschrift von Numeri 1,1 bis 10,10 literarkrtisch und traditionsgeschichtlich untersucht*, BZAW 120 (Berlin, 1970); S. McEvenue, 'A Source-Critical Problem in Nm 14, 26–38,' *Bibl* 50 (1969): 453–65; Negretti, *Settimo giorno* (n. 16 above): 173–79; as well as the works of Grelot, McEvenue and Ska listed in n. 16 above. It is legitimate to ask, as Wellhausen did and as G. von Rad, W. Groβ, P. Weimar and others have done more recently, whether earlier stages or materials inserted by P^g can be recognized. I doubt that a more precise reconstruction is possible. The following considerations do not, in principle, inquire beyond the document P^g as distinguished in this note.

30. Wellhausen himself took the position that P^g could not be demonstrated in Joshua; however, he first adopted this stance in *Prolegomena* (pp. 379–80), and not in his earlier publications. Still, his position was not accepted. Noth came to the same stance in developing his conception of the deuteronomistic historical work. See especially *Überlieferungsgeschichtliche Studien* (Tübingen, 2nd ed. 1957), 182–90; idem, 'Überlieferungsgeschichtliches zur zweiten Hälfte des Josuabuches,' *Alttestamentliche Studien F. Nötscher zum 60. Geburtstag gewidmet* (Bonn, 1950), 152–67. Everything

independent document, although what I am about to elaborate can be maintained, at least in part, even if one holds an hypothesis of expansion or redaction.[31] The author of the work was not only personally familiar

in Joshua that bears the stylistic marks of P (lists not being a part of it in any case), is, according to Noth, mutually unrelated additions to what are mainly secondary deuteronomistic texts from a later period. But even if we follow Noth in our judgment of the list material, the question remains whether we can dismiss the possibility of P^g being present because no priestly narrative of the taking possession of the land can be demonstrated. Should we really expect to find such a narrative? McEvenue, *Narrative Style* (see n. 16 above), 117–23, has shown that P^g has removed all the military aspects from the traditional war story of the scouts. According to A. Kuschke, 'Die Lagervorstellung der priesterschriftlichen Erzählung,' *ZAW* 63 (1951): 99–100, Israel's camp is also stripped of any military character. In all of P^g it is only the Egyptians who appear in military guise, but even they are not conquered in battle. P^g is, if we may use such an expression, 'pacifistic.' In any case, in describing the entry into Canaan, P^g may have been as succinct as in the story of the exodus from Egypt in Exod. 12:40–42. In addition, we need not proceed on the assumption that in Joshua P^g furnished the basis for redactional work in the same way as previously, in the Pentateuch, and that therefore it must be preserved as seamlessly in Joshua as elsewhere. Cf. S. Mowinckel, *Tetrateuch – Pentateuch – Hexateuch*, BZAW 90 (Berlin, 1964), 51.Thus the appropriate question is only whether the few texts in the style of P that are certainly present in Joshua, and that, on the basis of the narrative system in Joshua, can all be regarded as later insertions, really and necessarily presuppose their present context and – if not – to what extent they ought to be expected in light of the narrative system of P^g. In fact, Josh. 18:1a is to be anticipated, as a notice of the place in the Land where the tent of meeting was erected, and 18:1b provides the notice of fulfillment that supplements Gen. 1:28 (more detail on this in Part II below!). Cf. Josh. 14:1 and 19:51 with Num. 34:16 (which Noth wrongly denies to be part of P^g). If these verses are shown to be a probable part of P^g, notes like Josh. 4:19* and 5:10–12 are to be expected. Finally, we should perhaps reconsider whether something of P^g may not even be retained in the lists. However, that need not be the case, and even with the lists the conclusion of P^g after the death of Moses may have been quite brief and, in any case, have retained no scene in which God speaks. On this whole problem, see Blenkinsopp, 'Structure' (n. 21 above), 287–91.

31. The newer argumentation against P^g as an independent narrative can be summarized as follows: 1. P is, especially in the history of the patriarchs, too brief to be regarded as a narrative at all. 2. It would mean that indispensable content from the old sources was missing, such as an original sin or a convenant at Sinai. 3. P texts serve as headings for older material. 4. P texts depend on JE texts, and therefore presuppose them. 5. The statistical evidence establishing the attribution to P of many of the text fragments without which P would no longer be a continuous narrative is very dubious. To these points, let me briefly respond: To 1: Does this objection not rest on a postulate regarding genre that is derived, not from texts that are certainly P, but from the old sources? To 2: The 'facts' stated here are partly untrue: e.g., one cannot simply say that an original sin is absent in P. In addition, we find here an unfounded postulate: namely, that P must have narrated everything that JE had told. To 3: The

with the pre-priestly Pentateuch and at least the preliminary stages of the 'early' and 'later prophets,' but also presumed such knowledge on the part of his readers.[32] He did his writing most probably at the time when

functioning of P texts as headings and introductions, where the text is mixed, can be completely explained by the redactional activity involved in editing P and the old Pentateuch material together. To 4: Of course JE constitutes the principal model for P^g, and the author of P^g could presuppose that the readers were also familiar with JE. That is sufficient to explain the matter at issue here. To 5: Rendtorff, who develops these arguments, has undoubtedly put his finger on a whole series of problematic passages. But he exaggerates the demands of proof and works partly with rhetorical arguments. In turn, however, he himself should undoubtedly undertake the 'renewed careful examination' he demands, to determine whether 'something other than the reasons here presented favors the assignment of still other texts' to that 'priestly layer' that he himself has been forced to leave in place between Genesis 1 and Exodus 6 as a unified text system, and whether, after all, many other texts are also sown within this broader field of P. Quotations are from Rendtorff, *Pentateuch* (see n. 28 above), 162 n. 16. Every theory of expansion or redaction that denies a previous independent existence of P^g falls into difficulties that newer advocates of such theories are not inclined to explore: (1) In such theories, how can the redactional technique of combination in many texts, such as the Flood story or the narrative of the scouts, be reasonably explained? This kind of subtle meshing presupposes a number of pre-existing texts. Someone who intends to expand a text by interpreting it works in a different way. (2) The unusually rigid structure of P^g cannot have been intended, at the outset, for the text as it presently stands, since the combination with the older texts has made it, in large measure, invisible. (3) Important theological statements in P^g are structurally independent (for example, '*berit*' or covenant theology) and, as a result of the obliteration of the structure in the present textual context, are scarcely evident any longer.

32. JE (to retain the customary abbreviation) could already have been available to the author of P^g in its early-deuteronomic edited form. It precedes Dt/Dtr. On this, see recently and primarily D. E. Skweres, *Die Rückverweise im Buch Deuteronomium*, AnBib 79 (Rome, 1979). Especially if we regard the Abrahamic covenant in Genesis 15, which undoubtedly presupposes Genesis 17, as early deuteronomic (a preferred position at present), we are already supposing an early deuteronomic Pentateuch as an available model [Vorlage] for P^g. Its order of events must have had an almost canonical value for the author of P^g and his readers, for despite its freedom of treatment, his portrayal adheres essentially to what is found there. That this is true for the readers as well is evident from the many abbreviations of the account, the introduction of new persons and prerequisites for events as if they were well known, and the often concealed or reinterpretative plays on the text of the old sources. Parts, at least, of the material in the books of Joshua to 2 Kings must also have been familiar: as an example let me mention only the archaizing element of the ascension to heaven of the divine being who appears in Gen. 17:22 and Gen. 35:13, for which Judg. 13:20 is the only possible model known to us. For similar situations with respect to some of the prophetic books, especially Ezekiel, see, for example, M. Oliva, 'Revelación del nombre de Yahweh en la "Historia sacerdotal": Ex 6, 2–8,' *Bibl* 52

it was first becoming possible to return from the Babylonian exile.[33]

Hence this writing should be investigated in its historical aspect. Does it intend to narrate history? What is its view of history? The first question addresses the document's intention to make a historical statement. The second concerns the underlying philosophy of history, if we may be permitted the use of this word in such a context. Of course, we could ask an additional question, namely whether P^g provides historical information that is useful to modern historians. But we know the essentials of the

(1971); 1–19; Ska, 'Les plaies d'Égypte' (n. 16 above); L. Van den Wijngaert, 'Die Sünde in der priesterschriftlichen Urgeschichte,' *ThPh* 43 (1968): 35–50. What is least clear is the dependency relationship between P^g and Deutero-Isaiah: see n. 25 in Eitz's dissertation. A. S. Kapelrud's thesis in 'The Date of the Priestly Code (P),' *ASTI* 3 (1964): 58–64 does not appear to me to be definitely proved.

33. In dating, I rely primarily on dependence on texts of the exilic prophets and on the paradigm of exile and diaspora. The renewed linguistic discussion has, for the moment, led to theses that are partially opposed to one another. See especially R. Polzin, *Late Biblical Hebrew. Toward an Historical Typology of Biblical Prose* (Missoula, Montana, 1976); A. Hurvitz, 'The Evidence of Language in Dating the Priestly Code. A Linguistic Study in Technical Idioms and Terminology,' *RB* 81 (1974): 24–56. A comparison of these two approaches can be found in Polzin, pp. 168–69. The type of criteria in Hurvitz's work unfortunately permits no comparison with what is properly deuteronomic material. In addition it is questionable whether something that typologically stands before the book of Ezekiel is necessarily pre-exilic as well. As Polzin's study shows, the linguistic distinction between P^g and P^s is relevant. But Hurvitz does not distinguish between the two corpora; consequently, his material should be investigated again. If Polzin's chapter 3 cannot be disproved, we must still take into account that, at the level of cultic terminology, P^g consciously adheres to old language. It is possible that the influence of earlier models is visible here. Hence, until the linguistic discussion reaches a greater degree of clarity, everything depends on the most sensible historical ordering of the paradigm of the narratives in P^g and on the question of the relationship to exilic prophetic writings. Since this paradigm, at need, would also be conceivable after the fall of Samaria, in the end everything depends on the relationship to the prophetic writings. Anyone who is not ready to accept this should, to be consistent, remain open to theses like those of Y. Kaufmann. In relation to the question of the relationship between P^g and prophetic writings, Deutero-Isaiah presents a special problem. If Deutero-Isaiah presupposes P^g, the origin of P^g must be placed earlier. But if this is not the case, a somewhat later dating would accord especially with the results of my study, 'Die Ursünden in der priesterlichen Geschichtserzählung,' in G. Bornkamm and K. Rahner, *Die Zeit Jesu*, Festschrift for H. Schlier (Freiburg, 1970), 38–57 (Chapter 4 in this book). However, since in essence the address is to a diaspora that is already in a position to return home, but hesitates to do so, even later situations for the writing are conceivable. On the other hand, one should not bring the date down too far, since then the composition and

sources of P^g; hence for this third question we may always turn to the sources themselves, and in regard to P^g itself we may leave it aside.

1. The Re-translation of History into Myth

According to our way of thinking, an author who intends to write history thinks that the things narrated really happened and that they occurred in the same temporal sequence and in the same order of cause and effect as described. There would be a still closer approximation of our modern understanding if the author gave narrative expression to categories like causality, development or progress. But it may suffice here to inquire whether the author intended to tell what really happened, and to say that these things occurred as a single, connected sequence in time.

There can be no doubt that the old sources of the Pentateuch, no matter how we conceive them individually, had this intention, despite the underlying kerygmatic[34] motives and genre-specific unwieldiness of their own materials.[35] They wanted to give Israel information about its past. Did the author of P^g have the same purpose in mind?

insertion of H and of everything that in turn depends on it would be pushed to a still later date. Cf. N. Lohfink, 'Die Abänderung der Theologie des Priesterlichen Geschichtswerks im Segen des Heiligkeitsgesetzes,' in H. Gese and H. P. Rüger, *Wort und Geschichte*, Festschrift for K. Elliger (Neukirchen–Vluyn, 1973), 129–36; A. Cholewinski, *Heiligkeitsgesetz und Deuteronomium* (Rome, 1976), especially 138–39. Both the new arguments for pre-exilic beginnings, such as those of Y. Kaufmann and his school, and also those for massive post-exilic beginnings, such as J. G. Vink, 'The date and origin of the Priestly Code in the Old Testament,' *The Priestly Code and Seven Other Studies*, OTS 15 (Leiden, 1969): 1–144, usually refer to a general 'priestly literature' without a developed discrimination of layers, or else to a finished 'priestly codex,' which they hesitate to analyze further. Thus it is common either to employ arguments that in fact do demonstrate the age of many aspects of content, materials, traditions, and models, but do not in themselves establish the time of composition of P^g, or else to apply arguments that are only valid for final additions and redactional revisions. Incidentally, Y. Kaufmann remained completely open to the possibility of later literary work on old legal material, as is clear, for example, in his exchange with E. Auerbach near the end of his life: cf. 'Der Kalender und das Alter des Priesterkodex,' *VT* 4 (1954): 308–9.

34. Classical studies include: H. W. Wolff, 'Das Kerygma des Jahwisten,' *EvTh* 24 (1964): 73–98; idem, 'Zur Thematik der elohistischen Fragmente im Pentateuch,' *EvTh* 29 (1969): 59–72.

35. Cf. here, for example, what G. von Rad wrote about the genre of 'saga,' which shapes a major portion of the JE material, in 'Offene Fragen im Umkreis einer Theologie des Alten Testaments,' *ThLZ* 88 (1963), cols. 410–14.

This author could have had the intention to write history in this sense, even if the sources used were, in fact, inadequate, so that we would today in large measure reject as unhistorical the results of his authorial work. We are only asking here about his intention.

At first it seems as if the author of P^g really meant to write history. After all, at least in its major features, the story follows the old Pentateuch narrative that did have that intention. This author also begins with creation, is aware of a primeval period and a Flood, speaks of the ancestors Abraham, Isaac, and Jacob, tells how their family followed Joseph into Egypt, describes the deliverance of Israel from Egypt and the years in the wilderness, tarries long at Sinai and finally leads Israel into the land promised to the ancestors. Is the adherence to the thread of the narration not necessarily also an acceptance of the related intention to make a historical statement?

The author not only takes up this narrative thread, with its focus on historical connections. He also introduces names, numbers and order: names through the genealogies and the tables of nations and tribes,[36] numbers through a well-constructed chronological system,[37] and order

36. Genealogies: Gen. 5:3–27, 28*, 30–32; 9:28–29; 11:10–26, 32; 21:5; 25:7, 8*, 26*, 35:28–29, (22–26); 47:28, 33; (Exod. 1:1–5). This is the principal genealogy, which is not carried through for Jacob in a clear schema and then is not continued for his twelve sons, the ancestors of the twelve tribes, once the fulfillment of the blessing of procreation has been witnessed in Exod. 1:7. The narrative notes and extended narratives are attached to this genealogy. See, for example, on the Flood: McEvenue, *Narrative Style* (n. 16 above), 36–41. This is also true of genealogical asides. In addition to the linear principal genealogy there are also the tables of nation and tribes as segmented genealogies. These are found in Gen 10:1–7, 20, 22–23, 31–32; 25:12–13, 16; 35:22–26; 36:40–43; Exod. 1:1–5. Apart from the lists of the sons of Jacob, these latter serve to remove the corresponding progeny from the sweep of the narrative in P^g. For literature, see C. Westermann, *Genesis 1–11* (Darmstadt, 1972), 55–67; idem, *Genesis I* (Neukirchen–Vluyn, 1974), 436, 468, 662–63, 741. Important new works include: A. Malamat, 'King Lists of the Old Babylonian Period and Biblical Genealogies,' *JAOS* 88 (1968): 163–73; M. D. Johnson, *The Purpose of the Biblical Genealogies* (Cambridge, 1969), 14–28; R. R. Wilson, 'The Old Testament Genealogies in Recent Research,' *JBL* 94 (1975): 169–89.

37. A principal, continuous chronological system in P^g can be established from the data in the following texts: Gen. 5:3, 6, 9, 12, 15, 18, 21, 25, 28, 32; 11:10, 12, 14, 16, 18, 20, 22, 24, 26; 21:5; 25:26; 47:28 (from which one may calculate when Jacob came to Egypt); Exod. 12:40–41 (on the basis of Gen. 47:28, the year of the exodus can be calculated here); Deut. 1:3; Josh. 4:19. The numbers in MT, Sam and G are sometimes widely different, and it is probable that no single series of numbers reflects the original as a whole. More detail on this may be found in n. 61 below. In addition

through a variety of structural systems within the whole that sometimes contain one another and sometimes overlap. The most comprehensive division, defining the structure of the whole work in ten major portions, though of differing length, is indicated by the *toledot* formulae.[38] The tenth part, the *toledot* of Jacob, which quantitatively makes up the whole second half of the document, is again divided by eight notes on wandering, each concluding a section and leading to the next, which occurs in a different place.[39]

But a greater value seems to be placed on those texts in which God

to the texts mentioned above, there is also a body of redundant information that P^g expands still further. Subsystems, sometimes detailed down to days, are found for the creation (week), the Flood (solar year), the lives of Abraham and Jacob, the period of the wilderness wandering and the entry into Canaan (in part cultic dates). Cf. Johnson, *Genealogies* (n. 36 above), 28–36, 262–65 (bibliography). See also the literature on the calendar of jubilees and that of Qumran.

38. See Table I. I count the following ten *toledot* formulae as originally part of P^g: Gen. 2:4 (concluding formula); 5:1; 6:9; 10:1; 11:10, 27; 25:12, 19; 36:1; 37:2. I consider Gen. 36:9 and Num. 3:1 as part of P^g. The older literature is cited in detail by P. Weimar, 'Die Toledot-Formel in der priesterschriftlichen Geschichtsdarstellung,' *BZ* 18 (1974): 65–93. Weimar has shown that the *toledot* formulae in P^g, including the other formulae attached to them, are ordered to the whole text up to the next such formula (or to the end of the work). This seems to me the only possible conclusion from his observations. Then in P^g *toledot NN* means something like: 'what happened beginning with and because of NN.' Gen. 37:2 thus introduces the whole text from the departure for Egypt until the entry into Canaan. All this is 'the fate of Jacob.' The quantitative misfit does not contradict this. Earlier, as well, the individual *toledot* texts were of very different length. Of course, the Jacob *toledot* then has to be structured by different means. The notes on the wandering serve this purpose: see the following footnote. The *toledot* formulae have one advantage over all other modern efforts to define the structure of the work: they are structural signals that were placed in the work by the author himself.

39. See Table II. In the notes on wandering in Genesis belonging to P^g, the typical verbs are *lqḥ, yṣʾ, bwʾ* and *yšb*. Beginning with the exodus of Israel, there are new verb combinations, especially with *nsʿ, bwʾ* and *ḥnh*. Some of the assignments to P^g are not entirely certain, but still probable. Some notes have been preserved only in a mutilated form. But in any case, we can discover eight 'wanderings' of Israel. The conclusion of a unit by a change of place is an ancient representative technique in epic, adopted here by P^g. In the resulting sections there is again evidence of a clear structural aim, with a preference for pairings, as previously in the *toledot* divisions. Selected recent literature: M. Noth, 'Der Wallfahrtsweg zum Sinai,' *PJ* 36 (1940): 5–28; E. Weidner, 'Assyrische Itinerare,' *ArOr* 21 (1966): 42–46; V. Fritz, *Israel in der Wüste* (Marburg, 1970): 33–34; G. W. Coats, 'The Wilderness Itinerary,' *CBQ* 34 (1972): 135–52; Cross, *Myth* (see n. 28 above), 308–17; G. I. Davies, 'The Wilderness Itineraries: A Comparative Study,' *Tyndale Bulletin* 25 (1974): 46–81.

speaks. One could call them the 'theological texts' of P^g. They are placed in paired relationships.[40]

Gen. 2:4	*Toledot* of heaven and earth	Narrative	Blessing
Gen. 5:1	*Toledot* of Adam	Genealogy	
Gen. 6:9	*Toledot* of Noah	Narrative	Blessing + *berit*
Gen. 10:1	*Toledot* of Noah's sons	Table of nations	
Gen. 11:10	*Toledot* of Shem	Genealogy	
Gen. 11:27	*Toledot* of Terah	Narrative	Blessing + *berit*
Gen. 25:12	*Toledot* of Ishmael	Table of tribes	
Gen. 25:19	*Toledot* of Isaac	Narrative	Blessing
Gen. 36:1	*Toledot* of Esau	Table of tribes	
Gen. 37:2	*Toledot* of Jacob	Narrative	Wanderings

Table I: The *Toledot* Division of P^g

40. See Table III. The 'theological texts' in this survey can only be distinguished with the aid of the structural signals furnished by the *toledot* formulae and notes of wandering already mentioned, as well as the fact that God speaks. In Exodus 6–11 and Exodus 24 to Numbers 4, we can distinguish still further sub-units. The first to point to the special character of these texts was McEvenue, 'Fulfilment' (see n. 24 above), 105. Within these 'theological texts' there are again two groups, one of which is italicized in the overview. Only these contain genuine narratives of appearances. God appears to Abraham and to Jacob, and then returns to heaven (Gen. 17:22; 35:13). After the exodus from Egypt the glory of YHWH appears, first from the wilderness, then on Sinai, and then in the sanctuary. Literature: N. Lohfink, 'Die priesterschriftliche Abwertung der Tradition von der Offenbarung des Jahwenamens an Mose,' *Bibl* 49 (1968): 1–8; Oliva, 'Interpretación' (see n. 16 above); C. Westermann, 'Die Herrlichkeit Gottes in der Priesterschrift,' in H. J. Stoebe, ed., *Wort – Gebot – Glaube,* Festschrift for W. Eichrodt (Zürich, 1970), 227–49 (too strongly systematized and therefore not adequate as regards Exodus 16); Oliva, 'Revelación' (see n. 32 above); H. Mölle, *Das 'Erscheinen' Gottes im Pentateuch* (Berne and Frankfurt, 1973); M. Oliva, 'Las revelaciones a los patriarcas en la historia sacerdotal,' *Bibl* 55 (1974): 1–14.

Israel in Egypt	Exodus from Egypt	Exod. 12:37a, 40-42; 13:20
Destruction of the Egyptians	To the wilderness of Sin	Exod. 15:22aα, 27; 16:1
Revelation of the sabbath	To the wilderness of Sinai	Exod. 17:1a,bα, 19:1, 2a
Revelation of the sanctuary	To the wilderness of Paran	Num. 10:11-13; 12:16b
Sin of the people	To the wilderness of Zin	Num. 20:1aα
Sin of Moses and Aaron	To the mountain of Hor	Num. 20:22b
Death of Aaron	In the plains of Moab	Num. 21:4aα, 10-11; 22:1b
Death of Moses	Entry into Canaan	Josh. 4:19aβ, b; 5:10-12; 18:1

Table II: The Wanderings of Israel in P^g

Genesis 1	The creation of the world
Genesis 6–9	Flood and Noachic covenant
Genesis 17	*Abrahamic covenant*
Genesis 35	*Blessing of Jacob*
Exodus 6–11	Mission of Moses and Aaron, miracles before Pharaoh
Exodus 14	Destruction of Pharaoh in the sea
Exodus 16	*Quail and manna: Revelation of the Sabbath*
Exodus 24–Numbers 4	*Sinai: Revelation and Building of the Sanctuary*, Camp
Numbers 13–14	*Scouting the Land: Sin of the people and their leaders*
Numbers 20	*Gift of water in the wilderness: Sin of Moses and Aaron*
Numbers 20	Installation of Eleazar, Death of Aaron
Numbers 27–Deuteronomy 36	Installation of Joshua, Directions for taking possession of the Land, Death of Moses

Table III: The 'Theological' Text Fields in P^g

At the beginning of the work, in Gen. 1:28, there is a kind of program for history, whose realization or non-realization is then confirmed from time to time in the course of the narrative.[41] By this means and, as soon as one goes more into detail, in many other ways,[42] the history described in P^g is shaped into a sequence by which one can locate every point cleanly in time and space.[43] Does this not indicate an intention to produce as clear and reliable a historical description as possible?

Unfortunately, the result is a little too much order. The figures and events are distributed through space and time according to principles that are more aesthetic than anything else. Consequently, the more one penetrates the heart of this document the more one doubts whether it possesses the kind of humility in face of the fact that is ultimately decisive for an intention to write history.

Almost everything is portrayed through pairs. Creation and Flood are the two events from primeval times that are described in individual detail. Noah and Abraham are the two recipients of a covenant. Among the patriarchs, Abraham and Jacob each encounter a revelatory appearance. Moses and Aaron are the two leaders of Israel in deliverance and

41. For more detail, see Part II below.

42. However, I cannot regard the 'cutting of covenants' in Genesis 9 and 17 as signals for divisions in the narrative, as so many do, despite their importance for the theology of P^g and despite the clear evidence that they are related to one another. The same applies to the different names of God that appear in P^g. Here, of course, the facts are more complicated than is generally supposed. The 'narrator' has already used the name YHWH once in the important verse Gen. 17:1 (and there is no reason to postulate a redactional alteration at that point). In the story of the patriarchs, he continues to speak of Elohim, and only the self-manifested divinity and people who speak of such appearances use the name El Shaddai for God. The revelation of the name of YHWH in Exodus 6 does not have the dignity of an appearance narrative. G. von Rad, *Priesterschrift* (see n. 11 above), 167–86, tried to demonstrate a structure of 'three mighty concentric circles' by means of a repetition of the narrative. In this regard, Noth, *Überlieferungsgeschichte* (see n. 15 above), 260–61, wrote that this 'whole conception' was 'already established in the tradition,' and the three circles resulted 'less from a comprehensive view of history than from a variety of details in the older tradition.' I see no structural signals capable of supporting this threefold division. Even the notices of leading out and leading in, on which Blenkinsopp, 'Structure' (see n. 21 above) primarily supports his argument, do not really subdivide the narrative, despite the important expressive function they acquire when seen from another point of view.

43. The 'space' is established in Genesis 1, and the table of nations in Genesis 10 makes a first approach to filling it with inhabitants. (Further differentiations are added later in the lists of tribes.) The wanderings that are narrated set it in motion and fill it with life. Most of these have to do with correcting wrong distributions of human beings within the common space.

wandering. The manna and Sinai pericopes are the two stories establishing the cult: the one for the Sabbath, the other for the sanctuary and its liturgy. There are two sins: at the sending of the scouts and at the cliff from which water springs. Aaron must die, and Moses must die. Eleazar is installed, and Joshua is installed. There are many other such pairs.[44] Then there are schemata of sevens: seven days of creation, seven days until Moses is called up the mountain into the fiery cloud. Or there is the number ten: ten generations between creation and flood, ten generations between Noah and Abraham, ten *toledot* headings. Is it not true that here the feeling for the bewildering and opaque complexity of historical facticity has been banished, and certainly any feeling for that incalculable and unpredictable turning point in the course of humanity where freedom and chance are at work?

The old Pentateuch sources, despite their distance from modern ways of dealing with history, still had a feeling for all these things. It is reflected in the confused association of the heaped up, only slightly edited masses of tradition. P^g did not impose any such restraint on himself. The author created a lovely form by doing violence to his sources. He omitted, revised, changed, and exercised complete freedom in inserting new things.

I can do nothing more than offer examples. To develop the pairing of Abraham and Jacob, this author knitted together the stories of Isaac and Joseph. Since he did not wish to treat the topic of 'sin' before the wilderness wandering, he excised from the story of Jacob the tale of his deceitful acquisition of his father's blessing and the enmity between the two brothers (Gen. 28:1–45). He found a different reason for Jacob's journey to the East: Jacob's parents sent him to Paddan Aram so that he would not marry a Canaanite woman.[45] This motif was not an invention, but in the sources it was told of Isaac.[46] Hence Isaac was not needed, but

44. The preference for pairs is even more evident in small details. Thus in the *toledot* of Terah we find a wandering of Terah and a wandering of Abraham, the birth of Ishmael (and his circumcision) and the birth of Isaac (and his circumcision), the death of Sarah (and her burial) and the death of Abraham (and his burial). Statements of time play a role as dividers between these smaller units.

45. Gen. 26:34–35; 27:46; 28:1–9.

46. Genesis 24. There it is not Isaac himself who travels eastward to find a wife among his kindred, but rather his father's servant. For the principal motif, see Gen. 24:3–4. In all likelihood it would not have appeared in Gen. 25:20, the comparable passage from P^g, in spite of the fragmentary nature of its present state. For the overall treatment of tradition in the Jacob narratives in P^g, see Groβ, 'Jakob' (n. 29 above), 339–40. On the way in which tradition is handled with regard to the motifs of guilt and punishment in P^g as a whole, see Lohfink, 'Ursünden' (n. 33 above), 41–47.

merely a motif from his saga, and the motif was transferred to Jacob. Here there is apparently no reference to history as such, but only to the constellation of events and the problem they express: where should a man find his wife, among the nations or within his own people? Many other examples can be offered of this kind of transplantation of events that, in and of themselves, had a fixed place in history: minutiae like the changing of Sarah's laughter into a laughter of Abraham in Gen. 17:17,[47] and more serious matters, like the silence about the Sinai covenant, which have truly important theological consequences.[48] This last shows that in all these matters what was at issue was not simply the aesthetics of the presentation, but rather that the latter was itself intended to be the vehicle for some very precisely conceived theological statements.

Something similar can be said about the genealogies and chronology. P^g was written at a time when learned mythographers in Ionia had already produced their system of family trees, and one of them, Hecataios of Miletus, working backward with the aid of the genealogies and an average estimated length for each generation, had for the first time attempted to establish an absolute chronology for the heroic period.[49] We cannot fail to recognize a similar chronological technique in P^g: the average length of a

47. Old sources: Gen. 18:12–15. On the dependence on the old sources, see most recently McEvenue, *Narrative Style* (n. 16 above), 145–46.

48. On this, see especially W. Zimmerli, 'Sinaibund und Abrahambund,' in his *Gottes Offenbarung* (Munich, 1963), 205–16. H. Cazelles, who assigns Exod. 19:3b–8 to P, nevertheless sees here only a 'renewal' of the Abrahamic covenant: 'Alliance du Sinai, Alliance de l'Horeb et Renouvellement de l'Alliance,' in H. Donner, ed., *Beiträge zur alttestamentlichen Theologie*, Festschrift for W. Zimmerli (Göttingen, 1977), 69–79. One can scarcely agree with Kutsch, 'Gott' (see n. 16 above), 386 that when P^g does not use the term *bĕrît* for the events at Sinai it offers 'nothing new' in contrast to the older tradition, since the idea of a Sinai covenant 'did not exist at all' in Israel. For even if, as Kutsch supposes, all the instances of *bĕrît* in the non-priestly parts of the Sinai narratives are to be assigned to the 'deuteronomic-deuteronomistic field,' we can still place them within the traditions available to P^g. Moreover, it is not simply a question of the word *bĕrît*, but also of the older connection of the Sinai tradition with the proclamation of the law. The excitement produced even in priestly circles by this dismantling of the Sinai covenant is evident from the very prompt reversal produced by the insertion of H. On this, see Lohfink, 'Abänderung' (n. 33 above).

49. On Greek mythography, which reached its high point in the 6th/5th centuries BCE, see W. Speyer, 'Genealogie,' *RAC* 9 (Stuttgart, 1976), 1166–70 (with additional bibliography). The work of Hecataios of Miletus was entitled 'Historiae,' but also 'Heroologia' or 'Genealogiae.'

generation seems to have been 100 years.[50] But on the whole, P^g stands more in the tradition of the ancient Orient, even in the genealogies and numbers.[51] This is indicated by the arrangement of the linear genealogies around the Flood as a central axis,[52] and perhaps also by the role of the number ten,[53] but in any case by its employment of a myth of origins to trace all its facts to a single beginning.[54] In detail, one is never certain in this very field at what point we are looking at tradition that P^g has incorporated, and where it is the author's own construction. But if it is tradition that is being used, then we must apply Wilson's assertion that ethnology furnishes no evidence 'that genealogies are created for the purpose of making historical record,'[55] and where we find the author of P^g

50. On the calculation of generations, at least in P^g in the MT, see n. 60 below.

51. See the works cited above in n. 36, as well as M. Ramlot, 'Les généalogies bibliques, un genre littéraire oriental,' *Bible et vie Chrétienne* 60 (1964): 53–70. A further dimension of the dependency on Mesopotamian science emerges if M. Barnouin is correct in his tracing of the numbers in Genesis 5 and in the muster lists of Numbers to Babylonian mathematics and astronomy. Cf. M. Barnouin, 'Recherches numériques sur la généalogie de Gen. V,' *RB* 77 (1970): 347–65; idem, 'Les recensements du livre de Nombres et l'astronomie Babylonienne,' *VT* 27 (1977): 280–303.

52. This corresponds to the structure of the Sumerian list of kings. On this, see especially T. Jacobsen, *The Sumerian Kinglist* (Chicago, 1939).

53. That ten generations represent the ideal genealogical depth is maintained by Malamat, 'King Lists' (n. 36 above). Wilson, 'Genealogies' (n. 36 above), contradicts this position. In the Bible, the primary comparison would be with the ten-generation list of David's ancestors in Ruth 4:18–22. Through the division of the whole work into ten '*toledot*,' it may be that P^g even represents itself as something like a '*toledot*' to the tenth power.

54. Certainly, this was seldom done in antiquity so consistently and obviously as in P^g. Still, as a basic principle it may be found even in a work like the 'catalogues of women' or 'Eoiae' attributed to Hesiod, in which different great races are traced to different women ancestors; however, these all had sexual relations with the gods.

55. 'Genealogies' (see n. 36 above), 189.

56. Methuselah, the father of Lamech, in Gen. 5:21 P^g is undoubtedly identical with Methushael, the father of Lamech, in Gen. 4:18 J. It may be that the author of P^g did not make an independent change, but instead that there were two alternative forms of the same name. Thus M. Tsevat, 'The Canaanite God Šälaḥ,' *VT* 4 (1954): 41–49, who sees in the second element of the name the name of the god of the underworld: *šelaḥ* or *šĕʾōl*. But even then, P^g might have chosen the form Methuselah, or retained it against J, because it appeared to contain the element *šelaḥ* (missile, spear), and this corresponded to the fact that the Flood in which Methuselah died

himself at work, he reveals intentions that are other than historical. The Yahwistic Methushael is introduced as Methuselah, so that his very name will make him recognizable as a sinner and it will be clear that the Flood was the consequence of sin.[56] The ages of the people before the Flood are given in such a way as to indicate that sinners like Methuselah themselves died in the Flood,[57] and also so that all the primeval ancestors could simultaneously experience the assumption into heaven of the perfect man, Enoch.[58] All the ancestors beginning with Noah, ten generations in all, could be present when Abraham saw the light of day, and only then did they each successively die.[59] The numbers thus served simply to underscore certain figures and events. The whole chronology in the Masoretic text fixes the Exodus *anno mundi* 2666. That seems to be two-thirds of a cosmic year of 4000, and thus the *annus magnus et mirabilis* would be, if we call on other biblical and extrabiblical information that was available in the time of the Maccabees, the year 164 BCE in our chronology, hence the year of the rededication of the Temple.[60] Of

had its origins in *ḥāmās* (violent deeds). For further information on the forms of the names in the genealogy in P^g, still useful is K. Budde, *Die biblische Urgeschichte (Gen. 1–12, 15)* (Gießen, 1883), 98–100.

57. According to the numbers in MT, Methuselah died in the year of the Flood (born *anno mundi* 687, age 969 years; the Flood happened in *anno mundi* 1656). According to the numbers in Samaritanus, this is also true for Jered and Lamech, and this may be original: see n. 61 below. In that case, the whole second half of the ten-person pre-Flood genealogy (with the exceptions of Enoch and Noah, of course) consists of sinners who were killed in the Flood. We can scarcely avoid thinking that P^g has used this means to express the inbreaking of sin. On the other hand, we should be skeptical of the ever-recurring assertion that the diminishing length of life expresses the increase of sin. This opinion can hardly be verified from the text: cf. Van den Wijngaert, 'Sünde' (n. 32 above), 36–37. On the whole, see Budde, *Urgeschichte* (n. 56 above), 92–103.

58. According to the MT, Enoch was taken away in *anno mundi* 987. In that year, all the pre-Flood ancestors were still or already living, except Adam, who died in 930, and Noah, who was not born until 1056. According to Samaritanus, which probably has the original numbers, Enoch was taken up in 887, and even Adam, who died in 930, and Noah, who was born in 707, were able to witness it.

59. According to MT, which probably has the original numbers here, Abraham was born *anno mundi* 1946. Noah died in 2006, Shem in 2094, Shelah in 2124, Eber in 2185, Peleg in 1994, Reu in 2014, Serug in 2047, Nahor in 1995, and Terah in 2098 – thus all after Abraham's birth.

60. See, most recently, Johnson, *Genealogies* (n. 36 above), 32–33. The 2666 years before the Exodus can be designated as the time of the 26 2/3 generations from

course, that can only be a system tucked into the text in the Maccabean period. But we have reasons to suppose that the original number system was also transparent for an *annus mirabilis*, probably when Solomon's temple was built.[61] We have lost the key to most of the genealogical and chronological material in P^g^, and yet the few doors we are still able to open do not lead us into a history.

If this is the case with the names and numbers, what should we think of the words and deeds? Elliger has spoken of the transparency of the presentation in the priestly document. It is true that the narration is in the past tense. But what is narrated corresponds to situations, opportunities, experiences and problems of the target audience. In the guise of the past, it offers them aid for their own lives and possible solutions for their problems. This state of things can often be demonstrated from the fact that at many points there is a terminological allusion to prophetic texts from the period of the exile.

The story of the scouts in Numbers 13–14 may serve as an example.[62] The sin committed by Israel's tribal representatives and the whole people in the wilderness of Paran has a specific name: *dibbat hā'āreṣ*, 'slandering the land' (Num. 13:32; 14:36–37). The slander is also quoted, and the crucial formulation is: *'ereṣ 'okelet yôšĕbêhā hî'*: 'a land that devours its inhabitants is this' (Num. 13:32). If we take the two formulations together, we are forcibly led to Ezek. 36:1–15, the prophecy 'to the mountains of Israel.' These mountains have become desolate and the possession of other peoples. They have fallen to the *dibbat 'ām*, the 'slander of the people' (Ezek. 36:3). YHWH now makes them a promise to bring the people Israel back to them and cause them again to live there happily and in great numbers. How had the people slandered the

Adam to Eleazar (but for the last two and two-thirds generations only with the aid of the levitic genealogy in Exod. 6:16–25 P^g^), if we reckon the generations at 100 years. (As a possible basis for this, see Gen. 15:13–16.)

61. The reconstruction of the original chronology of P^g^ that seems to me most plausible is by A. Jepsen, 'Zur Chronologie des Priesterkodex,' *ZAW* 47 (1929): 251–53. According to this, the numbers in Samaritanus would be original for the time before the Flood, and those of the MT for the time afterward. Reasons for this can be derived from a comparison of the various sets of numbers. In that case, the Exodus should be placed in *anno mundi* 2320. Since Solomon's temple was begun 480 years after the Exodus (according to 1 Kgs. 6:1, a text that should already have been available to P^g^), we come to the *annus mundi* 2800 as the *annus mirabilis*.

62. On what follows, see especially McEvenue, *Narrative Style* (n. 16 above), 90–144, and Lohfink, 'Ursünden' (n. 33 above), 52–54.

mountains of Israel? They had said, as quoted near the end of the oracle, *'okelet 'ādām 'atti*, 'you devour people.'[63] The connection between these two texts should be obvious.[64] Apparently the readers of P^g could also recognize it. They lived at a time when it was possible for them to return to the land. But it may be that such a return was not interesting for many of them. In such a context, this play on the text of Ezekiel means to say that a resistance to returning and a justification of that resistance by demeaning talk about the land was nothing other than a sinful adoption of the judgment passed by other nations.

If we see this, we can also recognize the meaning of the changes P^g has made to the narrative of the scouts in contrast to its earlier appearance. McEvenue has shown that P^g has banished every warlike element from the old narrative of spies and warfare.[65] What is described here is a peaceful inspection of the land they are about to enter. This also makes the story transparent to the situation in the Persian empire. Nothing has to be conquered, but it is conceivable that first of all some delegates must go ahead of the people to study the possibilities for new settlements, and that only after that would larger caravans be organized for the return. Obviously, a good deal would depend on the judgment such a delegation gave when it returned.

In similar fashion, it could be shown for many other narratives and motifs in P^g how little they have to do with the facts of the past, and how much, instead, depends on making the presentation as transparent as possible for the world of the readers. Even the primeval history was joined to the present in this fashion. The Flood was brought about by the sin of 'all flesh.'[66] This sin, apparently the fundamental sin of humanity itself, is also given a special name. It is *ḥāmās*, 'violence.'[67] This certainly includes

63. Ezek. 36:13; cf. 36:14.

64. The most recent discussion of the question whether P^g also derived the words of the blessing of fruitfulness (*prh* and *rbh* in Gen. 1:22 and frequently elsewhere) from Ezek. 36:11 may be found in M. Gilbert, 'Soyez féconds et multipliez (Gen 1,28),' *NRT* 106 (1974): 733.

65. On the 'pacifism' of P^g see n. 30 above.

66. For what follows, cf. McEvenue, *Narrative Style* (n. 16 above), 20–32 and 41–42; Lohfink, 'Ursünden' (n. 33 above), 48–52, but especially (despite Westermann's verdict in *Genesis I* [n. 36 above], 559, that it 'has no basis in the text') Van den Wijngaert, 'Sünde' (see n. 32 above), 40–48.

67. Gen. 6:11, 13. On the reference of this term, within the priestly writing, to Gen. 1:29 and 9:2–3, see the further discussion in Part II below.

the sin of Cain and the vengefulness of Lamech (Gen. 4:1–16, 23–24). But again there is also a pointer to Ezekiel. The group of terms used in Gen. 6:9-13 to introduce the Flood creates a bridge to Ezek. 28:1–19, the third saying against the king of Tyre. I cannot explicate this in detail here. In any case, this oracle against Tyre makes use of an old myth about the fall of a primeval being from heaven. Its original sin, pride, is here interpreted in light of what Tyre has done as *ḥāmās.*[68] In this concretization, and by omission of the original pride, P^g offers his readers a subtle play on the old myth of the Fall. The thing that formerly spoiled God's good creation[69] was the violence on account of which, now, prophetic oracles must be delivered against the nations. Today, in fact, the Flood really should be repeated – that is the conclusion the readers should draw. Thus here the fall of primeval humanity through sin and the distant Flood at the world's dawning are drawn out of the past, by way of the bridge formed by an oracle from Ezekiel, and made to be present realities.

One could comment almost the whole of P^g in this fashion. Every event is transparently narrated. What once was can also return. The structural congruence illuminates the readers' present – and perhaps every possible present.

What should we call the intention behind such a narrative? It talks about something that has already happened, and yet it is indifferent to the issue of when that event happened, what relationship it bears to everything that has happened before, and how it influenced everything that came later. What is more important is that all that once happened can be repeated in the readers' own time. In this way, the Then can illuminate the Now. This is an understanding of history for which there is, in a certain sense, a storehouse of paradigmatic world situations, all of which existed at one time and can recur again. It is worth telling about them because, when they return, a knowledge of them can be useful.

In Mesopotamia, the omen literature probably presupposed a similar understanding of history.[70] Naturally, it expected not only that world

68. Ezek. 28:16. On the word itself, cf. H. J. Stoebe, '*ḥāmās* Gewalttat,' THAT I (Munich, 1971), cols. 583–87.

69. Cf. the root *šḥt* in Gen. 6:11, 12, 13.

70. For an overview, see A. L. Oppenheim, *Ancient Mesopotamia* (Chicago, 1964), 206–24. The most important publications are in H. Hirsch, 'Akkadische Wahrsageliteratur,' *Kindlers Literaturlexikon* I (Zürich, 1965), cols. 341–43. For our context, the most significant are the 'historical omens,' although quantitatively, to be sure, they are a marginal phenomenon. On the concept of history, see H. Gese, 'Geschichtliches Denken im Alten Orient und im Alten Testament,' *ZThK* 55

constellations can be repeated, but also that there will be a correspondence between world situations writ large and the state of the omens. Moreover, it normally disposed its material according to other points of view than that of temporal succession, and in this sense it tends to isolate situations quite differently from the priestly writing. Thus, in the end, one hesitates to introduce them for comparison here. Nevertheless, more distant relationships in mental attitude are not out of the question. In Israel, too, the priests were entrusted with oracles, and one of God's last dispositions in the priestly narrative is the subordination of Joshua to the priest Eleazar, who can make use of the Urim oracle (Num. 27:21). In P^g scarcely anything happens that has not previously been predicted or ordered by God.[71]

However that may be, in what follows we will take another route in determining the intention behind the transparency of the narrative of the past in P^g, namely a comparison with mythical speech, especially the primeval myth.[72]

This myth tells of things that happened in the timelessness of primeval time, things that are true always and everywhere and therefore can also explain the Now. It can even happen that historical figures are subsumed in the myth. But the myth is not concerned with whether or not its figures once lived.

In contrast, the priestly narrative, apart from the primeval history in the old sources, rests on a broad historical substratum, and despite its freedom it remains true to that basis, for example in the sequence of the principal events. And yet it narrates everything as if it were recounting myths. In a sense it converts history back into myth. Therefore we get the impression that, in spite of the temporal sequence, we are in the last analysis looking at a great picture collection assembled on artistic principles. It derives from history, and yet its tendency is toward paradigm. It does not go

(1958), 132: 'The idea of history . . . is as follows: every situation or kind of age has already occurred once in the incalculable range of situations, and each will come again, but the sequence as such is indeterminable . . . There is no thought of a development from one situation to another over time, to say nothing of the idea that history might have a goal and purpose.'

71. Here, certainly, some differentiation is in order. See McEvenue, 'Fulfilment' (n. 24 above). In addition, in this connection the Mesopotamian conception of the determination of fate by the gods should be introduced. Cf. W. G. Lambert, 'Destiny and Divine Intervention in Babylon and Israel,' *The Witness of Tradition*, OTS 17 (Leiden, 1972): 65–72.

72. Literature on the theme of 'myth and the Old Testament' is listed in Dequeker, 'Noah' (see n. 21 above), 120 n. 19.

so far as to isolate the two from one another altogether. It even develops the genealogies and introduces a chronology, apparently in a conscious effort to counter the isolationist tendency of its narrative and under no circumstances to permit the thread of events to be broken. But there are chains of individual myths in the primeval myths also, for example in the Atrahasis myth, which we will discuss presently. Perhaps we can state our preliminary conclusion: In P^g the primeval era did not end with the Flood; instead, it extends throughout the entire narrated history.

2. The Rejection of a Dynamic World

One may ask even of a storyteller who intends to write paradigms rather than history what kind of notion of history, or 'philosophy of history' he or she has. Even this kind of author must make sense of the way in which the present of his or her addressees relates to the past and the future, and the author can express this in individual paradigms or in the total composition. How much more is this true of the priestly historical narrative, which rests on historical works and, despite its different narrative intention, has no wish to repudiate its origins.

The old sources of the Pentateuch contained a philosophy of history. Gen. 12:1–3 placed Abraham against the background of a humanity that had fallen under a curse, and made of him the beginning of a new blessing, emanating from God, for all nations.[73] The history of the ancestors and, at least from the time of the early deuteronomic redaction of the Pentateuch, the whole history of Israel until its entry into the Land is interpreted in the categories of promise and fulfillment.[74] Deuteronomy and the historical

73. Cf. especially Wolff, 'Kerygma' (n. 34 above).

74. There is a good introduction (although P is placed in the same line as JE) in G. von Rad, *Theologie des Alten Testaments* 1 (Munich, 7th ed. 1978), 179–89 [= *Theology of the Old Testament* 1, 165–75]. This category runs like a leitmotif through the works listed in C. Westermann, *Probleme alttestamentlicher Hermeneutik* (Munich, 1960). The newer discussions concerning the redactional classification of the theology of promise in the Pentateuch were provoked primarily by J. Hoftijzer, *Die Verheißungen an die drei Erzväter* (Leiden, 1956), though with a few later sparks as well. The restrictions in the text are made in view of Rendtorff, *Problem* (see n. 28 above). But see also J. Van Seters, 'The Yahwist as Theologian? A Response,' *JSOT* 3 (1977): 17–18. That it was in no way necessary that the theology of the promise of the Land to the ancestors had simply to be adopted is evident from the theology of history in the 'little historical creed' in Deut. 26:5–9. On this, see N. Lohfink, 'Dtn 26,5–9: Ein Beispiel altisraelitischer Geschichtstheologie,' *Geschichte, Zeugnis und Theologie* [= *Kerygma und Mythos* VI–7] (Hamburg–Bergstedt, 1976), 100–107.

work attached to it, as well as some things in the Sinai pericope, introduce the category of a 'contract' between YHWH and Israel as a principle of interpretation.[75] Hence we cannot avoid the question of P^g's attitude toward all this.

Still another question immediately arises. A great deal, at least in the paradigmatic pericopes in P^g, has to do with exilic and post-exilic 'hope for return.'[76] In this way, the author of P^g joins the chorus of the prophets of his time, for they also chant the hope for return. But in the prophets, this is combined with what we might call a dynamizing of history. The future will be greater than the past ever was. A new action of YHWH is imminent, something that surpasses anything in the past. The time-line is on an ascending curve. The essential, the real thing has not yet happened. Deutero-Isaiah, in particular, dynamizes the understanding of history in this fashion, but not he alone. Is P^g also part of this movement, since it proclaims hope for return?

This question did not arise as long as the history narrated by P^g was regarded only as a legitimation of the post-exilic cultic community. But more recently it has contributed to the suspicion that the priestly cultic community in the wilderness may not represent the original form, but rather a future ideal, or even an eschaton.[77] What about all this?

Since the author of P^g ordinarily says clearly what he wants to say, we should look for reflex utterances. In doing so, it is appropriate to begin with the interpretation of history that was contained in his models. He did not take up the theme of 'Abraham as beginning of the blessing for all

75. I deliberately say 'contract' and not 'covenant,' or 'order,' as E. Kutsch, *Verheißung und Gesetz, Untersuchungen zum sogenannten 'Bund' im alten Testament*, BZAW 131 (Berlin, 1973) would prefer to do, with somewhat too great a fixation on the meaning of the word *bĕrît*. Despite a number of individual considerations, we must agree with the fundamental thesis of an obvious theology of covenant in the deuteronomic and deuteronomistic literature, as developed by L. Perlitt, *Bundestheologie im Alten Testament* (Neukirchen–Vluyn, 1969). On the connection with neo-Assyrian ideology of the state and the process (as understood by sociology of knowledge) that led to the development of this theology of contract, see N. Lohfink, *Unsere großen Wörter* (Freiburg, 1977), 24–43 [= *Great Themes from the Old Testament* 17–37]; idem, 'Deuteronomy,' *IDB Supplement* (Nashville, 1976), 231.

76. See nn. 19 and 21 above.

77. The question of the 'effectiveness of the messianic idea' in the priestly document was proposed even at the time when the older notion of P was commonly held, but it was motivated primarily by a kind of desire for completeness, and not much was made of it. See Holzinger, *Einleitung* (n. 9 above), 338. For more recent literature, see n. 17 above.

nations.'[78] He apparently rejected the deuteronomic theology of covenant and therefore connects a different statement with the word *bĕrît*.[79] It is another matter, however, with the category of promise and fulfillment, whose role in the entire sweep of narrated history is all-pervasive.[80]

This theme does not make its first appearance with the patriarchs, but in the context of creation itself.[81] Steck has shown that the words of the creator God in Genesis 1 are not commands that are immediately realized, but something like projections of the final state of the world envisioned by God; the creator's own activity in many cases only produces a beginning from which, in the course of time, the final state will result.[82] This is especially true for the second work of the sixth day, the last and highest in all creation. Here, in the blessing of humanity in Gen. 1:28, God sketches a project for the whole chain of events that is subsequently described in the historical work.[83] To this blessing, which is repeated in

78. There is reason to believe that the author of P^g^ wished to give his readers the opportunity to share in the experience of his elegant scotching of this theme, since he takes up the key word 'nations' in connection with the promise to Abraham, but only in the sense that a multitude of nations is to be descended from Abraham: Gen. 17:4–6. There is also a 'blessing of the nations,' but no longer for 'all' the families or peoples of the earth. Gen. 17:16 makes it clear that this blessing only applies to Sarah's descendants, and thus is very narrowly limited. For textual criticism of this verse, see N. Lohfink, 'Textkritisches zu Gen 17,5.13.16.17,' *Bibl* 48 (1967): 439–40. Gen. 17:20 underscores this, since Ishmael is to become a great, but only a *single* nation. In contrast, the promise is renewed with emphasis to Jacob: Gen. 28:3; 25:11; 48:3. In addition, the association of *gôy* and *qĕhal gôyim* in Gen. 35:11 makes clear that the reference is only to the people Israel. Thus the blessing for all the nations of the earth slowly but surely becomes an assurance that the people of Israel (very numerous, of course) is to descend from Abraham. On the traditio-critical problem of these formulae, see Groß, 'Jakob' (n. 29 above), 326–27.

79. See n. 48 above, as well as R. Clements, *Abraham and David* (London, 1967), 71–78.

80. In this connection, the most important stylistic elements are described by McEvenue, 'Fulfilment' (n. 24 above), and Blenkinsopp, 'Structure' (n. 21 above).

81. It is true that there were some promise-motifs even in the old sources for the primeval history (cf. Gen. 3:15; 4:15; 8:21–22), but they are of a different type and are not developed in a literarily comprehensible fashion in the later history of Israel.

82. O. H. Steck, *Der Schöpfungsbericht der Priesterschrift* (Göttingen, 1975).

83. To the extent that P^g^ has no further concern with the other works of creation (except from the threat posed to them by the Flood), and thus omits them from his description, the human beings present a special case that has deeply influenced the overall shape of Gen. 1:26–31, as Steck describes in detail in *Schöpfungsbericht*, 129–58. The most recent study of the theme here under discussion is Brueggemann,

part, and renewed, in the course of the description, correspond later notices of fulfillment.[84] Thus we may now ask, in light of a suspected eschatology in P^g, whether in Gen. 1:28 something is announced whose fulfillment is not described in the work itself, and that may still not have existed in the exilic or post-exilic period.[85]

		BRK	PRH	RBH	ML''RṢ	KBS'RṢ	RDH (beasts)
Blessing	Gen. 1:28	X	X	X	X	X	X
	9:1, 7	X	X	X	X		
	17:2, 6, 16	X	X	X			
	28:3	X	X	X			
	25:9, 11	X	X	X			
	48:3-4	X	X	X			
Fulfillment	Gen. 47:27		X	X			
	Exod. 1:7		X	X	X		
	Josh. 18:1					X	
							YR' + HTT
Revision	Gen. 9:2						X X

Table IV: Genesis 1:28 as a Project for P^g

First of all, according to Gen. 1:28, humanity, so small at the beginning, is to reproduce and spread out over the surface of the earth:

'Kerygma' (see n. 21 above), but he reads in Gen. 1:28 too immediate a statement about Israel and its hope to return from exile into its land. My own analysis of Gen. 1:28 may be found in N. Lohfink, ''Macht euch die Erde untertan'?' *Orientierung* 38 (1974): 137–42 (Chapter 1 of this book); cf. idem, 'Die Priesterschrift und die Grenzen des Wachstums,' *Theologisches Jahrbuch* 1976 (Leipzig, 1977): 223–48. The interpretation given there of human rule over the animals should, however, be revised in light of what now follows.

84. On what follows, see Table IV. It does not contain the formulae that refer to the increase of the animal world or to the marginal lines of Abraham's descendants. In addition, the focus is only on the vocabulary of Gen. 1:28.

85. This is the case, for example, in J, since the the 'fulfillments' of Gen. 12:1–3 that Wolff has demonstrated within the story of the patriarchs are only something like 'fulfillments *in nuce*,' and the complete accomplishment of the blessing of the nations was certainly not yet present at the time when J was written, no matter when one dates it.

pĕrû ûrĕbû ûmil'û 'et-hā'āreṣ.[86] This blessing is repeated after the Flood, at a time when humanity is once more at a beginning point, and then is given again especially to Abraham and Jacob, from whom the people Israel is to descend. Its fulfillment is confirmed twice, in Gen. 47:27 and in Exod. 1:7. The second of these notices of fulfillment, at least, refers simultaneously to the blessing on Abraham and Jacob and the blessing of all humanity.[87]

The blessing of procreation in Gen. 1:28 accompanies the further promised blessing that the nations that will come into existence through that increase will each take possession of their own land. It appears to me that the imperative *kibšuhā* must be so understood.[88] This motif of promise and blessing reappears beginning with Abraham, but with a different vocabulary: here it is the promise of the land of Canaan to Abraham and Isaac, and there is a continuing reference to this in the continuation of the priestly narrative.[89] Once the blessing of procreation has been dealt with once and for all at the beginning of the book of Exodus, the promise of the land determines the course of events, as is evident especially in Exodus 6. Israel is not yet in its land and must be brought there. The fact that this really is the extension of what was said in Gen. 1:28 to all humanity is clear from one of the last sentences in P^g. For in Josh. 18:1 the words of Gen. 1:28, not used at all in the intervening text, are recalled: 'Then the whole congregation of the Israelites assembled at Shiloh, and set up the tent of meeting there. The land lay subdued before them' (*wĕhā'āreṣ nikbĕšâ lipnêhem*). This is the literary parenthesis around the whole work.

There then remains only one other element from Gen. 1:28, human

86. On this, see especially Gilbert, 'Multipliez' (n. 64 above).

87. We should not be surprised that a notice of fulfillment is given twice, since P likes to present important things twice over. The fact that the second notice *per modum unius* refers to the blessing at creation is clear from two expressions that are present here, but were not part of the blessing of Abraham and Jacob: *šrṣ* (cf. Gen. 9:7), and *ml'*, 'land' (cf. Gen. 1:28: 9:1). The sequence is chiastic with respect to Gen. 9:1, 7.

88. Cf. Lohfink, 'Erde' (n. 83 above), 138–39.

89. There is an analysis of the relevant texts in Cortese, *Canaan* (see n. 19 above). The terminology differing from that in the blessing of fruitfulness depends on the traditional promise of the land and on special priestly ideas about the sacro-legal character of Israel's possession of the land. It appears that here not everything is to be applied to humanity as a whole, hence the different terminology in Gen. 1:28.

rule over the animals.[90] There is no notice of its fulfillment in P^g. But that is not because we find here, at last, an eschatological future that is still unrealized, despite the possible parallels with a messianic peace among the animals that we might seem to see in it.[91] Instead, this theme is resolved in P^g not by fulfillment, but by a revision of the world plan. Regarding governance of the animals, the human beings have 'their fate determined' anew, to speak in Mesopotamian fashion.

The vegetarian instruction for nourishment both of humans and animals that follows immediately after Gen. 1:28, in verse 29, shows that human governance of the animals was certainly intended as something altogether peaceful and paradisiacal. But that very thing is destroyed by the sin of *kol bāśār*, 'all flesh' – an expression that includes both humans and beasts – the sin that provoked the Flood.[92] That sin is, after all, *ḥāmās*, 'violence.' Both human beings and animals have begun to kill, apparently in order to nourish themselves on flesh, contrary to God's order. After the Flood God will promise Noah never again to send another Flood.[93] But in order to do so, God must first reduce, in some sense, the mass of possible violence. This is accomplished by permitting human beings, from this point on, to eat meat. That is the meaning of the introduction of a state of enmity between human beings and animals, couched in the language of holy war, in Gen. 9:2: 'The fear and dread of you shall rest on every animal of the earth, and on every bird of the air, on everything that creeps on the ground, and on all the fish of the sea; into your hand they are delivered (*bĕyedkem nittanû*).'[94]

90. On the meaning of *rdh*, which may not be interpreted on the basis of the questionable occurrence in Joel 4:13, see Lohfink, 'Erde' (n. 83 above), 139.

91. E.g., Isaiah 11:6–9.

92. Against A. R. Hulst, 'Kol baśar in der priesterlichen Fluterzählung,' *OTS* 12 (Leiden, 1958): 28–68, and without the complicated explanation in J. Scharbert, *Fleisch, Geist und Seele im Pentateuch* (Stuttgart, 2nd ed. 1964), 53–54, according to which the human being as 'pinnacle' of all flesh is, in a certain sense, 'all flesh,' since the animals are thus implicated in the judgment on human beings.

93. Gen 9:8–17. For an analysis, see especially McEvenue, *Narrative Style* (n. 16 above), 72–78, and Groß, 'Berit' (n. 16 above). Most studies impede their own access to this text by failure to note its system of tenses and stylistic figures.

94. For the association of the paired words *yr'* + *ḥtt* with war, cf. Deut. 1:21; 31:8; Josh. 8:1; 10:25; 1 Sam. 17:11; 1 Chr. 22:13; 28:20; 2 Chr. 20:15, 17; 32:7. For the application of this linguistic form to the war of YHWH, cf. Deut. 2:25; 11:25. There is no need to discuss the fact that *ntn bĕyād* was the fixed expression of the oracle of salvation in war.

Thus the last element in Gen. 1:28 does not point beyond the history that is narrated in P^g. There is no hint of a promise that is not fulfilled within the story. The promise that Abraham and Jacob will be the ancestors of kings has long been fulfilled, at least as far as P^g's readers are concerned.[95] The same is true of the promise that YHWH will be God for them and their descendants.[96] Thus we can comfortably say that P^g knows of nothing more that will carry beyond the realities described in the history that has been narrated. Once Israel has crossed the Jordan, P^g is unaware of any dynamic history that continually surpasses itself and aims toward an undreamed eschaton.

Instead, the vegetarianism of Paradise and its abandonment after the Flood reveals a descending course of development. Could Ewald have been right after all when he compared this to the generally pessimistic view of history embodied in the theory of the four ages of the world? It is true that it is never apparent in P^g itself, but it could well be that P^g sees the course of history as an analogous decline from a 'best' world to a new, but only 'second-best' state.

In a certain sense this seems to me to be an accurate assessment. In any case, we are in a position to apply a much closer parallel than is provided by just any text about a descent from a golden age to an age of iron. I am referring to the Atrahasis myth (cf. p. 143 n. 26 above).

As we know, this work proceeds quite rapidly to the creation of humanity, the first great event described, and then goes on to depict the history of human beings and the gods until shortly after the Flood. At that moment, the groups of gods who had quarreled about the Flood and the rescue of the flood hero Atrahasis hammer out a compromise that establishes a new rule for human existence in the world. Apparently there is still disagreement among Assyriologists about exactly what it was that led to the gods' decison to destroy human beings by means of a flood. Was it human rebellion (so G. Pettinato),[97] or a grasping at greater things than

95. This promise is found in Gen. 17:6, 16; 35:11. It indicates that the Abrahamic covenant in P^g is placed within the tradition of the promise given through Nathan, which was understood as a Davidic covenant and in the immediate sense was not to be thought of in deuteronomic categories. On this, see Clement, *Abraham* (n. 79 above).

96. This is fulfilled at Sinai, when God takes up a cultic residence in the midst of Israel. This is unmistakably expressed at a strategic point in the Sinai revelation by means of the usual P^g technique of repetition, with Exod. 6:7 as a bridge to Exod. 29:45–46.

97. 'Die Bestrafung des Menschengeschlechts durch die Sintflut,' *Or*, n.s. 37 (1968): 165–200. Lambert and Moran have criticized Pettinato's position rather sharply.

had been planned for humanity (so, for example, W. von Soden),[98] or was it the purely biological fact that human beings were increasing too rapidly and thus becoming overly numerous (so A. D. Kilmer and W. L. Moran)?[99] Perhaps it was both sin *and* biology. But if we adhere to what appears clearly in the text as available to us, namely the compromise formulae arrived at after the Flood, what comes most obviously to the fore is the problem of overpopulation. The compromise concerns means by which the number of human beings can be kept smaller than before.[100] In any case, according to the Atrahasis myth a new world was established after the Flood because the first had not been successful, and this seems to me to provide a clear parallel to the priestly narrative, no matter how different the reasons given in the two works for the coming of the Flood.

What significance does this have for P^{g}'s idea of history? The Atrahasis myth evidently describes a restless phase of the world still groping for perfection because it wishes to explain the present world of stability as it now exists.[101] And the priestly document does nothing different, except that it pursues the path from a dynamic to a static state twice over. The first time it parallels the Atrahasis myth up to a first stabilization after the Flood. Now the world edifice stands fast and will never again be shaken. But for the human inhabitants of the structure there follows a second dynamic period. They are essentially exemplified in

98. 'Der Mensch bescheidet sich nicht. Überlegungen zu Schöpfungserzählungen in Babylonien und Israel,' *Symbolae Biblicae et Mesopotamicae Francisco Mario Theodoro de Liagre Böhl dedicatae* (Leiden, 1973): 349–58.

99. Moran, 'Atrahasis' (see n. 26 above); Kilmer, 'The Mesopotamian Concept of Overpopulation and Its Solution as Reflected in the Mythology,' *Or*, n.s. 41 (1972): 160–77.

100. It is possible that the number of human beings is to be reduced to a third of the previous total. The means to this end are the barrenness of many women, the Pāšittu-demon (infant mortality), and the institution of childless priestesses. The text (speech of the god Enki to the mother goddess Nintu) is translated by Kilmer as follows: 'He opened his mouth to speak, saying to the Lady of Birth, the Mother-womb: O Lady of Birth, Creatress of the Fates, (Let there be for the peoples . . .) [about five broken lines in which unknown stipulations are made]. Moreover, let there be a third-category among people (? or: only one-third of the people?). (Let there be) among the people bearing women and barren women, Let there be among the people a Pāšittu-demon, Let it seize the baby from the mother's lap. Establish *Ugbabtu*-priestesses, *Entu*-priestesses, and *Igiṣītu*-priestesses, They shall indeed be tabood, and thus cut off child-bearing' (Kilmer, 'Overpopulation' [see n. 99 above], 171).

101. These reflections are more broadly developed in N. Lohfink, 'Die Priesterschrift und die Grenzen des Wachstums,' *Stimmen der Zeit* 192 (1974): 435–50.

Israel. Humanity has once again a task before it: the same as the one proposed for it on the morning of creation, with minor revisions. It must grow to its proper number, and then each nation must take possession of the land assigned to it. This again is something dynamic, a history striving toward a greater future. But eventually the status proposed by God is achieved. Here the narrative stops, just as the Atrahasis myth concluded with the compromise after the Flood. The world is now the way it should be, and needs no further changes. Nor is there an absence of the formal narrative elements of a catastrophe at the end of the second dynamic phase and a revision of the old order by God's word. The sin of the people in the story of the scouts and the sin of the spiritual leaders in the narrative of the water from the rock have led to the death of an entire generation in the wilderness, together with their principal leaders. Who could fail to think of the Flood at the end of the primeval period?[102] And in Numbers 27 the leadership structures in Israel are revised for the time after the taking possession of the land: in the dynamic phase, Moses spoke with God, and Aaron was subject to him; now Eleazar the priest will tell Joshua, the successor of Moses, what God has communicated to him in oracles.[103]

The stability of the world, which God has brought to its perfected form in two stages, is guaranteed by the double covenant. The covenant with Noah guarantees the stability of the world itself, and the covenant with Abraham establishes the number of the people, their possession of the land, and the presence of God in the sanctuary in the midst of Israel. In both cases this is a *bĕrît ʿôlām*, 'an eternal promise.'[104] Its validity is no longer dependent, like that of the deuteronomic *bĕrît*, on the fidelity of human beings to the covenant. If a human generation sins, of course, it excludes itself, and punishment falls upon it. But God withdraws nothing, and the next generation can return to the stable, final state of the world.

Israel in exile, that is, the audience of the priestly narrative, has fallen away. The situation in the wilderness is again present, or even the situation in Egypt. But there is also hope for return, and it rests neither on

102. We could even wonder whether the themes of the plagues and the Sea of Reeds should not also be included in this context.

103. Ordinarily, all that is offered as an explanation for the redistribution of power in Israel is the priestly claim to authority in the post-exilic period. No doubt it existed, but in that case why were things not told from the very beginning in such a way as to reflect the later situation? The matter looks different as soon as we introduce the structural analogy to the primeval myth.

104. On the *bĕrît* theology of P^g, no other aspects of which, apart from this formal statement, can be discussed here, see the literature listed in nn. 48 and 93 above.

some kind of eschatology nor on the expectation of new arrangements by God in the future that will surpass everything previous. Instead, it is founded on what our world has already received from God since the crossing of the Jordan and, as far as God is concerned, can never lose. The fact that the stories narrated in P^g are paradigmatic is directly connected with the fact that the world can fall repeatedly from its perfect form into the imperfection of becoming. Then, in a sense, the paths of the dynamic phase must be trod once again. This connects the result of the first part of our reflection with what has been developed in the second part regarding the philosophy of history in the priestly writing.

This concept of history serves the same purpose for Israel in exile as does an eschatologically inspired prophet: it offers hope. But in doing so, it does not arouse in human hearts the inextinguishable unrest created by the prophets. That in itself may be a reason why we at the present time, when humanity seems to have arrived at the 'limits of growth,' should take a greater interest in the vision of a static world offered us by the priestly historical narrative.

However, this vision is so differentiated that the former alternative of 'law or history' no longer exists. The past that is narrated by no means simply legitimates things as they are. After all, the readers of the priestly document did not live within the glorious and peaceful order that had been planned by God and that could be theirs. But on the other hand their expectations are not projected dynamically toward a new, still unknown, and wholly surprising eschaton. The ideal shape of the world is known; it has already existed before. From the point of view of God it is always present, and all that is necessary is to return to it.

One might ask whether the overburdening of the priestly historical narrative with legislative material has not, after all, pushed the weight to the side of the 'law,' or whether, in the final form of the Pentateuch, the much more 'historical' narration in the old sources or the deuteronomic theology of covenant has not prevailed, with the result that P^g's peculiar treatment of history is no longer visible. Hence the question with which I began is still open here, at the end. Beyond this, it needs to be posed once more on the basis of our understanding of the canon, whether Jewish or Christian. But in any case, we will only be able to deal with it if, in treating such highly nuanced structures as that of the priestly historical narrative, we drop the use of unreflective ideas like that old favorite, 'salvation history.'

7

The Strata of the Pentateuch and the Question of War

1. Introduction

1.1 *The relativity of the idea of hostile occupation of the land, as exemplified in ChrG*

Even someone who maintains that the beginning of the tribal union of 'Israel' was simply a gradual and absolutely peaceful settling down of shepherds and goatherds who had tired of a migratory life; that is, someone who holds the most nonviolent of all the historical theories yet proposed for the origins of Israel, will scarcely question that, at least from the deuteronomic period onward, everyone in Israel was convinced that all Israel had once lived, for many generations, in Egypt, and that afterward it had taken possession of the land given to it by YHWH its God through a violent campaign of conquest. The military capture of the land appears as a principal feature of the Old Testament credo, and one that is simply taken for granted.

And yet quite recently Sara Japhet has shown, in an extraordinarily precise and persuasive analysis, that the Chronicler's historical work clearly and openly contradicts this article of faith, not only through omissions, but even through positive counter-statements, although these may be cautiously introduced and concealed within verbal asides.[1] Ephraim and Manasseh, the sons of Joseph who according to the older writings were born and died in Egypt, in Chronicles are said to have lived not in Egypt, but in the land of Canaan. The genealogy of Ephraim is interrupted in 1 Chronicles 7 by the narrative of his tribe's dealings with Gath, which reduce it to mourning. And we learn that Joshua is part of the tenth

1. S. Japhet, 'Conquest and Settlement in Chronicles,' *JBL* 98 (1979): 205–18. On Ephraim and Joshua, see pp. 213–16.

generation, born long after these events that took place in the land of Canaan (1 Chr. 7:14–29). There can be no doubt that the Chronicler intends to tell us that there never had been a violent invasion of the land by the people of Israel.

I begin with this observation based on the very late historical writings in the Old Testament in order to plead from the very beginning for an openness to the possibility that there were within the Old Testament very different ideas about the way in which the land came into Israel's possession. It seems necessary to make a case for such receptivity. I have already repeatedly expressed my opinion that the priestly document rejects war, and that for that reason, even if we suppose that that writing contains an account of the taking possession of the land, we should under no circumstances expect to find there a description of a military conquest. In doing so, I have regularly encountered friendly but determined skepticism among my colleagues. It appears to be unthinkable that a Pentateuch source that gives any account of the entry into the land of Canaan would not depict it as an expedition of conquest. That is how much the present book of Joshua dominates the fantasies of scholars.

The revision of sacred history by the Chronicler should endow our thinking with a greater degree of flexibility. Chronicles by no means eliminated Joshua's conquest of the land from its historical picture because it was opposed to 'holy wars.' On the contrary: nowhere in the Old Testament are there such devoted descriptions of holy wars as in Chronicles.[2] According to Sara Japhet, their interest is quite different. Israel and its land belong together. They cannot simply have come together at some point or other in history: Israel must be seen as an autochthonous nation in the land provided for it by its God.[3] But even if the reason for the Chronicles' rejection of the book of Joshua is not to be sought in a pacifistic attitude, in any case it was still possible, even at this late period, simply to eradicate the deuteronomistic theology of 'war and conquest' as the first of 'YHWH's gifts' to youthful Israel.[4] Consequently,

2. See G. von Rad, *Der Heilige Krieg im alten Israel*, AThANT 20 (Zürich, 1951), 80–81. On the other hand, there are very well founded reservations to be expressed against David's wars: cf. M. Bič, 'Davids Kriegführung und Salamos Bautätigkeit,' in *Travels in the World of the Old Testament*, Festschrift for M. A. Beek, SSN 16 (Assen, 1974), 1–11.

3. Japhet, 'Conquest and Settlement' (see n. 1 above), 218.

4. The expressions in quotation marks are from W. Zimmerli, *Grundriß der alttestamentlichen Theologie*, ThW 3 (Stuttgart, 2nd ed. 1978). There war and conquest are described even before the land and its blessing as gifts of YHWH.

we should anticipate a greater degree of flexibility in historical description by this author for earlier periods as well.

1.2 *The novelty of the question*

As regards the portrayals that are combined in the Pentateuch, it is notable that Gerhard von Rad, in his classic work on the 'holy war in ancient Israel' makes no mention of their various attitudes toward the military occupation of the land. Of course he has something to say about Deuteronomy, but beyond that only Exodus 13 receives a somewhat more intensive treatment, as a 'spiritualized war story' from the realm of 'post-Solomonic novel writing.'[5]

I have not encountered any other treatment of the Old Testament's statements regarding war that aims at a complete overview and in which the literary strata of the Pentateuch are examined to determine whether there is any variation among them on this subject.[6] The difference that is usually mentioned is between the reality and theory of the wars of YHWH in Israel's earlier centuries as retrievable from the individual narratives, songs and other indications in the Pentateuch on the one hand and the deuteronomic theory of holy war on the other.[7]

There are reasons for this state of things. If, for example, one inquires about the 'kerygma' of the Yahwist, Elohist, or priestly writing,[8] war

5. Von Rad, *Der Heilige Krieg* (n. 2 above), 45–47.

6. The nearest to this would be F. Stolz, *Jahwes und Israels Kriege. Kriegstheorien und Kriegserfahrungen im Glauben des alten Israel*, AThANT 60 (Zürich, 1972). Stolz aims at completeness in his treatment of texts that speak of YHWH's war, and he always establishes the source for texts from the Pentateuch. But he does not pursue the question of typical overriding points of view in individual strata.

7. Somewhat different is the treatment by L. Perlitt, 'Israel und die Völker,' in G. Liedke, ed., *Frieden – Bibel – Kirche*, SFF 9 (Stuttgart, 1972), 17–64. In dealing with the topic of 'war,' he treats successively the historical questions (pp. 19–29), the theory of YHWH's war in the post-Davidic literature (pp. 38–50), and the 'deuteronomic theology of separation,' as evident in the book of Deuteronomy, which is said to be an out and out 'theology of the state' (pp. 50–56). He himself adduces deuteronomic texts to illustrate the 'theory of YHWH's war.' But he supposes that this theory originated in the tenth century (p. 39). On the attitude toward war in the Yahwist's narratives of the patriarchs, see M. Rose, '"Entmilitarisierung des Kriegs"? Erwägungen zu den Patriarchen-Erzählungen der Genesis,' *BZ* 20 (1976): 197–211. I will address this in more detail below.

8. This designation rests on a number of influential essays by H. W. Wolff, which may be found in his *Gesammelte Studien zum Alten Testament*, ThB 22 (Munich, 1964; complete only with the 2nd ed. of 1973). They are translated, interpreted and augmented in W. Brueggemann, *The Vitality of Old Testament Traditions* (Atlanta, 1975).

scarcely appears as a noteworthy element, even when these works contain individual war stories or war songs.[9] The sabre rattles even less if, in drawing the literary-critical boundaries of the source documents, one is left only with a kind of mini-Yahwist and mini-Elohist.[10] It may then happen that, except for the miracle at the Reed Sea in J, there is no more trace of war and battle to be found.

Now, all this should really attract some attention. For if we suppose that in the pre-literary narrative and lyric material there was a rather frequent odor of war and the sacking of towns, and that in the mean time, in the deuteronomic stratum of the Pentateuch, there was a perfectly ruthless theology of war, the fading or, still more, the complete absence of war in the other strata would certainly count as a 'remarkable silence.' It would be a silence at points in the traditional course of the narrative where we really expect to hear something about war. In the syntax as given, it would constitute a non-statement – and therefore a statement.

Consequently, I think it is sensible to compare the various strata of the Pentateuch again with regard to their attitude toward war. What is at issue is primarily the attitude toward Israel's violent occupation of its land. My principal interest lies in the difference between the deuteronomic-deuteronomistic layer and the priestly stratum.

1.3 *Literary-critical presuppositions of the investigation*

I want to be brief in my remarks on what Julius Wellhausen called the 'Jehovist historical book' – what remained after everything belonging to the priestly writing and the deuteronomic corpus had been subtracted. As the discussion now stands, it is not possible to presume any consensus regarding assignment to different layers or time locations within this field of literature. Nor is it possible to develop one's own theories in this framework. I would like merely to establish one point: I regard the 'Jehovist historical book' as existing prior to the deuteronomic-deuteronomistic texts, and certainly the priestly writings, and at most in the case of certain individual texts am I prepared to debate whether they

9. Consider the laconic remark of W. Caspari, 'Was stand im Buch der Kriege Jahwes?' *ZWTh* 54 (1912): 110–58, at 123: 'But probably even the Elohist was only a civilian.'

10. As, for example, in P. Weimar, *Untersuchungen zur Redaktionsgeschichte des Pentateuch*, BZAW 146 (Berlin, 1977); idem, *Die Berufung des Mose. Literaturwissenschaftliche Analyse von Exodus 2,23–5,5*, OBO 32 (Freiburg in Breisgau, 1980).

might belong to a late redaction of the Pentateuch.[11] The principal or final redaction of the historical book, or at least its last, interpretive glossing, was probably in deuteronomic hands, and consequently was the very activity with which the 'deuteronomists' took their first tentative steps.[12]

Regarding the 'priestly writing,' I presuppose that P^g, the 'priestly historical narrative,' was more than a series of expansions added to the 'Jehovist historical book.'[13] It was, rather, an independent work produced toward the end of the Babylonian exile or shortly thereafter, as an alternative to the 'Jehovist historical book' and intended to replace it.[14] It was the literary basis for the redactional composition of the Pentateuch and its enhancement with a great variety of legislative material. In this last phase glosses, additions, and whole pericopes were inserted, even in the narrative material.

2. The 'Jehovist Historical Book' and Warfare

First of all I will set forth some theses, and then offer a rather detailed analysis of an essay by Martin Rose on the 'demilitarization of war' in the patriarchal narratives of Genesis.

2.1 *Six Theses*

2.1.1 *History: War and the factual beginnings of Israel*

Factually, Israel's beginnings were probably a good deal more combative

11. Differently in recent years: J. Van Seters, 'Confessional Reformulation in the Exilic Period,' *VT* 22 (1972): 448–59, according to whom JE is to be placed after D, on the basis of the key phenomenon of its treatment of the promise of the Land to the patriarchs; H. Vorländer, *Die Entstehungszeit des jehowistischen Geschichtswerkes*, EHS.T 109 (Frankfurt, 1978), 369: 'After the deuteronomist historical work had proposed an "etiology of loss of the land," the Jehovist work offered an "etiology of possession of the land;"' M. Rose, *Deuteronomist and Jahwist. Untersuchungen zu den Berührungspunkten beider Literaturwerke*, AThANT 67 (Zürich, 1981): The 'Yahwist' extends the deuteronomistic historical work backwards by successive additions to the beginning. None of these three works does justice to the findings, particularly in the book of Deuteronomy. In response to Van Seters, see especially D. E. Skweres, *Die Rückverweise im Buch Deuteronomium*, AnBib 79 (Rome, 1979); to Rose, my reivew in *ThPh* 57 (1982): 276–80; see also n. 66 below.

12. Thus Wellhausen, as early as his *Composition des Hexateuch.*

13. This was first stated by K. H. Graf. For a complete bibliography, see N. Lohfink, 'Die Priesterschrift und die Geschichte,' *Congress Volume. Göttingen 1977*, SVT 29 (Leiden, 1978): 189–225 (Chapter 6 in this book), at p. 197 n. 28. For my delineation of the boundaries of P^g see p. 198 n. 29.

14. See ibid. 199–201 nn. 31–33.

and bound up with war than was long believed. There was rather too much fascination with the theory of gradual and peaceful settlement by powerless shepherds and goatherds.[15] Gerhard von Rad's study of holy war in ancient Israel gave still further impetus to this idea, since there even the wars of the 'time of the judges' were interpreted as purely defensive.[16] Since then, doubts about the peaceful character of these events have arisen, even when it is presumed that Israel's existence can be traced to the settlement of nomadic groups.[17] These doubts increase at the point when the layers indicating destruction of Canaanite cities in the transition from the Late Bronze Age to Iron Age I are seen, on the basis of the cultural change and shifts in the history of settlement at the same period, as connected with the first footholds of the later entity called Israel.[18] Finally, the military camp again becomes truly the 'cradle of the nation' (though in

15. The classical study: A. Alt, 'Erwägungen über die Landnahme der Israeliten in Palästina,' *PJ* 35 (1939): 8–63 (also found in his *Kleine Schriften zur Geschichte des Volkes Israel* I [Munich, 1959], 126–75). The basis was laid beforehand in his 'Die Landnahme der Israeliten in Palästina,' *Reformationsprogramm der Universität Leipzig 1925* (also found in *Kleine Schriften* I, 89–125). According to Alt, military operations were part of a second stage, the 'expansion of the land.'

16. *Der Heilige Krieg* (see n. 2 above), 26: 'These wars appear . . . in fact to have been exclusively defensive in nature.' He refers to Caspari, 'Buch der Kriege Jahwes' (see n. 9 above), who attempted to give a thorough demonstration of this thesis.

17. First clearly expressed by R. Smend, *Jahwekrieg und Stämmebund*, FRLANT 84 (Göttingen, 1963); then see, for example, Perlitt, 'Israel und die Völker' (n. 7 above), 20: 'Occupation, extension and securing of the land . . . are unimaginable without a certain measure of military activity . . . occupation of land implies an international (and to a certain extent also a practical) conquest. Extension of the land means more or less violent subjugation of the defensively prepared Canaanite cities, alongside which the tribes could certainly not live in peaceful separation for very long. Securing the land very soon meant, in contrast to these first stages of establishment and expansion of settlement, both defense against other, succeeding nomadic tribes that were a dangerous threat to the new settlers, and a war of liberation against the Philistines.' Thus for him there can be no doubt 'that the initial experience of Israel was made up of struggle and war in the greatest variety of magnitudes and motivations.'

18. Let me point to three recent essays: Y. Yadin, 'The Transition from a Semi-Nomadic to a Sedentary Society in the Twelfth Century B.C.E.,' in F. M. Cross, *Symposia Celebrating the Seventy-Fifth Anniversary of the Founding of the American Schools of Oriental Research (1900–1975)* (Cambridge, Mass., 1979), 57–68; M. Weippert, 'Canaan, Conquest and Settlement of,' *IDB Supplement*, 125–30; A. Mazar, 'Giloh: An Early Israelite Settlement Site near Jerusalem,' *IEJ* 31 (1981): 1–36, esp. 33–36. For the history of settlement, see T. L. Thompson, *The Settlement of Palestine in the Bronze Age*, BTAVO.B 34 (Wiesbaden, 1979); idem, 'The Background of the Patriarchs: A Reply to William Dever and Malcolm Clark,' *JSOT* 9 (1978): 2–43, esp. 28–38.

a different sense from that used by Wellhausen, who thought entirely in categories of desert nomadism), if we pay attention to the sociological interpretations of the origins and early period of Israel that have been developed recently, especially in North America.[19]

The 'period of the Judges' was anything but peaceful. At the time of Saul and David, war was part of the daily routine. Hence it is highly improbable that the Israelites' memories of their past as they existed around the time of David and Solomon and as they were handed on in that period were not filled with wars and battles. This, of course, does not exclude the possibility that at the same time there existed memories like those in the stories of the patriarchs focusing on tribal ancestors, the hope for progeny, quarrels between women or between brothers, or strife between masters and servants, for these subjects are also indispensable for an egalitarian, acephalous farming society with segmentary organization, such as Israel seems to have been in the time before it became a political entity.[20] But that the military theme was more prominent at the time of David and Solomon is evident from what the books of Samuel, as literature from that time and about that time, have retained.

2.1.2 *War in Israel's pre-Pentateuchal traditions*

It is absolutely clear from what we can glimpse of older, pre-literary material in the Pentateuch and the books from Joshua to Samuel that even in the epoch of David and Solomon (the earliest period usually considered at which a collection of Pentateuch sources might have been made) a great variety of traditional material was available in which battle and warfare (sometimes connected with the conquest of land) played a major role, and in which YHWH was celebrated as the God who conducted Israel's wars and won Israel's victories.

19. First in: G. E. Mendenhall, 'The Hebrew Conquest of Palestine,' *BA* 25 (1962): 66–87; now monumentally developed in N. K. Gottwald, *The Tribes of Yahweh. A Sociology of the Religion of Liberated Israel 1250–1050 B.C.E.* (Maryknoll, N.Y., 1979). On the latter, see my review in *ThPh* 58 (1983).

20. Gottwald, *Tribes of Yahweh* (see previous note), especially parts VI–IX; F. Crüsemann, *Der Widerstand gegen das Königtum. Die antiköniglichen Texte des Alten Testamentes und der Kampf um den frühen israelitischen Staat*, WMANT 49 (Neukirchen–Vluyn, 1978), 194–222. The observations from social anthropology which Crüsemann, in particular, applies as a source of analogy are most easily accessible in F. Kramer and C. Sigrist, eds., *Gesellschaften ohne Staat*, vol. 1: *Gleichheit und Gegenseitigkeit*; vol. 2: *Genealogie und Solidarität* (Frankfurt, 1978); C. Sigrist, *Regulierte Anarchie. Untersuchungen zum Fehlen und zur Entstehung politischer Herrschaft in segmentären Gesellschaften Afrikas* (Frankfurt, 2nd ed. 1979).

Text groups that deserve special mention include: (a) Victory hymns and other types of military lyric, for example the Song of Deborah or the Song of Miriam,[21] at least partly collected and presented in the 'Book of the Wars of YHWH' and perhaps also in the 'Book of the Valiant;'[22] (b) Stories of war and conquest, often containing information about the war *ḥerem*;[23] (c) Tribal sayings that often contained references to the military prowess of the group being praised, or to their success in war;[24] (d) Cultic texts of the type of the manifesto of the law of privilege in Exod. 34:10-26, which grounded the conquest of the land, the prohibition of alliances, and the promise of the driving out of enemies in Israel's special relationship with YHWH.[25]

21. Since Albright, North American research in particular has occupied itself with these texts. The key may be found in the dissertation first prepared in 1947–1948 but published only in 1975 with an afterword and bibliographical notes: F. M. Cross and D. N. Freedman, *Studies in Ancient Yahwistic Poetry*, SBLDS 21 (Missoula, Montana, 1975). For our particular question, see especially P. D. Miller, *The Divine Warrior in Early Israel*, HSM 5 (Cambridge, Mass., 1973). Critical remarks on the method applied are to be found in D. W. Goodwin, *Text-Restoration Methods in Contemporary U.S.A. Biblical Scholarship*, Pubblicazioni del Seminario di Semitistica, Ricerche 5 (Naples, 1969).

22. For the 'Book of the Wars of YHWH,' see Num. 21:14; for the 'Book of the Valiant' ('Book of Jashar') see Josh. 10:13; 2 Sam. 1:18. Regarding the contents of the 'Book of the Wars of YHWH,' F. Schwally, *Semitistische Kriegsaltertümer, I. Der heilige Krieg im alten Israel* (Leipzig, 1901), 4, presents the usual opinion: 'According to Num. 21:14 there was a work on YHWH's wars in which the battles for the conquest of Palestine were described.' A highly detailed attempt to refute this idea is that of Caspari, 'Kriege Jahwes' (see n. 9 above). Interesting, although by no means certain, is the reconstruction of the quotation from the 'Book of the Wars of YHWH' in Num. 21:14–15 by D. L. Christensen, 'Num 21:14–15 and the Book of the Wars of Yahweh,' *CBQ* 36 (1974): 359–60. In that case it would have been the description of YHWH's appearance for battle in a theophany, similar to that in the Song of Deborah. N. H. Tur-Sinai, 'Was There an Ancient 'Book of the Wars of the Lord?'' [in Hebrew], *BIES* 24 (1959/60): 146–48 lacks foundation.

23. There is a thorough analysis of these narratives in Stolz, *Kriege* (see n. 6 above). On references to *ḥerem* in these texts, see N. Lohfink, '*ḥāram*,' *TDOT* 5: 180–99, especially 194.

24. See H.-J. Zobel, *Stammesspruch und Geschichte. Die Angaben der Stammessprüche von Gen 49, Dtn 33 und Jdc 5 über die politischen und kultischen Zustände im damaligen 'Israel'*, BZAW 95 (Berlin, 1965).

25. The most recent monograph on this subject is that of J. Halbe, *Das Privilegrecht Jahwes Ex 34,10–26. Gestalt und Wesen, Herkunft und Wirken in vordeuteronomischer Zeit*, FRLANT 114 (Göttingen, 1975). Earlier literature is listed there.

2.1.3 *Ancient Oriental parallels in the theology of war*

The theologizing of wars and victories was not an invention of Israel, in which case one would have to wait for the prophets or look for an appropriate situation of origin in the deuternomic or exilic period. It is a common feature in the Oriental heritage. Statements indicating that everything accomplished in battle is really effected by divine terror, or that the divinity alone is the real agent, while human beings need only trust, were probably available to Israel from the very beginning, together with the idea that the divinity might turn against his or her own people.[26]

2.1.4 *The 'natural' attitude to war in the 'Jehovist historical book'*

If we presuppose all this, the attitude toward war, and also toward the idea of a violent conquest of the Land or individual parts of it, as described in the 'Jehovist historical book' can be identified with that which was regarded in a certain sense as 'natural' at the time of David and, of course, at later periods as well.

If the 'Jehovist historical work' ended with stories of the conquest of the Land, these wars of YHWH were the natural high point of the prehistory of the people, as directed and controlled by YHWH. If it ended earlier, it at least contained references to the people's later place of residence, and in fact to its attainment of its full extent in David's kingdom. At least in poems like the victory hymn in Exodus 15 or the oracle of Balaam in Num. 24:15–19 there was sufficient indication that YHWH's promises would be fulfilled through David's warlike deeds.

I wish to pursue the further details of this subject in the following theses, with reference to the classical sources. If anyone rejects this classification of the sources, what is said will of course apply, *mutatis mutandis,* to the 'Jehovist historical book.'

2.1.5 *The 'natural' attitude to war in the Yahwist work*

Regarding the traditional distinction between J and E, it is true of J that the 'natural' attitude toward war and the occupation of the Land, as defined above, can be observed roughly from the book of Exodus onward. In contrast, there are no wars in the primeval history or in the stories of

26. See the parallels in Stolz, *Kriege* (n. 6 above), 187–91; M. Weippert, '"Heiliger Krieg" in Israel und Assyrien. Kritische Ammerkungen zu Gerhard von Rads Konzept des "Heiligen Krieges im alten Israel,"' *ZAW* 84 (1972): 460–93; M. Weinfeld, '"They fought from Heaven" – Divine Intervention in War in Israel and the Ancient Near East,' [in Hebrew], in M. Haran, ed., *H. L. Ginsberg Volume,* EI 47 (Jerusalem, 1978), 23–30. On a divinity's turning against his or her own people, see Num. 21:29, a verse from one of the oldest biblical texts.

the patriarchs.[27] In the primeval history there is not even a mythology of battles between the gods, or of a struggle with chaos, which elsewhere in the ancient Orient serve as models to legitimate earthly wars. Their absence is probably connected with the worship of YHWH alone. In terms of content, this mythology has been transferred, at least in intimations, to the event at the Sea of Reeds, where it is historicized. The highly peaceful character of the stories of the patriarchs may in part be connected with the interests of these traditions, which are entirely typical of segmentary societies (see 2.1.1 above). But even if the traditions of the patriarchs are supposed to have contained military elements before they were edited into the Yahwist work, there would be a literary strategy at work here. The stories of the patriarchs are placed, chronologically and genealogically, before the traditions of the exodus, the wilderness, and (possibly) the occupation of the Land. Consequently, no conquests can be depicted in them. I will return to this subject immediately, in discussing Martin Rose's essay.

2.1.6 *The 'natural' attitude to war in the Elohist texts*

There is no lack of wars in the texts traditionally assigned to the Elohist source of the Pentateuch: for example, the battle with the Amalekites in Exodus 17 or the defeat of Sihon in Numbers 21. We cannot demand anything more, given the fragmentary state in which this writing has been preserved (if, indeed, it ever was an independent document).[28] On the other hand, if it is denied that these and comparable texts belonged to E, the question may arise whether the remaining texts are not affected by a fundamentally anti-military attitude.

2.2 *On Martin Rose, '"Entmilitarisierung des Kriegs"?'*

Now let us turn to M. Rose's 'Erwägungen zu den Patriarchenerzählungen der Genesis' [Propositions concerning the narratives of the patriarchs in Genesis], as regards a 'demilitarization of war' said to be found there.[29]

27. References to authors who emphasize the peaceful character of the Yahwist and Elohist works can be found in Vorländer, *Entstehungszeit* (see n. 11 above), 297, 322, 328, 331. The point at issue is, in each case, the foundation for particular datings.

28. The most recent monographs that posit an originally independent Elohist source are K. Jaroš, *Die Stellung des Elohisten zur kanaanäischen Religion*, OBO 4 (Freiburg, 1974): see the literary-critical table on pp. 23–37 and the bibliography on pp. 435–96; and A. W. Jenks, *The Elohist and North Israelite Traditions*, SBLMS 22 (Missoula, Montana, 1977): see pp. 67–68, 'The E-Texts in the Pentateuch').

29. Rose, 'Entmilitarisierung' (see n. 7 above).

This essay deserves to be recognized as the first ever to have raised the question of the attitude toward war in a particular aspect of the 'Jehovist historical book.' In it, the author defends the thesis that the patriarchal traditions were by no means as pacific as they now appear, but instead have been artificially 'demilitarized.'[30]

2.2.1 *The argument from the 'Yahwist' texts under scrutiny*

A first series of proofs rests on traditional material that has been edited within the patriarchal narratives. Here Rose finds remnants that point to an originally military character. However, with the exception of the divine names *'ăbîr ya'ăqōb* and *paḥad yiṣḥāq*, the etiology for Mahanaim in Gen. 32:2–3, the story of Dinah in Genesis 34 and the saying about Jacob in Gen. 48:22 (that he took the piece of land at Sichem from the Amorites 'with my sword and with my bow'), the passages he discusses are not usually assigned either to the Yahwist or to the Elohist: I mean principally Genesis 14 and 15. But he thinks that such chapters could not have been connected with a person who offered 'not the slightest point of connection' in the tradition. I agree with Rose's argument, and I would like to append some additional observations that Rose adduces somewhat later: the bridal blessing for Rebecca in Gen. 24:60 (cf. 22:17), '. . . may your offspring gain possession of the gates of their foes,' and the 'terror from God' that, according to Gen. 35:5 E, travels protectively through the land with Jacob. One should also note that the only surviving inscriptional witness, possibly referring to a patriarch, documents nothing other than a feud between nomads and an Egyptian military action against groups involved in military trade. For the smaller stele of Sethos I from Beth Shean presents the group of Abrahamic nomads (if it is they who are the subject) as engaged in a military conflict with a group of Hapiru.[31] Hence there really is some evidence that the Yahwist retelling of the old stories of the patriarchs has deliberately omitted the warlike elements.

2.2.2 *The argument from redactional texts of the 'Yahwist'*

Rose's second group of proofs for his thesis proceeds, instead, on the basis of redactional and theological interpretive texts in the patriarchal

30. The word 'demilitarization,' used as an idiolect, undergoes a change of meaning in Rose's writing. Here it refers to the removal of all statements about battle and war from a particular textual corpus. In his later work, *Deuteronomist und Jahwist* (n. 11 above), it can also serve to characterize war stories that, though theologized, have remained in the text. In that case its meaning is equivalent to 'theologizing.'

31. Cf. M. Liverani, 'Un' ipostesi sul nome di Abramo,' *Henoch* 1 (1979): 9–18.

narratives. Here he thinks it possible to demonstrate that linguistic elements from the terminology of holy war have in some sense been altered into a nonviolent form. This he considers a deliberate action on the part of the redactor, that is, the 'Yahwist.' However, it does not seem to me that he has proved that the formula of encouragement, 'do not be afraid,' existed only in war oracles. The formula 'I will give you the land' should never have been compared to the formula in the war oracle for handing someone or something over, 'I will give so and so into your hand.' The other 'clans' or 'peoples' are *not* introduced as enemies in the genuinely Yahwistic texts. For the assurance of support, as well ('I will be with you') it appears to me that its sole appearance in the context of war is not demonstrated. Finally, in the ancient Orient there were other occasions besides a victorious war for building an altar or stele. Thus Rose's second set of proofs appears to me to be questionable. Still, the first is sufficient for us to give serious consideration to the idea of a deliberate 'demilitarization' of the patriarchal traditions by the 'Yahwist.'

2.2.3 *Rose's conclusions*

However, Rose concludes from all this that such a tendency would not have been acceptable in the era of David and Solomon. He then searches for appropriate periods and, after discussing various possibilities, finally arrives at a narrow time period between Isaiah and Deuteronomy. It is clear that he himself is not persuaded by this line of argument, since subsequently, in his book *Deuteronomist und Jahwist*, he proposes an exilic or post-exilic origin for the 'Yahwist.' In fact, the first question that arises is whether one may really draw conclusions about the time of writing of the whole Yahwist work on the basis of some findings in the patriarchal narratives. Beginning with the departure from Egypt, the 'Yahwist' has no problem about rattling the sabre. Consequently, the explanations drawn from narrative strategies, described above, offer a more likely interpretation of the findings. A necessary consequence of the decision to give a temporal sequence to narrative blocks that were originally unconnected and simply placed alongside one another was that the block of tradition containing 'stories of the patriarchs' could not have anything to say about a conquest of the Land.

But even if one believes it possible to propose questions about time of composition simply on the basis of the patriarchal narratives (perhaps thinking more in terms of a fragment or documentary hypothesis), the conclusion from a 'demilitarized' narrative to a time of composition free from the turmoil of war is by no means necessary. It is especially in the hardest times that the dream of a golden age can arise, the vision of a time when human beings all behaved peacefully toward one another.[32] And H. W. Wolff, in his essay on the kerygma of the Yahwist,[33] has at least shown that, precisely from this point of view, the peaceful stories of the patriarchs could fit very well in the situation of the time of Solomon. Since Wolff's essay, a whole series of publications in line with his has given further support to this notion.

Thus we may derive from Rose's presentations the conviction that, if we accept the existence of an older Yahwist historical work distinct from the late 'Jehovist historical book,' the stories of the patriarchs given there have been deliberately painted in pacific tones, and that warlike features apparently contained in the traditions incorporated in the work have been eliminated. The motive for this first appears clearly as a necessity of narrative strategy: in the narratively constructed 'patriarchal period' the conquest of the land was not yet called for. But especially if we suppose the time of composition to coincide with that of David and Solomon, there could be an additional, paradigmatic purpose: the Israelites and non-Israelites, living more closely together in the Davidic kingdom than before, are to be presented with a model of peaceful relationships with one another.

2.3 *Summary*

In the 'Jehovist historical book' as a whole there are a good many more military features in evidence, even in the narratives of the patriarchs. Thus in conclusion we may still maintain regarding this literary complex that, while the military theme was not central, it was still in some sense 'natural.' War is something that is described as a matter of course, along with everything else, and as such it does not present problems either for the author or for the anticipated readers. If YHWH willed the existence of Israel, then YHWH must also have willed war, conquest and destruction.

A question that is certainly raised by the description of the miracle at the Sea of Reeds is: who is it, ultimately, who makes war? Is it Israel, or YHWH its God? But the fact that YHWH destroys the Egyptians for Israel's sake does not present any problem. That YHWH can even turn against YHWH's own people is also discussed – in Numbers 13–14, for example – but this, too, is a concretization of a commonly accepted

32. See Vorländer, *Entstehungszeit* (n. 11 above), 297–98, with references to Holzinger and Mowinckel.

33. *EvTh* 24 (1964): 73–98; also found in his *Gesammelte Studien* (see n. 8 above), 345–73.

theologoumenon verified in Israel's history even before the creation of the state.[34]

The deuteronomistic writings will weight these matters differently. In particular, they will spend a great deal more energy on the theory of war. It is to these writings that we now turn.

3. War in Deuteronomy

3.1 *Statement of method*

In what follows I am attempting to summarize and extend my previous preliminary work on this subject.[35] I encountered the deuteronomic theory of war first of all in connection with research on words that were to be included in the *Theologisches Wörterbuch zum Alten Testament.* These were the root *ḥrm,* the verbal forms of which are probably denominatives from *ḥerem,* 'dedication to destruction,' and the root *yrš,* 'take possession of,' which in the *hifil* probably does not mean 'drive out,' as is usually supposed in the German tradition (shaped by Luther's interpretation), but instead, in alignment with the tradition of the old translations and Anglo-Saxon exegesis, should be translated 'destroy.' Deuteronomy's theory of war can be brought into rather clear focus on the basis of these two roots. They direct our attention immediately to what they have in common: the brutality, the comprehensive radicality and the close connection with taking possession of the land promised to Israel. This last is, in reflex, given statutory authority in the law of war in Deuteronomy (Deut. 20:10–18), which makes a clear

34. Consider, for example, the events treated in the story of the Ark and there interpreted in this sense. See especially A. F. Campbell, *The Ark Narrative (1 Sam 4–6: 2 Sam 6). A Form-Critical and Traditio-Historical Study,* SBLDS 16 (Missoula, Montana, 1975).

35. N. Lohfink, 'Darstellungskunst und Theologie in Dtn 1,6–3,29,' *Bibl* 41 (1960): 101–34; 'Die deuteronomistische Darstellung des Übergangs der Führung Israels von Moses auf Josue,' *Schol* 37 (1962): 32–44; '*ḥāram*' (see n. 23 above); 'Kerygmata des Deuteronomistischen Geschichtswerks,' in J. Jeremias and L. Perlitt, eds., *Die Botschaft und die Boten,* Festschrift for H. W. Wolff (Neukirchen–Vluyn, 1981), 87–100; N. Lohfink, '*yāraš*,' *TDOT* 6: 368–96. There are extensive bibliographies in the two lexicon articles. A recent work that concentrates strongly on the question of war, but is not especially helpful, is U. Köppel, *Das deuteronomistische Geschichtswerk und seine Quellen. Die Absicht der deuteronomistischen Geschichtsdarstellung aufgrund des Vergleichs zwischen Num 21,21–35 und Dtn 2,26–3,6,* EH XXIII, 122 (Berne, 1979). Not accessible to me: S. Siwiec, *La guerre de conquête de Canaan dans le Deutéronome,* Diss. Studium Biblicum Franciscanum/Antonianum (Jerusalem and Rome, 1971).

distinction between more distant cities and those of 'these peoples that YHWH your God is giving you as an inheritance' (v. 16). Only in these cities must the *ḥerem* be carried out: the complete destruction of everything that breathes, which in this context means all human beings.[36]

3.2 *'DtrL' as the relevant stratum*

This whole theory of war does not appear to be something that was present from the beginning in the deuteronomic-deuteronomistic tradition and was gradually developed there. It does not appear to have existed in the pre-Josian and Josian law. It is first found in deuteronomistic strata of the law and in the deuteronomistic parts of the book of Deuteronomy, and underlying the law as such. This, certainly, is based on the supposition that the text of the deuteronomic law could have been stylized before the oldest deuteronomistic layer, but not yet as a speech of Moses delivered immediately before the people crossed the Jordan to begin a violent occupation of the Land. However, such a stylization would not have been created first of all through a 'deuteronomistic historical work' in Martin Noth's sense, a work that would have extended from Deuteronomy to 2 Kings and could only have come from the period of the exile. Instead, I suppose that this historical work integrated a number of preliminary writings in itself, each of which only depicted brief periods of time, and all of which were somewhat older. The preliminary stage that interests us here is a description of Israel's taking possession of the Land, and contains the major part of the present text from Deuteronomy 1 to Joshua 22. I call it DtrL (= deuteronomistic narrative of the occupation of the land).[37] Here the genuine deuteronomistic theory of war is developed.

DtrL was composed around the deuteronomic law and incorporated it. This law was itself revised and expanded within the framework of DtrL. At this stage, it was stylized as a farewell address of Moses to Israel, immediately before his death and before the crossing of the Jordan under Joshua. Hence DtrL has two themes: the law, and taking possession of the Land. These correspond to the two primary interests of King Josiah, as we know them, in his later years. He desired to renew his state within, through the law that would restore the primeval age of Israel, and, with respect to the restoration of ancient Israel to its appropriate magnitude, he wished to extend that law outward in all directions, but especially

36. See Josh. 11:13–14, where, probably within the same stratum, we find the same formula, with the exception that livestock is expressly excluded.

37. For more detail, see Lohfink, 'Kerygmata' (n. 35 above), 92–96.

northward. Hence I posit that DtrL stems from the late years of Josiah's reign, that it was prepared at his order, and that it is intended to be several things at once: a new synthesis, transparent and enlightening to all, of the most important traditions of Israel about its social structure and territorial rights, a kind of strategic planning document of the king, and a type of propaganda writing that is meant to plead the case for the king's purposes and legitimate his actions.[38]

3.3 *The ideas of DtrL about Israel's holy war of conquest on its entry into the promised land*

The deuteronomistic theory of war was also formulated in the context of this DtrL. There already existed something like a preliminary, basic idea of 'holy war.'[39] It marked the pattern, already existing at that time, according to which wars were conducted. It underlies the old narratives in the 'Jehovist historical book' and other traditions, including those that were later reworked in the new version, especially within the book of Joshua. It is possible that these traditions already existed in the form of a collection of sagas. Using all these materials, DtrL now systematized a fixed schema of the course of a YHWH war for the conquest of the Land. If in individual cases, especially in the book of Joshua, the old materials did not quite fit into the schema, they were approximated to the normative model by means of additions: one example would be the story of the capture of the city of Ai. In what follows, we will discuss some of the important elements of this systematized presentation.[40]

38. On the function of the whole deuteronomic and deuteronomistic literature, see N. Lohfink, *Unsere großen Wörter. Das Alte Testament zu Themen dieser Jahre* (Freiburg, 1977), 24–43 [= *Great Themes from the Old Testament*, 17–37, 'Pluralism. Theology as the Answer to Plausibility Crises in Emergent Pluralistic Situations, Taking the Deuteronomic Law as the Basis for Discussion']. For these considerations, I owe a great deal to the sociologist and pastoral theologian F. Menneke. The two of us conducted a summer seminar in Toronto in 1972 on this topic. Among the participants was P.-E. Dion, who has since published an article on this question: 'Quelques aspects de l'interaction entre religion et politique dans le Deutéronome,' *ScEs* 30 (1978): 39–55.

39. 'Holy war' is not necessarily 'war of YHWH,' since of course there was a considerable store of ideas common to the peoples of the ancient Orient, and since at that period the conduct of war and talk about war were no doubt strongly influenced by Assyrian culture.

40. The background is always the classic description of the 'theory of holy war' in von Rad, *Heiliger Krieg* (see n. 2 above), 6–14, where the DtrL material entirely shapes the presentation. Consequently, we need not treat the subject exhaustively in the following remarks.

3.3.1 *What triggers the war*

A war must begin with an offer to the opponents of an opportunity to surrender. This is what the law of war says (Deut. 20:10–11), and that is how the model narrative depicts it (Deut. 2:26). Israel may only begin the war if its offer is refused. Of course, DtrL believes that, during the conquest of the land, YHWH constantly hardened Israel's enemies, so that in fact they always subjected themselves to the mechanisms of war. This is expressly stated in the summary in Josh. 11:19–20.

The war is YHWH's war. YHWH sends terror against Israel's foes. But in DtrL, Israel is not simply passive on this account. Israel must believe and have courage, but it must also go into battle and fight. If in Isa. 7:9 'faith' means abandonment of the normal ways of power politics, that in Deut. 1:32 it represents readiness to go forth to a violent conquest of the Land.

3.3.2 *The ḥerem*

Despite what Gerhard von Rad thought, the *ḥerem*, the dedication to destruction, did not originally form part of this holy war, nor was it associated with YHWH's war. The deuteronomists found in their model documents and old sources a limited number of *ḥerem* stories and *ḥerem* notices. We can only detect them in Numbers 21, Joshua 6–7, 1 Samuel 15 and Joshua 10–11. But beyond these, they apparently had access to an old list of peoples containing the names of nations that no longer existed. Beyond these, there was also an ancient promise from YHWH to drive out the inhabitants of the Land. We can observe it in Exodus 23, Exodus 34, and Judges 2. In fact, Exod. 23:23 spoke not only of banishment, but of destruction. It is possible that the deuteronomists even possessed a text containing a command to drive out or destroy other nations. Deut 20:17 contains a formula referring to a commandment of destruction, but such a commandment cannot be verified from the demonstrably older texts we possess. Still, the reference formulae in Deuteronomy are not all drawn from thin air; they are genuine literary references.[41] It appears to me that the deuteronomists combined these varied materials and systematized them. In this way they arrived at the idea that YHWH had given a command, before the conquest of the Land, that its inhabitants should be entirely destroyed. This would have been the commandment of *ḥerem*.

This *ḥerem* would, of course, no longer have been what it once had,

41. See Skweres, *Rückverweise* (n. 11 above). On the basis of the backward reference in Deut. 20:17, see his discussion on pp. 43–47, which in my opinion concludes with a *non liquet*.

when it was still practiced: a particular renunciation of looting based on a special vow or a special prophetic saying in individual campaigns, but by no means in all. Now the basis of the *ḥerem* was a general commandment of YHWH applying to the whole conquest of the Land. The object of destruction was no longer the spoils of war, but the inhabitants. The material goods and livestock were to be spared and simply taken. In this way, the word *ḥrm hifil* in deuteronomistic language lost its specific meaning ('to dedicate to destruction and to carry out this consignment to destruction'). It became a synonym for the many other words for destruction that DtrL, and later strata as well, employ.

3.3.3 *The whole population as objects of destruction*

Norman K. Gottwald has presented striking arguments for thinking that in Israel's historical beginnings the *yōšĕbê hā'āreṣ*, to whom the promise of banishment referred, were not the 'inhabitants of the land,' but the 'rulers of the land,' since *yōšeb* with the name of a place could also designate the ruler of a city, and the plural would refer to the patrician class in some place.[42] Thus there seems to be a well-founded suspicion that the acknowledged deuteronomic-deuteronomistic list of peoples originally designated ethnic groups that made up the ruling elite in the Canaanite cities.[43] It may be, then, that in historical reality the issue was only the driving out of ruling elites in the Canaanite cities, and thus of bringing down the dominant social and political systems. The institution of the *ḥerem* would have nothing to do with it. The *ḥerem* was a renunciation of spoils, sometimes vowed to the divinity in war, and primarily applying to material goods. It was only the systematizing of traditions in the deuteronomistic writing that made of it an eradication of the whole population commanded by God.

3.3.4 *The juristic and theological conception of acquisition of territory*

Another part of any war was its conclusion with a cultic victory celebration and return home. These elements recede completely into the background

42. Gottwald, *Tribes of Yahweh* (see n. 19 above), 507–34.

43. On the meaning of ethnicity as a social category transcending other systems in the ancient Orient, see especially K. A. Kamp and N. Yoffee, 'Ethnicity in Ancient Western Asia During the Early Second Millennium B.C., Archaeological Assessments and Ethnoarchaeological Perspectives,' *BASOR* 237 (1980): 85–104. It is easily imaginable that some of the groups mentioned in the list of peoples constituted the patrician class in different city-states that were not politically related, and that at the same time these groups maintained a consciousness of their ethnic identity. For an attempt to discern a geographical arrangement of the individual nations in the list, see N. Lohfink, *Die Landverheißung als Eid. Eine Studie zu Gn 15*, SBS 28 (Stuttgart, 1967), 67–68.

in DtrL. They are replaced by a new climax to the whole process: the acquisition and occupation of the conquered territory, of course with all the property existing therein. Therefore one of the most frequently appearing deuteronomistic words is *yrš*, 'take possession of.' Naturally, this word was not absent from older war narratives, but it was by no means a necessary element. Now, in the deuteronomistic theory of the conquest of the Land, it becomes indispensable. Moreover, it is incorporated into an extended juristic presentation.

In the ordinary theories of war in the ancient Orient, and consequently also in that of ancient Israel, the god of a nation fought for his or her people in war. If the victory was gained, the object fought over belonged to the god and that god's nation. That took care of the legal question concerning, for example, captured territory. The victors quite simply were in the right by the very fact that the victorious god was on their side.[44] We find this model of legitimation for the possession of a particular territory, for example, even in the argumentation (so deuteronomistic-sounding, but really, at least typologically, pre-deuteronomistic) of Jephthah's messengers to the king of the Ammonites in Judg. 11:24: 'Is it not so, that you enter into the possession of the one whom Chemosh, your god, destroys? And should we not enter into possession of everything that YHWH, our God, destroys by our attack?'[45] This is the law of the national god. In contrast, the deuteronomists developed a system that might be called 'the law of the world god.'[46]

In DtrL, the 'taking possession' of the conquered territory is clearly related to YHWH's oath to the ancestors to 'give' the land to their offspring. But it is not only the Israelites to whom, in DtrL, land is given

44. On this, see especially G. Furlani, 'Le guerre quali giudzi di dio presso i Babilonesi e Assiri,' *Miscellanea G. Galbiati III* (Milan, 1951), 39–47.

45. [Translation following the author's German.] For Judges 11, the most persuasive analysis still seems to me to be that of W. Richter, 'Die Überlieferungen um Jephtah Ri 10, 17–12,6,' *Bibl* 47 (1966): 485–556. See p. 538: 'The argumentation in Judg. 11:16–26 shows no influence from Deuteronomy, and thus is prior to it in time; it faithfully follows the view of history witnessed in Numbers 21.' But even an all-too-subtle division of strata, such as the recent one offered by M. Wüst, 'Die Einschaltung in die Jiftachgeschichte, Ri 11, 13–26,' *Bibl* 56 (1975): 464–79, ultimately arrives at an ancient typological age for Judg. 11:24. For, according to Wüst, the latest stratum in Judg. 11:24 derived its argument 'from verse 23, which is part of the fundamental stratum' (p. 477).

46. Richter, 'Jephtah' (see n. 45 above), 546, speaks (somewhat misleadingly) of a 'centralization' of the idea in Judg. 11:24 by Deuteronomy. 'Here YHWH makes a sovereign decision, no longer in conflict with the gods of other nations' (p. 547).

as a possession. The Edomites, Moabites and Ammonites have each been given their own land to possess, not by their own particular gods, but by YHWH, according to Deut. 2:5, 9, 19. Thus YHWH is above all nations and gives each its own land. They are entitled to take possession of it – if necessary, by conquest and destruction of the previous inhabitants.

We are dealing here with a theologizing of a kind of concept of land based on 'royal law.'[47] As the ruler of a land gives out fiefdoms,[48] so YHWH gives territory to the different nations. In the special case of Israel, YHWH has taken on an obligation to do this, in the past, by swearing an oath to the people's tribal ancestors.[49] Now YHWH 'gives' Israel its territory. Just as, in Babylonian commerce, a clear distinction is made between the act of transfer and that of assuming ownership,[50] so here all that remains to be done is for Israel to take possession of its territory. This is described with the word *yrš*, which in itself evokes the connection with conquest. Thus Israel's war of conquest is, from a theological and legal point of view, comparable to the action of the recipient of a fiefdom in response to the act of donation on the part of the divine ruler of the world. The victor's right is bound up in an encompassing law of divine distribution of the world's territory.

3.4.1 *The justification of Josiah's policy of territorial expansion*

We must ask what may have been the purpose of such a 'juridical theology,' with its refinement of previous ideas. If we start at the time of Josiah's initiative, and consider the connection with his real interests, the following may be said: if one thinks in terms of the law of the national god, who goes to war for his or her people, and of the right of the victor

47. It should be placed alongside the two concepts ('historical' and 'cultic') developed by Gerhard von Rad, 'Verheißenes Land und Jahwes Land im Hexateuch,' *ZPDV* 66 (1943): 191–204, repr. in his *Gesammelte Studien zum Alten Testament*, ThB 8 (Munich, 3rd ed. 1965), 87–100.

48. In the OT, cf. 1 Sam. 8:14; 22:7; 27:6. On the *našû-nadānu* documents, which are of great importance for the distribution of land, and the influence of their terminology, see the recent work of J. C. Greenfield, '*našû-nadānu* and its Congeners,' in M. de Jong Ellis, ed., *Essays on the Ancient Near East in Memory of Jacob Joel Finkelstein*, MCCA 19 (Hamden, Conn., 1977), 87–91 (with bibliography).

49. The combination of all three elements (oath to the ancestors, 'giving,' and *yrš*) is found in DtrL at the following locations: Deut. 1:8; 10:11, and Josh. 21:43–44 – thus precisely at the framing positions.

50. The fundamental study is by M. San Nicolò, *Die Schlußklauseln der altbabylonischen Kauf- und Tauschverträge*, MBPF 4 (Munich, 1922).

that is bound up with that law, it was perfectly legitimate that the northern parts of Israel's land had been in Assyrian possession for more than a century. The Assyrians had conquered them; consequently, they had a right to possess them. Josiah could lay no claim to them. Of course, he could attempt to conquer them. But then they could also be as quickly reconquered, as soon as Assyria was strong enough, and with a revival of the Assyrians' former legitimate title to them. Moreover, it does not seem to have been the case in any sense that Josiah extended his borders northward by a genuine war of conquest. At any rate, we have no evidence of it. Instead, he gradually absorbed an area that had been emptied of authority by imposing a new government, something like the legal notion of the appropriation of ownerless property. But this idea was probably too weak, or too inappropriate to serve as a public legitimation for his actions. However, the very idea of law developed in DtrL was ideally suited for the purpose: not for the Assyrians, of course, in case they should regain their power, but at any rate for his own population in Judah as well as for the people in the annexed northern territories. For according to this notion the Assyrians, even though they had conquered the northern territories, had no legitimate right to be in the land. That land had been given to Israel by YHWH, the lord of all lands, and Israel had also taken possession of it long ago. Josiah, as the possessor and representative of the ancient rights of the people of Israel, was positively obliged to reannex the land of Israel. He even had law on his side if he was forced to bring about the repossession of the land through a war of conquest, even if it took on the violent features of the kind of *ḥerem*-war that distinguished the original conquest under Moses and Joshua. This last was probably more sabre-rattling than a weapon actually drawn. But it did serve to focus on eventualities that were not really envisaged, and in any case it could legitimate severe action in individual cases, such as in Bethel (cf. 2 Kgs. 23:15–20). Thus, all in all, DtrL could serve to make it clear to the population of Judah as well as to the people of the North that Josiah of Jerusalem, in pursuing his policies, was not engaged in some kind of private adventure, but was doing exactly what the divine sphere expected of him.

3.4.2 *The rebuilding of structures of plausibility in Judah*

There must have been a further reason for the harshness and brutality of the original war of conquest described in DtrL – beyond what has already been said, but very closely connected to it. DtrL associates YHWH's command to destroy with the names of peoples that no longer existed at the time of Josiah. This of itself shows that the intention here is not to present a model for military campaigns that Josiah was actually planning. It is probably more a matter of a kind of moral armament and strengthening of the population of Judah, who had grown timid and aimless after a century of Assyrian domination. We know that Assyrian propaganda of that period worked deliberately and massively to instil in the people a sense of fear and anxiety in face of the military power of Assyria and its god. The conquest stories in DtrL act as counter-propaganda. The even more dreadful terror of the God of the entire world, who is on Israel's side, is narratively described. No one in Israel needs to fear when what is at issue is the land that YHWH had promised to the ancestors. But since everything is written in such a way that it can no longer be seen as giving directions for present action, these present-day Israelites need not be afraid that circumstances will arise in which they will be called upon to perform such slaughters and bloodbaths.

Hence the deuteronomistic theology of war, as it entered the Pentateuch in the book of Deuteronomy, appears originally to have had a very precise application to concrete action. It was intended to restore the structures of plausibility in the society of Judah that, first in the royal era and then once again under the cultural and political shock of Assyrian dominance, had gotten spiritually out of joint. To that purpose, some operating space had to be created for Josiah's activity as head of state in the eyes of the population on whose personal assent he had to depend.

3.5 *The deuteronomistic theory of the war of conquest and of the internal connection between law and violence*

One result of this was to create a very close connection between the categories of law and violence. Law is established through violence, and behind it all stands the divine authority. It seems to me that we find revealed here in a clarity that is seldom seen elsewhere the extent to which law, even the law of nations, rests on violence, and the way in which it constantly threatens to release violence anew. The God who emerges in this theology is like an earthly ruler in that this God can only establish the desired system of justice by the application of violence and the destruction of life. This calls for a great deal more thought. In particular, it appears to me to be important in this context to consider that the deuteronomistic movement, at least under Josiah, represented the first and, until the Maccabean movement, the greatest single attempt to institutionalize the unpolitical, or even anti-political social plan of early Israel in the form of a political state.

Historically, the attempt failed. In contrast, the priestly document implies a completely different social initiative.

4. The Priestly Document and War

4.1 *The relationship between P^g and earlier works*

The account of events in the priestly historical narrative (P^g), which I wish to treat separately for the moment, presumes both the 'Jehovist historical book' and the exilic 'deuteronomistic historical work.' In addition, it expects its readers to be acquainted at least with the 'Jehovist historical book,' since it frequently introduces characters without preparation and takes for granted certain facts that readers could only know from the 'Jehovist historical book.'[51] These things should be expressly stated, since they alone make the absence of war in P^g truly relevant.

4.2 *The absence of war in P^g*

There is no war in the priestly historical narrative.

4.2.1 *Primeval history and the history of the patriarchs*

This is not so surprising in primeval history, or in the stories of the patriarchs, since even in the 'Jehovist historical book' the topic of 'war' is only occasionally mentioned in those periods. Even so, the theme of 'strife,' in a general sense, appears three times: in the story of Cain, in that of Jacob, and in the Joseph novella. Cain does not appear in P^g. The story of Jacob has been altered in such a way that there are no longer any conflicts between Jacob and Esau or between Jacob and Laban.[52] The story of Joseph has been condensed so severely that there is no trace of the principal theme of the old novella.

4.2.2 *Destruction of the Egyptians in the Sea of Reeds*

The first great narrative of holy war in the 'Jehovist historical book' is the destruction of the Egyptians at the Sea of Reeds. There is now a very

51. Examples include: Appearance of persons without introduction: Moses in Exod. 6:2 (which may well have been – together with the more elaborate definition of Aaron's importance – one of the reasons for the later addition of Exod. 6:13–30); Reference to information from JE that is omitted in P^g itself: allusion to Kadesh-Barnea in Num. 20:12 (P^g must have placed the event before the negotiation with Edom narrated in Num. 20:14–21, prior to the departure from Kadesh; probably P^g also made the identification of Meribah in Exod. 17:7, the model for the story of the water miracle, with Kadesh, an identification that was later made specific; P^g itself did not expressly locate the story in Kadesh, because Kadesh was supposed to be part of the promised land: cf. Num. 34:4 P^g; there is a later harmonization, for example, in Num. 27:14; Deut. 32:51).

52. Read the reasons given in the priestly writing for Jacob's journey to Laban in Gen. 27:46; 28:1–5, and the peaceful separation of Jacob and Esau after Jacob's return home in Gen. 36:6–8.

detailed investigation by Jean-Louis Ska of the way in which P^g has altered this story.[53] It is true that the Israelites, as they depart from Egypt, are called 'YHWH's armies,' and there is an emphatic use of technical military terms for Pharaoh's troops in Exodus 14 (army, horses, chariots, riders). But in spite of all this, no war occurs. 'There is neither a battle between Israel and Egypt nor a victory of Israel over Egypt; there is only a self-revelation of YHWH before the eyes of the Egyptians.'[54] P^g's models for the events are YHWH's 'judgments' on the nations as proclaimed by the prophet Ezekiel. In succumbing to these 'judgments,' the nations recognize who YHWH is. Even in the 'Jehovist historical book,' the holy-war narrative in the story of the Sea of Reeds was stylized in such a way as to depict the sole activity of YHWH in the struggle. But it remained a war story. Here war is omitted entirely; it does not even serve as a frame of reference for what is said.

4.2.3 *The order of the camp*

P^g then hurries over the story of the manna to arrive at the broadly expanded Sinai pericope. Toward the end of it, in Numbers 2, there is an order given for the Israelites' camp. But in the tradition, the camp is repeatedly mentioned from the moment of departure from Egypt, and from the descriptions of the battles with the Philistines until the deuteronomic law, the camp of Israel is always a military camp. Here again, P^g has made some basic changes. Let me refer at this point to Arnulf Kuschke's study in comparative tradition history. In all the aspects he treats, he repeatedly concludes that 'military features are completely absent from the camp in the P narrative.'[55]

4.2.4 *The story of the scouts*

The first narrative in the 'Jehovist historical book' that P^g treats at length after the departure from Sinai is the story of the sending of scouts in Numbers 13–14. Sean E. McEvenue has made the necessary comparative study of this story.[56] The sending out of spies to examine the southern

53. J.-L. Ska, 'La sortie d'Égypte (Ex 7–14) dans le récit sacerdotal (P^g) et la tradition prophétique,' *Bibl* 60 (1979); 191–215.

54. Ibid., 203 n. 21.

55. A. Kuschke, 'Die Lagervorstellung der priesterschriftlichen Erzählung. Eine überlieferungsgeschichtliche Studie,' *ZAW* 63 (1951): 74–105; the quotation is from p. 99.

56. S. E. McEvenue, *The Narrative Style of the Priestly Writer*, AnBib 50 (Rome, 1971), 90–127. On this text as a 'narrative of sin,' see N. Lohfink, 'Die Ursünden in der priesterlichen Geschichtserzählung,' in G. Bornkamm and K. Rahner, *Die Zeit Jesu*, Festschrift for Heinrich Schlier (Freiburg, 1970), 38–57, at 52–54 (Chapter 4 of this book).

part of the land, which has a military purpose in the 'Jehovist historical book,' becomes a kind of festal procession of delegates through the whole of the promised land of Canaan, with one representative from each tribe. This is not a matter of spying in advance of a planned campaign of conquest. Instead, the land that has been promised as YHWH's gift is to be inspected and evaluated. That is the sense of the key word *tûr* that P^g introduces into the story. It is precisely in carrying out this duty that the delegates fail. Therefore they and their whole generation must die in the wilderness. P^g has created a story of sin that aims primarily at a paradigmatic portrait. It has nothing to do with war; in that case it would be a question of lack of courage and weakness of faith, as in Deuteronomy 1. Instead, the sin is *dibbat hā'āreṣ*, 'calumny of the land,' a negative judgment on the good and saving gift offered by YHWH.

4.2.5 *The installation of Joshua*

The next text in P^g in which military matters could be discussed is Num. 27:12–23.[57] Here, in a scene immediately preceding the death of Moses, the question of succession is introduced and provides the occasion for saying a few remarks about offices in Israel. Moses asks God for a successor, and receives Joshua. This corresponds to the situation in Deuteronomy 31, part of DtrL. There Joshua is ceremonially installed as Moses' successor, and his duties are defined as the conquest and division of the land.[58] He is thus entrusted with the war of conquest that will be described in the first half of the book of Joshua. The dependence of P^g in Numbers 27 on the text of DtrL in Deuteronomy 31 can be demonstrated down to the linguistic level. In Deut. 31:2, Moses justifies the installation of Joshua because of his own age. He says: *lo' 'ûkal 'ôd lāṣē 't wĕlābô'*, 'I am no longer able to go out and come in.' In Num 27:16–17 Moses asks YHWH to provide a man for the congregation, *'ăšer yēṣē' lipnêhem wa'ăšer*

57. For the intermediate journey as far as the 'plains of Moab,' the locus of Moses' final acts before his death, see J. Wellhausen, *Die Composition des Hexateuchs und der historischen Bücher des Alten Testaments* (Berlin, 3rd ed. 1899), 108: 'This report seems to know nothing of difficulties with neighboring peoples; it treats the terrain like a *tabula rasa.* The Israelites travel from Kadesh directly eastward through Edom and settle down unmolested in the Arboth of Moab.' For Num. 27:12–53, S. Mittmann, *Deuteronomium 1,1–6,3 literarkritisch und traditionsgeschichtlich untersucht*, BZAW 139 (Berlin, 1975), 110–11, has presented an analysis that I find off the mark: in it, typical linguistic procedures in P^g are deprived of their elements of internal tension by being immediately dissolved into literary-critical 'stratigraphy.'

58. See Lohfink, 'Übergang' (n. 35 above).

yābō' lipnêhem wa'ăšer yôṣî'ēm wa'ăšer yĕbî'ēm, 'who shall go out before them and come in before them, who shall lead them out and bring them in.' The formula, 'to go out and come in' in Deut. 31:2 surely has a particular reference, in the context of DtrL, to Moses as military leader.[59] Under Moses, Israel had conquered the land east of the Jordan, and Joshua is to be his successor as general in conquering the lands west of the Jordan. P^g leaves the scene in the same place and at the same time: in the plains of Moab, beyond the Jordan, near Jericho (cf. Num. 22:1), and immediately before the death of Moses (cf. Num. 27:13). But Moses has led Israel to this point without a word having been said about military conquest. Nevertheless, the plea that Moses now expresses is clearly a request for a military leader for Israel. The development of the meaning of the formula 'to go out and come in' gives it a still more decisively military tone.[60] And yet the answer Moses receives from YHWH is crucial. Moses is to install Joshua as his successor, but he is to be subordinate to Eleazar the priest. Eleazar is to inquire of the Urim on his behalf. And then it is said that *'ăl pîw yeṣĕ'ŭ wĕ'ăl pîw yābō'û*, 'at [Eleazar's] word they shall go out, and at his word they shall come in,'[61] *hŭ' wĕkol bĕnê yiśrā'ēl 'ittô wĕkol hā'ēdâ*, 'both he and all the Israelites with him, that is,[62] the whole congregation' (Num. 27:21). Here not only is the general subordinated to the priest, but even his generalship is in some sense washed out of the

59. Cf. for Joshua, in the same literary stratum, Josh. 14:11, where *lammilḥāmâ* confirms the military meaning. For more on this double expression, see J. G. Plöger, *Literarkritische, formgeschichtliche und stilkritische Untersuchungen zum Deuteronomium*, BBB 26 (Bonn, 1967), 178–81; H.-D. Preuß, *yāṣā'*, *TDOT* 6: 225–50, at 229 (for Num. 27:17, 21, 'reinterpreted in a cultic sense').

60. For *yṣ' lipnê* NN in the sense of the royal head of the army going ahead of the troops in war, cf. 1 Sam. 8:20.

61. Samaritanus and Vulgatus read the verbs in the singular. The LXX supports the plural of the MT. This latter is certainly the *lectio difficilior*. Since the Vulgate normally does not correspond to Samaritanus, the singular *lectio facilior* may have developed independently in two places. It is true that the LXX witnesses to the plural reading, but by making a change at another place it has also managed to retain the picture of Joshua as general and supreme commander of Israel. It translates, 'And he shall stand before Eleazar the priest, and *they* [plural!] shall inquire of *him* [probably Eleazar, instead of 'from him,' i.e., 'for Joshua'] about the decision of the Urim, and at his word [which can now be understood to refer to Joshua] they shall go out and at his word [the same!] they shall come in: he and the sons of Israel together with the whole congregation.'

62. This seems to be an emphatic and summary Waw, since otherwise *bĕnê yiśrā'ēl* would be in parallel to *'ēdâ*.

language. It is true that the word-pair 'go out' and 'come in' remains. But Joshua no longer goes out and returns 'at their head.' He is even coupled immediately with them into a single unit, and then the unit is analyzed into its parts in an appositional phrase. But then the unit is brought together again right away, through the word *'ēdâ*, 'congregation.' According to Leonhard Rost's thorough study of this word, 'There is never any report of a military action by the *'dh*. Instead, at the one place where the *'dh* concerns itself in a war (Numbers 31), an *'m* is separated out from it, which then, after the victory is gained, reports to the *'dh*.'[63] It must be clear by now that at this very point P^g employs a highly referential language game to interpret out of existence the tradition of the violent conquest of the Land under Joshua.[64]

4.2.6 *Entry into Canaan*

Then Moses dies. At this point, according to the opinion of Martin Noth (and Wellhausen before him), an opinion shared by most exegetes today, P^g comes to an end. But if, after all that has been said, one must doubt that P^g could have contained the wars of conquest under Joshua, the small number of text fragments in the book of Joshua that appear to wear the garments of the priestly vocabulary no longer present a major problem. It is easily imaginable that a priestly account of the entry into Canaan would have been relatively brief; such an account may well have existed, though lacking in war trumpets. And one really expects it, since so much in P^g was pointed toward this moment.[65] Since P^g certainly no longer served in the

63. L. Rost, *Die Vorstufen von Kirche und Synagoge im Alten Testament. Eine wortgeschichtliche Untersuchung*, BWANT 76 (Stuttgart, 1938), 84. Numbers 31 is not part of P^g, but is later. Nevertheless, it can certainly be adduced as a witness to the linguistic flavor of the priestly writing.

64. Let me draw attention also to the following: In his request, Moses speaks of a military successor, a leader for the *'ădat YHWH*, in Num. 27:17. This word combination is a *hapax legomenon*. It can best be interpreted as a deliberate reformulation, on the part of the priestly writer, of *'am YHWH*, and in the particular sense of YHWH's levy. Here P^g lets Moses, in a certain sense, attempt before God to create a military variant on the concept of the congregation of Israel. In that case, the summary expression *wĕkol hā'ēdâ* in Num. 27:21 is the divine answer: the 'congregation,' whose characteristics have already been fully described, remains intact; no military element is to be added.

65. For example, if one reads the book by E. Cortese, *La terra di Canaan nella Storia Sacerdotale del Pentateucho*, SupplRivBib 5 (Brescia, 1972), one can understand, on the one hand, that the great authority of Martin Noth restrains the author from posing the literary critical questions he has developed for the book of Numbers with

book of Joshua, as it had in the Pentateuch, as a basis for the great redactional combining of sources, it is also easily imaginable that only a series of fragments from such an ending of P^g was retained, and not virtually everything, as had been the case in the earlier books. The verses in P-style that are scattered throughout the book of Joshua and could stem from the final part of P^g are: Josh. 4:19; 5:10–12; 14:1–2; 18:1; 19:51. The fact that they are really to be explained in this fashion seems to me to be established especially by Josh. 18:1, for there two themes that were assigned a major role in P^g are finally brought to a conclusion. On the one hand, the holy tabernacle is set up at a fixed location within the Land, in Shiloh. On the other hand, it is declared that the Israelites had taken possession of the Land, but the verb used is not *yrš*, but the less usual *kbš*. This word had been used in programmatic fashion immediately after the creation of human beings in Gen. 1:28: 'Be fruitful and multiply, fill the earth and take possession of it (*wĕkibšuhā*) [NRSV: and subdue it].' The word never appears again in the whole intervening text of P^g, but now in Josh. 18:1 we read *wĕhā'āreṣ nikbĕšâ lipnêhem*, 'and the land had been given into their possession [NRSV: The land lay subdued before them].' All the other declarations in Gen. 1:28 had been taken up in the course of the narrative and either fulfilled or extended. Each fulfillment was established by an express notice. All that was lacking, as far as the narrative was concerned, was the taking possession of the earth. Here, of course, it is not established for the whole of humanity, but it is confirmed for the people of Israel, to whom the second half of the narrative was limited. The example of Israel also reveals the truth of this element of the divine word given at creation. At this point, the last of the arcs drawn from the beginning has reached its end. These observations alone are sufficient for us to recognize the hand of P^g in Josh. 18:1. But in that case, P^g must have narrated the entry of Israel into the promised land of Canaan, though surely with the brevity that this document commands in such masterly

respect to the book of Joshua also, but one will be increasingly skeptical about the supposition that P^g broke off its presentation with the death of Moses. At the crucial passages, Noth's logic is not compelling. He notices in Num. 27:15–23 that P 'is very deliberately silent' when it comes to the formulation of Joshua's future task of occupying the land west of the Jordan, and does not mention 'the duty of conducting the war.' He concludes from this that the theme of occupation of the land must have lain 'outside the body of material he had chosen for his work' (M. Noth, *Überlieferungsgeschichtliche Studien* [Tübingen, 2nd ed. 1957], 191). All that follows logically is that no military occupation of the land was contemplated. Thus one could also discuss the possibility that the occupation of the land was taken into account, but not as a military affair.

fashion, and with a deliberate omission of any military action. The most important note, for P^g, in connection with the entry into the land of Canaan, which also constitutes the end of a narrative arc, is probably contained in Josh. 5:10–12: in Gilgal, and nowhere else, the Israelites celebrated the passover, as they had done immediately before leaving Sinai in Num. 9:1–5 P^g. On the next day the manna ceased, and they began to nourish themselves with the produce of the land. There is a preparation for this note as early as Exod. 16:35.[66]

4.2.7 *Conclusions*

Thus P^g eliminated war from the story it tells, with paradigmatic intent,[67] of the beginning of the world, the history of humanity and of the people of God. It is not that it is depicted as factually present and then condemned as evil. It simply does not exist. Where it might occur, in the events at the Sea of Reeds and at the installation of Joshua, its beginnings, which even thrust themselves forward in the language itself, are transformed by divine initiative into something quite different. The world of P^g is a world without war.

66. The latest and most comprehensive treatment of Josh. 5:10–12, in Rose, *Deuteronomist* (see n. 11 above), 25–53, despite a long bibliographical note that documents the long-developing consensus on the assignment of the text to P (p. 25 n. 18), is so fixated on a dispute with E. Otto and E. Zenger that the reasons for the earlier consensus are not really brought forward. The only argument worth discussing against an assignment of the whole text to P^g seems to me to be the indication of time, *bāʿereb*, in Josh. 5:10 (as in Deut. 16:4, 6, in contrast to *bên hāʿarbayim* in the comparable P^g texts Exod. 16:12; Num. 9:3, 5). But on the level at which Rose, who also adduces P^g, argues, the case against the possibility of *bāʿereb* in P is not entirely solid. He has overlooked the fact that *bāʿereb* also occurs in Exod. 12:18; 16:(8), 13; Lev. 6:13; 23:32, all texts ascribed to P and, with the exception of Leviticus 6, also all chapters from which Rose draws the examples to show that P's typical formula is *bên hāʿarbayim.* One of the counter-examples even comes from P^g: Exod. 16:13. This is the fulfillment notice for the announcement in Exod. 16:12, where *bên haʿărbăyim* is found. It seems to me to follow from all this that one must not even restrict P^g to this expression; at this point it appears that P^g itself has introduced a variation. Thus it is at least not out of the question for Josh. 5:10 that *bāʿereb,* too, was already in P^g. Moreover, it is entirely possible that here, either during the redactional insertion of the P texts into the book of Joshua or in the course of the later transmission of the text the less distantly removed deuteronomic festival laws exercised a harmonizing influence. In any case, it appears to me that the expression *bāʿereb* is not a strong enough basis to support the theory of a deuteronomistic, or of a post-priestly and/or post-deuteronomistic hand.

67. On this point, see Lohfink, 'Priesterschrift' (n. 13 above).

4.3 *The sanction for upsetting order according to* P^g

But now we must explain what this implies. If there are no wars in P^g, that does not mean, for example, that there are no deaths. God establishes God's own order in the world, and this process is often a matter of life and death for human beings. But for all of it, God needs no human armies as instrument. God can do all of it alone.

4.3.1 *Connections with earlier theologies of war*

If we want to understand the priestly writing's idea of the way in which God transforms world history into the judgment of the world genetically, from the perspective of war, it is best to begin with the concept of holy war in which human activity is increasingly pushed into the background and divine activity in war gradually moves toward the idea of the divine power as the sole agent. The Reed Sea narrative in the 'Jehovist historical book' has already developed quite far in that direction. The classic representative of this concept is the prophet Isaiah. If one pursues his idea of holy war to the farthest extreme, and at the end even erases the idea of war itself, substituting words like 'judgment' or 'punishment,' one probably arrives at what P^g has in mind. There are four narratives[68] concerning sin and punishment in P^g. In the Flood, God acts alone to put an end to the violence that has filled creation. At the Sea of Reeds, God alone prepares an end for the Pharaoh who has oppressed and exploited the Israelites. In the wilderness God prepares an end for the generation of Israel whose delegates have calumniated the land of Canaan. Finally, before a new generation can enter the land of Canaan, God also brings an end for Aaron and Moses, the leaders of Israel who have not believed God and glorified the divine name. Thus guilt truly meets its punishment, but God alone brings it about. For this, God needs no human soldiers or courts of law.

4.3.2 *Connections with the declaration made at the time of creation*

God's punitive extinguishing of human existence is directly connected with God's uniqueness as the creator. This is made clear at least in the first two narratives of guilt and punishment, since both the Flood and the

68. In my article on original sins in P^g (Lohfink, 'Ursünden,' see n. 57 above) I counted three narratives, excluding the story of the exodus from Egypt and the destruction of the Egyptians (pp. 43–46). A study by J.-L. Ska, 'Séparation des eaux et de la terre ferme dans le récit sacerdotal,' *NRT* 113 (1981): 512–32 has convinced me that we should take four narratives into account. On their system, see idem, 526 n. 30: purification 'of the universe' (Genesis 6–9), 'of Israel and the nations' (Exodus 1–14), 'of Israel alone' (Numbers 13–14), and 'of the elite of Israel' (Num. 20:1–13).

destruction of the Egyptians are, each in its own way, a retraction of the region of dry land made by the creator, as the chaotic water advances to swallow it: 'Chaos has come to reclaim what belongs to it,' namely a society that has become chaotic.[69] The other two stories of guilt and punishment take place in the desert. As a result, the symbolism of chaos/water does not appear, and the death of the guilty is brought about directly by God, in Num. 14:37 by means of a *maqqēpâ*, a 'blow' caused by divine touch. In the case of the aquatic notion of chaos in Genesis 1, Genesis 6–8 and Exodus 14 there can be no doubt that the myth of the battle with chaos, between the creator god and the water god (such as that between Baal and Jammu in Ugarit) is in the distant background. Besides this myth, there is also that of the battle with the god of death, of drought, of the earth, of the underworld – in Ugarit, the battle of Baal with Mutu.[70] One may at least consider whether, in Numbers 13–14, P^g is not playing with this mythological background of the creator's struggle with the earth-monster. The scouts describe the land shown to them for their evaluation as the earth-monster, which is identified with death and the underworld: 'It is an earth that devours its inhabitants' (Num. 13:32).[71] The people who received this message would be stricken with fear of the death-dealing monster, so that they would prefer death 'in this wilderness' (Num. 14:2). And this wish would be fulfilled through a kind of fairytale word magic:[72] 'I will do to you the very things I heard you say: your dead bodies shall fall in this very wilderness' (Num. 14:28–29). The story of Dathan and Abiram, probably recorded already in the 'Jehovist historical book,' contained in a most explicit form the idea of the earth-monster that, through YHWH's creative act,[73] appears to swallow alive the gang of

69. Ibid., 525.

70. For the connection between the two monster-figures and for biblical examples of the idea of earth monsters (none of them from P^g), see M. K. Wakeman, 'The Biblical Earth Monster in the Cosmogonic Combat Myth,' *JBL* 88 (1969): 313–20; idem, *God's Battle with the Monster. A Study in Biblical Imagery* (Leiden, 1973).

71. For possible connections to texts from Ezekiel, see Lohfink, 'Ursünden' (n. 57 above) 53; S. McEvenue, *Narrative Style* (see n. 56 above), 135–36.

72. See McEvenue, *Narrative Style*, 127–44.

73. See Num. 16:30. It is true that this connection of the verb *br'* with a punishing action of YHWH is unique, as is the noun *bĕrî'â* which precedes it in the etymological figure. Moreover, the LXX seems to have read a different text. It could therefore be the case that here we are faced with a later, interpretive alteration of the text.

rebels (see Num. 16:28–34). P^g did not incorporate this story, but it would have been typical for P^g to let motifs from this narrative context echo in another. If it did so, then only in a very subdued form. But it appears that, on the whole, water remains its symbol for chaos. Thus the last two stories of guilt and punishment remain at a rather abstract level. But undoubtedly it is true here also that it is YHWH, as the creator, who by a word reduces sinners again to nothingness.

4.4 *The removal of war and the proposal for a holy society*

4.4.1 *The problem of what P^g intends to say*

Of course, it is possible to ask whether the disappearance of war from the stock of narrative elements is more than a result of heightened abstraction. Is not the handing over of the Egyptians to the water of chaos and the death of rebellious people in the wilderness effected by God's word really nothing but a kind of interpretation (the idea being that, ultimately, it is God the creator who is at work here) applied to certain events in human history in which the immediate subjects of the action really were human beings, and which we ordinarily describe in terms of war and the punishment of criminals? And to that extent war would not have been eliminated, but only discussed in a different way and from another point of view. It might, in fact, be more 'divinized' than in any other imaginable theology of war.

With this question about the real statement that is made by the action in P^g, which, on the surface at least, is undoubtedly free from war, I have arrived at what is by far the most difficult part of my discussion. Can it be that, in this historical narrative, all that is depicted is a deeper dimension of our well known, war-soaked history? In that case, the statement would be: of course there is war, but if we see it more clearly it is really not human war; rather, it is divine, creative judgment. Or can it be that another society is being portrayed, a society that is imaginable from God's perspective and that is, in fact, really somehow present in the midst of visible society? Can it be this society whose history is described, a description that attracts attention so powerfully that the other, war-soaked society and history fades from view? It might even be possible to imagine a combination of both these intentions.

I think I can see some indications that the second possibility is the correct one. P^g thinks in terms of a society, and therefore a structure of the world that, at least among human beings, functions or could function without the use of violence. It is a world that has become peaceful through worship, and that can be kept peaceful by the power of ritual.

4.4.2 *'Holy war' between human and animal in* P^g

We can best approach this issue from the observation that war has not been completely eliminated from P^g. It no longer exists between human beings, but there is still war between human and animal.

At creation, human beings were given authority over the animals (Gen. 1:26, 28). According to Walter Groß, this is precisely what makes the human the image of God.[74] This governance is intended to be nonviolent, as is evident from the fact that both humans and animals are restricted to vegetable food (Gen. 1:29).[75] Evidently governance is regarded as concerned direction, and not as destructive exploitation.[76] The killing and eating of animals is not included.

It is not simply the corruption of humanity that brings on the Flood. Rather, 'all flesh' is corrupted, that is, human and animal (Gen. 6:12). All have committed *ḥāmās*, 'violence,' and have filled the earth with it (Gen. 6:11, 13).[77] Thus there must have been violent killing of human beings by other human beings, of animals by other animals, and mutual killing by human beings and animals. I think we must conclude from the revision of the original order of the world that is established after the Flood that, in the opinion of P^g, that inundation of the world with violence that evoked the Flood must primarily have arisen between humans and animals.

The revision consists in the assigning of a limited space to violence: human beings may kill animals and eat them (Gen. 9:2–6).[78] That is the

74. W. Groß, 'Die Gottebenbildlichkeit des Menschen im Kontext der Priesterschrift,' *TQ* 161 (1981): 244–64.

75. Of course Gen. 1:29–30 is in continuity with notions about an original vegetarianism that existed in a variety of cultural areas and that from time to time appeared in other contexts besides that of the relationship of sovereignty and subordination between human and animal. But the formulation in P^g is independent and must in any case be understood from the context in which it is placed in P^g. Cf. C. Westermann, *Genesis*, BK I:1, 223–25.

76. See Westermann, *Genesis*, 227: 'existence on behalf of those under subjection.'

77. For a review of the meanings of *kol bāśār* in Gen. 6:12, see A. R. Hulst, 'Kol Basár in der priesterlichen Fluterzählung,' *OTS* 12 (1958): 28–68. According to him it is at least not certain that animals are included. Among those recent writers who include only human beings are Westermann, op. cit., 560, and J. Scharbert, *Fleisch, Geist und Seele im Pentateuch*, SBS 19 (Stuttgart, 2nd ed. 1964), 53–54. It seems to me that the totality of the statements in P^g that are in play here can be included in a logically consistent system only if the animals are included.

78. McEvenue, *Narrative Style* (see n. 56 above), 68–71, has revived the thesis of Rudolf Smend and Heinrich Holzinger that Gen. 9:4–6 was not part of the original text of P^g. I do not find the contrary reflections of Westermann, *Genesis* (see n. 75 above),

post-Flood form of human rulership over the animals. And this arrangement is now expressed in the traditional terminology of holy war! For the words of God that establish the new order are, in a certain sense, an 'oracle of holy war.' We hear that 'the fear and dread of you shall rest on every animal of the earth, and on every bird of the air, on everything that creeps on the ground, and on all the fish of the sea; into your hand they are delivered. Every moving thing that lives shall be food for you' (Gen. 9:2–3).[79]

4.4.3 *The killing of animals as a condition that makes cultic sacrifices possible*

What strikes us particularly in this narrative sequence, so strange to us as it seems, is the degree to which human beings and animals are united in a kind of common 'society.' It is true that the humans' imaging God, and their position of authority, distinguish them from the animals, but at the same time these things join human and animal in a community on whose functioning the death and life of the universe depend. The central problem is violence. In our own day, this brings us very quickly to fundamental ecological ideas, and justly so. But within the context of our question concerning the real reasons for eliminating war from human history, a quite different observation is in order.

In the world from which P^{g} comes, people normally ate only meat

621, convincing. In any case, if we accept Walter Groß's thesis that human beings' imaging of God consists in their governance of the animals (see n. 74 above), we should assign Gen. 9:6b to P^{g}. The problem here, namely that God makes a personal reference in the third person, exists even if we do not suppose that any additions have been made. In Gen. 9:6b, in any case, a free quotation from Gen. 1:27 is placed in God's mouth. If Gen. 9:2–3 gives a new order to the modalities of human rulership over the animals, Gen. 9:6b would supply the appropriate conclusion. For the question I am dealing with here, the assignment of Gen. 9:4–6a remains a secondary matter.

79. For the association of the roots *yr'* + *ḥtt* with war, see Deut. 1:21; 31:8; Josh. 8:1; 10:25; 1 Sam. 17:11; 1 Chr. 22:13; 28:20; 2 Chr. 20:15, 17; 32:7. The closest parallel formulations for the statement complex in Gen. 9:2a,bα are to be found in two deuteronomistic divine promises of the success of the war of conquest: Deut. 2:25 and 11:25. *ntn bĕyād* NN in Gen. 9:2bβ is the fundamental expression of the sacred oracle in war. Thus Gen. 9:2 as a whole sounds like a sacred oracle legitimating and inaugurating the warfare of human beings against the animals. Gen. 9:3 then makes explicit the purpose of the war: the animals are given as food for human beings, which is an alteration of the original order for nourishment. What remains throughout is the governance of human beings over animals, that is, their imaging of God (Gen. 9:6b). See McEvenue, *Narrative Style* (n. 56 above), 68; Westermann, *Genesis* (n. 75 above), 619. Groß, 'Gottebenbildlichkeit' (n. 74 above), 261, speaks of the human 'reign of terror' over the animals.

that had previously been offered to a divinity in a cultic ritual.[80] And the ritual that P^g is thinking about, in turn, is not imaginable without animal sacrifice.[81] But how could animals be ritually killed and eaten by human beings, so long as the original instruction for vegetarian nourishment in Gen. 1:29, with its implication of nonviolence between human and animal, was in effect? This means that the war between human and animal established by God in Gen. 9:2 in the context of a blessing provides the condition that alone makes it possible for God to plan and create the congregation of Israel in the form that was to be characteristic of it: shaped by cultic worship and hence by the presence of God among the people. We must admit that there are no positive indications of this connection within the text of P^g itself. On the other hand, it seems to me scarcely imaginable that the author of P^g did not see, and did not positively intend this essential connection between the initial topic and the principal theme of the narrative.

4.4.4 *The killing of animals and the problem of war*

But let us go a step farther. The author could have described how it became possible for human beings to kill and eat animals without using forms of language that were bound to awaken thoughts of the holy war of conquest under Joshua, a war whose deuteronomic description this author had used every artistic means at his command to eliminate from his own portrayal. Thus when he did what he did, he may indeed have seen a connection between the elimination of war from the world he describes and the introduction of warfare into the relationship between human beings and animals.

4.4.5 *The absence of war and the presence of God*

A third fact of note: whatever replaces war in P^g's version of things is

80. In this connection we can ignore the deuteronomistic introduction of private slaughtering of animals, since the law in the priestly document revokes it. We can also set aside the fact that according to P^g the cult exists only within the people of God, and not in humanity as a whole; moreover, the cult exists in Israel only from Sinai onward. The question whether P^g implies the idea of election, or whether it depicts it by using the descendants of Israel as an example of what really should be true of all humanity, does not appear to me to have been fully clarified. But even apart from this, P^g is particularly concerned with that nation that lives on the basis of the cult given it by God, and that suffices for our reflections here.

81. It is true that the sacrifices are a marginal matter in P^g. But they are certainly a matter of course, and the whole spectrum of sacrificial laws was very quickly incorporated into P^g. That is surely no accident; it indicates the strong affinity with the sacrificial ritual that was present from the very beginning.

always closely connected with the presence of the glory of God. At the Sea of Reeds, YHWH gains *kābôd*, 'honor, glory' (Exod. 14:17) through the destruction of the Egyptians. In the manna story, YHWH's *kābôd* appears for the first time, and at Sinai it becomes possible for YHWH's *kābôd* to remain permanently in the midst of the congregation. From that point on, the community will be given everything, wherever the *kābôd* leads it, and finally, it is from the *kābôd* that the destruction of all that is sinful proceeds. Surely, there is no more war because Israel lives under the *kābôd*. But among the things that make possible the abiding presence of the *kābôd* and strip it of its mortal threat is the bloody ritual of sacrifice.

4.4.6 *Summary: the project for an archaic type of sacred society*

At this point we can, at most, pose one more question, since P^g itself does not draw any lines of connection. Is it possible that the author saw here a connection between a society liberated from war and violence, the cult at its center that effected this liberation, and the violent behavior of human beings toward animals?

With this question we have come very close to the elements of René Girard's theory, especially those related to archaic societies based on ritual. In such societies, according to Girard, the universal human tendency to violence is preventively smothered by being acted out in symbolic fashion within rituals employing the device of the scapegoat. The slaughter of the sacrificial victim is crucial, whether it be a human being or an animal substitute. For participants in this ritual, the sacred action effects a reduction of aggressiveness, a reconciliation, and a restoration of peace.

Obviously, this kind of theory is not developed within P^g itself. The sacrifice remains uninterpreted; the visible hints of an interpretation are directed elsewhere.[82] But it is part of Girard's theory that the real mechanism by which violence is reduced must remain hidden in order to be effective. The question presented to our text can only be whether we can discern within it a total constellation from which one may conclude to a social project that, in an underground fashion, derives from these archaic mechanisms. This seems to me to be highly probable.

In that case, while P^g on the surface only deals expressly with the problem of violence in its primeval history, which is oriented to all humanity, and in fact to all animal life, on the whole it eliminates war

82. For the most recent interpretation of the priestly writing's notion of sacrifice, see A. Schenker, *Versöhnung und Sühne. Wege gewaltfreier Konfliktlösung im Alten Testament. Mit einem Ausblick auf das Neue Testament*, BBB 15 (Freiburg, 1981), 81–119, with a list of older titles. See especially nn. 132, 135 and 138.

from the world as described, and constructs the society it portrays on the basis of the presence of the Holy that is achieved through the cult. As a result, even when it reaches its climax it is still continuing to treat the problem of violence without expressly saying so. In fact, a refusal to be explicit belongs to the essence of the projected solution.

4.5 *The sacred society of P^g as an exilic and post-exilic project*

4.5.1 *The sacred society as regression*

With respect to society, this is something like regression. P^g factually presupposes a world that already has a system of justice and a theory of war for the regulation of international relations, all designed to control violence. Its own solution – peace among human beings through the blood of animal sacrifices – points backward to archaic cultures in which human and animal still constitute a unity, and problems of human rivalry are projected toward the animal kingdom. There war continues, even if it no longer exists in the human world.

4.5.2 *Ancient roots*

This point of view is undoubtedly rooted in priestly traditions that may themselves stem from archaic times. They lived on in the interpretation of the rites that continued to be performed in the sanctuaries, and perhaps even perdured solely in the ritual itself, which continued to be carried out without being understood.[83] For all this to be suddenly revived toward the end of the exilic period or even after the exile, for it to explode the narrow limits of sacred actions and professional priestly knowledge and become the central, internal idea shaping a new historical narrative in radical competition with the important versions of Israel's history already in existence – for these things to happen, there must have been a very special reason.

4.5.3 *Farewell to the state*

I can discern this reason only in the loss of national political status and the conviction that there would never again be a national state, together with the solid belief in God's continuing desire that the people continue as God's own special society within the world of God's creation. This inner

83. By way of comparison, we may point to the discoveries of J.–M. de Tarragon concerning Ugarit, in his *Le culte à Ugarit d'après les textes de la pratique en cunéiformes alphabétiques*, CahRB 19 (Paris, 1980). Many archaic aspects of cultic interpretation found in the texts of the priestly document simply cannot be documented there, such as the distinction between clean and unclean.

constellation had, at that time, yielded a variety of different projects for Israel's future and the form it would take. A figure like Deutero-Isaiah is as much a part of this phenomenon as were the ideas expressed in the edited versions of the books of Jeremiah and Ezekiel. P^g may well have had the most peculiarly individual shape. In the first place, its totally uneschatological character is most striking.[84] But what has emerged from our investigation seems to me still more important: the archaic and cultic foundation. Evidently, there is a presumption that Israel will soon be able to resume life in its own land; and at that point it is to exist, to the fullest extent, as a society centered on a sanctuary and on the practice of the cult that takes place there. Then the problems of human violence would be solved in a fashion completely different from those in use everywhere else in the world.

4.5.4 *The function of the project for the post-exilic Temple congregation*

In fact, this conception made an essential contribution to the third major form assumed by Israelite society in the course of its history. In the wake of the egalitarian, but externally fortified and even aggressive tribal agrarian society, there had been an attempt to create a just state whose king would rule, according to the pattern of other kings, in the name of YHWH. The final ideological elaboration of this society was the deuteronomic project. After the collapse of the state, what emerged was a strongly sacralized sub-society, living around the Jerusalem temple as a kind of enclave within the larger framework of an imperial world society. P^g's conception undoubtedly exercised great influence on the self-understanding of that form of Israelite society, but its actual form was not shaped by P^g alone. Only in a weakened sense can we speak of a delayed experiment with a society based on an archaic sacral system. An external sign of this is the fact that the basic document of this society did not consist of P^g alone, nor even of the P^g writing augmented by many other priestly texts, but instead, in the form of the 'Pentateuch,' was redactionally composed from a variety of existing texts – even though P^g, in a sense, provided the literary basis for the whole. Still, with this restriction, one must say that P^g made effective a concept of society based on the idea that war could be eliminated from the life of humanity. That was a demand that neither the tribal society of the early period nor the subsequent state had had even a remote idea of proposing for itself.

84. On this, see Lohfink, 'Priesterschrift,' (n. 13 above).

5. Late Redactional Strata and War

Wellhausen liked to speak of an 'epigonic diaskeuasis.' In fact, the 'Jehovist historical book,' the 'deuteronomistic historical work,' and the 'priestly historical narrative' were revised and expanded before, during, and after their redactional combination, and today we might prefer to avoid the word 'epigonic,' since it all too easily takes on a pejorative note. In what follows, we intend to examine texts in this group concerning their attitude toward war, and in particular the violent conquest of Canaan. Do they follow the source that is last in time, P^g, or do older conceptions again prevail? My aim is not to achieve completeness; I will only offer examples that seem to me of special importance.

5.1 *The retention of the attitude toward war in the phase of mutual accommodation of the Pentateuch sources still existing as separate works*

Before the redaction of the Pentateuch there was undoubtedly a phase in which the various works, still existing independently of one another, underwent some mutual adaptation. The priestly document was tailored to make it more like the deuteronomistic work, and Deuteronomy was made to approach the thought and language of the priestly writing. Sometimes this was accomplished through rather extensive expansions, and it often affected central theologoumena and linguistic features of the two works. And yet, oddly enough, in the first phase the distinctive attitudes of the two documents toward war were maintained.

5.1.1 *The holiness code does not acknowledge a war of conquest*

The 'deuteronomizing' of the priestly document was accomplished primarily through the incorporation of the holiness code into the Sinai pericope.[85] By this means, for the very first time a social order in the form of a project described in terms of laws, in analogy to the deuteronomic law, was introduced into the context of the priestly document. By means of a conditional promise and conditional curse, the priestly document's theology of covenant was accommodated to the deuteronomic idea in the final, twenty-sixth chapter of Leviticus,[86] and a paraenesis comparable to the deuteronomic type was intoduced into the laws.

85. The most recent monograph on H is by A. Cholewinski, *Heiligkeitsgesetz und Deuteronomium. Eine vergleichende Studie,* AnBib 66 (Rome, 1976): see the bibliography there. The 'incorporation' of H may well have implied its 'collection' as a first step.

86. See N. Lohfink, 'Die Abänderung der Theologie des priesterlichen Geschichtswerks im Segen des Heiligkeitsgesetzes. Zu Lev. 26,9.11–13,' in H. Gese and H. P. Rüger, eds., *Wort und Geschichte,* Festschrift for K. Elliger, AOAT 18 (Kevelaer, 1973), 129–36.

In the legal regulations in H, in contrast to the deuteronomic law, the topic of war is not mentioned. In Leviticus 26 a future war is introduced: it was probably in the model document, and it was necessary for the curses to contain a kind of preview of history up to the time of exile and return.[87] Of special importance for our subject is the paraenesis in the crucial stratum in Lev. 20:22–24 (a chapter on capital crimes) and earlier in Lev. 18:24–30 (a chapter on sexual immorality), for here, from a supposed location at Sinai, a connection is drawn with the promise of the Land and the entry into the Land. Is the priestly document's elimination of a war of conquest under Joshua maintained here, or not?

As in DtrL, so also in Lev. 20:24 it is YHWH who has given the Israelites the land for their possession. But the text avoids saying that YHWH or the Israelites have destroyed or eliminated the inhabitants of the land. The wordplay between *yrš qal* and *yrš hifil* would have been appropriate at this point. But instead it is said that YHWH has 'sent away' the inhabitants of the land at the coming of the Israelites: *'ăšer 'ănî mĕšallēaḥ mippĕnêkem* (Lev. 20:23; cf. 18:24). At most, a semi-mythical image is in use: the land has 'vomited out' its inhabitants (Lev. 18:25, 28; cf. 20:22). Thus despite the close association with deuteronomistic paraenesis, we still find here P^g's old aversion to a military view of Israel's occupation of the Land!

5.1.2 *The 'reviser' of Deuteronomy 7–9 holds to a war of conquest*

The adaptive strata in the book of Deuteronomy are quite different. The closest approach to the theology of P^g is shown by the hand that edited Deuteronomy 7, inserted Deuteronomy 8, and placed the story of the renewal of the covenant after its breach at Horeb in a new context of interpretation by the insertion of Deut. 9:1–8, 22–24.[88] In contrast to the usual deuteronomic practice of introducing the category of 'covenant' first

87. Both in the texts that are customarily assigned to the outline model and in those usually said to be located in the redactional strata that interest us here, the clearly personified 'sword' plays a role. It is mentioned seven times: Lev. 26:6, 7, 8, 25, 33, 36, 37. Of these, Lev. 7:33a (and perhaps v. 6 as well) are assigned to the model. The question of this model document, which in my opinion has not really been resolved, cannot be pursued here (cf., for example, Lev. 26:33a with Ezek. 5:12; 12:14). Could this talk of a 'sword' reveal the effects of a tendency to make war an almost mystical work of YHWH? In Deuteronomy 28 the 'sword' no longer appears. (In Deut. 28:22, following the Vulgate, a re-vocalization must be made to *ûbăḥoreb*; the Masoretic reading is probably occasioned by a desire to harmonize with Leviticus 26.)

88. N. Lohfink, *Das Hauptgebot. Eine Untersuchung literarischer Einleitungsfragen zu Dtn 5–11*, AnBib 20 (Rome, 1963), 167–218; idem, 'Kerygmata; (see n. 35 above), 99–100.

at Horeb and at the proclamation of the deuteronomic law itself, in these chapters, as in P^g, the 'covenant' is already recognized in God's oath sworn to the ancestors, in which Israel can trust despite its own sin, since it was given without condition: cf. Deut. 7:12; 8:18, as well as Deut. 7:8; 9:5.[89]

However, the late deuteronomistic reviser develops a theology of covenant and grace more closely allied to that of the priestly writing in connection with the theme of violent conquest of the land, the topic of the texts before him. As early as Deut. 7:17–24 he appears to have expanded an older text[90] to such an extent that Gerhard von Rad believed he saw here, despite its 'obviously late and theoretical' character, a 'formula' for 'war orations' as, in his opinion, they might have been declaimed in front of the restored armies at the time of Josiah.[91] But probably, at this point, the reviser only wanted to establish the basis for his crucial remarks in chapter 9,[92] which are practically an advance formulation of Pauline teaching on the justification of sinners by grace alone. For the fact that Israel is utterly immersed in sin and has no rights before its God is demonstrated from its behavior during the time in the wilderness,[93] and the reason why YHWH nevertheless bestows salvation is (besides the sin of the former inhabitants of the land) only the promise to the ancestors;[94] nevertheless, salvation itself is concretely depicted as the success of the war of conquest, effected by YHWH, a success that, according to deuteronomist historical fiction, is about to take place immediately after the time

89. On the closeness to P^g, see also N. Lohfink, 'Die These vom "deuteronomischen" Dekaloganfang – ein fragwürdiges Ergebnis atomistischer Sprachstatistik,' in G. Braulik, ed., *Studien zum Pentateuch*, Festschrift for W. Kornfeld (Vienna, 1977), 99–109, esp. 103 n. 15.

90. Cf. Deut. 7:20 with Exod. 23:28; Deut. 7:22 with Exod. 23:29–30; Deut. 7:23 with Exod. 23:27; Deut. 7:24 with Exod. 23:31. There are especially striking connections with *ṣirʿâ* in Exod. 23:28 and with the reasons given for the prolonged conquest in Exod. 23:29–30. See the most recent treatment of the problem of dependency: G. Schmitt, *Du sollst keinen Frieden schließen mit den Bewohnern des Landes. Die Weisungen gegen die Kanaanäer in Israels Geschichte und Geschichtsschreibung*, BWANT 91 (Stuttgart, 1970), 13–24. The most recent study of Exod. 23:20–33 is Halbe, *Privilegrecht* (see n. 25 above), 483–99.

91. G. von Rad, *Deuteronomium-Studien*, FRLANT 58 (Göttingen, 1947), repr. in his *Gesammelte Studien zum Alten Testament* 2, TB 48 (Munich, 1973), 109–53, 36–39 = 138–41.

92. In G. von Rad, op. cit., 37 bottom = 139, '8:1' should be corrected to read '9:1.'

93. Deut. 9:7–8, 22–24.

94. Deut. 9:5.

when Deuteronomy is proclaimed.[95] Here there is a mixing of the greatest variety of older strata: cf. Deut. 9:1–2 with Deut. 1:28, and Deut. 9:4 with Deut. 6:19.[96] The wordplay with *yrš* is carried through a whole series of variations: there are seven instances of this root in Deut. 9:1–6!

5.2 *In the combining of the 'Jehovist historical book' and the priestly document, the deuteronomistic idea achieves dominance*

Thus both in the priestly document and in Deuteronomy, despite all their mutual adaptations, the individual ideas about the occupation of the Land – with or without war – remain untouched. This changes at the moment when written works that previously existed as separate entities are brought together in a single whole. Even if there was first a redactional combination of the 'Jehovist historical book' with the priestly document, with the deuteronomistic historical work temporarily left aside, still at this early stage the priestly document's presentation of a world without war must have been called into question. For, at least according to the most popular position to date, the 'Jehovist historical book,' even before the death of Moses, contains material about wars of conquest in the land east of the Jordan (in Numbers 21) and about the settlement of Gad and Reuben there (in Numbers 32); and if one supposes a Jehovist 'Hexateuch,' one must even presuppose reports of conquest in the land west of the Jordan as well. Were these different points of view simply ranged in unconnected fashion alongside one another, or were linking texts created to form a bridge between these contradictory pictures? The latter seems to be the case. In the process, the picture of a military conquest prevails.[97]

95. Deut. 9:1–3; cf. 9:4, 5, 6. On the theology of grace in this text, see G. Braulik, 'Gesetz als Evangelium. Rechtfertigung und Begnadigung nach der deuteronomischen Tora,' *ZThK* 79 (1982): 127–60.

96. On Deut. 6:19 as part of DtrN, see Lohfink, 'Kerygmata' (n. 35 above), 98–99. (See also n. 111 below.) The reviser in Deuteronomy 7–9 is thus reworking an edition of DtrG that has already undergone a striking theological revision.

97. Since the whole question of the redaction of the Pentateuch and its phases remains highly hypothetical, the same may be said also of the linking of the texts treated in the following pages with R^{JEP}, to use the classic symbol. Still, scarcely anything in the results of the following presentation would change if we were dealing with texts from a later stage of redaction, or even posterior to the principal redaction of the Pentateuch. For, as will appear, DtrG was in any case already part of the picture, even if it was not inserted at the same time. The fact that I posit, precisely in the area of Numbers 32 and 33, some expansions in a redactional stage previous to the inclusion of the book of Deuteronomy, is connected with the other fact that, at the moment when one regards Deuteronomy as already an integrative component in the Pentateuch, these

5.2.1 *Numbers 32–34 as a field of investigation*

Let me make this clear on the basis of texts from Numbers 32–34. If we follow the thread of P^g, by Num. 22:1 Israel has already arrived on the plains of Moab, and in Num. 27:12–23 Moses has been instructed to climb the mountain on which he is to die, and has already installed Joshua as his successor. Thus nothing is lacking except God's final words to Moses, and his death. The divine delimitation of the land of Canaan that now stands in Num. 34:1–12 would have been located immediately after Num. 27:23. But now the notes about the settlement of Gad and Reuben in the land east of the Jordan, taken from the 'Jehovist historical book,' have been inserted between the installation of Joshua and the delimitation of the land west of the Jordan, and constitute the main part of Numbers 32. It is not possible for me to analyze the chapter in detail at this point.[98]

expansions in fact appear rather meaningless, since they only anticipate and duplicate texts from Deuteronomy. For the most recent study of the redactional history of the last part of Numbers, see M. Wüst, *Untersuchungen zu den siedlungsgeographischen Texten des Alten Testaments, I. Ostjordanland*, BTAVO.B,9 (Wiesbaden, 1975), especially 213–21. However, I am not persuaded by all of his proofs.

98. Martin Noth, *Das vierte Buch Mose. Numeri*, ATD 7 (Göttingen, 1966), 204, is fundamentally of the opinion that the substance of the older sources of the Pentateuch is at this point 'so tightly combined with later revisions and additions that it is not possible to carry out a clear and persuasive literary-critical division.' In fact, Wellhausen offered an analysis in *Composition* (see n. 57 above), 113–15, and then simply withdrew it in the addenda to the third edition (idem, 352), in response to an article by A. Kuenen, 'Bijdragen tot de critiek van Pentateuch en Jozua I–III,' *Theologisch Tijdschrift* (1877): 465–96, 545–66 (at 478ff.; 559ff.) – but without suggesting what his new opinion was. Kuenen himself, however, in the subsequent second edition of his *Einleitung*, offered no more precise analysis, and coolly expressed an opinion that here the redactor who joined JE and P may have created a narrower text combining both traditions and their language: cf. A. Kuenen, *Historisch-kritische Einleitung in die Bücher des Alten Testaments hinsichtlich ihre Entstehung und Sammlung* (German tr. by T. Weber) I:1 (Leipzig, 1887), 97–98. The most recent analyses are those of Mittmann, *Deuteronomium 1,1–6,3* (see n. 57 above), 95–104, and Wüst, *Untersuchungen* (see n. 97 above), 91–118. In Wüst's work, at p. 94, there are summaries of the opinions of other authors. Wüst draws attention to a series of weaknesses in Mittmann's analysis. I would mainly add, apart from some minor details, that the reasons for the division of Num. 32:6–15 into two strata are not persuasive. (Unfortunately, on this point Wüst follows Mittmann.) Moreover, Num. 32:12–15 and 32:20–23 cannot belong to the same stratum, since the consequences of sin in the one case are said to affect all Israel, and in the other case only the sinful tribes. Wüst supposes a somewhat more extensive basic layer than does Mittmann, and this is surely correct. But his suggestions about the strata of editing and expansion seem to me in part to be questionable also. For example, his reasons for supposing an extensive secondary expansion within Num. 32:20aβ–23 do not seem at all plausible

But in the following section I want to point out a passage from a stratum in the revision that presents a deuteronomistic theory of conquest for the land west of the Jordan in combination with priestly linguistic elements. Hence it was probably seen to be necessary to precede the existing priestly delimitation of the land in Num. 34:1–12 with a clear divine command to occupy the land through a war of extermination, and Num. 33:50–56 probably owes its origin to that circumstance.[99]

5.2.2 *Numbers 32:20–33*

In Numbers 32 the idea of a violent seizure of the land from east to west was already given on the basis of the text of the 'Jehovist historical book.'[100] The expansion in Num. 32:20–23, the only passage I intend to

to me. The division creates more difficulties than it solves, and there are positive reasons for connection rather than division. So much for critique of the most recent proposals. I am not going to treat, in this context, the section Num. 32:6b–15, which I take to be a unit. It seems to me to originate with the principal redaction of the Pentateuch. The idea behind it may be to make all of Numbers 32 into a counter-narrative to Numbers 13–14. If at that time the failure of a group from Israel had led to the death of a whole generation of Israel in the wilderness, so now, a generation later, there was an analogous danger that a group would fail; but this danger is averted and the occupation of the land can proceed.

99. In assigning Num. 34:1–12 to P^g, as I have done above, I am following Cortese, *Terra di Canaan* (see n. 65 above), 41–51. He refutes Noth's arguments for a dependence on and connection with Joshua 13–19. Cortese, however, wishes also to add Num. 33:50–56 to P^g (ibid., 51–58). That cannot be. As Wellhausen had already correctly seen (*Composition* [see n. 57 above], 115), there appears here 'a foreign element in Q.' The detailed facts were already well presented by B. Baentsch, *Exodus-Leviticus-Numeri*, HKAT I, 2 (Göttingen, 1903), 683. To these more linguistic observations may be added those of redaction criticism. Within Num. 33:50–56, v. 54 may not be regarded as a still later addition, for the whole section Num. 33:51b–56 constitutes a part of the frame for 34:1–12, and precisely through the relationship between 33:54 and 34:13. In addition, the number seven for the *hā'āreṣ* in Num. 33:51b–56, which is scarcely accidental, will no longer be present if 33:54 is eliminated. On the other hand, Num. 33:54 is undoubtedly secondary in relation to Num. 26:52–56 (a text that is more recent than P^g and contains within itself a number of layers). On this, see Noth, *Studien* (n. 65 above), 203 n. 2; Wüst, *Untersuchungen* (n. 97 above), 198–99 and n. 627. This requires that all of Num. 33:50–56 come from a much later initiative than P^g, and in turn accords with the fact that here, in contrast to P^g, the occupation of the land is depicted in as martial a fashion as possible.

100. This is true even of the extremely narrow 'foundation layer' which Mittmann posits: Num. 32:1, 16, 17a, 34–35, 37–38 (after removal of later expansions in all these verses), since in v. 17a the Gadites and Reubenites declare: 'We will take up arms as a vanguard before the Israelites, until we have brought them to their place.' Of course, the interest of the text was focused entirely on the settlement of the two tribes in the land east of the Jordan, and their assistance to the tribes west of the Jordan presented no major problem.

treat in the following brief study, introduces ideas and linguistic elements both from the deuteronomistic and from the priestly sphere into this context. Before Moses permits the Gadites and Reubenites to establish cities and sheepfolds in the land east of the Jordan (Num. 32:24), he obligates them through a conditional blessing (Num. 32:20aβ–22) and a conditional threat of punishment (Num. 32:23) to take part in the conquest of the land west of the Jordan. This is a typically deuteronomic form of establishing an obligation. The concrete formulation of Num. 32:20b, 21a in the first conditional clause cannot be understood except as a formula modeled on Josh. 4:13.[101] It is followed in v. 21b by *yrš hifil*, with YHWH as subject,[102] another typically deuteronomistic expression. But instead of attaching the statement about the west Jordan tribes' taking possession of the land with the usual deuteronomic word play employing *yrš qal*,[103] the text continues with the characteristic priestly verb *kbš* (Num. 32:22a).[104] Certainly, the redactor is thinking of Josh. 18:1, for it is only in light of the placement of the tent of meeting in Shiloh, described there, that the phrase 'when the land is subdued before YHWH' is completely comprehensible.[105] In the consequent clause in Num. 32:22b, possession

101. The formula, 'to go before YHWH for the war' is quite unusual. If I am not mistaken, only in Josh. 4:13 do we find the formula, 'to cross over [the Jordan] before YHWH armed for war.' There it means that the Israelites, or more precisely the tribes east of the Jordan (cf. v. 12) passed by the ark, which had been stationed in the middle of the dry riverbed, in order to make war on Jericho. In Num. 32:20 it was necessary first to take up the verb from v. 17, and then to attach the rest of the formula from Josh. 4:13. But what emerged was apparently so unusual that then, in Num. 32:21, everything had to be repeated with the proper verb and the mention of the Jordan, shortened only by the omission of 'for the war.' The twice-repeated 'before YHWH' then immediately became a connecting formula to hold the whole unit together (note its repetition in Num. 32:22a and b).

102. It is also possible that *kol ḥālûṣ* could be the subject. In that case, we would already have here what certainly must be asserted of Num. 33:50–56, namely the transfer of the declaration of extermination from YHWH to the Israelites.

103. In the parallel passages Deut. 3:20 and Josh. 1:15, we find *yrš qal*. For this word play, see Deut. 9:3, 4, 5; 11:23; 18:12; Josh. 23:5; Judg. 11:23, 24.

104. This word frames P^g: Gen. 1:28; Josh. 18:1 (see section 4.2.6 above). The *nifal* is otherwise found only in Num. 32:29; 1 Chr. 22:18, and (in another context) Neh. 5:5.

105. In Josh. 18:1 the land lies subjugated before the Israelites. Thus Num. 32:29, which belongs to the same or a later stage of redaction and is not forced by any connecting expression to use the phrase 'before YHWH,' has also adopted it. There is also talk of drawing lots for the land 'before YHWH' in Josh. 18:6, 8, 10; 19:51. In those passages the background is always Shiloh.

of the land east of the Jordan is then described with a word typical of the priestly writing, *'ăḥuzzâ.*[106] The threat in Num. 32:23aβ begins with what is probably a literal borrowing from Deut. 9:16, thus elevating the situation to the level of Israel's original sin, the making of the golden calf.[107] Finally, what is said about sins that the sinners in some sense 'seek' and then 'find' seems to reflect the tone of deuteronomistic speech.[108] On the whole, then, what we have here is a passage that has been deliberately constructed out of a mixture of deuteronomistic and priestly linguistic elements. The distinction between the two worlds of thought and speech has been eliminated. Israel's military conquest of the land west of the Jordan gains entrance into the sphere of the priestly writing.

5.2.3 *Numbers 33:50–56*

This is even more clearly evident when, in Num. 33:50–56, the divine definition of the land of Canaan, which is being given to Israel, is preceded by an express command to seize it by military conquest. The construction of the sentences is in the priestly manner. The fact that what is at issue is the military destruction of the inhabitants of the land is discernible from the reprise of this theme in a conditional curse, which belongs more to the deuteronomistic tradition: it concludes the text at

106. An expression reading *'ăḥuzzâ lipnê YHWH,* however, cannot be found. Here it seems that the connecting phrase 'before YHWH' is simply meant to give a full close to the first conditional clause. But it is also possible that this phrase, taken together with 'you . . . return' earlier in the verse, may have been intended to produce a kind of contrasting reference to Deut. 1:45 in which, after a military expedition not sanctioned by YHWH that ended in defeat, the text reads: '*When you returned* and wept *before YHWH,* YHWH would neither heed your voice nor pay you any attention.'

107. Deut 9:16: *wĕhinnēh ḥăṭā'tem laYHWH 'ĕlōhêkem;* Num. 32:23: *hinnēh ḥăṭā'tem laYHWH.* I posit a literal borrowing, although the word *ḥṭ'* is quite common. In the priestly writing and Ezekiel this verb is used absolutely, not with *l* (Ezek. 14:13 being the single exception); on the other hand, it is often used with *lĕ* in deuteronomic texts. There it is found in the first person, which probably represents the original usage proper to it (Deut. 1:41; Josh. 7:20; Judg. 10:10; 1 Sam. 7:6; 12:23; 2 Sam. 12:13) or, for reporting, in the third person (Deut. 20:18; 1 Sam. 2:25; 14:33; 1 Kgs. 8:33, 35, 46, 50; 2 Kgs. 17:7). In the second person it is found only in 1 Sam. 14:34, a passage whose subject is rather different, and then also in Deut. 9:16, where there is a literal correspondence. The parallel Exod. 32:33 points to the same context of sin involving the golden calf. There the accent is on the premise that only the guilty should be punished.

108. Comparable texts are: Deut. 4:30; 31:17 (twice); 31:21; Judg. 6:13; 2 Kgs. 7:9; Ps. 119:143; Job 31:29; Esth. 8:6.

Num. 33:55–56.[109] In individual phrases we encounter a recognition that it is necessary to speak of the violent conquest in the language of a particular tradition, that of 'Gilgal.'[110] While it originally referred to the expulsion of the inhabitants of the land, in deuteronomistic theology this had become their destruction. An exilic editor of the deuteronomistic historical work, whom Rudolf Smend discovered and named the 'deuteronomistic nomist' (DtrN),[111] must have taken it particularly to heart. He apparently introduced the already existing older text of Judg. 2:1–5 into the work and formulated his own key text, Josh. 23:1–16, on the basis of this tradition. This latter text, in particular, seems to be reflected in Num. 33:50–56, for Num. 33:55, *liṣnînim bĕṣiddêkem*, 'thorns in your sides,' appears to be the reworking of a rather peculiar formulation in Josh. 23:13.[112] As in Deuteronomy 7, so also in Num. 33:52, the command to destroy the inhabitants is coupled with an order to destroy their cultic objects. But the objects to be destroyed are described, not by means of concepts from Deut. 7:5 and Deut. 12:3, but instead with expressions that are found in the holiness code.[113] Thus here again the mixture of elements from the priestly

109. In itself it would be conceivable that the conditional clause in Num. 33:51b continues for the moment, and that the consequent clause begins only at v. 54. The decision depends on Num. 33:55–56, and the continuation of the chain of events beyond the destruction of the land's inhabitants to the division of the land is explained by the interest in connecting the text to Num. 34:1–12, a connection that is accomplished by the linking of Num. 33:54 with Num. 34:13 (see n. 99 above).

110. I called it 'the Gilgal tradition' years ago, borrowing from Judg. 2:1: see Lohfink, *Hauptgebot* (n. 88 above), 178. The most important studies since then are Schmitt, *Keinen Frieden* (see n. 90 above), and Halbe, *Privilegrecht* (see n. 25).

111. R. Smend, 'Das Gesetz und die Völker. Ein Beitrag zur deuteronomistischen Redaktionsgeschichte,' in H. W. Wolff, ed., *Probleme biblischer Theologie*, Festschrift for Gerhard von Rad (Munich, 1971), 494–509.

112. For the connection between these two verses, cf. also Num. 33:55, *tôtîrû*, with Josh. 23:12 (the conditional clause to v. 13), *bĕyeter*. Num. 33:55, like Josh. 23:13, speaks of the eyes and the *ṣiddêkem* ('sides?'), but the instruments or objects that cause the damage shift. The *ṣĕninîm* move from the eyes in Josh. 23:13 to the sides (?) in Num. 33:55. It is possible that behind these ideas, which are no longer completely intelligible to us, there stands the word *ṣiddîm* in Judg. 2:3, which might originally be connected, not with Hebrew *ṣad*, 'side', but instead with Akkadian *ṣaddu*, 'sign, portent' (cf. BHS ad loc.), a word that, by the time of the editing, was no longer understood.

113. For *maśkiyyôt*, cf. Lev. 26:1; *massēkôt*, Lev. 19:4 (but also in a Gilgal text: Exod. 34:17, and frequently in DtrG, although always in the singular with the exception of 1 Kgs. 14:9); for *bāmôt*, cf. Lev. 26:30 (of course also frequently in DtrG); *ṣelem* (Num. 33:52) is a word from P^g, although in a different context there; in the sense employed here it is found in 2 Kgs. 11:18, but especially in Ezek. 7:20; 16:17.

and deuteronomistic writings in this piece of text is palpable. But as regards content, the deuteronomistic theory of a military conquest of the land of Canaan has been introduced into a context that, before this, was deliberately devoid of military elements.

The subject is even given a new expression. In Num. 33:52, the verb *yrš hifil* is used: *wĕhôraštem 'et kol yōšĕbê hā'āreṣ mippĕnêkem*, 'you shall drive out all the inhabitants of the land from before you.' In the following verse (Num. 33:53), this is repeated, probably in exactly the same sense, although in a shortened formulation.[114] Thus this verb is emphatically placed in a position that it did not have in the deuteronomistic tradition. It is true that there had been old reports in which it was said, descriptively or even with regret or displeasure, that the Israelites had not been able to 'destroy' the inhabitants of particular areas in the course of the conquest. These are found in Judges 1 and within Joshua 13–17. There were also formulations of the command to destroy using other verbs. But *yrš hifil* was the typical word for a promise: YHWH will be the one who, when the Israelites march into the land west of the Jordan, will 'destroy' the inhabitants of the land. DtrN placed a condition before this promise. Only if Israel observes the law will YHWH destroy them all. Numbers 33:50–56 also speaks in conditional fashion. But in the conditional clause, Israel's duty is not pronounced to be fidelity to the law, but rather the destruction of the land's inhabitants, something that formerly was YHWH's own task. If Israel does not carry out the bloodbath it will experience the consequences in the misery that the surviving inhabitants will visit upon Israel. In light of what we have uncovered in the history of the tradition at this point, this is shockingly untheological. The authors must have found it so themselves, because in the final verse, Num. 33:56, they attempt to supply the previously forgotten theological dimension: 'And I will do to you as I thought to do to them.' It is only necessary to compare Num. 33:50–56 with the text of Judg. 2:1–3, which at first glance appears so similar, to recognize the difference in viewpoint.[115]

114. On the text-critical problem in Num. 33:53, cf. N. Lohfink, 'Textkritisches zu jrš im Alten Testament,' in P. Casetti et al., eds., *Mélanges Dominique Barthélemy*, OBO 38 (Fribourg, 1981), 273–88, at 277.

115. Let me, however, point out that the shift in linguistic treatment of *yrš hifil* already begins with the deuteronomistic hand, which (in debate with DtrN) revised Deuteronomy 7–9 and introduced there an antinomistic theology of grace. In Deut. 7:17 Israel is confronted with the question how it will be possible for all these superior nations to be destroyed (*yrš hifil*). But the answer given is that YHWH will do it. In Deut. 9:3–5, the destruction of the people of the land is predicted three times, with the help of *yrš hifil*: twice it is YHWH who is the subject of the prediction, but once it is Israel.

In terms of its strata, this passage is too independent for us to be able to say on the basis of a broader context whether one ought to detect, behind its new nuancing of the old idea of a war of conquest at the beginning of the people's history, a real contemporary background with a special intent. Perhaps it is only a matter of a purely literary job of combining that was not fully adequate to its models. On the other hand, there may well be a new situation of the post-exilic community, and a new concern, behind the chapter on the war with Midian which we will discuss in the following section.

5.3 *The post-exilic actualization of the deuteronomistic theology of war within the redaction of the Pentateuch as a whole*

5.3.1 *Literary-critical location of Numbers 31*

Even if W. F. Albright and O. Eissfeldt were correct in saying that Numbers 31 contains some very ancient and significant pieces of information about a Midianite kingdom with the right of protectorate over neighboring realms at the end of the second millennium BCE,[116] the chapter itself is one of the 'very late pieces of the Pentateuch' and probably represents a 'subsequent addition to the Pentateuch as a whole entity.'[117] The content of the beginning, Num. 31:1, attaches the chapter to Num. 25:17–18, a post-priestly text, but at the same time it presupposes the text of Num. 27:12–14. The beginning of Numbers 31 has thus been created for its present place in the book. The location after Numbers 25, where the war with the Midianites undoubtedly would have fit in better, was apparently no longer free, since the 'second census of the people,' also a late addition, was already firmly anchored there. The language of the narrative sounds more like the priestly writing, but in detail one can demonstrate other elements, including some that are

116. W. F. Albright, 'Midianite Donkey Caravans,' in H. T. Frank and W. L. Reed, eds., *Translating and Understanding the Old Testament,* Festschrift for H. G. May (Nashville and New York, 1970), 197–205; O. Eissfeldt, 'Protektorat der Midianiter über ihre Nachbarn im letzten Viertel des 2. Jahrtausends v. Chr.,' in his *Kleine Schriften* 5 (Tübingen, 1973), 94–105 (see also the expanded version of this essay, with the same title, in *JBL* 87 [1968]: 383–93). Along the same lines, see W. J. Dumbrell, 'Midian – A Land or a League?' *VT* 25 (1975): 323–37.

117. Quotations from Noth, *Numeri* (see n. 98 above), 198. Only G. von Rad, *Die Priesterschrift im Hexateuch. Literarisch untersucht und theologisch gewertet,* BWANT 65 (Stuttgart, 1934), 132–34, assigns part of the chapter (Num. 31:1–12) to the original priestly document. There is a refutation in Noth, *Studien* (see n. 65 above), 200–201.

deuteronomistic.[118] This narrative concerns itself with the campaign of extermination against the Midianites only to the extent that it can be made to serve as a peg on which to hang exemplary regulations describing the groups to be killed, the behavior expected when returning home after the campaign, the distribution of the spoils, and the voluntary expiatory offerings of returned soldiers. To that degree, we may suspect here an intention to expand, if not at certain points even to offer a corrective to the deuteronomic laws of war that occur later in the Pentateuch.[119] This already presumes that the deuteronomic law has been incorporated into the Pentateuch.

5.3.2 *Numbers 31 and the cultic-militant interests of the Jerusalem temple state*

The story is constructed in such a way that it can also serve as a model for wars originating from post-exilic Jerusalem. On the one hand, it takes place before the beginning of the theme of the conquest of the land west of the Jordan. Thus Joshua is also kept out of it, and one may not regard the war described here as a war to take possession of the land, which has been completed once and for all. Wars of this kind are conceivable at a later time as well. On the other hand, Moses has already been given notice of his end, and he no longer takes wars under his personal command, as for example in the retrospective look in Deuteronomy 1–3. Thus Eleazar, Aaron's successor, can take a more prominent place in the foreground of the story, and even undertake a part of the proclamation of the law in place of Moses (Num. 31:21–24). In addition, the priest Phinehas, the son of the high priest Eleazar, is made the leader of the campaign.[120] At

118. See the instances listed by Baentsch, *Ex-Num* (n. 99 above), 651.

119. As regards the content, for example: the Israelite troops adhered to the law in Deut. 20:12–15 (for wars against cities outside the promised land) and did not kill any women and children. Now, in Num. 31:14–18, Moses rules that only girls who have not yet had sexual intercourse are to be allowed to live. Still, the question of a fundamental intention to correct the picture is reopened when this rule is given a rationale based on a particular sin of the Midianite women (v. 16) and when the whole war is designated a war of revenge (v. 2). It remains open whether this is to be valid for all later wars against enemies outside the land of Canaan.

120. This is not stated so baldly. But what can Num. 31:6 mean (Moses sends the contingents of a thousand from each of the twelve tribes, along with Phinehas, to the war) in combination with Num. 31:14, and especially Num. 31:48 (the commanders of the army, or rather the commanders who were assigned to the thousands, then explained in apposition to be the commanders of thousands and the commanders of hundreds) except that Phinehas is the leader? According to Num. 31:13 Moses,

this point it seems very likely that there is a hint of the structure of the post-exilic temple state, in which the family of the high priest assumed the various functions of leadership in the persons of different members of the family. These functions certainly included political and military roles.

The interest of the chapter seems to me to focus primarily on two things. On the one hand, some of the cruelty of the war of extermination, which in the deuteronomistic portrayal was deliberately limited to the situation of conquering the land, has now been made permissible for later wars not tied to that situation. This is accomplished especially in Num. 31:15–18. The reason given there for the intensified cruelty toward the civilian population of the enemy, that the enemy women had seduced the

Eleazar and *kol nĕśîʾê hāʿēdâ* go to meet the returning troops. Hence it seems to me scarcely possible to dispute the appositional character of *śārê hāʾălāpîm wĕśārê hammēʾôt* in Num. 31:14, and especially in Num. 31:48. The older commentaries hasten to assert, in exegeting Num. 31:6, that Phinehas did not take the command. But why not? They give no reasons for their assertion. Perhaps at this point a glance at the war scroll from Qumran may be instructive, although of course one cannot prove anything about Numbers 31 on that basis. Obviously, the priests themselves, in this scroll, do not shed blood. But they are eager actors. Someone who may be identifiable from other Qumran documents as the Davidic messiah, *nśy(ʾ) kl hʿdh*, appears, but so sparingly that Y. Yadin, in his truly painstaking analysis of the war scroll, *The Scroll of the War of the Sons of Light against the Sons of Darkness* (London, 1962) apparently did not venture to say anything in detail about his function, nor to devote a chapter to the hierarchy of command. It is by no means certain that the 'great standard at the head of the whole army' (1QM 3 12) is the symbol of command of the *nśy(ʾ) kl hʿdh*, since the standards of the tribes each bear the name of the *nśy hš (bṭ)* (1QM 3 14), just as, apparently, the standards of the four camps each bear the name of the corresponding camp. (Here a lacuna in the manuscript must be filled, and the commentators are not in agreement about the exact words that should be supplied.) But on the 'great standard at the head of the whole army' stands only 'People of God,' and then the names of Israel, Aaron, and those of the twelve tribes (1QM 3 12–13). The name of the *nśy(ʾ) kl hʿdh* is not written there. This figure appears only at the very end of the account of the standards in connection with an object, not thoroughly described in hierarchical terms, at which point the reading is also, unfortunately, in dispute. Most people read *mgn*, 'shield,' but other suggestions are *ns*, 'banner,' *mṭ* = *mṭh*, 'staff, scepter,' *kly*, 'tool, weapon, garment' (1QM 5 1). On this stands his name and those of Israel, Levi, Aaron, the twelve tribes and the Sarim of the twelve tribes (1QM 5 1–2). Everything favors the supposition that this is a secondary literary element corresponding to nothing else in the war scroll. Cf. the exhaustive argumentation in this sense in P. R. Davies, *1QM, the War Scroll from Qumran. Its Structure and History*, BibOr 32 (Rome, 1977), 35–36. But even should this not be a late literary addition, the form of the *nśy(ʾ) kl hʿdh* is at least kept separate from the principal system of the military hierarchy, and this in the form of a placement at the end and not at the head. In Numbers 31 there is not even a comparable figure.

Israelites into falling away from YHWH, was not impossible even in the post-exilic period.[121] Whether there really were military actions in which the model of the Midianite war was followed is another question, and one that, because of the lack of sources, we cannot answer. But at least the theoretical possibility was created in Numbers 31. On the other hand, the interest of Numbers 31 is clearly directed toward cultic and ritual aspects of the conduct of war, such as the period of taboo and the purification rites for returning soldiers (Num. 31:19–24), and the portion of the booty that is to go to the sacral personnel and the temple (the principal theme beginning at Num. 31:25). This, too, reflects the post-exilic situation. On the whole, we must say that in Numbers 31 not only are the cultic interest of the priestly document and the radical ideology of war of the deuteronomistic literature, which were originally opposed to one another, melted together into a unit, but beyond this that the deuteronomistic war of extermination against the previous inhabitants of the land, originally conceived more as a depiction of the past and a myth designed to support the national identity, has suddenly become a mode of action that is conceivable even in the future.

6. War and the Pentateuch as a Whole

The texts that have just been treated, drawn from late strata of the Pentateuch, have led us to the final redaction of the work; in fact, in Numbers 31 we are already beyond that stage. As a concluding step, we must take a look at this final redaction itself.

6.1 *The production of the Pentateuch as a relativizing of the theory of a society without war in P^g*

The production of the Pentateuch meant, in any case, that the priestly document did not succeed as the exclusive theory of the social structure built up around the temple in Jerusalem, which we can qualify only in a restricted sense as a 'temple state.' The far more militant conceptions of the past laid down in the 'Jehovist historical book' and in Deuteronomy also entered the canonical text and cast their light over the priestly portions as well.

121. Cf. Ezra 9–10; Neh. 10:30 [31]; 13:23–29. Ezra, however, construes the sin as an offense against the prohibition of marriage with the original inhabitants of the land: cf., for example, Ezra 9:1 with Deut. 7:1–4.

6.2 *The exclusion of the book of Joshua from the canon of the Torah did not occur because of the military actions narrated there*

One could, of course, raise the question whether it might not be relevant in this context that the book of Joshua, the summit of military narrative from a deuteronomistic pen, was pruned away. Is it possible that someone did not wish to see this bloodthirsty beginning of the national history recorded as part of the basic canonical text for the new reality? Or were the Persian agencies of control in this minor neighboring province with a privileged religious status less than enthusiastic about allowing that kind of military self-interpretation?

One might have such thoughts, but in view of the late strata examined in the previous section, with their alteration of the priestly writing in the direction of the deuteronomistic picture of things, one is required to dismiss them quickly from one's mind. The fact that such harsh and victorious wars are narrated in the book of Joshua cannot have been the reason why it was not included in the fundamental canon.

It would seem that the final redactors of the Pentateuch had the task of putting together, from old documents, the laws on the basis of which the Jews in Jerusalem and in the Jewish communities within the Persian empire could continue to live. They accomplished their assignment in the most conservative fashion possible, by retaining in their original form as much as feasible of the old writings in which the laws were to be found. This was literarily possible because the giving of the law, even before their time, had been associated almost exclusively with the figure of Moses. Hence they could create a work that (apart from the antechamber formed by Genesis) simply traced the curve of Moses' life. When he died, all the relevant laws of Israel had already been uttered. The book of Joshua was no longer necessary. The question of military or non-military occupation of the land, of more or less war in Israel's early period, played no part in this context.

6.3 *The theology of war in the late strata and post-Pentateuch developments*

Attitudes to war are more clearly discernible from texts that were newly created in this phase of the redaction. But they show that it was by no means an accident that Chronicles, although they reject a conquest of the land by Israel, are certainly well acquainted with a war that is embellished with religious rites and supported by religious pathos; or when, later, the Maccabean revolt is set off and led by a priestly family; or when the community at Qumran could, finally, produce a document describing the war of the children of light against the children of darkness. This last, of course, is the depiction of a war that is expected in the last days, and it also implies that the intervening time until the eschaton is to be characterized by nonviolence.[122]

Even this community in the intervening time, living nonviolently, finds its basis in the Pentateuch, but not in the texts treated here; rather, that basis was in the laws themselves, the laws in the Pentateuch that project the social order of the people of God, especially in Leviticus 19.[123] Here, and not in the world without war of the priestly historical narrative, purchased through a system of bloody sacrifices and then repressed and painted over in the history of the Pentateuch itself, is the starting point for the project of a society without violence that is found in Jesus' sermon on the mount.

122. Cf. 1QS 10 16–19: 'I know that judgement of all the living is in His hand, and that all His deeds are truth. I will praise Him when distress is unleashed and will magnify Him also because of His salvation. I will pay to no man the reward of evil; I will pursue him with goodness. For judgement of all the living is with God and it is He who will render to man his reward. I will not [like the Zealots later] envy in a spirit of wickedness, my soul shall not desire the riches of violence [acquired through revolutionary action]. I will not grapple with the men of perdition [at the time of the Zealots, these were the Romans] until the Day of Revenge [i.e, the eschatological battle that will establish God's definitive judgment].' Translation from Geza Vermes, *The Dead Sea Scrolls in English* (New York, 1962), 71; explanatory notes in brackets by N. Lohfink.

123. For example, the phrase 'I will pay no man the reward of evil' in the quotation in n. 122 may well have the text of Lev. 19:18aα as its background, despite the difference in terminology. The remaining language is determined by the intentional parallelism to the retributive action of God, for which a terminology well grounded in the Bible is employed.

8

The Problem of Individual and Community in Deuteronomy 1:6–3:29

It is true that Deuteronomy 1:6–3:29 contributes nothing of major significance to an intellectual clarification of the problem of individual and community.[1] Nevertheless, it can throw new light on this much-discussed question, which it addresses from a rhetorical, educational, and authorial standpoint. This essay, after clarifying some preliminary questions by way of orientation, will undertake a brief investigation of the standpoint of that text.[2]

(a) Gerhard von Rad already pointed out that here, in contrast to the older sources of the Pentateuch, 'the people is made the subject and placed in the foreground.'[3] From a purely literary-critical point of view, that is, a stratum that is especially indebted to ideas of community overlays an older one that is more individualistically oriented.[4] The correction of the tradition is perhaps most evident in the divine speech in 1:35–40,[5] where the non-punishment of Caleb is set in sharp contrast alongside the

1. The most recent, very thorough and outstandingly documented work on the problem is by J. Scharbert, *Solidarität in Segen und Fluch im Alten Testament und in seiner Umwelt.* Publications to date: I. *Väterfluch und Vätersegen* (Bonn, 1958); cf. *Schol* 35 (1960): 93–96. For Deuteronomy 1–3 cf. especially pp. 187ff., even though there the different strata of Deuteronomy are considered *per modum unius.*

2. Let me refer, for further details, to my study of the descriptive artistry and theology of Deut. 1:6–3:29 (*Bibl* 41 [1960]: 105–34). The present essay is that promised on p. 106 n. 4 of that study. For textual and literary criticism of Deut. 1:6–3:29, see especially p. 107 n. 1, p. 127 n. 2, and p. 132 n. 2.

3. G. von Rad, *Das Gottesvolk im Deuteronomium* (Stuttgart, 1929), 18 n. 2.

4. Let me expressly emphasize that this literary-critical judgment says nothing about the age of the categories of 'community' employed by Deuteronomy at this point.

5. Only Deut. 1:39a (as far as *yihyeh*) is a latter addition.

extension of punishment to Moses ('on your account'). Neither Caleb nor Moses had participated in the people's sin. For Caleb, this is presupposed as already known from tradition; Moses' innocence had been brought out clearly by the earlier text. The exception of Caleb corresponds to the tradition (in which Caleb had once been the central focus of the narrative, before the emphases shifted); this element of tradition is not dropped, as are so many others, because it prepares for another story about Caleb that will be inserted at a later point.[6] It appears that the tradition connected with the narrative of the scouts, insofar as we can judge, does not contain a divine punishment pronounced against Moses. Here we seem to be facing the author's own contribution. This author's desire to think of history in a thoroughly theological sense, and his ability to consider the most varied elements of the tradition together, in a collection of representative individual narratives, is at work here.

(b) It would probably be inadequate to suppose that the categories of community had, of themselves, extended equally over the individual categories in the old sources, simply because they are forms of thought that are unique to the author. Instead, they were probably quite conscious and deliberate. This is evident from the fact that they play a major role in the very framework of the three chapters.[7] YHWH's speech in Deut. 1:6–8 introduces the theme of the narrative, and is presented as a word of command from God to the whole people, who are encamped and assembled at Horeb. In Deut. 1:35, YHWH enunciates a judgment on these same people; in Deut. 1:37 Moses also, although personally guiltless, is subjected to the same punishment, and in Deut. 1:38–39 a new plan for the future, again for the whole people, is proposed. In Deut.

6. This takes for granted the position (which has the greatest probability) that Deut. 1:6–3:29 represents the exordium of the historical work and was written by the Deuteronomist himself. The later Caleb story is found in Joshua 14 (cf. especially vv. 6–8): on this, see M. Noth, *Überlieferungsgeschichtliche Studien* (Halle, 1943), 32. It is not unusual for the Deuteronomist that, as a result of dependence on sources, different opinions can come to be placed alongside one another. In this case the fact that Moses, as the leader of the people, naturally stood within a different context of solidarity than Caleb, the head of a single clan, may have contributed to the situation. But the Deuteronomist does not work out the distinction unreflectingly. Apparently in the case of Moses he is not concerned with the special problem of his responsibility as ruler or mediator; rather, this is merely the concrete instance in which he is faced with the more fundamental problem of the arrangement of individual details within more comprehensive units.

7. This framework consists of Deut. 1:6–8, 34–40; 2:14–16; 3:18–29. For more detail, see *Bibl* 41 (1960), 132.

2:14ff. it is emphasized with the greatest solemnity (through a threefold repetition) that the old (sinful) generation had entirely died out before the beginning of God's saving activity on behalf of the new generation. In Deut. 3:18–20, Moses orders the tribes dwelling east of the Jordan to cross over with their 'brethren' to conquer the land west of the Jordan – apparently so that the whole community will share in this process of salvation.[8] Finally, God refuses Moses' request to be allowed to enter the land west of the Jordan along with the rest 'on your account' (Deut. 3:26–28). Thus the whole framework of this narrative is governed by categories of community.

(c) At issue are two kinds of community, but it must be said that, in the final analysis, both of them are theologically determined.

On the one hand, there is the people Israel. These are, of course, the people who are descended from Abraham, Isaac, and Jacob, but their identity is definitively established only by the oath YHWH gave to their ancestors, whose content was that they would be given a precisely defined land as their own possession. Thus the community comes into being as a result of a divine word of blessing that intentionally summons it forth.[9] Corresponding to this, there are other nations (Edom, Moab, Ammon) whose ancestors also received promises of land from YHWH; negative parallels are the nations of Sihon and Og, who cannot demonstrate any such promises and therefore may be punished not only during a single generation, but even by being completely exterminated.

The word 'generation' describes the second type of community. This word (i.e., *dôr*) is found in Deut. 1:35 and 2:14, the first time perhaps in a gloss. In any case, the thing itself is clearly present. YHWH condemns the sinful generation (and Moses with it) and transfers the occupation of the land to the next generation. Hence the wandering in the wilderness, lasting an entire human lifetime, at the end of which the sinful generation is dead. The new generation as a whole will cross over the Jordan, and the tribes that dwell east of the Jordan must also take part; in contrast, Moses, as a member of the old generation, must remain behind. It is true that, in one sense, such a generation is really what we also understand by the word 'generation,' but the crucial definition is theological: the one generation is defined by sin and God's word of punishment that it evokes, the other by

8. For Deuteronomy 1–3 the land east of the Jordan is not properly part of the promised land. For the proof and for bibliography, see *Bibl* 41 (1960), 131 n. 3.

9. The Deuteronomist is thinking here in juristic categories (oath, transfer of property, lack of willingness to make a contract). Cf. *Bibl* 41 (1960), 124–27, 130–31.

obedience and the resulting validation of the promise to the ancestors.[10]

The distinction between the two types of community ultimately rests on another distinction (valid at least in this phase of salvation history): between divine grace and divine wrath. God's grace is always prior; God's wrath only follows when that grace is rejected by the people. God's grace was bestowed on all the descendants of the patriarchs through God's promise to the ancestors. Thus God's wrath can only be directed at the generation that sins, and God's grace remains available to the generation that follows after.[11]

(d) After these preparatory clarifications, we may now address the principal question: why did the author so deliberately place the categories of community in the foreground of the presentation? He may have had personal ideas about the relationship between individual and community, as well as opinions about the personal responsibility of a mediating person for the actions or misdeeds of a society entrusted to him or her – but it appears that it was not his concern at this point to expound those ideas. Instead, he retrojects all these questions into the freedom of God, which is unpredictable, and for that very reason challenging to religious sensibility. Without giving a single reason, God associates Moses with the sinful generation, but then does not destroy him along with it; instead, God gives him new tasks in order, finally, to include him once again in the fate of that generation.

Thus it is not a question of theoretical clarification. The author is more interested in simply telling a story. But in telling it, he desires to influence, guide and educate the readers. His concern is about the readers' internal attitude, not their theoretical knowledge. The speech of Moses in these three chapters is permeated by a muted technique for winning over human minds. In the guise of Moses, the author takes the readers (of the time of the exile) by the hand, and leads them through the fate of Moses, so difficult to understand, showing them everything and gradually persuading them to abandon individualistic ideas of personal guilt or

10. None of this is new. G. von Rad developed it in a number of essays on the whole scope of deuteronomic theology. It is merely mentioned here in passing, in the first place so that it may be clear that it is not absent from Deut. 1:6–3:29, a section that for many reasons may be set apart from the rest of the book of Deuteronomy, and in the second place in order to show that at this point, for the Deuteronomist, the problem of individual vs. community was a genuinely religious one.

11. Given the theology of the author of Deuteronomy, what is said about Sihon at Deut. 2:30 (that YHWH 'hardened his spirit and made his heart defiant') could probably not be said about Israel in chapter 1.

innocence and simply to feel themselves united with the great and total guilt of the nation. This rhetorical-educative process should now be the subject of our reflections.

At the beginning, the narrative very facilely demonstrates Moses' innocence. Sin occurs despite Moses' solemn warning (Deut. 1:29ff.). After the report of this warning, Moses as narrator inserts his present judgment of events (vv. 32–33). Here, at the latest, it becomes clear to the readers that a line of division is to be drawn between Moses and the sinful nation. Thus at the beginning of the narrative the readers discover those individual categories of moral judgment that they themselves are probably accustomed to apply.

As a result, their reaction to the speech of YHWH that follows (Deut. 1:34–40) is assured. When God, in v. 35, condemns the sinful generation, the readers will find the judgment to be just. When, in v. 36, God excepts Caleb from the punishment, they will also feel the justice of it, given their individualistic ideas of justice. And correspondingly, they will expect Moses also to escape unpunished, or rather they will not even anticipate that any 'case against Moses' will be discussed at all. At this point the narrator interrupts the report of God's speech, inserts some words of his own, and then resumes. In the most compact form ('You also shall not enter there'), but with a reference to the underlying problem ('on your account'), he expresses the word of God that applies to himself. Undoubtedly, the narrative is many-layered and dense at this point. For a moment, the readers can sense the oppressive weight within the soul of Moses when he speaks of this word of God from the distant past. While Moses immediately becomes quite objective and calm again in his narrative, the problem has been introduced, and in the course of the narrative the utterly unexpected and dumbly accepted, unexplained, not yet realized judgment of God on Moses retains a secret and agitating actuality within the readers; from this perspective, they now see the further events through the eyes and feelings of Moses.[12]

As the readers begin to identify with someone condemned without personal guilt, they may at first feel how a spark of hope kindled in Moses when all the others had died and he was still alive. (Had God perhaps retracted the judgment?) They sense how that hope grew as Moses even received the divine command to begin the occupation of the land

12. Deuteronomy 1–3 may well be another case of what Erich Auerbach, *Mimesis* (Berne, 1946), 16–17 says, in a comparison between Homeric and OT narrative styles, about the many-layeredness and density of the latter.

himself.[13] Then they share with Moses the dark act of obedience by which he publicly proclaimed his own successor.[14] Here they learn from Moses how one should say 'yes' to the will of God, even in such difficult matters, but they may also sense how the decision to prostrate himself before God and beg for mercy had to ripen within Moses.[15] And so the readers' identification with Moses is complete when Moses stands as a supplicant before God.

This identification was the purpose of all the nets that the narrative has woven. Now the readers are imprisoned within Moses. They will not easily be able to separate from him again when Moses silently accepts God's answer rejecting his plea. They will understand all that is expressed by the note about the place of encampment with which the narrative rather abruptly ends, a notice that at first seems to say nothing and to be superfluous. This is quite typical of the subdued Hebrew narrative style, so penetrating in its very mutedness. The readers will understand it, and when they reflect that the new generation will soon cross over the river into the land of promise, leaving behind only a lonely altar, while the dark gate of death, behind which the shades of Moses' own generation are waiting, has opened before them, the readers themselves (readers who may also have awaited death far away from the land of their ancestors) will have learned a good deal: not something theoretical, but rather how one must act before God.

Thus narrating and not instructing, guiding and speaking in muted rhetoric,[16] the author of Deut. 1:6–3:29 also poses for readers of today the

13. Deut. 3:24–25, Moses' plea for himself, teaches us that Moses does not found his hope on a consciousness of individual worthiness, but rather on the divine comportment, which he thinks he may interpret as a faint sign of the beginning of a change in God's attitude toward him.

14. The transition from second person singular to second person plural in Deut. 3:21–22 makes the public nature of the event obvious.

15. The stylistic weight placed on this plea of Moses becomes fully evident for the first time when we reflect that in Deuteronomy 1 a prayer of Moses on behalf of the people that was found in the old tradition (cf. Num. 14:11–20) is ostentatiously omitted (using language drawn from the passage itself!). Cf. *Bibl* 41 (1960), 117–18.

16. Since Deut. 4:1–40, which, in the present form of the speech of Moses extending from Deut. 1:6 to Deut. 4:40, first introduces rhetorical elements as such, is probably to be located later in time than Deuteronomy 1–3 (cf. *Bibl* 41 [1960], 106 n. 2 and 134 n. 1), one must question how, in Deut. 1:6–3:29, the 'speech' of Moses can be placed ahead of the other deuteronomic 'speeches.' Dillmann (*Kurzgefaßtes exegetisches Handbuch*), who seems to have sensed the problem, assumed that the text had originally been a narrative in the third person and was only later

problem of individual and community. No statement is made. The problem is proposed, but not concluded with any doctrine. A fate is exposed. One may develop sympathy, one may enter into it and allow the borders between this story and one's own fate to blur. One may learn to permit God's word spoken over nations and generations to have validity for one's own self.

accommodated to its surroundings. This is impossible, since Moses' narrative perspective cannot be surgically removed from the text without loss of substance. But Moses' appearance as a purely historical narrator in 'I' style immediately before the powerful deuteronomic sermons on the law remains something of a stylistic problem. Nevertheless, certain stylistic characteristics show that Deut. 1:6–3:29 was created for its present location. The rhetoric emphasized in this essay, which is invested in the overall logic of the narrative, may perhaps create a kind of bridge to the following deuteronomic sermons, and the rest may have been accomplished by the consciousness that the narrative of the nation's history belongs before the sermon on the law existing from the beginning (even if the themes were originally organized around the exodus from Egypt). On this last point, compare G. Mendenhall, *Law and Covenant in Israel and the Ancient Near East* (Pittsburgh, 1955) (= *The Biblical Archaeologist* 17 [1954]: 16–46, 49–76), and K. Baltzer, *Das Bundesformular* (Neukirchen, 1960).

9

The Deuteronomistic Picture of the Transfer of Authority from Moses to Joshua
A Contribution to an Old Testament Theology of Office

Deuteronomic style, characterized by its rhythmic language, the internal rhymes that roll the meaning forward, the broadly undulant periods within, and finally by the tireless repetitions of formulaic combinations of words – this warmly surging, sometimes rushing style of levitical preaching often makes the language a kind of music. As we listen, we are borne away, drawn onward. The words, even the sentences lose their individual existence and seem like waves in a larger stream. What is true of the language is also true of the book as a whole. Objects and motifs appear, recede, reappear, turn and twist and always seem to be only variations on a few basic themes, always the same.

This impression is certainly correct. And yet it embraces only one aspect of the complicated phenomenon that is Deuteronomy. In conscious tension with what has been previously described, Deuteronomy and the writings dependent on it claim to be making sharply, often even legally exact pronouncements. Where a novice only hears cascades of verbal music in his or her ears, the experienced should make precise distinctions among the themes and motifs that are being developed.

Often, exegesis is still at an early stage in this respect. The exact meaning of many individual sayings still continues to escape us. While we know the dictionary meaning of the individual words, we are often not fully aware of their symbolic value in the deuteronomic context, and certainly we miss the meaning of many linguistic clichés and formula words. It is the very period of fine and subtle distinction among sources, the end of which is in view at the present time, that has unconsciously avoided the real problems: tempted by its own method to expect doublets and repetitions, it has often moved all too quickly to suppress the question of the precise meaning of individual texts. Thus there is at present a renewed need for very fundamental individual studies.

The present essay is intended to be a study of that nature: a single, small demonstration of the exactitude and precision of deuteronomistic formulation.[1] It takes up the chain of texts on the replacement of Moses by his successor, Joshua (Deut. 1:37–38; 3:21–22, 28; 31:2–6, 7–8, 14–15, 23; Josh. 1:2–9).[2] Its purpose is to show that they never say the same thing, that is, that we are never faced with repetitions and doublets.[3] Each

1. This work continues two other studies by the author directed to the same end: 'Darstellungskunst und Theologie in Dtn 1, 6–3, 29,' *Bibl* 41 (1960): 105–34; and 'Wie stellt sich das Problem Individuum – Gemeinschaft in Dtn 1,6–3,29?' *Schol* 35 (1960): 403–07 (Chapter 8 of the present book). Another study, on Deut. 28:69–32:47, will soon appear in *Biblische Zeitschrift* under the title 'Der Bundesschluß im Land Moab,' [*BZ* n. f. 6 (1962), 32–56] and a longer work on Deuteronomy 4–11 will soon (1962) be completed. This last attempts a new formal and literary analysis of these chapters, perhaps the most difficult to understand in their precise sequence of ideas. A knowledge of the elementary forms employed and of the stylistic techniques (e.g., commentary on older texts, montages of freely chosen elements from the covenant formula, framing of older texts with newer ones, etc.) creates the basis for investigation of the redactional work of composition that undoubtedly took place (no matter how deeply these very chapters are rooted in the tradition of oral preaching). It is only in this way that the intention of the chapters can be clearly understood. It is a question of an actualization of the 'principal commandment' of the covenant, achieved by combining a variety of traditions. At no point is there a vague and unplanned general preaching; at every moment, even though often in a way that is quite unfamiliar to us, precise individual statements are being presented.

2. When at this point texts from two different biblical books (Deuteronomy and Joshua) are regarded as parts of a single series, we do not necessarily presuppose Martin Noth's theory of a deuteronomic historical work (cf. M. Noth, *Überlieferungsgeschichtliche Studien* 1 [Halle, 1st ed. 1943]; for a commented bibliography, see E. Jenni, 'Zwei Jahrzehnte Forschung an den Büchern Josua bis Könige,' *ThRundsch* 27 [1961]: 1–32, 97–146, especially 97–118), although it is certainly the best explanation of the findings. It is sufficient here to think of a unified deuteronomistic layer within the 'framework' of Deuteronomy and Joshua, something that, practically speaking, has been acknowledged since the work of J. Hollenberg ('Die deuteronomischen Bestandteile des Buches Josua,' *Theol. St. u. Kr.* 47 [1874]: 462–506). While it is true that our investigation in some sense presupposes some such context, the results contribute further to increasing the certainty of some such hypothesis.

3. For a contrary example, see C. Steuernagel, *Das Deuteronomium und das Buch Josua*, HKAT (Göttingen, 2nd ed. 1923); cf. its presentation of Deut. 1:37–38; 3:21–22; 31:3–6; Josh. 1:3–9.

of these texts makes a stride forward. Each tells us something new, and it is only the sum total that constitutes the sharp and differentiated portrayal of the transfer of office. When this picture has been made visible we find revealed at the same time a clear-cut theological conception of office under the Old Covenant.[4]

1. Analyses

(a) We begin with God's speech in Josh. 1:2–9. A. Dillmann once characterized its content as follows: 'After Moses' death, Joshua is addressed by God, who calls upon him to begin the task of conquering the land with confidence and courage, and to act in accord with the teaching of Moses that he has heard.'[5] The expressions found in the best-known commentaries continue along this line. For example, the *Bible de Jérusalem*: 'Invitation à passer en terre promise. La fidélité à la Loi, condition du secours divin.'[6] *The Interpreter's Bible*: 'Joshua Assumes Command; He Is Given His Orders.'[7] La Sacra Bibbia: 'Ordine di penetrare nella terra promessa. L'osservanza della Legge.'[8] All these headings agree in seeing the beginning of the action of the book of Joshua in the divine speech in vv. 2–9. This seems to be the case also for Martin Noth, though he attacks the problem much more directly: 'In a short address to Joshua, YHWH points to the task now at hand of conquering the promised land west of the Jordan, the extent of which is briefly described on the basis of Deut. 1:7 (vv. 1–4), in order then . . . to repeat at this crucial moment the encouraging words of Deut. 31:7–8, in a slightly different arrangement (vv. 5–6).'[9] It is undoubtedly true that this divine speech sets the action of the book of Joshua in motion, as the immediately

4. The author owes the inspiration and basis for this investigation to the lectures of his respected teacher W. L. Moran, with whom he also had frequent opportunities to discuss this subject. Obviously, he alone is responsible for the final results. Important impulses also arose out of a discussion with E. Schächter.

5. *Die Bücher Numeri, Deuteronomium und Josua*, KeH (Leipzig, 1886), 442.

6. F.-M. Abel, *Le livre de Josué* (Paris, 1950), 15–16. [Invitation to enter the promised land. Fidelity to the law as a condition of divine aid.]

7. John Bright, in: *The Interpreter's Bible* (New York, 1953), 2: 553.

8. D. Baldi, in: *La Sacra Bibbia*, ed. S. Garofalo (Turin, 1960), 1: 473. [Orders to enter the promised land. The observance of the law.]

9. *Überlieferungsgeschichtliche Studien* (see n. 2 above), 41. For Noth, vv. 7–9 are secondary (loc. cit., n. 4).

following verses show. But it also has another function: it serves as introduction, overture, prologue, or whatever one wishes to call it.[10] Crucial motifs of the book that follows are briefly presented here, for example, the *leitmotif* of the first chapter: as YHWH was with Moses, so YHWH will also be with Joshua.[11] Or we may note the motif of following the Torah of Moses, something that will recur in three decisive passages.[12] At the same time, as is appropriate for the 'introduction' of a 'second volume,' there is a connection made back to the 'first volume,' Deuteronomy.[13] The backward references to Deuteronomy and the sounding of motifs to come continue throughout the first chapter of Joshua. The third function of an 'introduction' would then be to indicate the disposition of the book to come. This role is assumed not by the whole of Joshua 1, but by a part of this chapter, namely the divine speech in Josh. 1:2–9. It is this function of God's speech that will concern us in what follows!

If we ignore chapters 22–23 (and 24),[14] which tend to form a concluding part of the frame, the book of Joshua is composed of two major parts. The division lies between Joshua 12 and Joshua 13. Following F. Nötscher,[15] we may give headings to the parts as follows:

Joshua 1–12	Occupation of the Land West of the Jordan
Joshua 13–21	Division of the Land West of the Jordan

This disposition is immediately announced in Josh. 1:2–9. It seems that this has not yet been recognized; consequently, we must offer proof for it now.

10. In H. W. Hertzberg, *Die Bücher Josua, Richter, Ruth*, ATD (Göttingen, 1953), 14, this is noted, but not fully evaluated. The word 'prologue' is used once. See Noth, *Überlieferungsgeschichtliche Studien* (see n. 2 above), 41: 'Einführung [Introduction].'

11. Cf. Josh. 1:17; 3:7; 4:14; 6:27.

12. Josh. 8:31; 22:5; 23:6.

13. It is well known that this text is heavily dependent on texts from Deuteronomy. For vv. 3–5a, cf. Deut. 11:24–25; for v. 4, cf. Deut. 1:7; for v. 5a, cf. Deut. 7:24; for vv. 5b, 6, 9, cf. Deut. 31:6–8, 23; for vv. 7–9, cf. Deut. 17:14–20. Add to these the individual, highly 'deuteronomic' formulations.

14. Joshua 24, though ancient, is usually not regarded as an original part of the book of Joshua.

15. *Die Heilige Schrift in deutscher Übersetzung*, Echter Bibel (Würzburg, 1955), 1: 556 and 591.

(b) According to non-Deuteronomistic tradition also, Joshua had two duties: to be a general in the field and to participate in the division of the land.[16] In the book of Joshua, the two groups of themes thus described correspond to these two tasks. If the divine speech at the beginning of the book of Joshua is meant to indicate the division of the book, it would seem appropriate for this to be done by having God speak to Joshua about Joshua's two duties. Within the deuteronomic stratum this would, of course, be possible only on condition that the deuteronomic conception assigned precisely these two tasks to Joshua.

That is, in fact, the case. It is true that Joshua is here Moses' successor in a much fuller sense. No priest Eleazar appears at his side, whose oracle he had to consult or with whom he must cooperate in the division of the land.[17] Nevertheless, he has clearly conceived tasks, and they correspond to those in the rest of the tradition. They can be discerned from the vocabulary that is used within Deuteronomy in giving a preliminary view of Joshua's work:

1:38	*bw'*	enter (the promised land)
	nḥl hifil	distribute the inheritance
3:21	*'br*	cross over (the Jordan)[18]
	nhl hifil	distribute the inheritance
31:3	*'br*	cross over (the Jordan)[19]
31:7	*bw'*	enter (the promised land)[20]

16. General: Num. 27:17 (terminology: *yṣ'* and *bw' lipnê hā'ām* or *yṣ' hifil* and *bw' hifil 'et hā'ām*). Division of the land: Num. 34:17 (terminology: root *nḥl*, stem form shifting or text-critically uncertain). In our context it is not necessary to discuss the place of these traditions in more detail. From the point of view of tradition criticism, they are probably older than Deuteronomy. But even the question of time plays no significant role in our purely comparative reference. On the legal uses of *nḥl*, see F. Horst, 'Zwei Begriffe für Eigentum (Besitz): *naḥălâ* and *'aḥuzzâ*,' in *Verbannung und Heimkehr*, Festschrift for W. Rudolph (Tübingen, 1961), 134–56, especially 150ff.

17. It is different within the book of Joshua in 14:1, 19:51 and 21:1, where it is not the deuteronomic author himself who is speaking (P, or, according to M. Noth, a later expansion).

18. At this point Moses avoids what he really should do, that is, actually install Joshua in his offices.

19. The expression in Deut. 31:2, *lō' 'ûkal 'ôd lāṣē't wĕlābô'*, is important. Moses here applies the typical terminology for a field general to himself (cf. n. 16 on Num. 27:17).

20. M has the *qal*; Samaritanus, Vulgatus and a few Hebrew mss. attest to the *hifil*. The question may well remain open, since our texts know both stem forms in this context.

	nḥl hifil	distribute the inheritance
31:23	*bw' hifil*	lead (into the promised land)

Thus at three points there are two expressions placed alongside one another. The second is always the same: 'distribute the inheritance.' The first is more variable and seems at least sometimes to depend partly on the context.[21] In any case, it always refers to the conquest of the promised land. Joshua is here Moses' successor in the office of field general.

First of all (in v. 2), the speech of God in Josh. 1:2–9 takes up the first of the two expressions, in the form *'br 'et hayyardēn*, 'to cross the Jordan.' It thus speaks of Joshua's office as field general, his duty to go at the head of Israel to conquer the land that will be precisely defined in the following verses. All this is condensed within the first undertaking: the crossing of the Jordan. This is generally recognized by exegetes, as the descriptions in Josh. 1:2–9 quoted above make clear. On the contrary, it remains virtually unnoticed that at some point the topic changes, and that God's 'encouragement' to Joshua refers not at all to the task of conquest, but to the distribution of the inheritance. For in v. 6 we find a pointed use of the word *nḥl hifil*, 'distribute the inheritance.' If we consider the careful use of words in the Joshua texts from Deuteronomy listed above, and the non-deuteronomistic parallel traditions about Joshua's two tasks, we can scarcely continue to regard the statement in v. 6 as synonymous with that in v. 2, or place the one in some kind of logical subordination to the other. But if it is the case that Josh. 1:2–9 speaks successively of Joshua's two offices, then here in fact, and surely quite deliberately, the author has indicated the disposition of the narrative material that is to follow.

(c) The substance of this question was probably obscured primarily by the fact that, toward the end, the motif of fidelity to the law expands so significantly and apparently shoulders the principal theme aside. One need only compare the modern commentaries cited above. Martin Noth is probably closest to the matter in ascribing v. 6 to the deuteronomist while taking everything after v. 7 for a later addition.[22] For our present inquiry we may set aside the question whether in v. 7 the deuteronomistic author of the chapter continues to speak or whether a later insertion begins at this point. Instead, what is decisive is that the author of vv. 7ff. (whether the deuteronomistic writer or a later, expanding hand) in any case has clearly

21. This is the case in Deut. 1:38, cf. 1:34–37; or in 31:3, cf. 31:2b.

22. See n. 9 above. Only the designation of Deut. 31:7–8 and Josh. 1:6 as 'encouraging words' is inexact.

demarcated the section about the law as a digression from the principal theme!

To begin with, v. 7 takes up the words *ḥăzaq we'ĕmaṣ* from v. 6 as a short 'quotation' and point of contact that requires further commentary.[23] These imperatives require for their interpretation the 'paraenetic formula' of deuteronomic preaching on the law,[24] the basic form of which also begins with commanding-warning formulae, but here (precisely as an interpretive formula) is connected by means of an infinitive.[25] But the paraenetic formula is always only a formal element, a connecting link: here it connects to the real instruction that must be given, the directions for a constant interaction with the book of the law, speaking and reciting (v. 8 as far as *wālaylâ*). Now the movement of thought and speech reverses itself. Once more there is the paraenetic formula,[26] and then, introduced by a rhetorical question, the 'quotation' of the beginning:[27] thus v. 9a returns to the point that was left in v. 7a, and v. 9b can continue v. 6. The overall stylistic figure is a so-called 'concentric structure' (schematically: A + B + C + B′ + A′).[28] Elsewhere it by no means always serves only to highlight deviations, and it is certainly not merely the form for later insertions. Probably in this case as well vv. 7–9a should not be regarded as

23. It is emphasized by *me'ōd*. The connective particle is *raq*, which should probably be translated not as 'only,' but rather as 'in any case, and absolutely,' or something similar. At any rate, it is neither positively nor negatively evident from the continuation of the book that the office of distributor of the inheritance has been bestowed on Joshua only conditionally.

24. A typical formal element for the deuteronomist proper. The paraenetic formula consists of a warning and a promise. Fixed sequences of words are used, and the individual cases are filled out with deuteronomic clichés (principal elements: *šmr – 'śh* in the first part). For more detail, see the essays announced in n. 1 above on Deuteronomy 29–32 and on Deuteronomy 4–11. For one example, see the concluding paraenetic formula in Deut. 5:32–33.

25. Read *k'šr*, and eliminate *kl htwrh*. The reasons may be found in the commentaries, e.g. M. Noth, *Das Buch Josue*, HAT (Tübingen, 2nd ed. 1953), ad loc.

26. It is connected by *lĕma'an*, normally the conjunction between the two parts of the paraenetic formula. Therefore *kî 'āz* introduces the second part.

27. The root *ṣwh* can also have a technical sense of installation in office here. Cf. Deut. 3:28; 31:14, 23. The roots *'rṣ* and *ḥtt* expand the formula of encouragement, similarly to *yr'* and *'rṣ* in Deut. 31:6, and *yr'* and *ḥtt* in Deut. 31:8. This is probably already a deuteronomic reversal, perhaps in connection with the introduction of the terminology of war preaching.

28. For details, see Lohfink, 'Darstellungskunst' (see n. 1 above), 123.

an unimportant digression; it may be that these verses indicate the most important interest of the deuteronomic author. Still, from a formal point of view, they are an interruption built into another form that contains them and that needs now to be investigated: the form of Josh. 1:6, 9b.[29]

(d) Joshua 1:6, 9b can be divided as follows:

I. 'Formula of encouragement' (*ḥăzaq weʾĕmāṣ*)
II. Statement of a task (introduced by *kî ʾattâ*)
III. 'Formula of support' (key element: *ʿimmĕkā YHWH*)

The schema found here occurs three times in the deuteronomic Joshua texts: besides Josh. 1:6, 9b, it is also in Deut. 31:7–8 and Deut. 31:23. It is probable that the old text Deut. 31:23 served as a model for the other two. Although it is used only three times, the deuteronomic author sensed that the schema was a fixed form. This is evident from Deut. 1:38 and 3:28. There the author makes a play on this schema and uses the word *ḥzq* as a technical expression for the reality indicated by the schema. In Deut. 1:38, God commands Moses regarding Joshua: *ʾōtô ḥazzēq, kî hûʾ yanḥilennâ ʾet yiśrāʾēl.* Later this same command of God, only more intense, is pronounced in Deut. 3:28: *wĕṣaw ʾet yĕhôšuaʿ wĕḥazzĕqēhû wĕʾammĕṣēhû, kî hûʾ yaʿăbōr lipnê hāʿām hazzeh wĕhûʾ yanḥîl ʾôtām ʾet hāʾāreṣ ʾăšer tirʾeh.* Thus the word *ḥzq* has a very technical sense: one is reminded of our word 'confirmation.' Apparently the schema here under discussion exists as a fixed formula in the deuteronomic stratum of Deuteronomy and Joshua for a kind of installation in office which may be referred to by the use of the verbs of the 'formula of encouragement.' If this is correct, then part II of the schema must contain the naming of the office to be conveyed. The correct translation of Deut. 1:38 must therefore probably be: 'Strengthen (encourage) him (i.e., entrust him through installation in office) so that he may distribute (the land) to Israel as its inheritance.' All the other passages should be translated accordingly. Against the idea that we have here a kind of genre of installation in office one might object that the typical formula of encouragement, combined with a promise of support, certainly stands in Deut. 31:6 and Josh. 10:25 apart from any installation in office. Both of these are instances of monitory addresses to the whole nation, in which they are called to carry

29. The fact that in v. 9b YHWH makes a self-reference in the third person is not an adequate reason for regarding the verse as secondary: see, for example, Deut. 1:8. The phenomenon is frequently found both in the OT and in extra-biblical texts from the ancient Orient.

out the holy war. In response we may say that probably the background of these passages is the genre of the speech of the leader of a holy war.[30] The formulae of encouragement in both these different genres seem to be mixed together in the deuteronomic sphere.[31]

The deuteronomic schema of speech for installations in office being examined here does not appear to be purely literary (within the deuteronomic stratum of Deuteronomy and Joshua); rather, it seems to rest on a form of speech that was actually used for installations and decisions about actions to be undertaken.[32] This assumption is supported first of all by 2 Sam. 10:12. In the war against the Ammonites and Syrians, David's general Joab must divide his army. He gives his brother Abishai, who takes over the leadership of one part, the necessary strategic instructions (v. 11) and concludes: 'Be strong, (I) and let us be courageous for the sake of our people, and for the cities of our God, (II) and may YHWH do what seems good to him! (III)' In a whole series of post-exilic texts we find that, when people are being entrusted with particular duties, often at the end of fairly long speeches, the following schema appears: 'Be courageous! (I) Carry the matter through! (II)[33] YHWH will be with you! (III)' This schema is found in fairly pure form in Hag. 2:4 and 2 Chr. 19:11b; somewhat drawn out, but clearly recognizable, it appears in 1 Chr. 22:11–16 and 28:20 (cf. v. 10); Ezra 10:4 is probably only a reference to it, with a different sequence of parts. As the schema appears concretely, it can scarcely be derived from our deuteronomic passages, but must go back to a style of speech drawn from real life that is witnessed by the deuteronomic schema in another of its guises.

If we have correctly described the function of the schema used in Josh. 1:6–9 (interrupted by vv. 7–9a but not thereby destroyed) important consequences for the meaning of the verses must follow. It would be wrong to interpret the individual words and sections of the speech only in terms of their dictionary meaning. Thus it would be a distortion of the

30. Cf. Deut. 20:3–4; 1:29–31; 7:14–24; 20:1.

31. See n. 27 above.

32. The following texts, though with a somewhat different interpretation, were collected in a hectographed manuscript of W. L. Moran's lecture on Joshua (1961), at the Biblical Institute in Rome, pp. 13–17.

33. The fact that the verb *'śh* represents a separate part and may not simply be attached to the formula of encouragement is shown especially by the stylizing in Hag. 2:4. In this variant of the form, part II does not need (as in the deuteronomic variant) to be made concrete, since here there is always a preceding text.

substance if we were to place too much emphasis on the fact that YHWH here bestows courage on Joshua. That is, at least, not the central point of the expression. The form, with all its parts, constitutes a single statement: 'This is how an installation in office is done.' The content of the variable elements of the form (in part II) then serves to concretize it. Here we find the key word *nḥl hifil.* YHWH thus entrusts Joshua with the office of distributing their inheritance to the Israelites. That is the proper meaning of Josh. 1:6–9, to which a warning to remain faithful to the Torah is added as a kind of digression (even though one need not doubt that this idea was extraordinarily dear to the one who shaped the passage).

(e) Now the first part of God's speech attracts renewed interest, for here we do not find the form of installation in office that characterizes the second part, even though this part speaks of the other of Joshua's two duties.

To begin with, it is important that Josh. 1:2–5 also follows a particular form. A statement of fact (v. 2a: 'My servant Moses is dead') is followed by a command (v. 2b: order to cross the Jordan for the purpose of conquering the promised land); the two parts are linked by *wĕʿattâ.* The subsequent sentences (vv. 3–5) follow from the content of the command: they are the fundamental conditions that will make it possible: the transfer of title to all the lands that are to be conquered (v. 3), the description of the territory (v. 4), and the promise of support in battle (v. 5).[34] The principal form is thus made concrete in v. 2: it is the form of command.[35]

The fact that Joshua's task as general in Joshua 1 is only stated as a command, while his duty to distribute the land is associated with installation in office, can be readily understood if we reflect that within the deuteronomic stratum such an installation of Joshua has already been carried out by God in Deut. 31:23.[36] This installation, however, is (and here the detailed planning and formulation of the whole composition is evident) only an installation in the office of field general: '. . . for you shall

34. The promise of support in v. 5 is, at the same time, parallel to the promise of support in v. 9. This is a minor stylistic confirmation of our division of the text.

35. A related form (there is also an interjection placed at the beginning, hence the absence of *wĕʿattâ*) appears frequently in the same deuteronomic stratum. Cf. Lohfink, 'Darstellungskunst,' (n. 1 above), 124–25.

36. As a result of redactional work, the introduction to the speech does not make completely clear who it is that is speaking. But the text of the words of installation shows unmistakably that it is YHWH who speaks. For more detail, see my work on Deuteronomy 29–32 (n. 1 above).

bring the Israelites into the land that I promised them.' This limitation of the divine commissioning of Joshua in Deut. 31:23 is all the more striking because in the previous installation of Joshua by Moses (Deut. 31:7–8) Joshua had been entrusted with both offices in a single act of commissioning.[37] Since Joshua, then, according to the whole context of the work, had been installed by YHWH in the office of field general during the lifetime of Moses, after Moses' death all that could follow was the divine command that henceforward Joshua should assume his office and carry it out (Josh. 1:2–5). The genre of commissioning speech would be out of place here. But it was probably necessary for Joshua's second office, in which God had not yet formally installed him (Josh. 1:6–9).

(f) When one has once sensed how systematically the deuteronomic portrayal is composed at this point, one may directly inquire whether the installation in the office of distributor of the land is enhanced by a concrete command to exercise that office. Here one could, in a sense, test the correctness of our analysis thus far. Such a command would have to be found at the point where the distribution of the land begins, that is, at the beginning of the second part of the book of Joshua. And there we in fact find it, and it is embodied in exactly the same form.

Joshua 13:1b contains a series of statements ('You are old and advanced in years, and very much of the land still remains to be possessed'). In vv. 2–6 there follows an excursus, consisting at least partly of exposition of the key phrase 'the land that still remains.' Then the second part of the form is attached with *wĕʿattā̆*: this is the word of command for the distribution of the inheritance (v. 7: 'Now therefore divide this land for an inheritance to the nine tribes and the half-tribe of Manasseh').

(g) The analysis has thus revealed the following distinctions, which are important for understanding the deuteronomic portrayal of Joshua's replacement of Moses: Joshua has two different tasks (conquest and division of the land), which the text in part treats separately; in addition to Joshua's installation in office, there are divine commands to carry out the tasks associated with the office at the proper times; Joshua is installed in the same offices first by Moses, and then by God. We should also add:[38] it

37. The fact that a double installation of Joshua is reported, once by Moses and a second time by God in person, will have to be investigated later.

38. Here I may refer, for treatment of various fundamental matters, to two earlier essays: Lohfink, 'Darstellungskunst,' and idem, 'Individuum – Gemeinschaft' (see n. 1 above for both of these).

is because of a divine command that Moses installs Joshua in his offices; God's command to Moses to commission Joshua is given twice because between the two lies a last attempt by Moses to persuade God to let him enter the promised land along with the people. All this can be observed from purely literary evidence, and we have thereby isolated the elements from which we can now proceed to a synthetic reconstruction of the total picture as seen by the deuteronomist.

2. Conclusions

(a) How, then, according to the deuteronomic picture, was the leadership of Israel transferred from Moses to Joshua?

After the attempt to conquer the promised land from Kadesh Barnea, an effort that collapsed because of the people's lack of faith, Moses learns from YHWH that he too, along with the whole wilderness generation, will be unable to participate in the conquest of the land. Joshua, however, will be part of that conquest. Moses is given the task of installing Joshua in office, so that he may distribute the inheritance. Note: Moses is only authorized to install Joshua in the second office; there is merely a vague reference to Joshua's first duty. This unclarity of the divine command regarding the first office leaves room for the more personal interlude that begins for Moses at this point (Deut. 1:37–38).

After forty years of wandering in the desert, after the death of the whole wilderness generation, and after the conquest and distribution of the land east of the Jordan, Moses undertakes a series of concluding actions. We can only understand these if we presume that his hope of entering the promised land has revived. First he directs the tribes east of the Jordan to take part in the conquest of the land. Then he turns to Joshua, but instead of formally installing him in office as one would expect, he only promises him that YHWH will be with him and thus shifts rapidly to an address to the whole assembled people, whom we should picture as present before him.[39] This is understandable in light of his prayer to YHWH, reported immediately afterward, that he may after all be permitted to cross over into the promised land. Instead, what follows is God's sharp rejection of this request, an order to go up the mountain and look at the land from afar, and then finally a repetition of the command to commission Joshua. This time the command embraces both

39. In Lohfink, 'Individuum – Gemeinschaft' (see n. 1 above), 406, the full meaning of Deut. 3:21 has not yet been explored. Cf. *Schol* 36 (1961): 424.

of Joshua's tasks. Moses is told clearly and unmistakably that he should install Joshua in both offices (Deut. 3:18–28).

Moses carries out this duty in the larger context of the covenant-making ceremony that is presented in Deuteronomy 29–32.[40] In a war speech he proclaims to the people that Joshua will be their leader, together with YHWH, who is the real leader of their armies.[41] Then, before the whole assembly, he formally installs Joshua in both his offices (Deut. 31:2–8).

In this same worshipping assembly, a theophany occurs. YHWH calls Joshua and Moses into the tent and now YHWH personally installs Joshua in the office of field general. The office of distributor of the inheritance is not mentioned (Deut. 31:14–15, 23).

Moses dies. YHWH commands Joshua to enter into his office as conqueror of the land west of the Jordan. At the same time, YHWH formally installs him in his second office, as the one who will distribute the inheritance (Josh. 1:2-9).

Joshua immediately begins carrying out the command to conquer the land (beginning at Josh. 1:10). The people, represented by the tribes east of the Jordan, acknowledge him as their leader (Josh. 1:16–18; cf. Deut. 34:9, a non-deuteronomic passage). YHWH demonstrates, through Joshua's success, that this is the leader of the armies whom YHWH has appointed: this is the second Moses (especially Josh. 3:7; 4:14).

Toward the end of his life, Joshua receives in similar fashion a command from YHWH to enter into his second office, i.e., to carry out the distribution of the inheritance (Josh. 13:1, 7).

The above outline seems to demonstrate that the deuteronomic portrayal advances step by step and without repetitions. Nothing is repeated except certain formal elements and some technical vocabulary. But if we look more closely, we can distinguish a series of precise distinctions that, in each case, determine the exact meaning.

(b) Undoubtedly a good deal of effort was devoted to depicting the

40. For more detail, see the essay on the redactional history of Deuteronomy 29–32 cited in n. 1 above. K. Baltzer, in *Das Bundesformular* (Neukirchen, 1960), 71–90, has performed the service of demonstrating the necessity of a confirmation of the covenant when the office of leadership in Israel is transferred from one person to another. This context is very important and must necessarily be taken into account as background for my presentation in this essay, but cannot be discussed in detail here.

41. This is probably how the parallel statements in v. 3 should be understood. The customary excisions should probably be subjected to testing from a stylistic point of view.

transfer of reponsibility from Moses to Joshua. What interest underlies that effort? What does the author want to say through this involved portrayal, which apparently explicates a fundamentally historical sequence of events in terms of juristic and theological principles?

It would seem that the whole problem of continuity in Israel's leadership under the covenant with YHWH is to be presented here in terms of a prime example. First we encounter the personal problem of the departing leader who cannot yet come to terms with the fact that his term of office is ending, and who seeks to extend it. Here YHWH remains unbendingly firm. Then we meet the fact of a twofold installation in office, first by Moses and then by YHWH. Is this intended to explain the essence of such a process of installation? – that on the one hand, God desires a commissioning for office by human beings, but on the other hand it is God who accomplishes it? It would certainly be an unjustified exegetical minimalism to be unwilling to grant the presence of theological thinking behind this type of double depiction in which the two scenes are so precisely aligned with one another.

We encounter YHWH's concrete command that introduces the carrying out of the tasks involved in the office that has been bestowed. God not only gives an office, but remains the driving force in the history of God's people. It is God who leads the officeholders.

Finally, we are faced with the fact that the text does not speak abstractly of an office of leadership in Israel, but instead that concrete tasks associated with salvation history are presented: the conquest and distribution of the land. Certainly, this is in part conditioned simply by the special traditional material related to the story of Joshua. But is the motif not also deliberately employed in order to emphasize the individual call that is present in every bestowal of office, even when the office itself is handed on from generation to generation?

That office also involves an element of confirmation through success and of acceptance of leadership by those in subordination was a fact probably present even in the traditional narrative material. Nevertheless, our deuteronomic stratum has underlined it, so that no one can assert that it tells us nothing about that layer and its intention. At the same time, these motifs remain associated only with the office of field general, and certainly they are not the central focus of attention in our stratum.

Thus we can see, in the background of this narrative, a complete theology of office. It is perhaps not unimportant to note, when we try to explain the role and transmission of office in the New Testament, that there were such things within the theological traditions that emerged from the Old Testament as well.

10

The Decalogue in Deuteronomy 5

I would like to make clear the purpose of these reflections by contrasting what I have to say with Henning Graf Reventlow's book, *Gebot und Predigt im Dekalog.*[1] Without doubt, this book has advanced research to a considerable degree. This can easily be demonstrated, since Stamm's excellent report on decalogue research in the last three decades had appeared shortly before.[2] The progress in Reventlow's work consists not only in individual insights, but primarily in its fundamentally new orientation. Stamm still focused on the 'ur-decalogue,' corresponding to the point of view in the literature he was discussing. He was able to include the 'additions to the original form' in a brief 'addendum,'[3] while the comparison between the Exodus and Deuteronomy versions occupied only two pages.[4] Reventlow, in contrast, emphasizes that the decalogue stands within 'a single history.' It is, he says, 'a continuing task of exegesis' precisely 'to illuminate this history and to continue to discover new aspects within it.'[5] This turn to the 'history' of the decalogue, to the expansive and late forms that appear together with the original form, is laudable in any event. The following reflections, too, are meaningful only within this frame of reference. We are concerned with a late phase in the history of the decalogue: with the origins of the special version of the decalogue in Deuteronomy 5.[6]

1. Gütersloh, 1962.

2. J. J. Stamm, 'Dreißig Jahre Dekalogforschung,' *ThRundsch*, n.s. 27 (1961): 189–239, 281–305.

3. Ibid., 203–6.

4. Ibid., 199–200.

5. *Gebot und Predigt*, 95.

6. Regarding the text: late versions of the decalogue that were able to revise the version already existing in Exodus and Deuteronomy or that treat the text with freedom must

The new orientation of interest led immediately, in Reventlow's work, to a more concrete picture of the history of the decalogue than can be found in the works of the older authors. The formulations of Eduard König may serve as an example. He made a thorough comparison of the Exodus and Deuteronomy versions of the decalogue,[7] in which he spoke of a 'subsequent revision' and 'stylistic perfecting,' and used expressions like: 'results of the advance in Israel's religious and moral experience,' 'secondary,' 'greater measure of humanity,' 'spiritualizing of the moral vision.'[8] In Stamm's little book on the decalogue, also, the concepts remain at that general level, even though the emphasis has shifted from intellectual history to matters of style: 'modernizing,' 'additions,' 'increased precision of content,' 'greater rhetorical fullness,' 'giving more attention to the place of the individual,' 'stylistic improvement,' 'different idea of the concept of coveting.'[9] In comparison to these, Reventlow shows a genuine development. He suggests four principal stages in the history of the decalogue.[10] 'Apodictic commandments' from two different 'series,' and 'unified Torah material' (the first stage) were combined, in a second stage, into a 'mixed picture,' the 'apodictic original form' of the decalogue that was used in the 'liturgical proclamation of the law.' At that point, in a third stage, 'priestly knowledge' in the form of 'explanations and precisions' was included. In a final stage, the 'sermon' 'wraps' the text of the third stage 'in a broad coating of paraenesis and personal advice.' This fourth stage in turn consists of 'a whole series of stages of exposition.' This was already true within the Exodus version of the decalogue. In the newer Deuteronomy version, then, the 'preachng expansion' has again 'advanced one stage farther.'

be eliminated as textual witnesses for this problem: I refer, for example, to papyrus Nash, Samaritan decalogue inscriptions, phylacteries, etc. On this, cf. Stamm, 'Dekalogforschung,' 197–98. Since a tendency to harmonizing may be presumed also in the Masoretic text, Samaritanus, and the ancient translations, we must apply the principle of the *lectio difficilior* in giving attention to those variants that drive the two versions apart. Practically speaking, this involves Deut. 5:21b, *'bdw*, and Deut. 5:10, *mṣwtw* (for details, cf. *Biblia Hebraica*). These two variants are unimportant for the considerations that follow; hence I will simply use the Masoretic text of the *Biblia Hebraica.*

7. *Das Deuteronomium*, KAT (Leipzig, 1917), 91–93.
8. Ibid., p. 92.
9. J. J. Stamm, *Der Dekalog im Lichte der neueren Forschung* (Berne, 2nd ed. 1962), 9.
10. All the following quotations are from his concluding summary: *Gebot und Predigt*, 93–95.

Reventlow achieves this concrete picture through a form-critical analysis of the individual parts of the decalogue. In doing so, he presupposes, with reference to Köhler, von Rad, Zimmerli, Mowinckel, Alt, and others, that the different forms discovered by analysis are each to be associated with different historical periods.[11] At least the 'preachers' belong to a much later period than do the 'old proclaimers of the law' from the 'original cult.'[12] This presupposition of Reventlow's method is perhaps not so secure as it might appear at first glance, and sometimes calls for a systematic proof. But it would at least theoretically be conceivable that a text like the decalogue was first put together at a time when paraenetic forms, as well as apodictic and priestly ones, were already available. In that case, the factual juxtaposition of these forms in the concrete text of the decalogue would not justify any conclusion about multi-phased development. We should further inquire whether we really have historical proofs that the 'sermon' only began at a relatively late time in history. The transfer of formal distinctions through time, in any case, requires a reflective justification. But for the purposes of the following reflections we may set aside these challenges to Reventlow, since I am concerned only with the very last 'stage' of development of the decalogue, the existence of which is in any case a certainty because of the difference between the Exodus version and the Deuteronomy version.[13]

Reventlow characterizes this stage as follows: 'Throughout,' the Deuteronomy version 'showed itself to be the later form, in which the process of expansion through preaching has already advanced one stage farther, and also the understanding of the content of some commandments had already shifted in comparison to their original meaning.'[14] Apart from the change in the understanding of the content of individual commandments, Reventlow is thus unable to give a concrete, unique motivation for the origin of the Deuteronomy version of the decalogue; instead, he must order this development within the more comprehensive process (in part already prior to the Exodus version) of 'expansion through preaching.' Naturally, such an ordering is already an important assertion.

11. Ibid., 13–22.

12. Ibid., 69–70.

13. It can be seen in the two versions even if the Deuteronomy text is not directly descended from the Exodus text, but if, instead, both of them are derived from a common prototype (as, by the way, I suspect to be the case). The detailed comparison must accordingly be carried out with appropriate caution.

14. *Gebot und Predigt*, 95.

But does it not, in a certain sense, remain general and abstract, much like the previously cited formulations about 'king' and 'tribe' – even if there is a relative progress in contrast to those? Interestingly enough, Reventlow has not inquired more closely into the question whether, behind the last great alteration of the decalogue text within the paraenetic intentions that had long been at work there might stand a single, concrete purpose that would explain all the changes at the same time.

A whole is more than the sum of its parts. Of course it remains possible that the more than twenty differences between the Exodus and Deuteronomy versions of the decalogue occurred sequentially and that the forces that can be identified behind them are a general paraenetic tendency and a changing understanding of details of content. In this case, Reventlow would have said everything that can be said. But it is equally possible that all the changes, or at least a major portion of them, go back to a single operation performed on the text, an intervention that resulted from a particular, concrete and unique intention. The individual changes would then not (or not only) each have a special meaning, but would ultimately have to be derived from the one, overall purpose behind the alteration of the text. The more we regard the decalogue as an official and sacred text, the less can we suppose that an unlimited number of alterations of its text would have been possible, and that every preacher would have been able, in some sense, to tinker with it; instead, we must posit a few, correspondingly intensive operations of a highly official character, done for a particular reason and with a particular purpose.[15] Hence one must make a serious investigation of the hypothesis that a great many of the 'additions' and 'changes' in the Deuteronomy version were parts of a universal phenomenon and can be traced to a single intention.

15. The freedom with which, only a few decades ago, people were able to speculate about the growth of the text of the decalogue may be illustrated by a quotation from the important essay by H. Schmidt, 'Mose und der Dekalog,' *Eucharisterion Gunkel* 1, FRLANT 36,1 (Göttingen, 1923), 93, on the conclusion of the decalogue: 'But it is easy to understand that *kl' šr lr'k* invited an explanatory gloss, a statement of what is meant by this. I would like to believe that this temptation took effect twice: once someone wrote in the margin *'št r'k w'bdw w'mtw wšwrw wḥmrw*, and a second time someone inserted *l' tt'wwh byt r'k [w]śdhw*, which seemed to him to be missing. This second gloss is, in the manuscript that underlies Exod. 20:17 (differing from Deut. 5:21), at the beginning of the commandments, and for that very reason entered the text through an accommodation of the verb to what was found there.' Here it is practically assumed that the decalogue was only transmitted in written form and was unknown to the copyists, so that the 'classical' mistakes of copyists could begin to enter the picture.

Whether the hypothesis can be sustained, only its success will determine. If it does not prove itself, it will always be possible to return to Reventlow's position, which in a sense represents a minimalist solution.

Using Reventlow's method, one could not obtain any picture of a hypothetical unity among the peculiarities of the Deuteronomy version of the decalogue, since the method isolates the individual parts of the text and then evaluates them form-critically as separate units. When Reventlow summarizes, at the end of an analysis, he only states totals. He does not even raise a further question about a whole that would be more than the sum of the parts. In what follows, then, our concern will be to inquire not only about individual forms, but primarily about the possible presence of a comprehensive form. Such a form must not necessarily be immediately connected with the old, elementary forms of proclamation of the law. It could also be a stylistic form introducing quite other principles of formation. Therefore one may also not demand a demonstration of 'parallel genres.' It could be that what we find here is a unique formation without genre. Hence the appropriate method is not (or at least not solely) 'form criticism,' but only the more comprehensive method of 'stylistic analysis.'

I will begin with the Sabbath commandment, which in fact reveals the greatest and most frequent differences from Exodus 20. Exod. 20:8 begins the Sabbath commandment with *zākôr*, Deut. 5:12 with *šāmôr*. Previous research has always attempted to answer the question of the relative age of these two formulations purely from the words themselves, without reference to their larger contexts. The result has been a division into two parties with diametrically opposite opinions.[16] Stamm therefore thinks that the question 'evades a definite judgment.'[17] Reventlow agrees with this opinion.[18] But new light is immediately shed on the problem if we take a look at the overall stylistic formation of the Sabbath commandment in Deuteronomy.

In fact, the beginning, *šāmôr 'et-yôm haššabbāt*, corresponds to the conclusion of the commandment, *la'ăśôt 'et-yôm haššabbāt*. Without doubt, what we have here is the stylistic technique of *inclusio*, by which a linguistic unit is placed in a frame. Thus the *šāmôr* at the beginning corresponds to a *la'ăśôt* at the end. This is not carelessness or accident, but rather the two verbs are closely associated in the deuteronomic cliché

16. Cf. Stamm, 'Dekalogforschung,' 199.

17. *Dekalog*, 8.

18. *Gebot und Predigt*, 24.

vocabulary. In Deuteronomy 5–28 alone, the chapters that form the core of the book, the combination of these two words is found 27 times. For details of this usage, let me refer to my treatment of this cliché in another place.[19] Within the 'framework' of the Sabbath commandment, then, we find a double expression divided between the two corresponding clauses. Both clauses thus dialogue with one another, and only in combination do they form the complete statement in the sense of deuteronomic paraenesis.[20]

Within the external inclusio there is an internal one: Deut. 5:12, *ka'ăšer ṣiwwĕkā yhwh 'ĕlōhêkā*, finds an almost word-for-word counterpart in Deut. 5:15, *'al-kēn ṣiwwĕkā yhwh 'ĕlōhêkā*. Within the internal space thus enclosed there are also chiastic correspondences between individual words. Overall, the picture is as follows:

5:12	Observe the sabbath day
12	as YHWH your God commanded you.
14	To YHWH your God
14	and your male and female slave
14	*so that* (as a mark of the turning-point of the text)
14	your male and female slave
15	YHWH your God
15	therefore YHWH your God commanded you
15	to keep the sabbath day.

No matter how much the text is gathered together out of different formal elements, it has been deliberately shaped into a new whole by means of corresponding key words and parallel clauses.

Reventlow posits a number of temporally distinguishable stages of development within the 'preaching layer' of Deut. 5:15. In particular, he thinks that Deut. 5:15b is 'a later stage of development in which the key word "Sabbath" is revived in an expression that, stylistically speaking, appears quite awkward.'[21] This view of things is lacking in probability, since the series of retrospective repetitions reaches its climax in v. 15. We

19. *Das Hauptgebot*, AnBib 20 (Rome, 1963), 68–70, cf. also p. 90 (on the role of the expression in the 'paraenetic schema').

20. For this observation on the association of *šmr* and *'śh* in the Sabbath commandment in the Deuteronomy version, I am indebted to a suggestion given me orally by W. L. Moran.

21. *Gebot und Predigt*, 58.

must rather suppose that the text, after *lĕmaʿan* (Deut. 5:14b) is a single expansion. In the course of this expansion, the half-verse Deut. 5:12b was also inserted. The word *šāmôr*, which begins v. 12, is also a necessary element in the overall formal context. This is important, for we can now recognize that overall formal context of the Sabbath commandment in Deut. 5:12–15 as a motif on the basis of which an original *zākôr* could have been changed to *šāmôr*. On the other hand, there is no motif in Exod. 20:8–11 that could have occasioned the alteration of an original *šāmôr* to *zākôr*.[22] Hence *zākôr* should represent the earlier, and *šāmôr* the later version of the beginning of the Sabbath commandment.

Thus the unified reshaping of the Sabbath commandment took place on the stylistic level by means of corresponding key words. This indicates the path we must travel in our attempt to organize further differences between the Deuteronomy version and the Exodus version of the posited comprehensive reshaping of the decalogue. For the moment, I will proceed on the basis of the differences in the two versions of the Sabbath commandment, since here we already have assurance that a unified intervention has taken place to give the commandment a new shape.

Deuteronomy 5:14b expands the series of subjects of the Sabbath obligation, already known from Exod. 20:10b, by adding two new members: 'and your ox and your donkey.' Reventlow considers it less likely that here we have an example of the 'conscious personal work of the preachers of this version;' the 'preachers' have simply 'quoted more fully' an adapted series, like that of the ten commandments.[23] I would like to take up Reventlow's reference to the series of the ten commandments. In the Exodus version there is an agreement in only two members between

22. Let me point out that the Sabbath commandment in Exod. 20:8–11, in its final form, is also framed by key words ('the sabbath day, to keep it holy' in 20:8, 11). Within this *inclusio* the schema 'six days – on the seventh day' is repeated twice. The second passage is introduced by *kî*, 'for.' It cannot be decided with certainty whether this full form preceded the Deuteronomy version, as an earlier stage. Probably the preliminary stage of Deut. 5:12–15 contained only a text corresponding to Exod. 20:8–10. For the more conservative one imagines the tradents of the decalogue to have been, the less will one expect them simply to have removed whole clauses or sentences and replaced them with others. Exod. 20:11 would thus be, first of all, a parallel to the Deuteronomy version of the Sabbath commandment, or perhaps an imitative expansion of it. Cf. E. Jenni, 'Die theologische Begründung des Sabbatgebotes im AT,' *ThSt* 46 (Zürich, 1956), 5. This, however, says nothing about the age of this explanation of the Sabbath as such. It is only a question of its penetration into the text of the decalogue.

23. *Gebot und Predigt*, 57.

the series within the Sabbath commandment and the series of the ten commandments: 'male and female slaves.' The expansion in Deut. 5:14b adds two more members that were already appended to the series within the tenth commandment in the Exodus version, after 'male and female slaves,' namely 'ox and donkey.' Whether or not there may be a fixed, preliterary series behind all these constructed lists,[24] in any case the expansion of the series in Deut. 5:14b establishes a clearer correspondence of key words between the Sabbath commandment and the final sentence of the decalogue in the Deuteronomy version.

This would represent a connection of key words between the middle and the end of the decalogue. From the simple requirements of symmetry, then, the question arises whether a possible key-word connection between the middle and beginning of the decalogue had to be newly created. The expectation is not disappointed. The Deuteronomy version's special explanation of the Sabbath commandment in terms of the leading of the people out of Egypt corresponds in its wording to the beginning of the decalogue. This is no accident; it is done deliberately. From a 'form-critical' point of view, Deut. 5:15 uses a cliché of deuteronomic legal commentary that is also attested in Deut. 15:15; 16:12; 24:18, 22.[25] The first member of this cliché demands recollection of having been a 'slave in Egypt,' and also, in two of the four instances, having been 'delivered' from there by YHWH (Deut. 15:15 and 24:18). The word *pdh* is used in these instances, and consequently one would expect to find *pdh* also in the application of the cliché in Deut. 5:15. But instead, what actually appears is the *hifil* of *yṣ'*. Why? Now, it was precisely this word that, from ancient times, had stood in the opening phrase of the decalogue, and to make the key-word correspondence with it clearer, it was preferred to the *pdh* that was more commonly part of the cliché.

This kind of key-word linking from the Sabbath commandment to the beginning and end of the decalogue does not exist in the Exodus version. It would, of course, be erroneous practice to trace the introduction of the motif of leading out of Egypt in the Sabbath

24. I have some doubts about positing a single, major series behind Exod. 20:10 and 17. In order to insert 'ox and donkey,' a *kol* had to be added before 'livestock' in Deut. 5:14. This looks as if 'ox and donkey,' as such, had not been planned for in Deut. 5:14. There may have been stereotypical pairs of words (such as 'son and daughter,' 'male and female slave,' 'ox and donkey'). But they did not exist within a single, fixed series; they could be freely combined according to circumstance.

25. The essential structural elements are *wĕzākartā kî* . . . *'al-kēn* . . . Cf. Lohfink, *Hauptgebot*, 126.

commandment *only* to a stylistic play of this kind. But we must maintain that this word game may have been played deliberately when the occasion called for the introduction of the Exodus motif into the Sabbath commandment. What intention may there have been behind it? For the moment, we pose this question in a purely stylistic sense.

The connection of the Sabbath commandment to the beginning and end of the whole text by means of key words at least has the effect of underscoring and emphasizing this commandment. Since the Sabbath commandment stands more or less in the middle of the decalogue, one may ask whether, in some sense, the center of the text is being emphasized here. That would be significant, since the pre-Deuteronomy version of the decalogue, as we suppose it existed, was undoubtedly top-heavy. The introduction and first commandment were broadly constructed; after that, the commandments became shorter and soon shifted to a list of short commands concluded by the somewhat longer tenth commandment. This is especially true if we must think of the explanation of the Sabbath commandment in the Exodus version (Exod. 20:11) as absent.[26] This is true even if, perhaps, the text of the first commandment (including the prohibition of images) was not yet as extensive as it now is in both versions.[27] Is it possible that, by the underscoring of the Sabbath commandment, the true basic form of the decalogue (a series with emphasis on the first member) was in some sense abandoned, in favor of a new basic form with emphasis at the center? That would be a revolutionary new concept. For example, in that case the number of *ten* commandments would no longer play a significant role, since the majority of the commandments follow the Sabbath commandment. Was there really an intention to relativize the short commandments of the ethical series, so weighty just because of their laconic brevity and parataxis?

This suggestion leads immediately to a further observation, showing that the previous reflections carried us in the right direction. We find, in fact, that the Deuteronomy version has eliminated the parataxis that, in the primitive form of the decalogue, helped to give emphasis to the short

26. No more than this need be excised. I agree with Reventlow, *Gebot und Predigt* 45ff., that the Sabbath commandment was never formulated in the style of the 'you shall not' series.

27. However, the development of this part of the decalogue was probably already complete when the processes that interest us were developing. This is favored by the almost complete agreement between the Exodus and Deuteronomy versions of this part of the decalogue, and then by an indication that the 'paraeneses' of Deuteronomy may be able to offer us. (See below for more on this point.)

commandments! Of course, the fact that the Deuteronomy version also distinguishes itself from the Exodus version by the introduction of the conjunctive particle *wĕ* in several places has always been noticed. But very few people have known what to make of this. When Stamm writes about the additions in Deuteronomy 5, as contrasted to Exodus 20, he says: 'However, seven of these consist only of the conjunctive particle *wĕ* (and); it is not necessary to indicate the passages in which it is found in Deuteronomy 5, differing from Exodus 20.'[28] Reventlow writes, in the same vein, that the 'sevenfold addition of the copula' is 'in any case meaningless as far as the content is concerned,' but does show 'a progressive development from Exodus to Deuteronomy.'[29] I myself can find nothing more to say about the *wĕ* in Deut. 5:9 that is additional to the text of Exod. 20:5; the same is true of the excess *wĕ* in Exod. 20:4, 17 (contrast Deuteronomy 5). But it is a different matter with the *wĕ* in Deut. 5:18, 19, 20, 21 (twice in v. 21), each time before the negation *lō'*. Important here is both the series-character of the phenomenon and the fact that the copula is not inserted before the first *lō'* of the series of negative commandments (Deut. 5:17). Thus while in the middle part of the series the joints between the individual commandments were filled in by the insertion of the copula, the separation from the preceding, differently constructed and more elaborate commandment regarding parents is maintained. The intention appears to be to connect the whole series stylistically, beginning with the commandment against murder, into a single block.

This confirms our suspicion that the Sabbath commandment was meant to receive an emphatic central place in the Deuteronomy version of the decalogue. Over the front-weighted series schema is laid a new, centrally-weighted configuration of five blocks of statements that can be schematically outlined as follows:

I	Worship of YHWH[30]	5:6-10	long
II	Name of YHWH	11	short
III	SABBATH	12–15	long
IV	Parents	16	short
V	Moral commandments	17–21	long

28. *Dekalog*, 7.

29. *Gebot und Predigt*, 24.

30. One might object that, by the hypothesis here presented, the copula should really be expected before the negations in Deut. 5:3, 4, and 5 also. But we must consider that the sentences in Deut. 5:7–10 are held together by other means. Think, for example, of the pronouns with backward reference in Deut. 5:9 that point back beyond 5:8 to

Since centrally-weighted structures are found quite often elsewhere in the Old Testament as well,[31] there need be no fear that the meaning of this reshaping would not have been understood by those contemporary to the operation.

But what could have been the meaning of this reshaping in the direction of an emphasis on the Sabbath? The simplest supposition is that this new version intended to assert about the Sabbath commandment what had previously been true of the commandment at the beginning of the decalogue: for in the old form of the decalogue that first commandment had been emphasized by its position at the beginning and by its extent. The Sabbath was thus, in a sense, declared to be the 'first commandment,' or better – to avoid a connotation of enumeration that would make no sense here – the 'principal commandment.' There can be no doubt at all that Israel's covenantal thought included the concept of a 'principal commandment' preceding all detailed obligations, and that, moreover, this 'principal commandment' could be reformulated and commented on at different times and in different situations.[32] The 'principal commandment'[33] arose directly out of the 'prehistory' of the covenant formula. In Israel, its essential content is the nation's being led out of Egypt. Therefore in the decalogue also the 'first commandment' is preceded by a notice about the exodus from Egypt. Now, in the Deuteronomy version of the decalogue the reworking of the text introduces the motif of leading out of Egypt into the Sabbath

5:7; cf. W. Zimmerli, 'Das zweite Gebot,' *Festschrift Bertholet* (Tübingen, 1950), 522–23. As a result, the parataxis here makes a quite different impression than in the final part, where it is an intensifying addition to a number of stylistic features that have a separating effect. For that reason, there may have been no felt need to eliminate the parataxis here as well.

31. To stick with Deuteronomy, let me refer to Deut. 1:6–8, 19–36 (cf. Lohfink, 'Darstellungskunst und Theologie in Dtn 1, 6–3, 29,' *Bibl* 41 [1960]: 122–23); Deuteronomy 8 (cf. Lohfink, *Hauptgebot*, 194–95), and Deuteronomy 29–32 (cf. Lohfink, 'Der Bundesschluß im Land Moab,' *BZ* n.s. 6 [1962]: 49–51).

32. Let me refer to my book, *Das Hauptgebot*, a literary analysis of Deuteronomy 5–11. These chapters in Deuteronomy are devoted solely to the treatment of the complex of problems surrounding the 'principal commandment.' The roots of the concept of a 'principal commandment' preceding all individual commandments go back to the second millennium in the genre of the formula of vassal contracts. K. Baltzer, *Das Bundesformular*, WMANT 4 (Neukirchen, 1960), has chosen the concept of 'declaration of a fundamental principle' for this phenomenon.

33. It begins with Exod. 20:3 = Deut. 5:7. Reventlow's somewhat different idea (*Gebot und Predigt*, 26–28) I do not find persuasive.

commandment, and it does so with a formula of words that corresponds exactly to the beginning of the decalogue. This can only underscore the suggestion, derived from the newly-created structure, that the Sabbath commandment is supposed to be presented here as the 'principal commandment.'

At what period would this kind of advancement in rank for the Sabbath commandment have been possible? When could it, in some sense, have become an *articulus stantis et cadentis ecclesiae*? [article by which the congregation stands and falls?] Certainly not until the exile or after it.[34] But this creates a problem regarding the textual context within which the 'Sabbath decalogue,' as I would prefer to call this version of the decalogue, has been transmitted to us, since Deuteronomy 5 seems with great probability to be pre-exilic. This problem can also serve to push us toward new knowledge!

The 'paraeneses' that precede the 'laws' as such in Deuteronomy serve to present and comment on the principal commandment of the covenant in its various formulations. Thus in the formulation in Deut. 5:6–7, 9bα the principal commandment is cited and commented in Deut. 6:10–25, within a text that, together with Deuteronomy 5, constitutes a unified[35] literary stratum.[36] The principal commandment in the formulation in Deut. 5:6, 8, 9a, bα is commented in the later text of Deut. 4:1–40, word for word, but avoiding any echo of Deut. 5:7.[37] The formulation of the principal commandment in Deut. 5:9a is introduced into the 'paraenesis' in Deut. 8:19 and 11:16,[38] and this is done by a hand that is probably later than that of Deuteronomy 5–6 and earlier than that

34. On the revaluation of the Sabbath during the Exile, see G. von Rad, *Theologie des AT* (Munich, 2nd ed. 1958), 1: 87; E. Lohse, 'Sabbaton,' *TDNT* 7:1–35; Roland de Vaux, *Das Alte Testament und seine Lebensordnungen* (Freiburg, 1962) 2: 338. (Originally published as *Les institutions de l'Ancien Testament*, 2 vols. [Paris, 1958–1960]; English translation by John McHugh under the title *Ancient Israel: Its Life and Institutions* [New York, 1961]; the passage cited is on pp. 482–83).

35. See the proof of this in Lohfink, *Hauptgebot*, 142–43.

36. The commentary proper is in Deut. 6:12–15. For proof, see (1) W. L. Moran, 'The Ancient Near Eastern Background for the Love of God in Deuteronomy,' *CBQ* 25 (1963): 85; (2) – independently – H. Graf Reventlow in an unpublished lecture from the fifteenth congress of German Orientalists, Göttingen, 1960; (3) Lohfink, *Hauptgebot*, 154–57.

37. The commentary proper is in Deut. 4:16–20. For proof, see W. Zimmerli, 'Das zweite Gebot,' 562–63.

38. The commentary on Deut. 5:9b[b], 10 is also found in the same layer (Deut. 7:8–10).

of Deuteronomy 4. Thus the relative chronology of the individual parts of the 'paraenesis' of Deuteronomy may be helpful, even by way of the various commented parts of Deut 5:6–10, for a reconstruction of the different phases of the growth of the formulations of the principal commandment at the beginning of the decalogue. I cannot pursue this question in more detail at this point. Here I am concerned about one conclusion only: in the whole 'paraenesis' in Deuteronomy, which is thus so deeply concerned, in all its different layers, about the 'principal commandment' in its varied formulations, there is no commentary at all on the Sabbath commandment.[39] Thus either the Sabbath commandment was never the principal commandment, or it only became such when the composition of Deuteronomy 1–11 was essentially complete. The second possibility harmonizes with the notion of an exilic or post-exilic origin for the Sabbath decalogue. But it also compels us to suppose that the recension of the decalogue now found in Deuteronomy 5 was only inserted in the course of the transmission of the text, in place of an older recension of the decalogue that was found there. That is entirely possible, since the decalogue surely led an independent oral existence, in addition to its literary existence in Deuteronomy. The more developed forms of the text that resulted could then, of course, have exercised influence on the literary citation of the decalogue in Deuteronomy, even when this created a certain tension with the deuteronomic context. There is even a positive indication that the recension of the decalogue that now stands in Deuteronomy 5 cannot simply be the one that the author of Deuteronomy 5–6 originally inserted in his text.

According to Deuteronomy 5–6, there is an essential difference between the decalogue and the other laws in Deuteronomy. The decalogue was promulgated by God directly, while the other laws were conveyed to the people through the mediation of Moses, who first received them alone on the mountain from God. Thus when the narrative of Deuteronomy 5 quotes the decalogue, what is at issue is the citation of

39. We must go even farther. In the 'laws' of Deuteronomy as well, the Sabbath commandment is not considered part of the decalogue! The commandments of the decalogue are reflected in the 'laws,' it is true, through those laws that contain the *b'r* formula. Reventlow, *Dekalog,* 61–63, has noted this already. (See the passages cited there.) J. l'Hour has treated these laws in detail in an article in *Bibl* 44 (1963): 1–28, which also addresses the problem of their relationship to the decalogue. It is true that not all the commandments of the decalogue are represented in these laws. Nothing corresponds to the commandments in Deut. 5:11 and 21, either. Still, it is striking that there is also no *b'r* law regarding violation of the Sabbath.

divine law, coming direct from YHWH and not derived from any earlier promulgation of YHWH's laws. But this directly contradicts a formula that appears twice in the present recension of the text of the decalogue in Deuteronomy 5: *ka'ăšer ṣiwwĕkā yhwh 'ĕlōhêkā* (Deut. 5:12, 16). In the cliché language of deuteronomic preaching, this formula indicates a reference back to a promulgation of a law of YHWH that has happened or been reported earlier; in most cases, this is the decalogue. It is in the preterite and can be clearly distinguished from a promulgation in the present tense: *'ăšer 'ānōkî mĕṣawwĕkā (hayyôm),* as W. L. Moran has shown.[40] Reventlow, in treating the Sabbath commandment, remarks concerning the 'phrase added by the Deuteronomy version in contrast to the Exodus version, "as YHWH has commanded you,": . . . this is unmistakably preaching style.'[41] At another point he says of the formula, that through it 'the preaching character of the Deuteronomy version appears more clearly.'[42] That is, of course, correct. But the question of the statement that this formula customarily makes within deuteronomic 'preaching' is not raised. In fact, it functions as a backward reference. It says that the law to which it is appended is not being presented for the first time, but rests on another law previously promulgated by YHWH. And by that very means it sets the recension of the decalogue as it now appears in Deut. 5:6–21 in genuine contradiction to the narrative in which it is embedded in the form of a quotation. That context requires a proclamation of the law from the mouth of YHWH for the first time and as a basis for everything else. This fact confirms our hypothesis that the version of the decalogue in Deuteronomy 5 worked its way into the text at this point only much later, while originally an older form of the decalogue was used here.[43]

40. 'Love of God' (see n. 36 above), 86. In n. 51 Moran also points out the resulting problem concerning the decalogue in Deuteronomy 5 that we are discussing here. See also the treatment of the formula of backward reference in Lohfink, *Hauptgebot*, 60–61.

41. *Gebut und Predigt*, 56.

42. Ibid., 24.

43. This penetration can be thought of as unofficial: a scribe created agreement between the text of the decalogue in Deuteronomy 5, which in his opinion was incorrect, and the version with which he was acquainted. But we could also suppose an official intervention in the text of Deuteronomy. This could have occurred, for example, at the time when the Pentateuch was put together. When it was seen that the decalogue would appear twice, the opportunity was seized to insert a different version in the second passage, in order by this means to salvage both versions.

In Deut. 5:12, the formula of backward reference is probably one of the elements introduced when the 'Sabbath decalogue' was created. In that case, the same would be true of the formula in Deut. 5:16. This leads us to still further insights regarding the Sabbath decalogue:

The Sabbath decalogue consciously understands itself not as the original form of the decalogue, but as a secondary version. It must refer for its legitimation to the original decalogue. It openly acknowledges that it contains secondary features. This self-understanding could be historical: the Sabbath decalogue knows that it was preceded by a decalogue with a different principal commandment. But it could also result from a difference in the *Sitz im Leben.* Could it be that, at a particular period, the old decalogue with its emphasis at the beginning was still being used in its ancient, cultic life-setting, while the Sabbath-centered decalogue was being used for another, secondary cultic celebration, let us say at the Sabbath worship service of the rising synagogues? One may pose these questions in order to indicate the possibilities that exist. It is not possible to answer them.

The formula of backward reference appears only in the Sabbath commandment and in the commandment regarding parents in the Deuteronomy version. These are two commandments in which genuine interventions were made in the older texts. The formula of backward reference may thus have the task of ensuring that here, in spite of the changes and additions that have been made, at bottom nothing is commanded that is not also in the older version. If we have correctly perceived this connection between the formula of backward reference and the changes in the text within the commandment under consideration, we may associate one last difference between the Exodus and Deuteronomy versions of the decalogue with the intervention associated with the creation of the Sabbath decalogue: the insertion of *ûlĕmaʿan yîṭab lāk* in the motivation for the commandment regarding parents (Deut. 5:16b).

If this addition is traceable to the Sabbath redaction, then we can draw limits for the temporal beginning of the Sabbath decalogue. This is true because the addition detaches the promise of long life from the concept of the *'ădāmâ.* The older version promised long life in the *'ădāmâ.* As a result of the insertion, it is now only long life, but without connection to the *'ădāmâ,* that is promised, and all that is associated with the *'ădāmâ* is 'it [will] go well with you,' but without any indication of time. This is most easily understood if the promise had to be accommodated to the situation of exile in which, while it was perhaps regarded as temporary, one still had to take into account at least for the time being a loosening of the connection between blessing and *'ădāmâ.*

This may sound oversubtle. But would it not have been one of those typical little tricks by means of which one can accommodate texts regarded as inviolable to changed situations by means of the smallest possible additions? The addition to the commandment regarding parents would thus point to a composition of the Sabbath decalogue during the Exile.

The greater portion of the differences between the Exodus and Deuteronomy versions of the decalogue is now associated with a single intervention that can, to some extent, be described in terms of its intention and time: the creation of a secondary form of the decalogue that, by means of a new stylistic placement of emphasis and additions to the content, presents the Sabbath commandment as the genuine principal commandment, corresponding to the needs of the exilic period.[44] There remains a whole series of differences that cannot be associated with this intervention.[45] Some of these may be accidents associated with the different textual traditions witnessed in Exodus 20 and Deuteronomy 5, but others may be, in line with the opinions of Stamm, Reventlow, and many older authors, individual changes that should be attributed to the development of the language or of different understandings of the content of the commandments. The latter would apply especially to some of the changes in Deut. 5:20–21. Since no one can ask that all the differences in the versions of the decalogue that have been transmitted to us within the Old Testament itself should be traceable to a single intervention, this remainder of differences that cannot be explained in terms of the creation of the Sabbath decalogue furnishes no objection to the hypothesis of the Sabbath decalogue itself. This hypothesis, developed primarily through stylistic analysis, again represents (as I think I may say) a major concretizing of the picture of this stage in the history of the decalogue, in

44. For that reason I have some hesitation about placing too much emphasis on the social factor in the 'deuteronomic' explanation of the Sabbath. It may be nothing more than a continuation of deuteronomic motifs that had long been customary (cf. Deut. 12:12, 18; 16:11–12). In the new version of the Sabbath commandment the only issue was introducing, as unobtrusively as possible, the stereotypical prehistory of the covenant as an explanation for the new principal commandment. The 'social element' served, in all this, as an elegant transition from the existing series of subjects of the Sabbath obligation. Note, besides the preference for the verb *yṣ'*, already mentioned, the strengthening of the Exodus motif by means of the cliché 'mighty hand and outstretched arm.'

45. In Deut. 5:8, *kol* instead of *wĕkol*; in 5:9, *wĕ'al* instead of *'al*; in 5:10, *miṣwôtāw* instead of *miṣwôtāy* (5:10 *ketib*); in 5:20, *šāw'* instead of *šeqer*; in 5:21, *'ēšet* instead of *bêt*; in 5:21, *tit'awweh bêt* instead of *taḥmōd 'ēšet*; in 5:21, *śādēhû*; in 5:21, *'abdô* instead of *wĕ'abdô* (see n. 6 above); in 5:21, *šôrô* instead of *wĕšôrô*.

contrast to the previous conclusion reached in the course of the history of research, that it was the preachers of Israel who were at work in producing the Deuteronomy version, and not only at that time, but earlier as well.

Of course, the 'Sabbath decalogue' remains an hypothesis. But this is one of those hypotheses that is a good deal more reliable than, for example, the reconstructed 'primitive decalogue,' since the latter must be based on certain postulates, such as that of an original purity of forms. Here, in contrast, it was only necessary to make the most intensive possible comparison between two existing recensions of the sme text. Since it is thought permissible to reconstruct 'primitive decalogues,' it may be considered at least as legitimate to speak, in hypothetical terms, of a 'Sabbath decalogue' fashioned during the Exile.[46]

46. I owe special thanks to W. L. Moran, who discussed the problems of the 'Sabbath decalogue' with me at length and with great interest, and to J. Haspecker, whose penetrating criticism of the presentation has added immeasurably to its value. If I have frequently cited H. Graf Reventlow, this should be seen as an expression of the many stimuli I received from his book. In a great many citations in which I distinguish my own ideas from his, he simply represents the most recent witness to opinions that were represented also by others before him.

11

The 'Small Credo' of Deuteronomy 26:5–9

For some years now it has been increasingly clear that the 'confessions of faith' stemming from the first Christian millennium have become almost incomprehensible to present-day people. Still, we recognize that we need such texts, and consequently we are in search of new ones. We have come to the point that the simplest way to indicate one's claim to be an important theologian is by publishing a 'short formula of faith.'

In this situation, historical investigations of the Christian 'confessions of faith,' and especially studies of their Old Testament predecessors, must seem rather pointless. Or might it be useful, precisely in such a situation, to ask anew when and how the old formulae originated and what their original purpose may have been? Trusting that these questions may receive a positive response from some readers, I intend in the following pages to undertake an investigation of the best-known and most important credal text of the Old Testament.[1]

1. State of Research

In 1983, Gerhard von Rad described the text of Deut. 26:5–9 (except for an easily distinguishable 'deuteronomic overpainting') as a very ancient witness to a cultic type of text, that of the 'small historical credo.' The other two ancient examples were said to be Deut. 6:20–24 and Josh. 24:2b–13, both of them also showing evidence of deuteronomic overlays.

1. This essay contains the detailed documentation for my address, 'Dtn 26, 5–9: Ein Beispiel altisraelitischer Geschichtstheologie,' to appear in French in the *Acta* of the colloquium sponsored by the Centre International d'Études Humanistes on the theology of history (5–11 Jan. 1971), ed. by E. Castelli [= *Archivio di filosofia* 39 (1971): 189–99].

According to von Rad, the 'credo' from the period of the Judges furnished the model according to which, in the Davidic-Solomonic era, the Yahwist organized his narrative material. In this way the old 'credo' became a formal principle for the whole of what, beginning with J as a basis, ultimately grew far beyond its original dimensions to form the Hexateuch.[2] This thesis served Old Testament research for decades as an imaginative model for the ordering of the most varied phenomena.[3]

For a long time, critical examination touched only a problem auxiliary to the principal thesis and subject to solution, namely the question of the original separation from or association of the Sinai tradition with the salvation-historical traditions.[4]

In recent years, however, the textual bases of the principal thesis have been called into question. A number of authors have independently investigated the three instances cited by von Rad as old witnesses to the 'small historical credo,' and in each case the result was to cast doubt on whether it was really possible to discover a text that originated before the Yahwist.[5] In 1967, W. Richter studied the stereotypical formulae of the credo texts and the combinations of those formulae on a much broader textual basis than that of von Rad. He investigated all the historical summaries in the Old Testament that could be dated before the Exile, as well as all the texts from these periods in which individual formulae from the summaries appeared. His conclusion was that, up to the time of the

2. *Das formgeschichtliche Problem des Hexateuch*, BWANT IV, 26 (Stuttgart, 1938) = G. von Rad, *Gesammelte Studien zum Alten Testament*, ThB 8 (Munich, 1958), 9–86.

3. It was especially critical that Martin Noth, in his work, *Überlieferungsgeschichte des Pentateuch* (Stuttgart, 1948) accepted this thesis, but in doing so pushed the origins of the 'credo' still farther back into the dark beginnings of Israel, since he posited a narrative still earlier than that of the Yahwist, which he called 'G'.

4. See, for example, A. Weiser, *Einleitung in das AT* (Göttingen, 1st ed., 1948; 5th ed., 1963), 81–86; C. H. W. Brekelmans, 'Het 'historische Credo' van Israel,' *Tijdschrift voor theologie* 3 (1963): 1–11; T. C. Vriezen, 'The Credo in the OT,' *Die OuTestamentiese Werkgemeenskap in Suid-Afrika* 6 (1963): 5–17; H. B. Huffmon, 'The Exodus, Sinai and the Credo,' *CBQ* 27 (1965): 101–113.

5. Deut. 6:20–24: see N. Lohfink, *Das Hauptgebot*, AnBib 20 (Rome, 1963), 159–63; Deut. 26:5–9: see L. Rost, 'Das kleine geschichtliche Credo,' in *Das kleine Credo und andere Studien zum AT* (Heidelberg, 1965), 11–25; Josh. 24:2b–13: see G. Schmitt, 'Der Landtag von Sichem,' *ATh* 1:15 (Stuttgart, 1964), 29–30; also W. Richter, 'Beobachtungen zur theologischen Systembildung in der atl. Literatur anhand des 'kleinen geschichtlichen Credo',' in *Warheit und Verkündigung, Festschrift für M. Schmaus* (Paderborn, 1964), 191–95; summarily on all three texts: G. Fohrer, *Studien zur atl. Theologie und Geschichte (1949–1966)*, BZAW 115 (Berlin, 1969), 69.

deuteronomic writing, there existed no schemata with canonical rank. The 'credo' is not at the beginning; instead, it presupposes J and E and a whole series of other developments. It is a 'formulaic simplification and abstraction.'[6] Even if one does not share some of Richter's presuppositions and for that reason remains skeptical of some details of his view, one cannot contradict the major conclusions of his study.

As a result, our task can only be to give, within the new overall view, a more precise definition of the origins and expressive intention of texts like Deut. 26:5–9.[7]

2. The Context (Deut. 26:1–11)

The law concerning the delivery of the first fruits of the earth contains a number of motifs or motif complexes that point to a relatively late period:

(a) Verse 1, the introductory conditional clause, which however does not describe a concrete situation as do the conditional clauses of the 'casuistical laws,' presupposes a more comprehensive context, according to which this law was given before the conquest of the land; we need not necessarily conclude to the deuteronomistic localization of this lawgiving in Moab, and yet this introduction to the law, which is strongly colored by deuteronomic language as well, cannot be much older than that. The

6. W. Richter, 'Beobachtungen,' 176–212. The quoted passage is from p. 212. Along the same lines: B. S. Childs, 'Deuteronomic Formulae of the Exodus Tradition,' in *Hebräische Wortforschung. Festschrift W. Baumgartner*, SVT 16 (Leiden, 1967), 39.

7. If, in what follows, questions that L. Rost appears already to have answered are taken up once again, it is because Rost's argumentation may not be persuasive at all points. His essay contains a whole series of careless mistakes (e.g., in Deut. 26:7 he apparently read *z'q* instead of *s'q*, and as a result he has made some statistical errors on p. 12; also on p. 12 he has not distinguished between *šm' 'et qôl NN* and *šm' bĕqôl NN*; the example of *yād ḥăzāqâ* in the Pentateuch sources is not mentioned on p. 13, nor are the instances of *'ôt* and *môfēt* in the old sources; on p. 14 there is a mistake in the translation of Deut. 26:5; n. 15 assigns Exod. 23:20 to the Yahwist). The linguistic-historical proof on pp. 12–13 will, as it stands, scarcely be adequate to the demands of methodology (cf. especially n. 18 and the factual conclusions). It is surprising to find that Num. 20:15–16 E, the closest parallel to Deut. 26:5–9, is nowhere mentioned (p. 16). The historical speculations on the last pages can scarcely be established on the basis of the preceding analysis of Deut. 26:5–9. In the meantime, R. P. Merendino, *Das deuteronomische Gesetz*, BBB 31 (Bonn, 1969), 359–63, has criticized Rost's presentation and has practically returned to G. von Rad's positions (so that it is hard to understand how, on p. 362, n. 65, he can agree with Richter). Since it appears that, despite the questionable nature of his argumentation, Rost is probably correct in his literary-critical conclusions, it appeared advisable to present my own argumentation at length.

preceding verse, Deut. 25:19, could have been composed with a view to later scenes in DtrG. Deut. 26:1 is connected to this preceding verse by related key words. This could, then, indicate that it was a deuteronomistic composition.

(b) In vv. 2b and 11 we find the motifs and clichés of the deuteronomic law of centralization, which can be traced, at the earliest, to the time of Hezekiah.

(c) In vv. 3–4 the Jerusalem priesthood is introduced, apparently in opposition to an older, priestless version still evident in v. 10b. This corresponds to an interest, observable elsewhere in deuteronomic laws, in explaining the priesthood's income. It is quite likely that it was also in this connection that the clarification in v. 3b, to be spoken by the Israelite who is presenting the offering, was introduced, since it is here that the motif of YHWH's oath to the patriarchs, so important for the deuteronomist, appears. In vv. 5–10 it is completely absent, even though, in conformity with deuteronomic style, it could easily have appeared at a number of points in those verses. It apparently had to be added at a later point.[8]

(d) In the whole law we find typical elements of deuteronomic language with greater frequency than in the preceding legal texts.

We may conclude from these observations that the whole law is relatively late, or that it consists in large measure of later expansions. Whether in the second case we should suppose a number of layers of augmentation, or only one, can remain open. The observation in (c) above compels us to posit at least two layers, even if the origins of the whole are relatively late.

The obligation to bring the first fruits of the earth to YHWH is old: cf. Exod. 23:19; 34:26.[9] We must suppose that there was a ritual, or even a number of rituals, for that purpose, and even that there was a fixed formula of offering as a part of such rites. But that is not to say that there must necessarily have been a formulated law for the ritual as well, describing the details of the rite and forming the basis for Deut. 26:1–11. It is just as possible that the custom existed even without such a law. Then only the prayer of offering would have existed as a fixed form of words. In the relatively late principal composition of Deut. 26:1–11, elements of the well-known ritual would have been described for the first time in terms of

8. Cf. C. Steuernagel, *Das Deuteronomium und das Buch Josua*, HAT (Berlin, 2nd ed. 1923), ad loc. Differing: R. P. Merendino, *Das deuteronomische Gesetz* (see n. 7 above), 352, who posits resemblance with regard to the land motif.

9. For further details, see O. Eissfeldt, *Erstlinge und Zehnten im AT*, BWAT 22 (Leipzig, 1917).

law. But whether there was a pre-deuteronomic law concerning the offering of the first fruits of the earth or not, it is certainly probable that an older prayer of offering existed in the context of an ancient ritual, and thus it is not impossible that the present prayer of offering in vv. 5–10 is very old, or at least that it contains ancient elements.

Since the following study concentrates only on Deut. 26:5–10, the history of the whole law need not be detailed further. The general framework of possibilities sketched here is sufficient.

3. The Change of Number in the Prayer of Offering (Deut. 26:5–10)[10]

At the beginning of the prayer of offering,[11] an individual ('my ancestor') speaks. Clauses 2–4 contain no elements that compel a different identification of the speaker. In contrast, with clause 5 a new self-understanding of the speaker begins. Now we read 'us,' and in clause 8 the subject is also in the first person plural ('we'). That continues until clause 13. Clause 14 then speaks again in terms of the 'I' of the subject and the 'to me' of the dative object.

10. Let me point out that this change of number has nothing to do with the phenomenon, frequent in Deuteronomy, of a shift in the form of address to Israel ('you' singular or 'you' plural). Here it is a matter of the first person ('I' or 'we'), and directly concerns not the whole of Israel, but a single, individual Israelite.

11. Since the verse division of the MT makes it difficult to identify individual clauses in the prayer of offering, in what follows I will use an *ad hoc* enumeration of the clauses. It is oriented to the appearance of *waw* + verb, and in the case of v. 10 to *wĕʿattâ.* The following 14 'clauses' result:

1 [5]A wandering Aramean was my ancestor;
2 he went down into Egypt,
3 and lived there as an alien, few in number,
4 and there he became a great nation, mighty and populous.
5 [6]When the Egyptians treated us harshly
6 and afflicted us,
7 by imposing hard labor on us,
8 [7]we cried to YHWH, the God of our ancestors;
9 YHWH heard our voice
10 and saw our affliction, our toil, and our oppression.
11 [8]YHWH brought us out of Egypt with a mighty hand and an outstretched arm,
with a terrifying display of power, and with signs and wonders,
12 [9]and brought us into this place
13 and gave us this land, a land flowing with milk and honey.
14 [10]So now I bring the first of the fruit of the ground that you, YHWH, have given me!

The singular subject at beginning and end is the individual Israelite head of family who brings the offering.[12] The 'we,' into whom the individual merges in the larger middle section, is Israel. This is clear also from the content of the clauses. At the end, the speaker is again an individual.

A temporary identification within a single prayer of the praying individual with his or her group is, in itself, not problematic. For example, Psalm 8 begins with 'we,'[13] meditates in 'I,' and ends again in 'we.' Nor need one conclude from the transition from 'I' to 'we' in Deut. 26:15 alone that vv. 13–15 contain two layers.[14] It is certainly striking that clauses 8–13 speak of the God YHWH, who is addressed in clause 14, in the third person, but if necessary this could still be explained stylistically as a shift from confession to prayer. But there is an additional phenomenon that can no longer be explained by a change of aspect: clause 1 speaks of 'my *ancestor*,' while clause 8 concerns YHWH, the God 'of our *ancestors*.' In this deuteronomic text it is clear that 'ancestors' refers to Abraham, Isaac, and Jacob. 'My ancestor,' on the contrary, as a deuteronomic formula for Abraham, Isaac, and Jacob, is unknown.

Once that is acknowledged, the further question arises: why does the text begin in the singular at all? It is understandable from the matter itself that clause 14, the statement of offering, should be in the singular of the one speaking. But it is no longer clear why the historical narrative first refers everything to a speaker in the singular, and then to the whole group to which the speaker belongs. At this point, the absence of an address to YHWH in clauses 8–13 takes on a new significance.

12. In deuteronomic language there is a possibility that utterances of all Israel can take the first person singular form: cf. Deut. 9:4; 12:30; 17:14; 18:16. But those are all marked citations, which are meant to characterize a juristically significant situation briefly and pointedly, in a style that we find, for example, in documented speech from the ancient Orient as well. The context shows clearly, in each instance, that the 'I' refers to all Israel. Here, in contrast, the context does not call for an official speaker for all Israel, but for the individual head of family who comes to the sanctuary to offer thanksgiving for the harvest. Moreover, there does not seem to be an instance anywhere in Deuteronomy for a shift from 'I' = Israel to 'we' = Israel within a single citation.

13. H. J. Kraus, *Psalmen*, BK, 66, concludes that the psalm was recited by those playing different roles, beginning and end by 'a number of singers,' and the middle part by 'a single voice.' That is possible, but this supposition is not necessary to explain a change of number.

14. When G. von Rad, *Das fünfte Buch Mose*, ATD, 114–15, nevertheless supposes a number of layers at this point, he does so on the basis of observations regarding the content.

Hence we are drawn to the suspicion that in clause 1 a pre-existing formula is being employed. Whether clauses 2–4 were also part of it is a question that must remain open. At least from clause 5 onward we are looking at the work of a second hand. Clause 14 could come, once again, from the first hand. At this point, we need to test whether other observations will support or falsify this hypothesis.

4. The Rhythm of Three in the Prayer of Offering in Deut. 26:5–10

Deuteronomy 26:5–10 is not a poetic text. It lacks the typical characteristic: the *parallelismus membrorum* within verses of more or less equal length. Instead, it represents a very solemn and often broadly sweeping prose. Closer analysis leads us to a rhythm of threes, steadily increasing in dimension, that extends throughout almost the whole of the text.

Clause 1 consists of three words, each beginning with the same letter ('). Words one and three are also connected by an internal rhyme. With this, a sharp rhythm of three is immediately introduced.

The rhythm continues in the connected group of three clauses numbered 2–4. Their common subject is the 'father' from clause 1. The length of the clauses increases steadily. The third and longest contains, in the three adjectives attached to *gôy*, a subordinate, concluding set of three.

The next three clauses are again connected by a common subject: the Egyptians. This group is also distinguished from what precedes and follows by its brevity, achieved by a progressive shortening from clause 5 to clause 6. In clause 7 it concludes with a somewhat longer phrase, but this is not sufficient to constitute another subordinated group of three. Clauses 5–7 are also distinguished from those that precede them by their identification of the speaker with the Israelites ('us').

Clause 8 introduces a new element, namely the deity: YHWH. To this point the text was, as one might say, secular and this-worldly. The three clauses 8–10 do not have the same subject (8: 'we,' 9 and 10: YHWH), but this is related to the fact that YHWH is introduced as the object of clause 8, and then is taken up as subject in clause 9. In regard to the length, the principle of the preceding group of three (medium, short, long) is recapitulated, but as a whole the clauses are again longer than those in the preceding group. By this means, another subordinated group of three is introduced into the longest and concluding clause, 10. The three principal clauses and the subordinated threeness of the final sentence are, in addition, distinguished by a rhyme on *-ênû*.

In the three following clauses (11–13), YHWH remains the subject.

Probably in order to make clear that a new beginning is envisioned, YHWH is once again expressly introduced as the subject of clause 11. Clauses 11–13 constitute the longest group of three in the whole text. They are the climax and conclusion of the historical narrative. Again the middle clause is the shortest. A subordinated schema of three is found already in the first clause (11). Externally, this appears to be a series with five members. But since there are double expressions at the beginning and end that are clichés of deuteronomic language, the effect is automatically that of a rhythm of three, with the shortest member in the middle. The third clause (13) does not contain a secondary schema of three, but here, instead, the flow of the language is deliberately slowed by a method not previously employed: an appositional anadiplosis, 'and gave us this land, a land flowing with milk and honey.' The last three words are constructed almost entirely of 'a' sounds.

Clause 14 reveals almost no influence of the rhythm of three.

Within clauses 2–13, the rhythm of three is unfolded according to analogical principles. Clause 1 contains this rhythm in a different way, and clause 14 stands outside the schema. As in the analysis of the change of number, so here we find it easiest to explain our findings if we suppose that in clauses 1 and 14 we are dealing with an older text that has been secondarily expanded by the insertion of clauses 2–13. The internal rhythm of clause 1 provided the rhythmic motif for the formation of the addition. The connection between the end of the addition and clause 14 was not made at the rhythmic level, but in terms of corresponding words and motifs.[15] From the formation of the additional material in light of the special characteristics of the older text, we must conclude that the addition was not a previously existing text that was only introduced in a new context, but that it was newly formulated for this context at the time the text was expanded.[16] This, of course, does not exclude the possibility that

15. The matching begins as early as clause 12; it can be reduced to the formula: 'to bring . . . gave . . . land // to bring . . . land . . . given.' The subject and object of 'to bring' in both halves are contrasted, while the chiastically arranged elements 'to give' and 'land' are parallel in content. The same words are used for 'to bring' and 'to give' in the two corresponding halves, while different words are used for 'land.' This was apparently unavoidable, because of the necessities of the existing formula. Cf. J. G. Plöger, *Literarkritische, formgeschichtliche und stilkritische Untersuchungen zum Deuteronomium,* BBB 26 (Bonn, 1967), 125: in connection with the phrase 'flowing with milk and honey,' Deuteronomy consistently uses *'ereṣ,* and in connection with 'fruit,' it always uses *'ădāmâ.*

16. R. P. Merendino, *Das deuteronomische Gesetz* (see n. 7 above), 352ff., does not inquire about the kind of structures on the sole basis of which one might deduce the

it may have been modeled on another, older text. There are some indications that this model text is still in existence.

5. The Relationships between Deut. 26:5–10 and Num. 20:15–16

The following survey examines (in the body of the essay) the verbal framework of these two texts, and discusses (in the footnotes) other facts that are important for a comparison of the texts:

	Deuteronomy 26		**Numbers 20**
Clause 1	NS		–
2	*wayyēred miṣraymâ*	v. 15	*wayyērĕdû*[17] *miṣraymâ*
3	*wayyāqor*		*wannēšeb*
4	*wayĕhî šām lĕgôy*		–
5	*wayyārēʿû ʾōtānû*		*wayyārēʿû lānû*[18]
6	*wayʿannûnû*		–
7	*wayyittĕnû ʿālênû*		–
8	*wanniṣʿaq ʾel YHWH*[19]	v. 16	*wanniṣʿaq ʾel YHWH*
9	*wayyiṣmaʿ*[20] *qōlēnû*		*wayyišmaʿ qōlēnû*
10	*wayyarʾ ʾet-* . . .		–
	–		*wayyišlaḥ malʾāk*
11	*wayyôṣiʾēnû*[21] *mimmiṣrayim*		*wayyōṣiʾēnû*[22] *mimmiṣrayim*

disposition intended by the author, but instead develops the 'structure' of the text almost exclusively from the content; he then is amazed that some of the members of the text thus deduced are longer than others, and concludes from this to a simpler basic text, all of whose members correspond in length to the shortest one, a text without any theology, a simple listing of facts; finally he derives this text by the elimination of certain expressions and words. I see the problem with this method at the very first step, and also in the supposition that the 'primeval text' must have been constructed of parts of equal length. What is the foundation for such a postulate?

17. Subject: *ʾabōtênû*, in contrast to singular *ʾābî* in Deuteronomy 26.
18. Subject: *miṣrayim*, in contrast to *hammiṣrîm* in Deuteronomy 26.
19. Over and above Numbers 20, Deuteronomy 26 also has *ʾĕlōhê ʾăbōtênû*.
20. Over and above Numbers 20, Deuteronomy 26 also has *YHWH ʾet-*.
21. Over and above Numbers 20, Deuteronomy 26 also has *YHWH*, which here probably indicates the beginning of a new group of three clauses (see above).
22. The subject is presumably the *malʾāk* whom YHWH has sent. He is sent in response to Israel's cry, similarly to the way in which, in the stories in the book of Judges, the saviors are sent, in response to the cry of Israel, to effect Israel's rescue. For YHWH's *malʾāk* as subject of the leading out of Egypt, cf. Exod. 14:19a and Judg. 2:1; for the same as subject of their continued leading, cf. Exod. 23:20, 23.

12 *waybi'ēnû*[23] –
13 *wayitten-lānû* –
14 *(wĕʿattâ hinnēh)* *(wĕhinnēh)*

The field extending from clause 2 to clause 11 is comparable. Of the seven verbs in Numbers 20, there are six corresponding verbs in Deuteronomy 26, and in exactly the same sequence. Once, in clause 3, Deuteronomy 26 contains a more precise juridical term,[24] but all the other instances have the same verb. Only the statement about the sending of a *mal'āk* is missing, and as a result the subject of the statement of fulfillment is changed (clause 11). Here theological reasons may well come into play: Deuteronomy knows nothing of a *mal'āk* of YHWH. The small linguistic differences in clause 5 indicate an interval of time between the two texts and make it inadvisable to regard Num. 20:15–16 simply as the 'basic text' reproduced with expansions in Deuteronomy 26.[25] If there is a genetic connection between Num. 20:15–16 and our text, it is that Num. 20:15–16 was a model that was imitated and expanded in Deut. 26:5–8.

This position appears unavoidable. In accepting it, one recognizes the author's interest in expanding single expressions or pairs of expressions in the model text to form groups of three, as well as in broadening all the clauses. In later parts of this study we will show that there were not only stylistic interests at work in the preparation of the broader text of Deuteronomy 26, but also intentions regarding content, and in fact that the latter were dominant.

Of special interest is the singular subject in clause 2, which corresponds to a plural in the model text. In the model text, the introductory nominal clause is missing. There can be a logical reference to the departure of 'our ancestors' to Egypt, and the statement about the sojourn in Egypt can, connecting with the 'us,' immediately shift into the 'we' of the first person plural that first appears at clause 6 in Deuteronomy 26, and even there is surprising. It is easy to see that the nominal clause (1) already existed and was unalterable, and that, to begin with, it was by no means a simple matter to move from it to the point of view of the model

23. From this point onward there is no further correspondence in Numbers 20, since there the story only extends as far as the oasis of Kadesh, and the further events that are mentioned in Deuteronomy 26 have not yet taken place.

24. This change of verb will be explained in section VII below; cf. also n. 46 below.

25. This is how, if I see the matter correctly, R. P. Merendino, *Das deuteronomische Gesetz* (see n. 7 above) explains the parallels betweenm Deuteronomy 26 and Numbers 20.

text. This confirms the layering of the text that was previously demonstrated. If clause 1 had not already existed, an author who took Num. 20:15–16 as a model would automatically have spoken of 'our ancestors' when placing a clause of that nature at the beginning of the text.

The word *hinnēh*, a call to attention, appears to indicate a connection between Num. 20:16 and clause 14 as well. That would counter what we have previously said about clause 14. But this fact can also be easily explained within our hypothesis. In both cases the usage arises from its originating in a characterization of the present after the conclusion of a description of the past. The Hebrew language itself would have suggested the use of this word in such a case. Its appearance in both texts must not necessarily rest on a relationship of dependence.

Let me expressly indicate that none of the other pre-deuteronomic or deuteronomic historical summaries in the OT offers such a close parallel to Deut. 26:5–9.[26] Therefore Deut. 26:5–9 and Num. 20:15–16 cannot be mutually independent instances of the same stereotypical credo formula.

Wellhausen assigned Num. 20:15–16 to the Yahwist,[27] but more often it is attributed to source E because of *tĕlā'â* in v. 14 and *mal'āk* in v. 16.[28] It is also characteristic of E's narrative technique to insert glances fore and aft.[29] Numbers 20:15–16 is, in fact, a backward look at a major preceding narrative complex inserted by a narrator into a diplomatic message to the king of Edom, and not anything like a cultic 'credo.'

If the theory thus far developed regarding Deut. 26:5–10 is correct, there also results a *terminus ante quem non* for the expansion of the older prayer of offering by the insertion of the middle piece consisting of Deut. 26:5–9: namely, the composition of E. It makes good sense at this point, as a kind of counter-test, to inquire about the larger literary works to which those parts of the text that are newer than Num. 20:15–16 should be assigned.

26. Compare only the texts of Gen. 15:13–14; Judg. 2:6ff. and Deut. 6:20ff., suggested by L. Rost, 'Das kleine geschichtliche Credo' (see n. 5 above), 16, as models for our text.

27. J. Wellhausen, *Die Composition des Hexateuchs und der historischen Bücher des AT* (Berlin, 3rd. ed. 1899), 108.

28. Cf. Exod. 18:8 and Exod. 14:19a, both E.

29. H. W. Wolff, 'Zur Thematik der elohistischen Fragmente im Pentateuch,' *EvTh* 29 (1969), 70.

6. Deuteronomic Linguistic Characteristics in Deut. 26:5–10

Clauses 1 and 14 contain no features of deuteronomic language; in fact, they formulate differently from the way in which typical deuteronomic texts would speak. This applies to the singular 'my ancestor' in clause 1, and to the relative construction after 'land' in clause 14.

In clauses 2–13 the elements taken over from Num. 20:15–16 must first be eliminated. Thus *yṣ' hifil* for the liberation from Egypt (clause 11), despite the many instances in Deuteronomy, cannot be used as evidence for deuteronomic language, since it is already found in Num. 20:16 E and there are other pre-deuteronomic instances as well.[30]

In the remaining text we can make the following determinations:

Clause 3: *gwr* (for the stay in Egypt) is not deuteronomic. In Deuteronomy, the expression is *hyh gēr be'ereṣ miṣrayim*, cf. Deut. 10:19 and 23:8.

mĕtê mĕ'aṭ is not deuteronomic. While it is true that the expression reappears in Deut. 28:62, that is a very late, deuteronomistic context, and since in both texts there are references to the promises to the patriarchs that their progeny will increase, we may suppose that the expression in Deut. 28:62 was taken over from Deut. 26:5. The expression is not found anywhere else in the whole OT.

Clause 4: *hyh lĕgôy* cannot be found elsewhere in Deuteronomy. The comparable passage, Deut. 9:14, is not sufficient to allow us to speak in this instance of deuteronomic language.

gôy gādôl 'aṣûm wārāb presents a combination of three adjectives that is unique in the whole OT. There are, of course, connections both of *gôy* (Deut. 4:38; 7:1; 9:1; 11:23) and of *'am* (Deut. 2:10, 21; 9:2) with two of the adjectives used here. But those are not instances of promises to the patriarchs. The passages with *gôy* have *gôy* in the plural, and in each case it is a matter of a reference to the Enakites or of a comparison with the military strength of various nations.[31] The passage that resembles this one most closely would be Deut. 9:14, but it alone is not sufficient to verify that this is deuteronomic language, all the less so since Deuteronomy is accustomed to express the subject contemplated in clause 4, the fulfillment of the promise to the patriarchs of a numerous progeny, in a

30. Cf. W. Richter, 'Beobachtungen' (n. 5 above), 178–88.

31. On the word combinations with *gôy* and *'am* in Deuteronomy, see the article by Georg Braulik to appear in a forthcoming issue [post-1971] of *VT*.

very different way: cf. Deut. 1:10–11; 6:3; 10:22; 13:18; 28:62. The total of three adjectives must not necessarily indicate a late dating, since there is a stylistic reason for it in this text.

Clause 6: *'nh* II (for oppression in Egypt) is not deuteronomic. The word is used in Deuteronomy for an attitude of YHWH toward Israel during the wandering in the wilderness: Deut. 8:2, 3, 16; it is also used for sexual intercourse in Deut. 21:14; 22:24, 29. But it is never used for the behavior of the Egyptians toward Israel. Together with *ṣ'q* (clause 8) and *šm'* (clause 9) the introduction of *'nh* II produces a verbal series that is found in Exod. 22:22 (cf. v. 26) BB, in a legal context whose content corresponds to this one. The same legal motivation has a completely different vocabulary in Deuteronomy (cf. Deut. 15:9; 24:15).

ntn 'al is not deuteronomic. Deut. 1:15 is not comparable. The passage that is comparable, Deut. 28:48, belongs to a late stratum and, as the single genuine deuteronomic parallel, indicates no fixed deuteronomic linguistic usage.

'ăbōdâ qāšâ is not otherwise found in Deuteronomy.

Clause 8: *YHWH 'ĕlōhê 'ăbōtênû* is a deuteronomic formula: cf. Deut. 1:11, 21; 4:1; 6:3; 12:1; 27:3; 29:24. However, this formula is not exclusively or originally deuteronomic. It is already found in the old sources of the Pentateuch (Exod. 3:13, 15, 16; 4:5).

Clause 10: *wayyar'* etc. YHWH's seeing is elsewhere spoken of in this way only in Deut. 9:13 and 23:15, but there in other contexts. There are no other deuteronomic instances of the three words that describe the oppression in Egypt. Thus the clause contains nothing that is typically deuteronomic.

Clause 11: *bĕjād ḥăzāqâ ûbizrōa' nĕṭûyâ* The double expression is deuteronomic: cf. Deut. 4:34; 5:15; 7:19; 11:2, and there are no instances of it before Deuteronomy. *bĕjād ḥăzāqâ* alone can be found, for the leading out of Egypt, even within the old sources of the Pentateuch (Exod. 3:19; cf. the early deuteronomic passages Exod. 13:3, 9, 14, 16; 32:11) and it appears frequently in Deuteronomy (cf. Deut. 3:24; 6:21; 7:8; 9:26; 34:12). *bizrōa' nĕṭûjâ*, on the other hand, cannot be demonstrated before the deuteronomic writing; the expression stands alone elsewhere only in Deut. 9:29. But Deut. 9:26 and 9:29 could also be taken together as an *inclusio*. In that case, the second expression would occur in deuteronomic language only as an expansion of the first.

bĕmōrā' gādōl. This expression is also found in Deut. 4:34 and 34:12, in both cases also applied to the departure from Egypt. But both these texts belong to late strata and could be dependent on our text. However, the expression is not found in texts that are certainly pre-deuteronomic.

bĕ'ōtôt ûbĕmōpĕtîm. This double expression is deuteronomic: cf. Deut. 4:34; 6:22; 7:19; 29:2; 34:11, as well as (not referring to the departure from Egypt) 13:2–3; 28:46. Its first appearance in texts that can be dated with certainty is in Isa. 8:18 (again not with reference to the departure from Egypt). *'ôt* alone is found in the old sources of the Pentateuch in Exod. 4:8-9, 17, 28, 30; 8:19; 10:1–2. *mōpēt* alone is in Exod. 4:21. In Deuteronomy we find *'ôt* combined with another expression as *mōpēt* only in Deut. 11:3.

We also find the combination of some or all of these expressions more than once in Deuteronomy. Sometimes other expressions are added as well: compare Deut. 4:34; 6:21–22; 7:19; 11:2–3; 34:11. But we cannot exclude the possibility that our text is the oldest of such long combinations.

Clause 12: *waybi'ēnû bw' hifil* for the leading of the people into the land of Canaan is very frequent in Deuteronomy. The verb series *yṣ' hifil – bw' hifil – ntn* is found in an easily recognizable form elsewhere only in Deut. 6:23, the other historical summary in Deuteronomy. Expanded by intervening members, it also appears in the late text Deut. 4:20–21, 37–38, and similarly in Josh. 24:5–13, which should be located somewhere in the field of texts belonging to E.[32]

'el hammāqôm hazzeh is a common expression in Deuteronomy. It is found after *bw'* in Deut. 1:31; 9:7; 11:5; 29:6. But it is also so frequent in other texts of the OT, both older and newer, that one cannot call it a typically deuteronomic expression.

Clause 13: *wayyitten-lānû 'et hā'āreṣ hazzō't* is very frequent in Deuteronomy. But this formula is also found in the older sources of the Pentateuch: Gen. 12:7; 13:15, 17; 15:18, etc.

'ereṣ zābat ḥālāb ûdĕbāš is a deuteronomic formula: cf. Deut. 6:3; 11:9; 26:15; 27:3; 31:20. But this formula as well can be found in the old sources of the Pentateuch: cf. Exod. 3:8, 17.

The fund of certainly and exclusively deuteronomic linguistic material is a great deal smaller than had been expected, given the expressions of G. von

32. See, most recently, W. Richter, 'Beobachtungen' (see n. 5 above), 194–95.

Rad and L. Rost. In reality, it is only within clauses 11–13 that one may say with certainty that the addition of clauses 2–13 to the older prayer of offering (clauses 1 and 14) was done by a deuteronomic hand. Certainly, this demonstration is sufficient, if clauses 2–13 are to be regarded for other reasons as a unit, and if it can be discovered why a deuteronomic hand for the most part made so little use of its own clichés, even though they often lay near to hand. The fact that clauses 2–13 constitute a unit is strongly suggested by the rhythmic construction alone (see section IV above). In the following section we need to clarify the real source of the language in clauses 2–13.

7. Allusions to JE in Deut. 26:5–9

The historical facts listed in this passage are, whenever possible, described in formulaic language that appears in the narratives in the old sources of the Pentateuch. Often what we find here are allusions to texts that are usually assigned to source E, but there are also enough exclusive allusions to J that one may suppose that the author of our texts was acquainted with the combined sources JE, and perhaps with some expansions of those sources as well.

In the following section we will present the relevant results of a broader review of sources: that is, we will list the texts that presumably lay at hand for the author of clauses 2–13. The other instances of the corresponding formulations in the old sources of the Pentateuch will not always be listed in detail.

The background of clauses 2 and 3 should most likely be sought in the narratives of Jacob and Joseph. In fact, the Elohist preview of history in Gen. 46:3[33] contains the key words for clause 2 (and also for clause 4: 'great nation'); the Yahwist narrative of the audience before Pharaoh in Gen. 47:1–5a, 6b holds, in v. 4, the key word for clause 3. These contexts are also important for the interpretation: *gwr* does not simply mean 'to dwell,' but points to a very particular legal situation created by Pharaoh's decree and later broken by the Egyptians. Certainly, we ought to ask whether the association of *yrd* and *gwr* in the closely connected clauses 2 and 3 may not point beyond this context to still another text from the Abraham narratives in J, at Gen. 12:10, the only place in the old Genesis narratives where the two verbs are found close together. This suspicion is all the stronger if we add clause 4. The promise of progeny is frequently formulated in the stories of the patriarchs with *hyh / śym / ʿśh lĕgôy gādôl*

33. Cf. H. W. Wolff, 'Zur Thematik,' (see n. 29 above), 70.

(cf. Gen. 12:2 J; 21:18 E; 46:3 E). But only in Gen. 18:18 J do we find the expanded expression *hyh lĕgôy gādôl wĕʿāṣûm*, which is taken up in clause 4 and expanded by one member. But Gen. 18:18 is about Abraham. Here we again see how the deuteronomic expander of the old prayer of offering attempts to accommodate to the singular ancestor in clause 1, apparently an unalterable feature of the prayer. By allusions to known texts, the author immediately indicates that the reference is not only to Jacob, but that Abraham is also in view, and hence the whole patriarchal history, as clause 8 then attempts to state more clearly.

Since an additional adjective was needed in clause 4 to preserve the rhythm of three, the deuteronomic author reached back for a word stem that plays a major role in the promises of progeny given to the patriarchs and in the reports of the fulfillment of those promises during the sojourn in Egypt: *rb* (cf. Gen. 16:10; 22:17; 32:13; 48:16; 50:20; Exod. 1:9–10; 5:5).

Clause 5 was already given from Num. 20:15. But the deuteronomic author of our text may have seen clearly that E is there probably referring to Exod. 5:23 (E?). Clauses 6 and 7 were necessary to preserve the principle of three. For clause 6, the author took up the Elohist formula for the oppression in Egypt from Exod. 1:11a, 1 (cf. also the preview, usually assigned to E, in Gen. 15:13). For clause 7 no clear reference can be found, either in the old sources of the Pentateuch or elsewhere in any earlier text.[34] But it may be that Exod. 5:9, *tikbad hāʿăbōdâ ʿal hāʾănāšim* (E?), could be adduced.

The principal elements of clauses 8 and 9 were fixed by Num. 20:15. The deuteronomic author may also have known that E had formulated at that point with reference to Exod. 3:9 E, for the author took inspiration from that and the parallel passage, Exod. 3:7 J, for the expansion of the two clauses into a group of three with clause 10. The result was the use of the verb *rʾh* and, for the series of objects, the words *ʿŏnî* (Exod. 3:7 J; cf. 3:17; 4:31 J) and *laḥaṣ* (Exod. 3:9 E). No basis can be found in the old Exodus narratives for the word *ʿāmāl*, which is added to make up the series of three.

Clause 8 has also been expanded by use of a deuteronomic apposition to *YHWH*. This was certainly not done without the knowledge that this apposition played a role in the old narratives of the call of Moses (Exod. 3:13 E). There it is a short version of the longer formulae in Exod. 3:6, 15;

34. There are parallels in P (Exod. 1:14; 6:9), but these are more likely to be dependent on Deuteronomy 26 than the other way around. Cf. also the word sequence *ʿabōdâ – zʿq – šmʿ rʾh* in Exod. 2:23–24 P.

4:5 E and Exod. 3:16 J that explicate the 'ancestors' by naming them. These formulae serve in Exodus 3–4 to establish the connection with the story of the patriarchs, and the formula serves the same function in the present instance.

The expressions in clause 11 that expand the text are deuteronomic, as we have already established; it is possible that *mōrā' gādōl* first became a deuteronomic expression in this text. The deuteronomic expander may, however, have been cognizant of the fact that these expressions themselves take up terminological attempts at interpretation of individual parts of the exodus tradition that were already made in the old sources of the Pentateuch.[35] In Exod. 3:19 J and 6:1 JE, *bĕyād ḥăzāqâ* anticipates the Egyptian plagues.[36] The deuteronomic expansion of the expression with *zĕrōa' nĕṭûyâ* seems to encompass the Sea of Reeds narrative also, and is based on Moses' song of victory (on this subject, cf. Exod. 15:6, 12; for the word itself Exod. 15:16). The middle expression, *bĕmōrā' gādōl*, could have been inspired by the same song (Exod. 15:11). In that case, it would refer specifically to the miracle at the Sea of Reeds. *bĕ'ōtôt* takes up a word that distinguishes individual 'plagues' in J (Exod. 8:19; 10:1–2), and in E describes the authenticating miracles with which Moses is to introduce himself to the Israelites as the one sent by YHWH (Exod. 4:8–9, 17, 28, 30). The word *mōpēt* is found only in an addition to JE and refers to the 'plagues' (Exod. 4:21). It is clear from Deut. 6:22; 29:2; 34:11 (*bĕ*) that the double expression *'ōtôt ûmōpĕtîm* can also be restricted in Deuteronomy to a description of the miraculous events in Egypt before the exodus.[37]

While it is true that the linguistic material in clauses 12 and 13 with which the one who expanded our text has extended the summary in Num. 20:15–16 beyond its historical end point consists throughout of expressions that are frequently found in Deuteronomy, nevertheless the choice of the word *māqôm* in clause 12 may very well have been made in light of Exod. 23:20: *hinnēh 'ānōkî šōlēaḥ mal'āk lĕpānêkā . . . lahăbî'ăkā*

35. On the individual expressions see, most recently, B. S. Childs, 'Deuteronomic Formulae' (see n. 6 above), 30–39, with references to the earlier literature. Childs's hypothesis presupposes a theory of which texts in Deuteronomy are older and which more recent; the theory itself is not discussed.

36. In the early deuteronomic passages Exod. 13:9 and (somewhat differently) Exod. 13:3; 14, 16, this expression is especially connected with the eating of unleavened bread and the killing of the Egyptian firstborn.

37. M. Noth, *Überlieferungsgeschichte* (see n. 3 above), 52, refers the double expression to the events at the Sea of Reeds. This is scarcely tenable.

'el-hammāqôm 'ăšer hăkinōtî. This is especially likely since Num. 20:15 and Exod. 23:20 are also united by the motif of the *mal'āk* sent by YHWH, which our author has omitted. The land of Canaan is already called *māqôm* in Exod. 3:8 J, although *bw' hifil* is lacking there.[38] At this point we also find the phrase, 'a land flowing with milk and honey,' which concludes clause 13 of our text. It first appears in the old sources in the promises of the land in the book of Exodus. Typical of the promises to the patriarchs concerning the land, on the other hand, is the formula *ntn 'et hā'āreṣ hazzō't* (Gen. 12:7; 13:15, 17; 15:18, etc.). Clause 13 could be a deliberate combination of two typical formulae from two different series of promises of the land.

With very few exceptions, then, the linguistic material in clauses 2–13 may be seen as a retrieval of key formulae from the old sources of the Pentateuch, even at points when we find cliché-type expressions that are common in deuteronomic language. There can scarcely be any doubt that here we have a systematically thought out and artfully composed resumé of the patriarchal and exodus narratives from the old sources of the Pentateuch. This intention permits us to acknowledge that the indications that the author of these clauses must be called 'deuteronomic,' though small in number, are nevertheless weighty proof. At this point, the author was not concerned to speak as 'deuteronomically' as could be, but rather to formulate as far as possible on the basis of the old narratives, and to summarize their vision of history.

With this we may conclude our series of observations applicable to the literary-critical analysis of Deut. 26:5–10. The result: a deuteronomic author has taken an old prayer of offering from the ritual of presentation of the first fruits of the earth (clauses 1 and 14) and broadened it through an inserted text created by the author himself, based on the historical summary in Num. 20:15–16 E and expanded by many references to key concepts in the patriarchal and exodus narratives in the old sources of the Pentateuch (clauses 2–13) to form a salvation-historical confession of faith with a concluding formula of offering (clauses 1–14). Now, after all this, we can attempt an interpretation of the older prayer and its expanded version.

8. The Ancient Prayer of Offering from the Harvest Festival (Deut. 26:5*, 10a)

Presupposing the results of the preceding analysis, this prayer would have read:

38. On this, see W. Richter, 'Beobachtungen,' (see n. 5 above), 204ff.

A wandering Aramean was my ancestor –
but see, now I bring the first of the fruit of the ground that you, YHWH, have given me!

The phenomenon of 'Israel' in the sense of the twelve tribes does not appear to constitute the horizon of this text. It is fully explainable if the speaker is the head of a tribe and the 'ancestor' a physical parent or, at most, the first ancestor of the tribe. Between the 'ancestor' and the speaker lies the fact of settlement. The previously nomadic or semi-nomadic tribe has acquired land for its own possession. In this, the god YHWH plays a role that cannot be more precisely defined. In any case, through the presentation of the first fruits of the land, this god is thanked for the change in the situation of the tribe from nomadism to a life of settled agriculture.

At least the origins of this formula of offering are most readily explained in such a situation, quite soon after a peaceful or military acquisition of the land. The tribes among whom the prayer originated were aware of the Aramean origins of their ancestors, or else at that time the word 'Aramean' described not only a particular group of people, but also a style of life, something like our word 'gypsy.' Particularly in the latter case the prayer could have come rapidly into use, without alteration, among other groups of YHWH-believers who were not Aramean in origin.

The prayer is based on the contrast between 'nomadic' and 'agricultural.' Otherwise, its formulation is open to the widest variety of interpretations. If we take into account the conservative character of every fixed ritual, there is no difficulty in supposing that this prayer may have been spoken, unchanged, many centuries after the completion of Israel's acquisition of the land. One could, if one wished, hear in it without further elaboration a meaning applicable to all Israel. In that case, the Aramean ancestor would naturally be Jacob/Israel, and the *'ădāmâ* would no longer be the acres belonging to a single family, but the land of Canaan. But it is not at all necessary to postulate such a shift in meaning. It is just as easily possible that the ritual remained local and familial in nature up to the point at which the deuteronomic expander incorporated it in the text.

9. The Deuteronomically Expanded Prayer of Offering (Deut. 26:5–10)

The deuteronomic author who broadened the text introduced the aspect of all Israel into the prayer. This author took the lapidary statement about the nomadic ancestor and extended it to form a summary of history whose content rests on the narratives and formulae of the old sources of the Pentateuch and whose form is that of a confession of faith. What were the author's special intentions in this operation?

(a) A first clue to understanding the author's intention may be the *structure* that was given to the text in this process. It must, in light of the observations presented in section IV, be defined as a series of four groups of three verbal clauses framed by two individual clauses, a nominal clause and a declarative verbal clause isolated by *wĕʿattâ* and emphasized by *hinnēh*. On this basis we may abstract the following structure of the text:

I.	Clause 1	The landless patriarchs
II.	Clauses 2–4	Departure to Egypt and becoming a nation
III.	Clauses 5–7	Israel's distress in Egypt
IV.	Clauses 8–10	Israel's cry in Egypt; it is heard
V.	Clauses 11–13	YHWH's intervention on behalf of Israel
VI.	Clause 14	Statement of offering

Part V seems to constitute a special problem. Given its threefold structure, this group of clauses must be presumed to be intended as a unified part of the text. Given the theme of the previous parts, it seems probable that we should define it as we have just done: 'YHWH's intervention on behalf of Israel.' But according to our usual view of things, and on the basis of many other biblical texts, one would expect such a title to refer only to the leading of Israel out of Egypt.

This problem is all the more acute if we reflect that, while *māqôm* can be understood, with reference to older texts, to mean the whole land of Canaan, in a deuteronomic context the word referred to the center of the land, the temple at Jerusalem: for in the centralization laws in Deuteronomy, the temple is the special, designated *māqôm* that YHWH has chosen for YHWH's name.[39] Since Deut. 26:5–10 is expressly designated, through Deut. 26:2, as a prayer to be spoken in the central sanctuary, we must presume, at least under the supposition that the expansion of the prayer of offering did not occur earlier than the writing of Deut. 26:2b, 11, that the expression *hammāqôm hazzeh* is certainly to be understood as referring to Jerusalem and its temple. At least in deuteronomic times it was the common usage to speak of Jerusalem

39. Cf. Deut. 12:5, 11, 14, 18, 21, 26; 14:23, 24, 25; 16:2, 6, 7, 11, 15, 16; 17:10; 18:6; 31:11, but especially, in the same law: Deut. 26:2.

and its temple with the expression *hammāqôm hazzeh.*[40] If clause 12, then, refers to being led into the land of Canaan, but especially in the sense of being led up to its holy center, the temple of Jerusalem, then clause 12 (and, accordingly, clause 13 as well) encompasses the whole history of the nation up to the time of David and Solomon.[41] For it was David who first conquered Jerusalem, and Solomon who built the temple. This whole course of history, extending over many centuries until the building of the temple under Solomon, was thus to be understood as part of YHWH's intervention after the Israelites' lament in Egypt.

But such a view is not so far-fetched as one might at first suppose. Even the Yahwist formulated in Exod. 3:8, as response to Israel's lament in Egypt, a declaration of YHWH's intention that united the liberation from Egypt in a single, sweeping unity with Israel's being led into the *māqôm* of the Canaanites, etc. In the victory song in Exod. 15:1–18, which apparently was one of the model documents available to our deuteronomic expander (see section VII above), the march through the Sea of Reeds and the progress through the nations at the entry into the land of Canaan up to the sanctuary on the mountain are set in parallel and poetically identified.[42] The usual opinion is that this refers to the temple in Jerusalem, so that this document available to the deuteronomic expander already contained a comprehensive overview of history from the exodus to the time of David and Solomon. If Exod. 15:2 was also part of the available material, the expander even had at hand the interpretation of this whole course of history as a single, great *yĕšûâ*, 'salvation.' We can thus maintain the interpretation of clauses 11–13 that was suggested by the threefold structure. This part of our text speaks, to the end, of YHWH's intervention in response to the lament of the Israelites in Egypt.

Hence the connection between the groups of clauses in III, IV, and V consists not merely in their historical succession. Instead, in these parts

40. Cf. 1 Kgs. 8:30, 35; 2 Kgs. 18:25; 22:16, 17, 19, 20; Jer. 7:3, 6, 7; 14:13; 16:2, 3; 19:3, 4, 6, 7, 12; 22:3; 28:3, 4, 6; 29:10; 33:10, 12; 40:2.

41. That in the book of Deuteronomy an extension of the process of acquiring the land up to the time of David is possible, in connection with Jerusalem and the temple, is clear from Deut. 12:8–10. DtrG regards it as sinful, from the time of Solomon onward, if a king does not destroy the holy places on the heights. Only Deut. 12:8–10 can be seen as a legal basis for this idea. This text should be understood as a veiled reference to the fact that the centralization of the cult was expected only from the time of David and Solomon onward, at which point 'rest' really began (cf. 2 Sam. 7:1, 11; 1 Kgs. 5:18; 8:56).

42. See N. Lohfink, *Das Siegeslied am Schilfmeer* (Frankfurt am Main, 3rd. ed. 1966), 122–26.

the course of history is interpreted on the basis of a single imaginative model. The succession 'distress – lament – hearing of the lament by another – intervention of the other to relieve the distress' corresponds to a course of interaction that occurs repeatedly in human social life. Moreover, this course of interaction was transferred to religious behavior and could be experienced in part, in an institutionalized form, in the sequence 'distress – ritual lament – divine promise of salvation – divine termination of the distress.' Since this is the only model of historical interpretation that penetrates even the structure of the text, and since within that structure it encompasses the major part of the existing text, we may suppose that it is closely connected with that which the deuteronomic expander intended to express.

(b) To determine the writer's intention one may also ask what motifs from Num. 20:15–16, from the deuteronomic linguistic world and from the narratives of the patriarchs and of the exodus in the old sources of the Pentateuch may have been omitted or avoided by the deuteronomic author. In doing so, we may in part refer to our previous observations.

J and E connected the story of the patriarchs with that of the exodus and acquisition of the land by means of the category of 'promise and fulfillment.' This category thus encompasses the beginning and the end. The old prayer of offering contains no reference at all to a promise of progeny or land. The theologoumenon 'promise and fulfillment' was probably known to the deuteronomic expander of the text, since in clause 4 this author makes use of typical vocabulary from the promise of progeny, and in clause 13 of typical vocabulary from the promise of the land. In this way the author undoubtedly creates a reference to the promises to the ancestors, but avoids reflexively introducing the category of 'promise and fulfillment.' That would certainly have been possible, and might even have been expected in clause 13. Even E had employed this means, later to become stereotypical in deuteronomic language, in Gen. 50:24, where, after a statement about the people's being led into the land, a relative clause was inserted with the assertion that YHWH had promised this land to the patriarchs under oath. There is, in fact, a plurality of instances in which this relative clause could have been inserted between the word 'land' and the phrase 'flowing with milk and honey': Exod. 13:5; Deut. 31:20; Josh. 5:6; Jer. 32:22. This last text is especially revealing, since Jer. 32:21–23 was very probably dependent for its formulation on clauses 11-13 of our text, and in the process of composition the relative clause, which the author sensed was missing, was inserted. The other 'credo' in Deuteronomy (Deut. 6:21–24) also contains a reference to YHWH's oath to the patriarchs after the word 'land' in v. 23. Our author's avoidance of the category 'promise and fulfillment' has two effects: (1) it was thus possible to introduce YHWH for the first time in v. 8, within the text governed by the model 'distress – lament – hearing – intervention'; (2) the elimination of this competing model naturally caused the chosen model to emerge more strongly.

The statement in Num. 20:16 that 'YHWH sent us a *mal'āk*' is not repeated. This may be adequately explained by the fact that deuteronomic theology seems to have had no fundamental knowledge of a *mal'āk* in connection with the exodus from Egypt and the wandering in the wilderness. But it would at least have been possible to preserve the word *šlḥ* and to designate Moses (or Moses and Aaron, as in Josh. 24:5 and 1 Sam. 9:16; or Moses, Aaron and Miriam, as in Micah 6:4) as the person or persons sent by YHWH to the rescue of Israel, the person or persons through whom YHWH led the people out. This would correspond to the point of view that is dominant in E: In Exod. 3:10, 11, 12; 14:11; 17:3; 32:1, 7, 23 it is not YHWH, but Moses who leads Israel out of Egypt.[43] But this point of view is also avoided. It is apparently important to the one who is expanding this text that, immediately after YHWH's hearing of the Israelites' lament, YHWH alone should be depicted as the one who intervenes in history.

Thus the omissions by the deuteronomic expander suggest that this author's intention was to apply the historical-interpretive model of 'distress – lament – hearing – intervention' as clearly and uncontestedly as possible, and, while not making YHWH the exclusive subject of history anywhere outside the model, to say that, within the model, YHWH is in fact that exclusive subject from the moment at which YHWH hears the Israelites' plea.

(c) A third approach to a closer determination of the deuteronomic expander's intention can be the question whether this author has introduced anything into the text that is not derived from the principal available sources.

Here we may mention first of all the word *'amāl* in clause 10. The choice of this word is best explained by the fact that it is part of the vocabulary of the songs of lament.[44] It is thus connected with the verb *r'h* in Pss. 10:17; 25:18; and with *'ŏnî* also in Ps. 25:18. The addition of

43. This idea is also attested in Exod. 11:28 J; 33:1; Num. 16:13 J; Deut. 9:12; 1 Sam. 12:8 Dtr.

44. Examples in individuals' songs of lament: Pss. 7:15, 17; 10:7, 14; 25:18; 55:11; 94:20; 140:10; in songs of the nation: Ps. 90:10. Cf. also Judg. 10:16 and the context in Ps. 107:12.

ʿāmāl thus strengthens the historical-interpretive model of 'distress – lament – hearing – intervention.'

Beginning with clause 9, only YHWH is the subject of the statements. This, too, cannot be traced immediately to the deuteronomic expander's principal sources. The usual view of the 'small salvation-historical credo' as a lapidary listing of YHWH's mighty deeds in history makes this phenomenon appear to be a matter of course. But the reality is quite different. If one limits oneself to the historical summaries that contain genuine series of historical facts, and if one does not go beyond the deuteronomic era, the following can be said: a listing of all the events mentioned as deeds of YHWH only occurs when YHWH's actions are contrasted to the actions of Israel. This is the case in prophetic speeches of judgment and in related texts (Amos 2:9–11; Judg. 2:1-3; 6:8–10; 1 Sam. 6:18–19; Jer. 2:6–7), in corresponding confessions of guilt (Jer. 32:20–23), in an instance where the Israelites take an obligation upon themselves (Josh. 24:17–18), and in the catechetical foundation of the obligations of the law (Deut. 6:21–24). Where there is no such contrast ('I' and 'all of you,' 'you' singular and 'you' plural, 'YHWH' and 'we') or where it is not specially emphasized, a much more secular style of speech may appear. The preview in Gen. 15:13–16, usually ascribed to E, mentions once, in v. 14, the brief stroke of the judgmental action of YHWH, but otherwise everything, even the exodus from Egypt, is attributed to the descendants of Abraham. The retrospect in Num. 20:15–16 E, which is the basis for our text, has as deed of YHWH only the hearing of the lament and the sending of the *mal'āk* who leads Israel out of Egypt. In Josh. 24:2–13 the original image is difficult to extract; but even after the removal of the pieces that are usually regarded as additions there remains a multiple back-and-forth between human subjects and YHWH as subject of the events. In the historical retrospect in Judg. 11:16–22 YHWH only appears in vv. 21 and 23 as subject in the context of holy war. In the deuteronomic historical summary in 1 Sam. 12:8–12 the text shifts according to a fixed scheme between the human subjects and the punishing or saving God. That our text, Deut. 26:5–10, cannot be counted among those in which YHWH's actions toward Israel are contrasted with Israel's disobedient or obedient attitude toward YHWH is clear from the very fact that in clauses 1–8 YHWH is not the subject of the historical events. That YHWH is and remains the subject from clause 9 onward is thus relevant. The conclusion drawn earlier is again confirmed: apparently everything that happened after the hearing of Israel's lament is meant to appear as the accomplishment of a single divine intervention in history on behalf of Israel.

The two phenomena in the text that cannot be derived from the principal sources used by the deuteronomic expander thus again underscore the fact that everything in this text is pointed toward the summarizing of the course of history from the exodus to the time of Solomon in terms of the model 'distress – lament – hearing – intervention.'

(d) The interpretation of the exodus from Egypt with the aid of this model was already present in the old sources of the Pentateuch, and was found as well in the basic model, Num. 20:15–16. It is true that by adopting this model, and *only* this model,[45] the deuteronomic expander behaved selectively, but not un-conservatively. The author does not introduce a new category, but simply brings forward very clearly a particular category from the tradition that, in the author's own eyes, is especially appropriate.

Still, in doing so, the author applies the category in a new way, loosing it from its fixed connection with a particular historical hour and making of it a great metaphor embracing the whole history of the people up to the moment at which the prayer of offering is uttered; for YHWH's intervention in aid of the people extends, in the text as a whole, not only up to the time of Solomon, but is immediately at work in the fruitfulness of the land that YHWH gave to the Israelites as help when they were in distress in Egypt.

The extent to which a fundamental reflection on history and God's relationship to history underlies such a procedure on the part of the author can scarcely be determined. But it is possible that, in the case of such a late text, and one that so painstakingly organizes the most varied and far-reaching traditions within a single category, we ought to reckon rather with a good deal of theological reflection than with little.

It is also difficult to draw conclusions applicable to current discussion of Christian creeds. The late origins of the classical 'credo' of the Old Testament may encourage us late Christians to dare to make our own brief formulae of faith. Perhaps, in addition, the interaction of fidelity to tradition with bold new conceptions may offer us a model for our own action.

45. Let me point out that one other category from the traditional interpretation of the exodus was adopted and even expanded: the connection between 'enslavement' and 'liberation from slavery.' Clause 3 emphasizes that the Israelites in Egypt originally had the legal status of *gērîm*. The statements in clauses 5–7 imply that the Israelites were illegally deprived of that status and enslaved. 'Leading out' (clause 11) is a legal term for liberating from slavery. This can either be done by means of a payment made or by the use of power; in the second case, of course, this is only legal if the enslavement itself was illegal. That is true in this instance. Therefore YHWH legally freed Israel 'with a mighty hand.' This whole model, however, is inserted into the larger model of lament and hearing. It only makes concrete the nature of the distress and the way in which the hearing of the lament took place in its first phase.

Index of Modern Authors

Index of Biblical References